Beyond the Conceivable

WEIMAR AND NOW: GERMAN CULTURAL CRITICISM

Edward Dimendberg, Martin Jay, and Anton Kaes, General Editors

To my mother
Chana Diner, née Isakson

Beyond the Conceivable

Studies on Germany, Nazism, and the Holocaust

Dan Diner

UNIVERSITY OF CALIFORNIA PRESS

Berkeley   Los Angeles   London

University of California Press
Berkeley and Los Angeles, California

University of California Press, Ltd.
London, England

The chapters in this book are revised versions of the following studies: Chapter 1: "Constitutional Theory and 'State of Emergency' in the Weimar Republic: The Case of Carl Schmitt," *Tel Aviver Jahrbuch für deutsche Geschichte* 17 (1988): 303–21. Chapter 2: "'Grundbuch des Planeten': Zur Geopolitik Karl Haushofers," *Vierteljahrshefte für Zeitgeschichte* 32 (1984): 1–28. Chapter 3: "Rassistisches Völkerrecht: Elemente einer nationalisozialistischen Weltordnung," *Vierteljahrshefte für Zeitgeschichte* 37 (1989): 23–56. Chapter 4: "Die Katastrophe vor der Katastrophe: Auswanderung ohne Einwanderung," in *Zerbrochene Geschichte: Leben und Selbstverständnis der Juden in Deutschland,* ed. Dirk Blasius and Dan Diner (Frankfurt am Main: S. Fischer Verlag, 1991), 138–60. Chapter 5: "Aporie der Vernunft: Horkheimers Überlegungen zu Antisemitismus und Massenvernichtung," in *Zivilisationsbruch: Denken nach Auschwitz,* ed. Dan Diner (Frankfurt am Main: S. Fischer Verlag, 1988), 30–53. Its English version is "Reason and the 'Other': Horkheimer's Reflections on Anti-Semitism and Mass Annihilation," in *On Max Horkheimer—New Perspectives,* ed. Seyla Benhabib, Wolfgang Bonß, and John McCole (Cambridge, Mass.: MIT Press, 1993), 335–63. Chapter 6: "Jenseits des Vorstellbaren—der 'Judenrat' als Situation," in *Unser einziger Weg ist Arbeit: Das Ghetto in Lodz 1940–1944,* ed. Hanno Loewy and Gerhard Schoenberner (Vienna: Löcker Verlag, 1990), 32–40. Chapter 7: "Historical Understanding and Counterrationality: The *Judenrat* as Epistemological Vantage," in *Probing the Limits of Representation,* ed. Saul Friedländer (Cambridge, Mass.: Harvard University Press, 1992), 128–42. Chapter 8: "Rationalisierung und Methode: Zu einem neuen Erklärungsversuch der Endlösung," *Vierteljahrshefte für Zeitgeschichte* 40 (1992): 359–82. Its English version is "Rationalization and Method: Critique of a New Approach in Understanding the 'Final Solution,'" *Yad Vashem Studies* 24 (1994): 71–108. Chapter 9: "Historical Experience and Cognition: Perspectives on National Socialism," *History & Memory: Studies in Representation of the Past* 2 (1990): 84–105. Chapter 10: "Varieties of Narration: The Holocaust in Historical Memory," in *Studies in Contemporary Jewry: The Fate of the European Jews, 1939–1943,* ed. Jonathan Frankel (New York: Oxford University Press, 1997), 84–100. Chapter 11: "Nationalsozialismus und Stalinismus—Über Gedächtnis, Willkür, Arbeit und Tod," *Babylon: Beiträge zur jüdischen Gegenwart* 10–11 (1992): 110–24. Chapter 12: "Cumulative Contingency: Historicizing Legitimacy in Israeli Discourse," *History & Memory: Studies in Representation of the Past* 7 (1995): 147–67. Chapter 13: "On Guilt-Discourse and Other Narratives. Epistemological Observations regarding the Holocaust," in *History & Memory, Passing into History: Nazism and the Holocaust beyond Memory, In Honor of Saul Friedländer on His Sixty-Fifth Birthday,* ed. Gulie Ne'eman Arad (Bloomington: Indiana University Press, 1997), 301–21.

Library of Congress Cataloging-in-Publication Data appears at the back of this book.

Manufactured in the United States of America

08 07 06 05 04 03 02 01 00   10 9 8 7 6 5 4 3 2 1

The paper used in this publication meets the minimum requirements of ANSI/NISO Z39.48-1992 (R 1997) (*Permanence of Paper*).

CONTENTS

Introduction

The evidence has become notorious. As our chronological distance from Nazism and its phenomenal core—the mass extermination—has increased, the latter's historical weight has grown as well. No introduction can do justice to this paradox's many sources, some of which I explore in the chapters that follow. Let us here simply note that the growing centrality of the Holocaust has altered the entire warp and woof of our sense of the passing century. If, well into the 1970s, wide-ranging portraits of the epoch would grant the Holocaust a modest (if any) mention, it now tends to fill the entire picture. The incriminated event has thus become the epoch's marker, its final and inescapable wellspring.

The Holocaust's gravitational pull extends in many directions, affecting among other things those hermeneutic principles on which the study of society and culture is founded and, in particular, the domain of historical research—specifically, those areas where empirically directed historical reconstruction is bound up with alternate modes of understanding and cognition. Strikingly, within their natural environment of *German history,* reverberations of Nazism and the Holocaust can be felt at work in topics that would seem to have little to do, thematically or chronologically, with either. We see, for instance, problems related to long-term tendencies of German history—a context in which the rise of National Socialism is understood to be located—inevitably condensed into the familiar model of a German *Sonderweg* (special path); in turn, the debate over a purported *Sonderweg* transforms historical objects and questions deeply rooted in the nineteenth century into material for the prehistory of National Socialism.

In the realm of modern history, the opposition between interpretive models of continuity and contingency is never sharper than in the case of Germany. A dualistically charged question persistently confronts historians and the concerned public alike. To insist on the long term—to represent Nazism and the Holocaust as the endpoint of a continuous historical development—appears to invite the reproach of a negative teleology, cloaked in a mantle of historical scholarship: deception, in other words, that—however necessary it may be in the face of the horror—nonetheless wipes out the role of *contingency* in the catastrophe's unfolding. In any event, nothing else may occur to a historian confronting the abyss of mass extinction than to force all of German history into the procrustean bed of Holocaustal prehistory.

Whereas such a process—a recourse to nineteenth-century German history for an arsenal of facts that pave a path forward to the Holocaust—may, in fact, look all too far backward, the same cannot be said for research on the Weimar Republic. Unlike the generally social-historical *Sonderweg* debate, research on Weimar focuses on political history, with its necessary stress on ideological continuities and ruptures. At the same time, Weimar's temporal proximity to the catastrophe allows an identification of coherent causal connections and the ascription of responsibility. Nonetheless, historiographers may well find remarkable the extent to which strategies for research on Weimar Germany burden the period with its Nazi aftermath: namely, with the unceasing question of whether it had to come to that—if events before Hitler's takeover might have taken another turn. The question's subjunctive terms underscore the fact that research on Weimar can never settle for the epoch's simple reconstruction. Rather, historians of that fateful period constantly struggle to investigate the possible alternatives to every decision and action that, in their estimation, made the takeover nothing short of unavoidable. It is precisely on account of this fatefulness that hardly any political historical period has been investigated with the thoroughness devoted to Weimar—as indicated, not only in terms of events that transpired, but, in extenso, of those that might have and did not.

If the subliminal epistemological premises informing Weimar historiography can be traced back to the question, did it have to come to that?, the epistemological investment in Nazism and the Holocaust has come to be increasingly articulated under the sign of a schism. The contours of such a schism—so I argue, from different perspectives, in several of the essays that follow—form the respective experiential backgrounds of each of the two principal collectives bound up in the catastrophe. In their generally framed, universalistic approach, inquiries into the "how"—how could human beings do such things to other human beings?—tend to follow anthropological interpretive patterns and thus correspond to the experience of the collective implicated in the active execution of the deed. In contrast, inquiries into the "who"—who were the victims?—aim at clarifying the motives of the perpetrators and thus center on their choice of victims: the extermination of the Jews is understood as a result of anti-Semitic ideology; that of the Romany as a result of hatred of gypsies; that of homosexuals as a result of enmity toward that sexual orientation; that of the handicapped as a result of a eugenic weltanschauung. The proximity of such a focus on motives to a focus on the victims' collective memory seems apparent. Again, the epistemology and understanding of the particular, concrete circumstances surrounding any specific deed embrace the interpretive potential of a negative anthropology and tend to privilege questions of human disposition, whereas investigations into the motives of those carrying out these deeds stress continuities and collective responsibility. In brief, they argue on the basis of specific historical postulates—indeed, on the basis of history, *tout simple.* In the end, the crimes were both grounded in a distinct locus and reflected the impact of a national collective entity whose nature was anything but indistinct. Likewise, they were inflicted, not on an arbitrary collection of individuals, but on those with particular origins and lineage—on grounds, that is, of collective considerations.

When it comes to clarifying the history of the incriminated event, approached in its capacity as a unified interpretive complex, we are dealing with questions of German history. If only for the sake of narration and comprehension, both the relative brevity and the radicality of the event suggest clearly demarcated regions of time and space, which allow us to fix continuities, latencies, and causalities. The anthropological approach, however, paradoxically discovers its most suitable investigative object in the actions and reactions of the victims. For emerging from a nationally disposed Jewish perspective, and bearing the posture of self-accusation, a quasi-historical discourse has developed over the postwar decades to denounce the behavior of the Jews in the face of the Nazi machinery of murder—behavior purportedly revealing an inadequacy or incapacity of defensive response for which the victims themselves are to be held accountable. It is in relation to this sort of argument that the anthropological, "humanity"-centered approach to the Holocaust can supply a fitting corrective. With the help, above all, of micrological case studies focused on the behavior of victims during the catastrophe's course, this approach shows that people facing a *civilizational break* such as that produced by the Nazis, and the monstrous situation resulting from it, could behave no differently than they did—independent of ethnoreligious affiliations and of collective historical experience.

To a considerable degree, the answer to the question of the "correct" approach to Holocaust research depends on the terms in which we formulate the question. And the terms themselves are to no small degree bound up with affiliation to a mnemonic collective involved in the historical events. However, rather than advocate a relativism of standpoints preformed by particular ethnic identities, an approach that reflects on its own premises can take cognizance of a plurality of perceptions and strive for a maximum possible objectivity and universalization. The presence of differently positioned collective memories running parallel along differently gauged narrative tracks has in any event become something like a cultural commonplace. And yet Holocaust historiography's linkage between epistemological and existential premises is particularly striking. All said and done, we face an extraordinarily radical historical occurrence.

The remarkably extreme polarization manifest in historical representations and moral evaluations of the Holocaust should not simply be laid to the account of differing experiences of the event. It appears instead to have spilled over to such short-term vantages from a more deeply layered context of religiously, hence as it were timelessly grounded, perceptions and argumentative patterns—such perceptions and patterns being of utmost significance for the relationship between Christians and Jews. Questions about the singularity and comparability of the Holocaust seem, in other words, to be narrowly tied to models of theological discourse, distinguished by their centering on topoi of election and universalization. To this extent, the Holocaust has not merely set the principal stamp on our epoch: its primeval existential and epistemological meaning is rooted in the founding myths of our civilization itself.

The present volume includes essays of diverse origin assembled around a set of concepts—continuity and contingency, rationality and narrativity—related to modern German history and the representation of the Holocaust. In the first chapter I consider Carl Schmitt's influential career as a legal theorist, beginning with Weimar's presidential cabinets of 1930–33 and focusing on Schmitt's interpretation of Article 48 of the Weimar constitution. My chief concern here is to delineate the manner in which both elements of the constitution and Germany's long-standing political traditions aggravated Weimar's state of crisis; how, in the face of the self-obstruction signified by both the Reichstag's conservative fiscal policies and constant recourse to the ballot box, the increasing distance between executive power and parliamentary legitimation quickened the pace of societal polarization, in the end rendering anything possible—including power being passed on to Hitler. And yet, within contemporary political expectations and despite the prevailing historical view of the event in relation to a teleologically grasped German catastrophe, Hindenburg's appointment of Hitler as Reichskanzler represents a phenomenon of contingency rather than continuity.

In contrast, the following chapter looks at the geopolitics of Karl Haushofer in the context of intellectual and ideological history, thus tending to stress motifs of continuity: anti-Western and antimodern conceptual forms, articulating German ideals of continental European expansion that laid claim to geographical foundation. In this case the geopolitical metaphoric universe, emerging from nineteenth-century German ideas of expansion that made themselves manifest in the Weimar period as a revisionist discourse, extends down to Nazi ideology—without, to be sure, being identical with it. And chapter 3 examines the transformation, within German theories of expansion, from antiuniversalist to racist principles by means of the development of Nazi international legal theory. Despite the eventual defeat of that theory, its underlying premises thus still offer us a radical view of an ideological continuum: the evolution of specific notions that needed no invention by the Nazis. Here as well, the legal theory of Carl Schmitt serves as a fulcrum between conservative traditions and their Nazi execution.

In the fourth chapter I consider notions of historical continuity in relation to what is usually seen as a first, pivotal moment in the turn toward the annihilation of the Jews in Europe: November 1938. At this essay's center is an assessment—in light of the policies toward minorities in Poland and elsewhere in East-Central Europe—of the manner in which the representative contemporary Jewish organizations perceived early Nazi anti-Jewish measures. The essay also examines the hopes Jewish organizations invested in a politics of regulated emigration—and the perceptions within which they were, in the end, trapped. As an aspect of the Holocaust's preliminary history, the increasingly precarious situation of German Jewry thus comes within an East-Central European context: one marked by ever more pressing questions of national and minority status, now interacting with the reality of blocked emigration.

These studies in legal, political, and intellectual history, centered on Germany before and during the Nazi period and on Europe's Jews at the threshold of the war, are grounded in problems of mentality and of continuity. In turn, such problems form the basis for considering questions of theory and method: above all, the question of the rationality of an extermination campaign apparently not motivated by utilitarian concerns. A series of chapters consider this question from different angles: in relation to the shift in Max

Horkheimer's version of critical theory in the 1940s—played out in both the *Dialektik der Aufklärung* (Dialectic of Enlightenment) he wrote with Theodor W. Adorno and other texts—as a reflection of events in Europe (chapter 5) and in light of Jewish behavior in Poland's ghettos, where for a limited period the reality of extermination remained largely beyond the victims' knowledge (chapters 6 and 7). That behavior—often the subject of criticism on the part of intellectuals such as Hannah Arendt—can serve, I suggest, as a historiographical cornerstone in the epistemology of a phenomenon that unsettles our usual assumptions of behavioral and motivational rationality. And in turn, the counterrationality of Nazi actions that emerges from this analysis has implications for the cognitive categories of historiographical research. Explanatory categories of "rationality," carried to an extreme—in an unlimited rationalization of the economic sphere—become for some historians the mass extermination's utilitarian motor; in a followup to my methodological arguments, I subject one particular example of such monocausal historical reduction to extended consideration (chapter 8). That discussion underscores the debt of various approaches and methods in Holocaust historiography to differing narrative structures, themselves reflecting distinct horizons of collective memory and experience—the topic I then explore in detail in chapter 9.

The last chapters center around narrative and memory. Narrative structure, choice of perspective, and the specific material of different narrative traditions point to the presence of a discourse analogous to courtroom procedure informing the conflicting views of history (chapter 10). Frequently, explanatory strategies stressing negligence emerge from a collective memory of the perpetrators' experience; inversely, narratives stressing the guilt and responsibility of the same perpetrators emerge from the collective perspective of the victims' experience (chapter 13). A further look at the effect of conflicting mnemonic-experiential horizons on Holocaust narrative, and a consideration of the Holocaust's growing impact on Israeli historiography, both gravitate around that discursive center (chapter 12). Finally, I scrutinize the comparative historical discourse devoted to this century's Stalinist and National Socialist mass murder and reflect on the meaning of memory as a cognitive category in comparative genocide research (chapter 11).

The discussions collected in this volume represent something like a profile of my interest in the Holocaust, its prehistory, and its historiography as well as the unique relation between history and memory that is significant for this subject. The individual chapters reflect different stages of research, both with regard to contents and methodology. In putting them together in this volume, I have attempted to give a broad overview of the Holocaust discourse in the 1980s and 1990s.

I would like to thank friends and colleagues for their helpful comments and criticism offered when the various essays were originally written over the past years: Omer Bartov, Seyla Benhabib, Dirk Blasius, Detlev Claussen, Norbert Frei, Ulrich Herbert, Gertrud Koch, Cilly Kugelmann, Gulie Ne'eman-Arad, and Moishe Postone. My special thanks go to Saul Friedländer and Anson Rabinbach. Of course, any errors and omissions in the text are my sole responsibility. Particular gratitude is due to the translators of the essays, William Templer and Joel Golb. Joel Golb also accomplished the difficult task of editing and assembling the pieces into their present form. Edith Gladstone, on behalf of the University of California Press, did admirable work as the copyeditor of the book. I also thank Iris Nachum for her contribution in checking out the references. Finally, I am particularly grateful to Liliane Granierer for contributing much to the clarity of the text through her assistance in reviewing the final manuscript.

The publication of this book was made possible in part through the support of the Benyamin and Chaya Schapelski Chair of Holocaust Studies, Tel Aviv University.

PART I

Political Ideology and Historical Context

ONE

On the Brink of Dictatorship

Carl Schmitt and the Weimar Constitution

Nowadays, whenever the concept of the state of emergency comes into a discussion of the Weimar Republic's constitution, Carl Schmitt immediately springs to mind, almost as if in a Pavlovian reaction: the thinker or the ogre, depending on one's point of view. The simple combination of the First Republic's legally regulated political system, in its overall assemblage, with its abolition through the state of emergency, seems to lead us automatically to Schmitt, who may well represent the century's most important German thinker in constitutional law. His definition of the political as the *objectless* opposition of *friend* and *enemy* (not foe: *hostis* and not *inimicus*) could hardly be better verified than by the never-ending intellectual battle as to the importance that should be attached to Schmitt: two parties at eternal loggerheads.[1] Without wishing to add further grist to debate over Schmitt's person or his dubious fame, I argue that we must acknowledge his ambivalent importance. This importance lies in the fact that, as one of his critics, Heinrich Muth, put it, "he is a paradigmatic thinker of our century. . . . He serves as a point of focus in which the different paths, detours, and wrong turnings taken by the *Zeitgeist* meet";[2] Muth's remark applies, above all, to the *Zeitgeist* of the Weimar Republic. It is not by chance that Schmitt has been accorded a position in the fields of constitutional law and political theory equal to that occupied by Heidegger in philosophy.[3] Yet in terms of the effect he had in the Weimar period, Schmitt's ideas form a theoretical pendant to Kurt von Schleicher's practical politics.[4]

Carl Schmitt knew how to surround himself with an "arcane nimbus" of impenetrability—or ambiguity.[5] The robust juristic and political concepts functioned as the lever with which he lifted the theoretical system of the

Weimar legal order off its hinges.[6] At the same time, in a mythological, quasi-gnostic process of conceptualization, they functioned as a smoke screen—as dark hiding places to which the guerrilla forces of the mind could retreat, thereby avoiding the attacks of enemies and critics.[7] The intellectual endeavor of Schmitt, the avowed decisionist, focused exclusively on the concept of the exception—*die Ausnahme*—the sole point from which the normal, hence the norm, could be understood.[8] Schmitt opened his *Politische Theologie* with the following sentence: *Souverän ist, wer über den Ausnahmezustand entscheidet*. This scarcely translatable sentence—"sovereign is he who decides upon states of emergency"—laid bare the conceptual core of the real constitutional legal order at one fell swoop. Schmitt devised the concept of *Verfassungswirklichkeit* (constitutional reality)[9] in order to play it off against the constitution as such. When called on to account for himself, he resorted to the exculpating phrase of the contemplative intellectual, borrowed from Goethe: "but I've only thought it."[10]

Born in 1888, Carl Schmitt lived through four epochs in German history: the Kaiserreich, Weimar, the Third Reich, and the Federal Republic; he died in 1985 at the age of ninety-seven.[11] Not only did he experience the academic and political effects of his work and its reception, but he was also concerned with his posthumous fame. He appears to have guided the pens of his biographers, who have proposed something like an organic line extending from Schmitt's political Catholicism,[12] by way of the effect he had as an interpreter of the constitution of the Weimar Republic and of the presidential regime, on to Schmitt the agnostic and politically "neutralized" figure (*Gleichgeschalteter*)[13]—indeed carrying a party card under the Nazis, but exposed in 1936 as an opportunist by the *Schwarze Korps* and subsequently kept under observation.[14] He always insisted on mentioning his highly privileged form of "inner emigration," taking on—*ex captivitate salus*—the role of the behind-the-scenes interpreter of the Federal Republic's basic law through the agency of his pupils and disciples in the field of constitutional theory. And yet his presence is clearly felt not only among those on the right, such as Ernst Forsthoff and Ernst Rudolf Huber. He also left his mark on those on the left: Otto Kirchheimer and Franz Neumann both attended his seminars, and the former also did his doctorate under his guidance.[15] His heritage is so far-reaching that in the 1950s, Theodor W. Adorno saw fit to delete the footnotes referring to Schmitt's *Politische Theologie* from Walter Benjamin's famous, rejected habilitation thesis, *Der Ursprung des Deutschen*

Trauerspiels: as those responsible for Benjamin's estate, both Adorno and his wife had been left perplexed and helpless when faced by Benjamin's letter to the legal theoretician in 1930 in which he expressed the deepest admiration for Schmitt.[16]

Such opaqueness, such a glittering multiplicity of views, underscore the difficulties involved in specifying Carl Schmitt's importance for the Weimar constitution. The one camp regards him as the reactionary destroyer of that constitution; the other—including, above all, Schmitt himself—views him as the man who helped stave off the Nazis: a *katechon* who braced himself to stem the onslaught of the impending catastrophe.[17] Irrespective of the way he understood himself as an interpreter of the constitution, one thing can be said for certain: the convergence of Article 48, paragraph 2, of the Constitution of the Weimar Republic with Carl Schmitt's legal and political thought is remarkable: almost as if the one had waited for the other. In the person of Carl Schmitt, the state of emergency provided for in the Weimar constitution found its rightful interpreter. With respect to its intellectual legitimation, this "cold constitutional change" from a parliamentary democracy to an authoritarian presidential regime took its course by way of— inter alia—Carl Schmitt.

The state of emergency, the prerogative of the executive, is anchored in Article 48 of the Constitution of the Weimar Republic. The political and constitutional legal considerations that, as some would have it, led to the semi-dictatorship of presidential government, the destruction of the Republic from above, and finally to the rule of Hitler and the Nazis, hinged on this article. Others consider the emergency provisions of Article 48, paragraph 2, to be the opposite: namely, a means to hold off the Nazis. Article 48 would thus appear to be a double-edged sword: a weapon whose use was intended to prevent things from getting worse—and which in actual fact led to the worst.[18]

It was the prerogative of the president of the Reich to implement Article 48. In turn, he was supposed to represent a counterbalance to parliament—or at least this was the intention of the founding authors of the constitution. Weimar parliamentarianism was, in other words, restricted from the outset. The slogan was "a balance of powers" (*Gleichgewicht der Gewalten*); that is, according to Richard Thoma, a Weimar-period specialist on constitutional law, the president of the Reich, elected by plebiscite, was meant to "keep the degenerative potential of government by parliamentary party in check."[19] Hugo Preuß spoke before the National Assembly on the necessity of equipping the political system with a presidential authority democratically elected by universal suffrage, just as was the parliament.[20] The plan was supported by such intellectual figures as Max Weber,[21] Friedrich Meinecke, and Friedrich Naumann. Thus, in the eyes of the constitution, the Reichstag and president of the Reich were in like manner democratically legitimated representatives of the nation's populace[22]—and yet they were not. For in practice, parliament is defined as an arena in which opposing forces face each other. A multiplicity of interests are assembled there, a multiplicity hardly in a position to act together—or interested in doing so—to counter the authority of the president. Thus, the presumed equivalence in power between the Reichstag and the president of the Reich—the parliament could avail itself of the possibility of appealing to the people to vote the president out of office—was purely theoretical in nature. To this extent, it would be euphemistic to speak of the Weimar Constitution as possessing a "dualistic" power structure corresponding to the Weimar class compromise.

Nowhere are the marks of a monarchic constitutionalism more obvious than in Article 48.[23] And they are evident not only in its eventual extensive use, but already in the intentions of the constitution's founding authors. As late as 1923, Hugo Preuß warned against incorporating an implementation law (*Ausführungsgesetz*) into Article 48, something foreseen in paragraph 5. What was imperative was "to retain to the greatest extent possible the unrestricted freedom of action for the constitutional (and thus provisional) dictatorship."[24] No specific law was indeed forthcoming, and no judicial right of review over presidential measures whatsoever was envisaged. As Karl Löwenstein aptly put it,[25] a presidential form of government "was from the outset *dolus eventualis*": it was conditionally premeditated. Thus, the institution of provisional dictatorship by the president of the Reich was accurately recognized to be a point of entry—namely, one through which the Weimar constitutional compromise could be changed in the direction desired by the forces of the ancien régime; and what is more, it could be changed without an open breach of the constitution.[26]

Nevertheless, the understanding of what comprised a state of emergency, in the framework of both constitutional reality and the political practice on which that reality was based, had to be altered significantly before such a change could come about. Hence the field in which such an understanding came into play—in other words, the interpretation of the terms "disturbance" or "endangering public security and order"—underwent various stages of change:[27] from the classic, factual situation of the uprising in the early days of the Republic, via states of economic and financial distress, to the *Notverordnungen* (emergency decrees), down to what was termed the *Verfassungsstörung* (constitutional disturbance)—that is, to the blocking of the parliament's functions—in the last phase of the Republic.[28]

Two elements introduced to expand the concept of the exception are contained in Article 48: (a) the duration and (b) the purpose of the measure. In its classic sense, the state of emergency must, by its very nature, be an exception.[29] It must be brief and geared toward reestablishing the status quo ante.[30] This is clearly the case if the phrase "disturbance . . . and endangering public security and order" is interpreted in the context of a police action, even if it is carried out by the military. In contrast, bringing the phrase to bear in the area of economic and financial policies involves a transgression of its traditional meaning within a civil society—namely, a combating of civil unrest; more important, a measure such as the *Große Steuernotverordnung* (the emergency tax decree of December 7, 1923), executed in the domain of finance and economy, is quite clearly geared not toward brevity but toward duration.[31] The elements of urgency and distress can no longer be discerned in a context such as the decree concerning judicial structure and criminal law, the *Verordnung über Gerichtsverfassung und Strafrechtspflege* passed on January 4, 1924. Here, measure and law merge.[32] Small wonder that the constitutionally enshrined difference between a parliamentary-enabling act (*Ermächtigungsgesetz*) and measures in accordance with Article 48, paragraph 2, no longer existed in practice.[33] The legal institution of the state of emergency became an umbrella institution for decrees that took the place of legislation. The intention was, above all, to cater to the bureaucracy's desire to simplify legislation's inevitably complicated course: a tradition stemming partly from legal practice during World War I, partly from misgivings about parliament's capacity to pass laws in a reasonable period of time.[34]

In the early 1920s parliament was still functioning, and to that extent the above-described process unfolded with its approval; especially since Ebert and the parliament collaborated to supervise the process.[35] The nature of dictatorial powers and the politics of decrees—and, ultimately, the nature of the constitution itself—would change under Hindenburg, the Reich's new president, as a result of his antipathy toward both the parliament and the political parties.

In the summer of 1924 the era of the decrees waned. In the spring a discussion began on the use of Article 48 within the context of constitutional law. At the convention of the Union of German Constitutional Theorists (*Ver-*

einigung deutscher Staatsrechtslehrer) Carl Schmitt and Erwin Jacobi—which is to say the two members submitting reports—expressed the opinion that because dictatorial powers had not been limited by a specific law as foreseen by paragraph 5, the president's unlimited authority extended to the entire Weimar constitution.[36] This, they explained, was necessary to protect the constitution's "institutional minimum"—the office of the president itself, the parliament, and the government. Their interpretation did not receive the support of those constitutional lawyers present at the convention. The dominant doctrine remained, for the time, that the measures taken by the president were bound by the constitution, with the exception of those seven basic rights laid down in Article 48, paragraph 2.

In the autumn of 1924 the Deutscher Juristentag, focusing its deliberations on a topical theme, acknowledged the political necessity of emergency decrees but demanded simultaneously that the emergency laws accruing to the president be curbed through a provision on implementation law, and that any measures taken be dependent on the previous agreement of the Reichsrat and the Reichstag's standing committee.[37] Proposals for a specific law, introduced as a result of pressure from the Social Democratic parliamentarians, did not even get as far as the Reichstag. In 1926 the president of the Reich apodictically rejected an experts' draft, on the grounds of the limitations placed on his discretionary powers: a forceful presidential note to Chancellor Marx ensured that the proposal indeed came to naught.[38] Thus, regarding the dictatorial powers of the president, the opportunity was missed in the Republic's tranquil years to make provisions for harder years to come.

As a step toward further developments, following the end of Marx's fourth cabinet and the elections of May 1928 (which brought the Müller government, led by the Social Democrats, to power), circles close to the president deliberated over plans to create a cabinet of civil servants independent of the political parties—one independent of the left. Schmitt's essay "Der Hüter der Verfassung" (The guardian of the constitution), published in 1929, in which he pressed for the expansion of presidential emergency powers—one of his persistent themes—coincided with these deliberations.[39] Once Article 48 was in Brüning's hands, such a strategy of expansion became realizable: at von Schleicher's behest, Müller would not have been granted a presidential cabinet.

Indeed, the overall intention of the "expansionists" was to exclude the SPD (the German Socialist Party) from participating in government and to extend the parliamentary basis for the right. Whatever the case, the parliament's nullification of the emergency decree of July 16, 1930, led to its dissolution and, following the September elections, to a completely new situation. With the Nazis before the gates, the SPD decided to adopt a policy of toleration toward the government.[40] The parliament approved things—but decided nothing.

It was only in 1932 that people became aware of the fact that Article 48 was to be applied in the context of a new constitutional situation. In that year Johannes Heckel coined the term *Verfassungsstörung*, which refers to the difference between, on the one hand, emergency powers and an interconnected acute and widespread state of danger and, on the other hand, a constitutional emergency invoked on other, at heart voluntary, grounds. Admittedly, if only the institutions involved and the public at large passively accept the situation, what we have here is still formally a parliamentary government; but in actuality, the cabinet existed solely as a result of presidential confidence. The manner in which the Brüning cabinet fell offers testimony to this cold change in the constitution's nature.[41] The course of developments leading up to this collapse were merely the external sign of machinations by the Reichswehr, by the bureaucracy, and by financial and industrial circles aimed at a dissolution of the already tattered Weimar compromise—and thus of the parliament: its replacement by a presidential regime or a reinstated monarchy. The slogan of the day was Reform of Reich and Constitution [42]—and the means of reform was Article 48.

Dominating historical interest in the presidential government—above all, from the summer of 1932 up to Hitler's advent to power in January 1933— is the question: could the Nazi triumph have been prevented by the application of Article 48 or even its "extension," the declaration of a complete state of emergency—such as an actual *Verfassungsdurchbrechung* (overextension of the constitution, or coup d'état)? And if the president had declared a complete state of emergency (*Staatsnotstand*) by applying Article 48, would this have been sufficient tó prevent what occurred? All interest in the political history of the Weimar Republic is in fact an interest in the prehistory of the Third Reich. Carl Schmitt liked to see himself in such a context: the context of what he described as a variety of efforts to prevent, or at least delay, the Nazi seizure of power. In legal terms such efforts would inevitably tread the thin line between a state of emergency and a breach of the constitution. Schmitt forged the intellectual weapons of those who claimed to delay but in fact accelerated Nazi accession to power through their policy of undermining the Weimar compromise.

It was Schmitt's interpretative ability vis-à-vis Article 48 and the state of emergency that gave him access to the sources of governmental power. His stature grew with the changing concept of the state of emergency; or rather, the state of emergency made him great. During World War I he served in the War Department of the Army headquarters in Munich.[43] Two wartime essays resulted from his work there: "Diktatur und Belagerungszustand" (Dictatorship and state of siege) [44] and "Einwirkungen des Kriegszustandes auf das ordentliche strafprozessuale Verfahren" (The effects of the state of war on ordinary penal proceedings).[45] His first full-length study, which was both formidable and caused a considerable stir, was published a few years later: *Die Diktatur: Von den Anfängen des modernen Souveränitätsgedankens bis zum proletarischen Klassenkampf* (Dictatorship: from the beginnings of the modern idea of sovereignty to the proletarian class struggle).[46] Deeply impressed by the October Revolution, by Lenin, and by postrevolutionary developments in Europe, Schmitt concerned himself with the problem of *pouvoir constituant* and the distinction between "provisional" and "sovereign" dictatorship —a point that was to prove decisive for his later writings and the nature of their impact. Here the importance of Article 48 for Schmitt becomes apparent: it embodies the legal institution of the state of emergency as a means used by the provisional dictator, the administrator of *pouvoir constitué*, who can admittedly repeal the constitution, but only in order to preserve it, and is thus unable to introduce a new constitution.[47]

Schmitt's *Politische Theologie* appeared in March 1922. Although concerned with the questions of sovereignty and the state of exception, the book focused even more on the nature of Schmitt's juridical thought, diametrically opposed as it was to the sort of norm-based legal positivism propounded by Hans Kelsen, a later colleague of Schmitt in Cologne. In harmony with the approach of Georg Jellinek, and even sharpening it, Schmitt takes as his point of departure the juridical integration of the social and political spheres. Thus, a direct path leads from Jellinek's "normative power of the factual" to "juridically concrete thinking, conforming to the situation."[48] In his report on a conversation between Schmitt and Ernst Jünger, Armin Mohler glosses this "concrete thinking" as "every sentence is an answer—every answer replies to a question—every question arises from a situation."[49] In other words—Schmitt later brings the point to bear against Kelsen—a decision is made according to a situation and not according to a norm. A norm presupposes normality, yet there is no norm for chaos.[50] "One law cannot protect another law"—such is the sum and substance of Schmitt's constitutional doctrine of 1927.[51] Therefore, only individuals— and *not* norms—can be sovereign: namely, those individuals who must decide on the state of emergency. Although the constitution can determine who is empowered to decide on the state of emergency—according to Article 48, the decision is up to the president—it cannot specify when such decisions are to occur. As a *pouvoir neutre,* placed above all institutions through election by plebiscite, the *Reichspräsident* is the "guardian of the constitution." In a state of emergency, the president functions as provisional dictator, and it remains his prerogative to suspend the constitution up to the point of, as Schmitt terms it, an "institutional minimum."[52]

Small wonder that the attention of the powerful was soon drawn to this handy theory, so tailored to the needs of the executive. The president's letter to Chancellor Marx rejecting the demand for a specific law on Article 48, one limiting the president's prerogative, was permeated by Schmitt's mode of argumentation. The state secretary in the president's office, Otto Meissner, appears to have consulted Schmitt's works as early as 1926,[53] but Schmitt himself first gained access to the ruling powers in 1929, thanks to his acquaintance with Johannes Popitz. In 1928 Schmitt had gone to Berlin to succeed Walther Schücking, the follower of Hugo Preuß, in the chair for public law at the Berlin Handelshochschule. Popitz, at that time state secretary in the Ministry of Finance, was—with Schleicher—a confidant of Hindenburg. Schmitt's contacts to Schleicher himself were established via the latter's aides Erich Marcks and Eugen Ott.[54]

A converging evolution was at work here. In the winter of 1929 Schleicher embarked on practical efforts to bring about a presidential government; Schmitt was devising a theory to that same end. However, it would be unfair to characterize Schmitt as a mere lackey of opportunist constitutional revisions: let us recall that he had spoken out at a relatively early point—during Ebert's presidency—in favor of strengthening the office of the president. To this extent he was not only a forward-looking thinker for the powerful but was thinking ahead of power itself.

The assistance he gave Brüning's government was the *Gutachen* (legal opinion) issued on July 28, 1930, justifying presidential authority in situations of financial and economic exception. Although the measures had not passed through any legislative process, they had validity—as decrees representing law. Despite the fact that Schmitt upheld the distinction, so important to him, between "measure" and "law," it held true only in theory. In practical terms, the distinction could no longer be maintained—*situationsgemäß,* suiting the given situation. The presidential decrees (*gesetzesvertretende Verordnungen*) were now characterized as substituting for law. It was, of course, theoretically possible to annul the decrees by parliamentary majority. More important: the government could stay in office as a managing government, functioning through presidential decrees, a provision previously rejected by the Reichstag. Brüning was delighted by the *Gutachten.*[55]

To which of the cliques around Papen and Schleicher Schmitt belonged is a heated point of contention in the secondary literature. His theory of expediency would seem to suggest that no personal loyalty was in fact at play, but he was always at pains to make sure that posterity considered him politically one of Schleicher's men. Some Schmittian scholars, such as Heinrich Muth, have attempted to derive an ideologically grounded orientation from his writings: an affinity to the DNVP (the German National People's Party), along with a readiness to "reform" the Weimar constitution in harmony with those far-reaching plans being molded by reactionary circles. Quite a few others, like Schmitt's biographer Joseph Bendersky along the lines of George Schwab, draw a nonideological but politically all the more significant line, unmistakably running in one direction: Carl Schmitt as the antagonist of evil, a convinced constitutionalist who wished only to avert the destruction of the democratic order and foil a Nazi seizure of power.[56]

Ernst Rudolf Huber, a close collaborator of Carl Schmitt in the fateful months of summer and autumn 1932, also put forward this view.[57] Yet even Huber remains ambivalent when questioned about Schmitt's intentions concerning the options of *Reichsreform* and preservation of the constitution. But intentions are almost beside the point here: why should Schmitt have taken sides ideologically or strategically, when a full state of emergency, based on an "enlarged" Article 48, would have fused the two options, while quite prosaically solving the problem of legality? It is hardly imaginable that a return to the democratic substance of the constitution would have been possible after what amounted to a coup d'état. And even if the document had been formally preserved, it would have shriveled to a dictatorial core— one comprised of the notorious article.

There is, in fact, an indication that Schmitt may have leaned toward Papen's plans for "constitutional reform." Huber reveals that Schmitt must have known of the *Reichsexekution*—the plan to carry out the "strike against Prussia"—several days before it took place. It was not by chance, stresses Huber, that Schmitt had been asked by the government to take the leading role in representing the Reich's case against Prussia in Leipzig.[58] His involvement is first documented in the cabinet protocols when Papen mentions his name at the July 25 meeting with Jacobi and Bilfinger to discuss this case;[59] the meeting followed fast on the infamous coup of July 20, in which the government under Prime Minister Braun, the "Red Czar," was deposed: undoubtedly an important step in the reaction's plan to "reform" the Weimar constitution and restructure the Reich, in concord with the basic import of the 1871 constitution.[60]

Schmitt's prominent participation in this project seems to suggest an ideological closeness. Nevertheless, when addressing the Supreme Court, his mode of argumentation conveyed the intention of preserving rather than "reforming" the constitution. But in truth, who could argue otherwise in the framework of the court? He based his reasoning on an essay he had recently published on legality and legitimacy.[61] Its purpose was, apparently, a rescue of the constitution's substantive core, in the face of the danger of civil war, through those powers bestowed on the president by the other constitutional bodies. *Legalität und Legitimität* was the apotheosis of Schmitt's influence on constitutional theory, according to both the essay's author and his interpreters.

The essay, so important for the crisis-ridden summer of 1932, was written in the spring and published in July, with Schmitt's specific notation "completed July 10," stressing its prophetic character. In the essay Schmitt interprets the Weimar constitution as a sundered entity, consisting of a "purely functional," "value-free" segment and a substantive segment centered on "a decision about values." Whereas the second segment is to be regarded as inviolable, the first can be altered so as to protect the second.[62] Some of Schmitt's analytic arguments appear quite plausible—for instance, those against functional or purely procedural interpretations, say of Article 68, which declared that "Laws of the Reich are enacted by the Reichstag." It was generally accepted that neutrality was to be upheld in respect to the content of such legislation. This also held true for Article 76, which went so far as to grant the legislative the right to change the constitution, if a suitable majority could be found to do so. In his commentary on the Weimar constitution, Anschütz maintained that the powers of the legislative were actually unlimited: it could even change the form of government.[63] The problem was quite obvious: the constitution did not embody a clear "decision" about political values and their formal stipulation. The talk of constitutional reform within all camps was thus not surprising; its focus was the destructive phenomenon of "negative majorities." Ernst Fraenkel, a Social Democrat, wrote in *Die Gesellschaft* that it was unreasonable to allow for a negative parliamentary majority capable of bringing about the fall of a government, in line with Article 54, unless this majority had the right to appoint a chancellor.[64]

Nevertheless, the essential object Schmitt was aiming at was not simply the distinction between portions of the constitution, one purely functional and the other value-oriented—and therefore unchangeable. After 1945, he maintained that *Legalität und Legitimität* also represented his reaction to Hitler's "Oath of Legality" in the Scheringer trial, where Hitler had sworn he would take power and abolish the constitution by legal means alone. If we recall, however, that Hitler swore his oath in September 1930 and that *Legalität und Legitimität* was written in the spring of 1932, then doubts may arise as to whether Hitler indeed represented the focus of Schmitt's attention. His perspective appears to have been both more general and more ambiguous. In apodictic fashion, Wilhelm Hennis questions whether a theoretician of the state like Carl Schmitt, possessing such deep insight into the phenomenon of mass society and its radical form of democratization, could ever have hoped to be a *katechon* preventing the worst rather than someone seeking to realize a political decision by any means.[65]

In a letter to Schmitt dated September 6, 1932, Marcks, Schleicher's aide, wrote that "*Legalität und Legitimität* is an excellent arsenal for us in the struggle for the future."[66] His enthusiastic assessment appears to have been well founded. According to *Legalität und Legitimität*, the section on basic rights of the Weimar constitution had changed its meaning: the state—and no longer the individual citizen—was now the object to be protected. Henceforth, the constitution's second segment could become the backbone of a totally new constitution.[67] For Schleicher, however, such a development was equivalent to the emergence of a strong state in the form of presidential government, while for Papen and his minister of the interior Gayl, envisaging constitutional reform with a view to a "new state," this reinterpretation of the existing constitution would not be enough.

Papen presented his "reformist" intentions at a cabinet meeting on August 10. He wanted to limit suffrage and create an upper chamber. He and Gayl wished to adjourn parliament indefinitely over the summer, and to have a new constitution drawn up in the interim. Schleicher feared civil war —the Reichswehr's nightmare—and strongly rejected the plan.[68] Schmitt, however, declined to close the door on the idea of constitutional reform, rather speaking out in favor of an initial period of political stabilization.

Doubtless, Schmitt was heavily involved in the planning for a nonconstitutional state of emergency (*überverfassungsmäßiger Notstand*), as outlined by Eugen Ott of the Reichswehr ministry. Ott had been especially appointed by Major General von Bredow to elaborate several proposals for a "further application" of Article 48, in the sense of "extending" the character of the dictatorial authority embedded in the stipulation. Huber makes clear that it was Schmitt, together with Ott, who had established all the necessary steps for implementing a full state of emergency before dispatching Huber, at the time twenty-eight years old, to his flat in Berlin for a secret meeting on the night of August 28–29, 1932. There Huber met Ott and two other officers from the General Staff for a more or less technical task: the legal formulation of presidential emergency decrees (*Notverordnungen*) to be issued in the course of the state of emergency. Schmitt himself remained at his home in Plettenberg.[69]

During a second meeting on August 30, Ott made clear that Papen, Gayl, and Schleicher were going that same day to Gut Neudeck to obtain the consent of the president of the Reich for instituting the partially nonconstitutional state of emergency. This intended state of emergency was nonconstitutional because it included, along with other steps, the postponement of elections beyond the constitutionally stipulated time limit. In other words, Schmitt belonged to the initiators of the plan for gaining time (*Zeitgewinnplan*), aimed at circumventing the deadline laid down in Article 25, according to which elections to the Reichstag had to be held within sixty days. At a meeting with Ott during the September crisis, with Jacobi and Bilfinger also present, Schmitt intimated what his concept of stabilization was: namely that supported by the president's oath to "avert danger from the people," one could cite "authentic emergency powers." These arguments were based on very thin constitutional ice. In any event, the plan failed. On September 12 the government dropped its intention of not fixing a date for new elections, the core of the emergency plans, because it had become known that the Zentrum Party and the Nationalsozialistische Deutsche Arbeiterpartei (NSDAP) were planning to charge the president with breach of the constitution, in accordance with its Article 59.

Carl Schmitt had different assessments of the three attempts to declare full states of emergency on the part of the two chancellors, Papen and Schleicher. In his testimony, Huber makes clear that Schmitt, although very enthusiastic about the September plan, voiced his opposition to a November effort, because of the circumstances, the personality of Papen, and the negative evaluation of the military, and was not very sanguine about Schleicher's plans for January 1933. Nonetheless, according to Huber, he still regarded it as advisable to take all necessary risks and was very bitter that Hindenburg changed plans on January 27 and declined Schleicher's request to receive the means for a full state of emergency.[70] But did the turn of events on January 30 have any deep effect on Schmitt? Had his political principles been offended in some way?

Carl Schmitt characterized politics as being not "immoral" but rather "amoral." Ethics and morals had their place in religion, or in the private realm. In contrast, the medium of politics was power.[71] To this extent it is difficult to uncover deep-seated beliefs or convictions in Schmitt. With his origins in political Catholicism, he joined neither the democratic parliamentarian wing of the Zentrum Party nor its corporative state or antiparliamentarian wing.[72] In scrutinizing Adam Müller's position in his essay *Poli-*

tische Romantik,[73] he ridiculed the political romanticism that had entered into Catholicism in the second half of the nineteenth century via Heinrich Leo and Karl von Vogelsang and found its way into the state corporative wing of the Zentrum Party. He aligned himself more with the vehemently antiliberal Catholicism of the early nineteenth century: with Bonald, de Maistre and, above all, the Spaniard Donoso Cortes.[74] Schmitt was not really integrated into political Catholicism, though his writings appeared in Catholic publications at an early date.[75] And he was never really close to Papen, with his ideas of a system based on "corporate order." He had no genuine ideological affinity with Gayl, a Protestant and German nationalist whose improvisation on the corporate-order theme found few adherents. Schmitt's careful apology for the second chamber contained in his speech to the Rhenish Langnamverein of heavy industry in November 1932, "Gesunde Wirtschaft im starken Staat" (A healthy economy in a strong state),[76] does reveal an opportunistic inclination toward the Papen-Gayl plans for constitutional reform. Nevertheless, his demand that the government establish contacts with all "productive social forces" appears aimed, already, in the direction of Schleicher's *Querfront* (a front running "across the board").[77]

The *Querfront* plan was based on a quite insightful interpretation of the nature of modern mass society. Its principal assumption was that state power could no longer be founded on a thin social base but rather required mass support, even if that support was passive. After the conservative and reactionary circles had neutralized the Social Democrats and forced them out of the political arena, they were able to count only on the Nazis, whom they actually feared in 1932 because of their social demagogy. Schleicher hoped to circumvent the parties and construct the mass base for his presidential regime through a melange of different, at times antagonistic, political forces sharing the common ground of a program to create employment. The *Querfront* was to include the Social Democratic unions on the left, as well as the SA and the oppositional wing of the NSDAP under Gregor Strasser, Christian and free unions, the Stahlhelm, the Reichsbanner, and others. But Schleicher failed in this unique venture. Carl Schmitt, who was certainly in a position to understand the political impact of such an approach to social questions, was from the start skeptical concerning its success and kept his distance.[78] His attitude surely reflected his general propensity for avoiding any concrete political responsibility, while remaining eager to be a party to political events, regardless of their source.

When Schleicher was dismissed and Hitler appointed chancellor, Schmitt was briefly disappointed, "flustered"—"yet somehow relieved: at least a decision."[79] It was not long before he was made Prussian privy councillor by

Hermann Göring. Already on May 1, 1933, he had joined the Nazi Party, along with the majority of German academicians—in his case, as an "intellectual worker." Thus commenced his career within the Third Reich. According to both Schmitt's teaching and his personal inclinations, as reflected in the concrete political positions for which he opted, any form of rule was better than the civil war he so feared; the Nazis were thus neither any better nor any worse than all the others. He stuck with the maxim of Hobbes, his favorite author: *auctoritas, non veritas facit legem.* And he was, as the literary scholar Hans Mayer, who studied under both Kelsen and Schmitt in Cologne, described him: "a man for the season."[80] It seems almost superfluous to add: for any season.

TWO

Knowledge of Expansion
On the Geopolitics of Karl Haushofer

Any scholarly portrait of German geopolitics must acknowledge the uses to which the Nazis put the discipline. For that reason, geopolitics has been of interest chiefly to historians of Nazism.[1] Its most distinguished representative, the professor and World War I general Karl Haushofer, was therefore considered less a geopolitician *strictu sensu* than an accomplice with the Nazi regime. Albeit in reverse fashion, something similar is at work within the field of geography, above all the branch of political geography.[2] Here we observe a stern dismissal of Haushofer and his school. Resulting from Nazism's appropriation of geopolitics, the dismissal is apodictic and strict.

The reluctance to approach Haushofer too closely is first and foremost a result of one particular factor: as a preliminary fulfillment of national history and a syncretistic ideology, National Socialism was able to mold various traditions running parallel to Haushofer's own thinking, making use of them in a practical manner. As we confront the history of the Nazi catastrophe, taking up such strands is unavoidable. They often bear the shape of, yet are not necessarily identical with, the Nazi weltanschauung. Their complex relations are particularly apparent in the geopolitical interpretation of world politics and its patterns of power and domination. Possessing ideological origins similar to those of National Socialism, hence some of its features, geopolitics both anticipated that movement and—along with other political and ideological currents—was absorbed into its mainstream.

In exploring the historical origins of Karl Haushofer's geopolitics, we uncover images, metaphors, and particular forms of perception that emerged from a profound social and cultural crisis. Inversely, within that crisis, we perceive a striking mirroring of motifs that threaten to take on renewed virulence within disparate contemporary critiques of Western civilization. To be sure, the proponents of this motivational mix are often unaware of the historical reference points.

The following discussion focuses on the past strands of cultural ideological perception that came together as geopolitics. In their substance, the decisive moments of Haushofer's thinking involve an articulation of German continental imperialism: the geopolitics he founded thus emerges as an effort, both practically oriented and theoretical in nature, to legitimate the execution of specific, hegemonic intentions. A priori, the discipline's manifestly self-referential character stakes no theoretical claim to generalizable, hence universal validity. It stands in close proximity to other approaches of the time that were virulently narrow in their national and imperial interests. These approaches shared a propensity to balance off imperial realms against one another. The degree of ethnocentricism involved here runs parallel to a second propensity: the justification of a selfish ordering of outwardly directed political claims through a nationalistically amputated international law.

Such a perspective defines Haushofer's geopolitics as a "German discipline"—along with many other contemporary foundational efforts in the sciences and humanities. It conjures up a condition of naturalized durability, deliberately setting itself off, through geography, against approaches to state, territory, and world order that—on the basis of an ever more intense and abstract process of social integration—dissolve an individual's ties to the concrete and natural order. And in the face of (or rather, because of) an increasing abstraction and formalization of both the hierarchy of states and their communication and commerce, geopolitics represents an ideology legitimizing international domination through putatively natural, hence timeless or unchanging principles. To this end it makes extensive use of agrarian, preindustrial, and precapitalist metaphors, physiocratically spurning the meaning of modernity. Based on patterns of knowledge and interpretation that rely heavily on the notion of space, the discipline rejects social and historical thinking in favor of a deterministic biological materialism but operates, to be sure, within a domain of the social. For Haushofer, history is bound up with spatial-territorial durability; civilization and culture proceed by apparently natural laws, and politics becomes a scientifically prognosticable form of perception, since it is understood, in any event, as an extension of this determinism, with ontological cachet. Its universally situated opponent is the terrestrialization of the abstract, itself never manifest as a comprehensible form of abstraction. Defined concretely, this geo-politics is hostile to the Anglo-Saxon world and its maritime culture; it is ori-ented toward the continent and is both autarchic and anti-Semitic.

The antagonistic framework of Haushofer's geopolitics thus represents the apogee and endpoint of that ideology presenting itself as science—the "German science" of international politics. We can reconstruct its features through motifs persistently present in Haushofer's writings—motifs struc-tured by the dualistic opposition of agrarian and industrial, rural and ur-ban, natural (or organic) and abstract.

Although German geopolitics only gained public attention and political sig-nificance following the 1919 Versailles treaty—and hence possesses, quite unmistakably, the status of a revisionist ideology reacting to the Great War's outcome—as a form of thought its social roots lie deeper. They lie in the ex-periential and sentimental world of a bygone epoch, a world that had been socially undermined before its final military breakdown. What led to the real crumbling of faded, romanticized notions of community and culture was capitalist social formation—above all in its crisis-ridden mode during the last third of the nineteenth century. In a country marked—according to Western standards—by delayed development, the process was experi-enced as an intellectual and cognitive shock.

Reflecting this reaction, defiant *metaphors of immutability* opposed capital-ism's intangible reality: a reality that had torn apart and discarded the tradi-tional social fabric, granting prerogative to the urban way of life over that of the countryside, to industrial over agricultural rhythms—in short, privileg-ing abstract over concrete forms of social intercourse. Crucially, the immu-tability proclaimed its *biological* foundation. In this manner, it rejected the ever greater institutional formalization, the suppression of forms of legiti-macy based on family and lineage and the accompanying inherited loyalty, the growing amount of *functional* signification and, above all, its theoretical foundation in sociology, political science, and positivist legal theory—all were innovations alien in their very essence and stood against the putatively *organic* nature of societal relations.

When he defines geopolitics as the "biogeographic completion of a one-sided political science, alien to the soil," juxtaposing the abstract formal "political" entity of the state with its biological political complement of the people (*Volk*), Karl Haushofer finds his place in this tradition of naturalistic organic thinking.[3] For Haushofer, the state is a real "organism"—in the end a "biological" phenomenon.[4] "Pure" jurisprudence, on the other hand, is "hostile to the soil," and sociology is a true antithesis of the soil- and nature-rooted geographical sciences.[5] In general, the logic of this tradition views every formalization as a threat to the "national soil," the *Volksboden*.[6] According to this logic, a border is no mere abstract political dividing line but represents a zone to be endowed with living energy, insofar as a strong, "living spatial will [*lebendiger Raumwille*] does not fix itself in linear fashion." Rather, at the most it develops a transportation network "to improve border circulation" (*zur besseren Grenzdurchblutung*).[7] For this reason, the tradition frowns on the use of transportation in cross-border movement or a mobilization of resources removed from the soil. On account of modern technology's transnational consequences such as the cross-mixing of peoples, it calls for reducing the benefits of technology such as the train system—historically the classic connecting link of capitalist social formation.

In fact, for Haushofer, in their propensity to "open up territory," trains and transport in general directly imperil the *Volksboden*. He sees, for instance, a "Romanifying [*Verwelschung*] of the Wallis canton" as resulting from the Simplon tunnel—defined as the opening of an "incursive gate" for the French through traffic and "Italian undercutting." As Haushofer explains it, "we now better understand the Swiss resistance to trains through the Greiner and Splügen mountains; we are becoming familiar with the shadow side of tracks laid through the Brenner and Semmering passes, of the train-transport gateways linking the west to the Rheinland, of traffic arteries on the Rhein choking under the grip of foreigners, of the development of main traffic zones that are all too near the borders."[8] Haushofer is consequently against opening the borders—in particular the Reich's western border—by means of transportation technology. Rather, he advocates "raising the border's blood pressure," something to be accomplished through socially demobilizing land cultivation.[9] He thus greeted the Nazi *Erbhofgesetz* (law on inherited farms) as one of the "most notable admonitory pillars" in the "turn" (*Umkehr*) away from a social dynamic menacing the *Volksboden*.[10] For Haushofer, the "right of blood to its soil" realized by the *Erbhofgesetz*, "to be preserved through the indissolubility of the ties between the two," confirms "humanity's law of nature."[11]

Throughout Haushofer's work, we find the mystifying leitmotif of an agriculture linking the people to their *Volksboden* and functioning as a form of collective defense against surging modernism, in the shape of a mechanized world. He denounces industry as culture's fall from grace, as a way of life forced on the Germans from the outside: from "strangers to the national self," the *Volkstum*. Even after World War II, in his "Apology for Geopolitics"—a sort of political testament and justification of his writing activity, above all during the Nazi period—Haushofer indicates that the "inadequacy at the time of the distribution of Central European *Lebensraum*"—a plight representing the final, pseudo-empirical legitimization of German continental expansion—was the "result of excessive industrialization and urbanization."[12]

This argument involves a classic neo-Malthusian inversion; postulating a precapitalist agrarian relation between population and agricultural growth based on the assumption of *absolute* natural limits, it ascribes such limits to society and to the possibilities for social productivity. In the process, it necessarily fails to recognize that urbanization and industrialization, precisely through their intensification of agriculture and demographic concentration, are able to expand space qualitatively, albeit not materially. In themselves, industrialization and urbanization do not reduce space absolutely; rather, preindustrial mentalities confronted with the life worlds of urbanization produce a feeling of psychic narrowness that, projected onto a natural environment, appears to emanate from it.

Toward the end of the Great War, the form of consciousness reflected in Haushofer's antiurban, anti-industrial stance had become politicized to such an extent that, in the role of Bavarian patriot, he could even speak out vehemently against the unified state, as well as the industrial system. Not coincidentally, he also expressed heated political opposition to a proletariat incarnating the new way of life. This proletariat, we read, "drew huge salaries and accomplished pathetically little, while real men stood in the field. . . . We hope, then, to separate the decent remains of our [Bavarian] kingdom from the cursed industrial state, living simply and in poverty from what the native soil gives us, preferring to destroy industrial waste with a flail rather than make a pfennig's gain from it."[13]

To be sure, the rejection of bourgeois capitalist life and Haushofer's autarchic motifs all entail reactionary alternatives; an "immoral enslavement to capital" thus contrasts with a military subordination considered "morally justified."[14] In the final decisive phase of World War II, key representatives of geopolitics, wishing to elevate this position to "the state ideology of National Socialism,"[15] shaped it into a cluster of classical images that emerged as Hitlerian Germany's agrarian-ideological, pseudo-anticapitalist existential lie: that the Reich, as a transhistorical mode of being, exists "between the assault of the machine worlds of West and East. Common to both [machine worlds] is a glorification of technology and a lack of any reflection on how far and how long humans will still be able to bear its advancing blessings. Common to both is a detachment from both blood and soil."[16] During the transitional and formational period of the fin de siècle, the backward-leaning, anticapitalist critique of civilization—based on biological metaphors and a natural understanding of the social world—had sunk into the psyche of many Germans: a psyche marked by angst at a new, unknown world both harsh and appealing. Karl Haushofer ends up repressing the latter, intimate aspect of his engagement, which we need to understand, in the end, as informing his geopolitical ideology: "Personally the entire meaning of my life is a battle against myself and my true nature, which, I believe, is a liberal nature. If you take this from me, you render my entire life senseless and rootless."[17]

Haushofer's simultaneously rationalized and mystagogic rejection of and struggle against abstraction, seen as the product of Western capitalist social formation, is a concrete expression of this ideology; his traditional anti-Semitism is the internal or domestic manifestation of this rejection. Haushofer's anti-British stance, apparent in his attack on the "plutocrats," represents its external dimension. This antagonistic complex differs from the Nazi triad of archetypal enemies in that Haushofer's geopolitical speculation does not view "Bolshevism" in an unequivocally negative manner; hostility to Russia has no place in the dichotomy on which Haushofer's geopolitics is founded: continental blockade against a maritime "outer ring," a notion borrowed from Halford J. Mackinder's principle of a "pivot of history."[18]

When Haushofer mentions Jews, he draws a categorical distinction between German Jews and those from the "East," *Ostjuden*. The distinction vanishes when he elevates "the Jewish," *das Jüdische*, to a simple metaphor, signifying the social substance of industrialization and urbanization. The extent of the metaphorization process is manifest in the lack of any consistent direct link between Jews and "the Jewish": the concept covers Germans (along with "plutocrats": freemasons, intellectuals, leftists, and liberals) who can be associated with images of abstraction—with that which is secret, generalized, possesses qualities that cannot be immediately grasped—and dynamic social transformation.[19] Conservative social elements also fall eminently within the concept's venue when they represent organizations linked to labor such as unions or right-wing social democrats.[20]

The centrality of "the Jewish," hence of anti-Semitic imagery, to the foundational structure of Haushofer's geopolitics becomes clear in his category of *Raum*—a "space" not to be understood as geographical in the narrow sense, yet strongly informed by the discipline of geography and essential to the geopolitical project. Where "the Jewish" metaphorically defines negativity, *Raum* signifies a positive existential form that, while connected to reigning circumstances, stands opposed to them. Comprising one dimension of

Haushofer's backward-leaning utopia, it thus serves as the structural antithesis of his biologically founded anti-Semitism, which in its turn mystifies poorly understood social phenomena into eternal categories of nature.

In this manner, Karl Haushofer constantly ties urbanization and industrialization to the Jews, offering his geopolitical idea of *Raum* in opposition to the process. When he must speak of either Jews or urban congestion, he runs short of breath, has a sense of choking. Denouncing the Jews, in classically anti-Semitic fashion, as founders and agents of a nature-destroying world of machines, Haushofer fantasizes them into monsters of power that rule over menacing legions. The Western powers are merely the instrument of an all-encompassing conspiracy. The Jews have thus parceled the Western hemisphere into "strictly unnatural" realms. Therefrom, "the chosen people and its 'Golem' derive their power. For sadly, urbanized as it is, wherever it gains a position of power, the nation of Israel lays waste the natural landscape—with rare exceptions. Marx was such a notorious shut-in, estranged from both air and soil! This Hebrew alone spread such misery over the earth."[21] Through its constant and penetrating repetition, Haushofer's theme of "the human throngs in greater New York, with its more than ten million, its unhealthy agglomerations of peoples, including 2.5 million Jews," takes on a meaning transcending the exemplary.[22]

We find other anti-Semitic observations scattered throughout a rich range of Haushofer's writings, both private and public. His use of classically anti-Semitic images to describe social phenomena—images cast in the light of the political purpose of geopolitics—is manifest, above all, in the liminal region between unfiltered, spontaneous expression and precisely articulated ideas: for instance, when Haushofer compares the Jews with an omnicorrosive "poison tree," or when he speaks of international Jewry's "enmity" to all authentically Germanic expressions of power.[23] In this context, he sees a duty imposed on Germany, in its role of central, transitional land between East and West, to serve as a "filter of eastern Jewry between the Romance peoples and the Slavic world."[24] In the framework of a polemic against the "high treason" and "stab in the back" to which the Great War's German troops have fallen victim, Haushofer—drawing a distinction from German Jewry—refers to the "East-Semitic penetration of the ruling elites" and holds it responsible for all the evil.[25] Despite his partial sympathy for the Bolsheviks—a sympathy grounded in his geopolitical premises—he appraises Soviet leaders of Jewish origin in a pejorative manner. While, for instance, in taking account of Haushofer's work, Karl Radek unmistakably flattered the founder of geopolitics, he in turn passed for Haushofer as a "cunning *Ostjude*."[26]

Such judgments do not necessarily define Haushofer as a systemically racial anti-Semite. Rather, the assurance Rudolf Heß (formerly Haushofer's academic assistant in Munich and meanwhile promoted to the führer's deputy) offered Frau Martha Haushofer—herself of partly Jewish origin—in writing, to the effect that Nazi anti-Semitism was not aimed at all racial Jews, may well represent her husband's stance. As Heß formulated it: "No, my dear lady [*gnädige Frau*], I and my comrades in struggle direct our efforts at those who I believe spiritually poison the people (in the realms of politics, theater, film, 'art') in a deliberate manner, moving it ever further along the path of crass materialism—something that, regrettably, has partly succeeded all too well." And yet Heß is well aware "that the best Germans can even stem from a direct mixing of blood."[27]

Unusual in the context of racial anti-Semitism, the "political" distinction Heß seems to advocate between a "materialist corrosive" Jewish element and a "blood mix" posing little threat to the health of the German people, was in fact an existential distinction for the Haushofer family, since under the Nuremberg laws the Sephardic Jewish side of Martha (Mayer-Doss) Haushofer's family background defined the racial identity of her sons Albrecht and Heinz.[28] A letter of protection that Heß had issued was meant to protect them from any resulting hardship.[29] Clearly, an evaluation of the mitigating differentiation between the biological, hence absolute anti-Semitism of the Nazis and Haushofer's "conservative" anti-Semitism must take account of the family circumstances.[30] Such a differentiation involves ascribing innovative "scientific" consequentiality to the Nazis, and what amounts to a specific bundle of political concepts to Haushofer. This bundle has central status within Haushofer's weltanschauung; it consists, on the one hand, of Wilhelminian Germany's ordinary, latent anti-Jewish sentiments—simple resentment and unconscious angst—and, on the other, of ideologically refined social-Darwinist assumptions.

Karl Haushofer's many Jewish acquaintances, it is suggested, indicate that he was not a racial anti-Semite, but the qualification itself has strongly limited meaning. As is the case with Haushofer's marriage to a "half-Jew" and his belatedly expressed willingness to share suicide with her in the event of her persecution, such connections need not conflict with strong anti-Jewish sentiments or a collaboration with Nazi anti-Semitic policies.[31] The same can be said for Haushofer's acceptance of Hans Kohn (residing, to be sure, in Palestine since 1925) as an academic protégé and for his correspondence with Ernst Simon, with its positive remarks about the Zionist movement.[32] In fact, having achieved prominence under Nazism as an educator of the people, Haushofer effortlessly cultivated his traditional anti-

Semitism—while steadily and comfortably denying the racist basis of Nazi anti-Semitism, meanwhile directed toward mass extermination.[33] Without needing to be a "scientific" anti-Semite,[34] he brushed off the Nazi anti-Jewish measures through the proverbial German analogy with chips that fall when one employs a plane—an expression of political assent prompting his son Albrecht—working at the time in Joachim von Ribbentrop's *Amt Ribbentrop* as Rudolf Heß's protégé[35]—to make the following, despairing comment: "I don't know whether to envy or admire the blindness that doesn't see how close the plane is to ourselves."[36]

Despite his racially Jewish status, Albrecht's own stance toward the persecution was stamped with precisely that political-cultural resentment at the heart of anti-Semitism, to which German-Jews of "origin" were not immune. Until the actual execution of the Nazi policy of extermination, he shared the approach of those viewing a distinction between *Ostjuden* and *Westjuden* as a valid criterion for discrimination, with all its consequences. As did his like-minded contemporaries, Albrecht viewed the *Ostjuden*, in his own words, as "a foreign body, only to be digested in selected specimens."[37] As late as 1934, he wrote a memorandum that he hoped would lead to a moderation of Nazi anti-Jewish policies. His proposed historical-temporal and territorial-spatial criteria for granting the Jews in Germany either full or half citizenship—that is, for deciding when to limit their civil rights—show, in Ursula Laak-Michel's words, "that it was [Albrecht] Haushofer's intention to exclude the eastern Jewish segment of the population from the body politic of the German people."[38]

For those sharing Karl Haushofer's weltanschauung, anti-Semitic themes and images attacking Anglo-Saxon culture stem from the same cognitive source: a postulated dichotomy between the abstract and concrete, maritime and continental, palpable and impalpable—between a conspiracy bent on world domination on the one hand, and a principle of upright openness on the other. In its various expressions, the dichotomy's initial pole is one of the opaque forms of society's principles of exchange: *Tauschen* that Carl Schmitt linked, in an etymologically suggestive manner, with a principle of *Täuschen*—of deception.[39]

An image used by one of Haushofer's geopolitical colleagues to convey the reality of maritime, capitalist, and trade-oriented England typifies the mythic images inscribed on the anti-Semitic retina: England, we read, lies "like a huge spider in the middle of the cable network on the floor of all the oceans, and on their surface, it is building bridges with its flying squadrons."[40] Such mythic metaphors reduce the condensation and abstraction of the circumstances surrounding trade to concrete terms in order to explain their factual guise. Enmity to the principle of trade fastens on the trader—and raises the personification of circulation to the form of "dollar imperialism," thus presenting itself as true to reality.[41] It quickly collapses back into its irrational origins, however, with the clear manifestation of what has been termed "Haushofer's personal distaste for the 'democratic powers' England and America"[42]—for that invisible, intangibly operating dominion that exploits the various *Völker,* "again and again costing them blood and soil."[43] The Anglo-Saxons thus find themselves in constant struggle to maintain the "founding principle of their empire," their status as "pirate states," against a "Europe that is experiencing renewal."[44] Their means of subjugation, we learn, has always been economic penetration through a neutral, border-surmounting "company."[45] And similarly, when faced with impediments, they take recourse to forms of political conspiracy, and to war. In this way, it is the "trade swindle perpetrated by Anglo-Saxon plutocrats and large-scale capitalists who—together with the clans of higher nobility—we have to finally thank for all the misery of the European war."[46]

In light of such sweeping statements, we need to note Haushofer's care in differentiating among the Anglo-Saxons: his profound aversion to the American form of life sparks his most violent emotional outbursts, articulated as European cultural superiority. "In the case of England, existence is still at issue: there I'm content to let hate vie against hate. But the Americans are really the only people on earth who I consider with a deep, instinctive hate, as in the face of a false, voracious and sanctimonious, shameless carnivore, dissembling with every gesture and in reality simply snapping around for feed to satiate his bottomless belly, lusting for dollars—like a lovely alligator."[47] In the Great War he thus recommended "dying European style rather than decaying American style" (*lieber europäisch sterben als amerikanisch verderben*).[48] And he announced the Haushofer school's future political doctrine in his expression of regret at Japan and Germany not having formed an alliance "for mutual protection against the sea wolves. For after all, both countries possessed great cultural power. . . . Only together with Japan [can we] resist the will toward annihilation, the hatred and utilitarianism of the united Anglo-Saxons . . . if we do not wish to yield to them like France or Italy, or if a huge socialist wave does not free us from a suffocating Greater Anglo-Saxon [*sic*] capitalism and its plutocracy, simply veiled by '*democracy.*'"[49] Through an opposition, understood as fundamental, between land and sea—between the "essentially distinct concepts" held by oceanic and continental powers—Haushofer thus geopolitically rationalized, or rather mystified, Germany's political conflict with the English and Americans.[50]

Later Haushofer would see Germany fail to endure, in a military struggle he defined as fateful, as dominant continental power or—corresponding to his earlier notion—to form a "continental block" with Russia and Japan and defy the maritime strength of the Anglo-Saxons. Consequently, in the closing stages of World War II, Haushofer anticipated a situation that would come to seem permanent: the sandwiching of Germany and Central Europe between the dominant power of the Western maritime and Eastern continental ways of life: the region's conversion into a global "military border."[51]

In harmony with his geopolitical schema, Haushofer correctly assumed that a parallel process would unfold in the United States and the Soviet Union:

> [The Americans would appropriate a] more or less broad strip of the European western and southern coasts, thus fulfilling Cecil Rhodes's ideal of opposite coasts. What is at play here is the ancient effort by every maritime power to gain possession of the opposite coasts, thus completely ruling over the sea between them. In this case the opposite coast is at least the entire east coast of the Atlantic, and if possible—to complete control over all "seven seas"—the entire west coast of the Pacific. In this manner, America hopes to hold the most distant fortress close to its "fulcrum."[52]

> [And the Soviet Union would take] possession of all that remains of the European (and as much as possible the Asian) continent, with or without a usable window to the open sea, in order to advance its world political aims from this base. The realm of the German people retreats into that old, danger-filled zone [*Raum*] marked by territorial struggle and battle, caught between sea power and land power. Undivided or divided between "the Third World War's combatants," it confronts a hard fate.[53]

Haushofer's prognosis fits Mackinder's thesis of a transhistorical durable opposition between sea-based and continental powers. This schema, Hans-Adolf Jacobsen explains, maintains that "a central power had always existed on the Euro-Asiatic continental block, its expansive drive was always aimed at the sea coasts. Against it stood a maritime antagonist that attempted to form a ring around this central continental power, thus hindering its efforts at world rule."[54] Such basic assumptions about the establishment or prevention of world domination did not stay stuck on the playing field of geopolitical dreamers. Participating in the 1919 Paris peace conference, Mackinder cautioned—following the logic of his "pivot of history"—against the dangers that a continental rapprochement between Germany and Russia could pose for the maritime powers:[55] an alliance the other European states saw condensed into the cipher of "Rapallo."

Between the poles of the maritime belt and continental European striving for world domination, the German geopoliticians postulate a wavering "quake zone," persistently the ally of one power or the other, plundered and exploited by either the "robbers of the sea" or the "robbers of the steppe." Without consistently maintaining the position, Karl Haushofer assigned Germany foremost status among the victims.[56] Reflecting his steadfast Anglophobia, he pleaded for the formation of a continental block, stretching from Central Europe over Asian Russia to the Far East, possessing—in Laak-Michel's formulation—"Germany and Japan as the outer pillars":[57] with—Haushofer wrote—"the outwardly turned defensive power of two world regions, Asia and Europe, and a reassuring continental center."[58]

Haushofer's effort to realize such a constellation within the framework of geopolitics, as both an academic foundation for German foreign policy and a means of educating the people, was simultaneously facilitated and impeded by the real historical circumstances. Rapallo and German-Russian cooperation during the Weimar period aside, the Soviet Communist regime represented a principal military and political obstacle to both Nazism and Haushofer's continental schema. But for rather different reasons Japan, as well, did not fit effortlessly into the schema. The difficulties involved in a geopolitical definition of Japan corresponding, by and large, to the continental maritime opposition were quite evident. Doubtless, in its historical development, Japan's island status served to encourage an orientation toward the sea. But—the geopoliticians argued—such insularity does not inevitably produce a maritime people. Here, proof is at hand in the contrast agrarian Ireland offers to sea-plying, mercantile England.[59] By the same token Kyoto, that old capital "lying far from the sea," points to a social and cultural structure whose emerging orientation was firmly continental.[60] For this reason, even in its phase of imperialist expansion throughout the islands, Japan long hesitated to decide "which of its sides to consider fateful: the Asian continent or the sea."[61]

Haushofer's sympathy for the Japanese was not sure from the beginning. At the time of his stay in Japan before World War II, he was still insisting that for this people, elements of Western civilization, "notions such as time- and work-efficiency," were "more or less alien";[62] but in the course of the war and the enactment of the Anti-Comintern Pact he expressed satisfaction with the superficially successful "Westernization of the apparently so clever pupils."[63]

Japan and the German Reich were meant to work together on the military execution of a campaign of economic plunder: a campaign inevitably coming up against the rules of a world market defined by a principle of exchange and dominated by Anglo-Saxon principles. Their alliance was thus more pragmatically stamped than the ideological evocations of commonalty hoped to suggest.[64] As Laak-Michel indicates, the partners in the Anti-Comintern Pact united only in the "thrust of their opposition" to the maritime Anglo-Saxons, its concrete core being "for Germany, the system institutionalized by the Versailles treaty, and for Japan, the Washington Naval Agreement of 1922."[65] We find no suggestions that such cooperation possessed a geopolitical content in the sense of Haushofer's continental block—although Haushofer was certainly able to offer much support in preparing the Anti-Comintern Pact, owing both to his (distinctly unpolitical) relations with leading Japanese cadres and to the Japanese reception of his geopolitics.[66] Equally unfounded is the assumption that the August 1939 agreement between Molotov and Ribbentrop was guided by the notion of the continental block or emerged from its geopolitical premise. This assumption was in fact an Anglo-Saxon fantasy, above all represented by American geopolitical enthusiasts. Even before the war, they presumed a calculating "mastermind" named Karl Haushofer lurking behind Hitler's actions—the geopolitician even being said to have a superbly furnished geostrategic institute at his disposal in Munich.[67] In actuality, the Americans were the ones who increasingly entrusted the planning of foreign policy to research institutions—a reflection of the desire to predict and consequently master the complexities of an international society.[68]

Although there was no such institutional link between Nazi foreign policy and Haushofer's geopolitical vision, the idea of continental rule they held in common does suggest a shared ideological origin. But in its concrete, political execution, this identical origin might find different and even antithetical expressions. To be sure, both Haushofer and the Nazis assumed a geopolitical unity of Central and East-Central European realms. But as Franz Neumann suggests, the base for such a unity might be either the "signing of the nonaggression pact or . . . war against Russia."[69] Within the strict framework of territory-centered, geopolitical considerations, both possibilities were in fact available—and the Nazis tried them out, one directly after the other. Because of his understanding of space, Haushofer not only considered the attack on Russia a military catastrophe but saw it end his geopolitical vision of a Euro-Asiatic continental block based on mutual understanding between Germany and Russia.[70] He had even been willing to suppress his reservations about Bolshevism, since his antagonistic world historical schema —continental versus maritime—was open to any form of rule in Russia, all being fit for alliance.[71] He could not warm up, however, to the Nazis' racist visions in the east, their plans for *Lebensraum*.[72]

Alongside the shared—albeit contradictorily expressed—continental political approach to space, to *Raum,* both the Nazis and Karl Haushofer rejected colonization and colonies.[73] At the heart of this rejection was a mutual opposition to the Anglo-Saxon, maritime "outer ring."

The Nazi self-limitation on overseas colonies had its source, in part, in
Hitler's pragmatic desire not to make the British into enemies. As Klaus
Hildebrand explains it, "the renunciation of colonial and maritime politics
was meant to move Great Britain into an alliance with Germany, thus assur-
ing the Reich's European hegemony from the Atlantic to the Russian expanses."[74] But Hitler did not pursue his continental policy from reflective
caution alone. His preference for a European *Raumpolitik,* distant from any
political pragmatism and—despite far-ranging similarities—distinct from
a politics of colonialization, was more decisive. Already in the first section
of *Mein Kampf* Hitler discards the Wilhelminian Reich's foreign policy, its
"claims to maritime power, its politics of trade and colonialization." He reproaches Bismarck's heirs for having neglected a politics of the soil—a politics that, by its very nature, "cannot find its fulfillment, say in the Camer-
oons, but at present only in Europe."[75] At the beginning, such an exclusively
continental orientation was not self-evident in the ranks of the Nazi party—
in any event a dumping ground for various ideational currents.[76] The party
was, in fact, the scene of a struggle between the advocates of the "voyage
over the seas" under the stewardship of the Ritter von Epp—that is, the
colonial faction—and the followers of the program of Darré, the "knights
facing east," whose goal was the subjugation of the continent's eastern peoples and the founding of a racist hierarchic order of rule.[77]

Politically, Haushofer's concept of a geopolitical dualism between land
powers and sea powers took on concrete form in the suggestion that the
German Reich place itself at the head of the movement of colonial and
semicolonial countries struggling for freedom from domination by the
"outer ring." For this purpose, the former Central Powers were meant to
band together into a "pressure partnership" with the USSR, Turkey, China,
and Japan, in order to break the Anglo-Saxon system of world domination,
"chief obstacle to true self-determination by the [world's] various peoples."[78]
Solidarity with anticolonial movements such as that of the Rif-Kabylians
against French and Spanish domination was thus quite natural;[79] conflicts
of this sort contributed to a steady weakening of the maritime "outer ring."
As part of the process, Great Britain, leading power of the "outer ring"—
once its invisible yet potent ties with such territories were severed—was expected to "sink into the same insignificance once marking Venice's presence in the Adriatic."[80] The comparison of England with Venice reveals a

consistent and ideologically necessary misperception on Haushofer's part: he takes account only of the centrality of trade, that constitutive source of maritime power, and overlooks the meanwhile fundamental significance of industry for Anglo-Saxon political culture. In short, he ignores America.

A specific understanding of *Raum* is central for the pioneering German geopolitician. In Haushofer's writings, two concepts of *Raum* interact. On the one hand, we find *Raum* as a metaphor. It encapsulates a sense of life reaching back to the deep societal upheavals in Germany during the last part of the nineteenth century. On the other hand, this approach to *Raum*, having acquired the status of a conceptual current, mingles with concrete, political perceptions. The concrete sense of *Raum* takes on various shapes: for example, it informs the concept of a "Central European" territory founded for essentially economic reasons and dominated by the German Reich— a schema of political order overriding national identities, moving in the direction of a continental *autarchy*.

As the mode in which a deep civilizational transformation finds its expression, the metaphoric significance of *Raum* expresses a sense of constriction catalyzed by a still strange urban, industrial way of life—a sense that struggles to make sense of the world by using ideas and theories about communal life as natural structures. Before Haushofer, the political geographer Friedrich Ratzel—not coincidentally a zoologist by training—had so politicized the biological notion of *Lebensraum* that, as a geographically mutated and expanded notion, geopoliticians henceforth applied it to human communal structures.[81] In relation to the subsequent development of political geography, the social Darwinist framework of its reception, and the emergence of geopolitics, it is of interest that moments of societal "mass claustrophobia" are already present in Ratzel's conceptual schema;[82] such moments would come to typify the German geopolitical concept of *Raum*. Of significance in this context is the suggestive imagery of phrases such as "elbow room,"[83] "freedom to breathe," "spatial constriction" (*Raumenge*), and "demographic population pressure" (*demographischer Volksdruck*). From such phrases came Haushofer's evocation of a "natural right to *Lebensraum*," meaning a new, "more equitable" apportionment of the world.[84]

Strikingly, despite appearances, what is at work within the concept of *Lebensraum*—its geopolitical meaning—is not *simply* that demographic and Malthusian ideology, focused on colonial expansion, manifest in so many scurrilous forms over the nineteenth century. In the end, the metaphor's deeper content cannot be concretized as territorial expansion, however hidden. Rather, it is independent from actual, geographical *Raum*, signifying that sense of life believed lost in the wake of the new social structures. Hans

Grimm makes this distinction perfectly clear in his book treating "peoples without *Raum*"—a notorious work that saw print in the early thirties, far more popular than anything Haushofer ever wrote: "even with a slice of colony or some other sneaky swindle [*pfiffiger Betrug*] . . . constriction can never be turned into *Raum*."[85]

Haushofer's geopolitics was one of the hidden, ideological expressions for this antiurban, anti-industrial, and quasi-romantic nostalgia. As something like a political theory of international order, it laid a pseudo-concretist, pseudo-empirical claim to natural scientific predictability—hence to scholarly respectability. In the process it abbreviated the nostalgia from which it emerged into clear-cut geopolitical determinism, itself grounded in a privileging of Germany, and in the state's corresponding "sociological exclusion" of other national entities.[86] In this manner, it assigned different nations different, inherent geopolitical qualities; if restricted or truncated—the latter being Germany's case as a result of Versailles—these qualities would struggle to achieve renewed fulfillment in the geopolitical reality of their natural territorial distinction.

According to Haushofer, the "all-German sense of space" (*gesamtdeutsches Raumgefühl*) is "continental and potamic."[87] "As the inhabitants of water-rich ancient settlements," the Germanic tribes already had a special "relation to watercourse borders." In fact, rivers never represented borders for such peoples, the Germans inevitably settling, as a "river-dwelling people" on both banks of a river.[88] The potamic sense of *Raum* that Haushofer thus postulates can hardly be reconciled with political decisions severing ethnicity and territory—the fate of both the Vistula and Memel regions as a result of Versailles.[89]

For Haushofer, the naturally determined geographical situation appears especially explosive when a disproportion starts to emerge between demographic population pressure and *Lebensraum*. He uses a population "pressure quotient" to measure the "lack of *Lebensraum* and free flow of breath," the "border pressure and constricted space [*Raumenge*] stifling the breath of inner Europe."[90] In distinction to the Germans—"robbed of *Raum* and with a pressured populace" (Haushofer's term here is *volksgedrängt*)[91]—the other "great people of the earth, needing to protect and nourish, in their wide open spaces [*weiten Räumen*], populations with *population pressure numbers* [*Volksdruckzahlen*] per square kilometer of merely 7 (the Soviet Union), 9 (France and Belgium), 12 (Britain), 15 (the United States), 16 (Italy), 20 (the Netherlands)," assure themselves of "free, defensible passages on land and sea, self-determination concerning coasts and streams, a free beating of the arteries." "Only the Japanese empire," Haushofer asserts, "displays *pressure rankings* [*Druckstände*] similar to the German (150 and higher, in high-yield regions up to 969)."[92] With his premodern and agrarian, in themselves indeed neo-Malthusian ideas concerning overpopulation, inadequacy of nourishment, and lack of space, Haushofer overlooks the capacity of intensified production to qualitatively extend *Raum*.[93] Instead we find references to the "cultural-political effect of expanded *Raum*" at the cost of other peoples—for instance the "pushing of racially alien forces down from the forest regions of Central Europe."[94] What was needed, to be sure—Haushofer argues—was a new political order, a "Third Reich come down to earth," only "earned and merited" through a movement far beyond "formal political borders." "From a folkish political perspective," Haushofer suggests, such a movement would recuperate that which "is folkishly ours due to rights based on ancient land appropriation, centuries of hard toil and rootedness."[95]

Haushofer makes it clear that the concept of geopolitical *Raum* does not correspond to that of the modern, territorial state, grounded in a more abstract understanding of nationality and region. In contrast, *Raum* reflects a concept of Reich that preceded the nation-state's onset. Consequently, the fact that German identity took on state form only at a comparatively late historical moment, with a large number of ethnic Germans thus living outside the state's legal territory—outside its "state soil" (*Staatsboden*) and "Reich soil" (*Reichsboden*)[96]—represent a fundamental conflict of political historical vision. Haushofer displayed a steady interest in the German presence beyond the Reich's borders—in the German "scattered settlements" extending far to the east, "to the Caucuses and the Volga."[97] Parts of the German people—not to be brought, in any event, into harmony with the modern, Western national idea—lived, among other places, in foreign national and linguistic communities spread throughout Central and Eastern Europe. Until World War I, ethnic coexistence within a multinational body politic had enjoyed dynastic legitimation. As a continentally oriented geopolitician, Karl Haushofer hoped to inherit the bankrupt dynasty's assets by way of new concepts of order, placed under German political hegemony according to the central geopolitical principle of concord between state and national borders.[98] The assets would thus be relocated in a unified context resembling a Reich, its contours become visible in the continental imperialist idea of *Mitteleuropa* (Central Europe) under German hegemony.

Alongside its significance as a metaphor for a lost sense of life—gaining rapid concretization and politicization after the Great War; mobilizing naturalized, reactive images against formalized state and societal institutions—the notion of *Lebensraum* amalgamated supernational, continental plans for a political structure dominated by Germany and basically *economic* in nature (this the geopolitical concept of Mitteleuropa) and built on a geopolitical *principle of autarchy*.[99] Manifest here is a temptation to politically fuse two distinct phenomena: Germany's traditional economic expansion toward the east-southeast[100] and the areas of German ethnic settlement along the Donau: one more confirmation of the dictum that "geopolitics and ethno-politics go together."[101]

The concept of Mitteleuropa was developed by Friedrich Naumann (1860–1919).[102] Aside from the German Reich and the Dual Monarchy, it was meant to include Turkey, Rumania, Greece, and Holland. Although its designated organizational form was federative, plans were also made to hold the system together through military might, which inherently contradicted the federative intentions and pointed instead to a centrally oriented structure. In any case, a centralizing propensity is evident in Naumann's talk of a strong "state socialism" to oppose the capitalist, hegemonically Anglo-Saxon world market. Such a schema, amounting to a continental European *colonial autarchy,* has its precedents in the history of German efforts to achieve unity: for instance, in the writings of Friedrich List (1789–1846), who argues in "Das nationale System der politischen Ökonomie" (National system of political economy [1841]) for a united German national state whose primary role involves a protectionist politics.[103] A vehement advocate of the customs union, List speaks up for a self-sufficient economy drawing sustenance from the continent's wide expanses, thereby embracing under German leadership all extant German states, all Central Europe, and, finally, all the vast area's different nationalities. Within List's schema, Austria held the political and Prussia the economic reins.[104]

This conception of Mitteleuropa contradicts the dominant nineteenth-century idea of the territorial national state. It is quite analogous, in actuality, to the German idea of Reich, which does not postulate a formational identity between the (national) state's inhabitants and territorial boundaries.[105] The conception—which geopolitics made into its political vehicle—was eminently well suited to the realities of Central and Eastern Europe: the intermingling of various ethnicities in population centers and settlement zones throughout the area meant that any national or linguistic border demarcations were in fact impossible. From this reality sprang the predilection for a supranational German-oriented rule in the area, accompanied by a pseudo-objective idea of geopolitics: a rationalization of imperial domination revolving around an axis of closed economic spheres—around the autarchic schema.

This schema can be traced throughout the entire corpus of continental—that is, German-centered—geopolitical writings.[106] Rudolf Kjellén argues as early as 1924 that "as a natural region," a Reich—in distinction to a merely *formalized* state structure—must "be constituted [*geartet*] in such a way that it guarantees a fitting autarchy. That is the real determination of inwardly situated geographical individuality."[107] Fully articulating the traditional antiabstract and agrarian weltanschauung, Kjellén discovers the solution to the "general economic problem" in autarchy:[108] a "reaction to the nineteenth-century industrial *typus,* cosmopolitan in its essence, exposing the national economy to competition on the open world market, where as always the strong can swallow up the weak, in the name of free trade."[109]

Kjellén appeals for a "relatively closed off, self-contained zone of production and consumption, which in emergencies is able to exist on its own behind closed doors." He defines autarchy as "nothing but the state's economic individuality, just as the natural region represents its geographical and nationality its ethnic individuality. The consequences of economic policy thus merge with those of geopolitics." And, he suggests, with its demand "for a homogeneous, self-contained populace," ethnopolitics stakes a parallel claim to its geopolitical counterpart.[110] In doing so, it maps the world into imperial regions—but regions that, in contrast to the invisible abstraction of the world market's exchange system, are *geographically* clearly demarcated. According to Kjellén, "in its great imperium" England already possesses "its sphere of interests. . . . Germany, however, must still create its own sphere. . . . Here we encounter the concept of Berlin-Baghdad and Mitteleuropa on the basis of a free union of state organs, hence a closed sphere of interests in which the Levant's paramount trade activity is conceived as a complement to Germany's industry." Here Kjellén can cite historical predecessors: "Fichte's closed trading-state" is "merely another name for the closed, autarchic sphere of interests."[111]

Karl Haushofer located himself in the tradition of political geography extending from Ritter to Ratzel to Kjellén.[112] In Allied custody after the war, he justified the strategy of autarchy embraced by the Nazis as a constant of German history. Autarchic theories, he explained, were "already understood and prepared by Stresemann and Brüning."[113] Such theories concerned "the connection between freedom, self-determination of a *Lebensraum,* and its capacity for economic self-sufficiency (autarchy), in conditions of balanced population density. This contributed greatly to Central Europe's sustained economic capacity for resistance, even during the war, and Darré's organization of the Reich's food-distribution network lay along such lines."[114] By means of this schema, the "concentrated industrial zones [in the west] could be supplied with the surplus of raw materials from the ethnic German [*volksdeutsch*] east"—also including Transylvania and other such eastern regions.[115] On the basis of extended regional demarcations the schema defined as natural, it made the geopolitics following such a principle into a "kind of land registry for the planet," through which the world was to be newly—and at last justly—apportioned.[116]

With this end in mind, in 1928 the discipline of "geojurisprudence" begins to search for new legitimatory criteria, which it discovers within spatial political "natural law," a sort of *Naturrecht*.[117] In a manner similar to what we will observe in the next chapter, in greater detail, regarding the Nazi international legal theorists, geopolitical *Naturrecht* opposes traditional international law's abstract and universal norms and premises. As the basis for *Naturrecht's* new, spatially particular international law,[118] it primarily rejects the formal principle of the legal equality of states in their capacity as international legal subjects.[119] Geojurisprudence appeals for regional hegemony in the form of a greater territorial order [*Großraumordnung*] within "international law," constantly citing the Monroe Doctrine's theory and practice as an example of its geographical determinism.[120]

The deeper sense of the demand for the negation of universal, positivist formal international law—for a shift toward new, geopolitically determined natural legal premises—lies in a presumably unfavorable starting point in the contest of imperial powers to reapportion the world's natural resources: it lies, that is to say, in access to raw materials. What geojurisprudence proposes here is a legal theory implicitly emerging from autarchic *Raum,* thus staking a legal claim to *ground rent* in an international context.[121] Within the revision of international law invoking "natural" geopolitical circumstances, it directly connects law and the realm of territorial domination—which does not amount to extending that law's principle of sovereignty so that its exalted status applies to the economic power at the state's command. What is in fact at work here is the subordination of peoples within structures of rule organized geopolitically, hence in relation to *Raum,* and thus no longer deriving their legitimacy from universal, international legal principles. Examples of such structures from World War II are the sphere of "co-prosperity" announced by Japan and the "new European order" for which Hitler struggled.[122]

Debate over the extent of Karl Haushofer's real agreement with Nazi policy—or the use of his geopolitics as an instrument of continental imperialism, or the points of convergence and divergence with Nazi praxis—is pointless. Like many of his contemporaries, Haushofer was basically a "fellow traveler."[123] But who, measured against the "pure" Nazi ideology and an inner circle of fanatical initiates, was truly a Nazi? To the extent that the Nazis presented themselves as enthused German nationalists, we can discern far-reaching correspondences between Haushofer's weltanschauung and the Nazis' much more ambitious program. And whatever Haushofer's reservations about common values, he did not fail to make use of Nazi privileges.

Yet Haushofer never joined the Nazi party. In December 1938, in a letter to the dean of the University of Munich's faculty of natural sciences, he justified his distance from organized National Socialism as a result of the "concealment" (*Tarnung*) of his close relation with leading party figures that had begun in 1919.[124] Retrospectively, we can cast the "concealment" argument in Haushofer's favor, as an indication that at the time he needed an excuse for *not* joining the party that would seem plausible to the conspiratorially inclined Nazis. But his proximity to Nazi ideology and his officially promoted activity as *Volkserzieher* (educator of the people) for the promulgation of an expansive geopolitics both point to another interpretation: despite sympathies deep-seated enough to warrant party membership, Haushofer opposed such formal political commitment as a matter of principle. In this regard, he belonged to the class of educated Germans who considered themselves in principle "*a*political." As early as the 1920s we see a tendency emerging in Haushofer that would prove durable—a positive participation in, and strongest possible identification with, the "movement," accompanied by an avoidance of clear and direct responsibility. The tendency reveals itself, for instance, in Haushofer's maintenance of ties with the Bund Oberland (emerging from the Freikorps Oberland) while refusing to accept the offer of a leading role there.[125]

Apart from ideological affinities, Haushofer's closeness to the Nazi and state apparatus was furthered by his close friendship with Rudolf Heß—the figure he had in mind when he invoked 1919 and his acquaintance starting then with leading Nazis. As Hitler's deputy, Heß had become a commissioner for *Volkstum*, entrusted with oversight of relations with ethnic Germans living in the east. In October 1933 he founded the "national German council" (*Volksdeutschen Rat*), under the chairmanship of Haushofer, then made the council his chief consultative and executory organ.[126] Haushofer was also most closely connected with the Nazi regime through his presidency of the German Academy. The extent to which such ties were mediated by Heß is apparent in the fact that after the latter's famous flight to England in 1941 and, following an interrogation by the Gestapo in the same year, Haushofer found his role limited in every respect.[127]

Speculation that his geopolitics, rather than Haushofer himself, served as godparent of the Nazi plans for world conquest is quite unpersuasive. Doubtless, as we noted, both Haushofer's geopolitics and the Nazis' expansionary motif emerge from a sense of constricted space that can be considered a phenomenon of political consciousness. Hitler appears to have taken up the problem of *Raum* as a political conceptualization of Nazi plans to conquer and "Germanize" the east as early as 1920.[128] It is virtually certain that, as Klaus Hildebrand suggests, he "was familiar with the problem . . . since the days of the Landsberg internment, lamented German territorial constriction, and desired to compensate for this deficit through conquest of Russia's Jewish-Bolshevik expanses."[129] There is no positive proof that Hitler was directly familiarized with geopolitics and the *Raum* idea through Haushofer or his "elected son" Heß.[130] If theoretical speculation on *Raum* had any strong influence on Hitler, then most likely it came from Ratzel's *Political Geography,* one of the most frequently read books in the Landsberg fortress.[131]

To be sure, we know that Haushofer was a frequent visitor to Landsberg.[132] He was there, however, for the sake of Heß, to whom he felt a special closeness since the war began. True, Hess took down *Mein Kampf* from Hitler as dictation, and elements of Haushofer's geopolitics may have been assimilated in this manner into Hitler's written program and cultic project.[133] But the explanatory value of such a link is limited, particularly in light of Hitler's later highly negative remarks about Haushofer and his geopolitics.[134] Even before this point, Haushofer scarcely exerted any real influence on the process of political decision.[135] His son Albrecht kept him informed about the course of affairs in the higher echelons of the Nazi state, thanks to Albrecht's position in Ribbentrop's office.

Haushofer's role as educator, as apologist for the ideology of *Lebensraum* and an expansionist nationalist orientation, is far less benign.[136] As suggested, it placed him in natural alliance with the Nazis—up to a desired point of saturation. But the partnership was limited, because a sharp opposition between geopolitics and Nazi politics grew along with the "plans for a new order": namely, the opposition between a politics of *Volk* and race, on the one hand, and *Raum,* on the other, apparent already in the differences between Haushofer and the Nazis vis-à-vis the Soviet Union. Beyond this, any conquest and annexation of national territory inhabited by "alien blood" contradicted the political idea of ethnic homogenization, of the identity of geopolitics and ethnopolitics.[137] The call of *Heim ins Reich* and the continental imperialist, expansionist politics of *Lebensraum* were on a collision course.[138] In his ideas of a "greater Germanic Reich" and in the brand of expansionist, exterminatory politics linked to it, Hitler went far

beyond the expansionist national German concept[139]—itself even conflict-
ing on occasion with the *Volk*-centered policies of the "Alliance of Germans
Living Abroad," which Haushofer headed.[140] Particularly in the case of
South Tyrol, this divergence in views would have negative consequences for
Haushofer.

For the sake of his alliance with Italy, in 1939 Hitler's decided to transfer
50,000 ethnic Germans to the northern side of the Brenner and to plan
their later settlement in the Crimea: a decision marking the subordination
of population politics to long-term, continental imperial *Lebensraum* planning. In his role as national ethnic policy advisor, Haushofer took up the
cause of the South Tyroleans, protesting against measures deemed "conceivable in the course of greater territorial, world-historical land cleansing
[*Flurbereinigung*]," yet here judged unjust.[141] When his book *Grenzen* was
published with some passages casting doubt on the Italian claim to South Tyrol, the Reich's Ministry for Propaganda banned it at Italian prompting.[142]

Haushofer's career advanced because geopolitics occupied the center of
Nazi educational efforts in the realm of foreign policy. He justified his ties
to the regime in terms of the influence he could exert on it. If only by virtue of the affirmative proximity in which he stood to Nazism, he could realize the intent he expressed through the English phrase "Let us educate our
masters."[143] This proximity, and not his documented stance toward the
Nazis, made him a "regime-conforming sympathizer," excluding any plans
for overt or covert resistance.[144]

Karl Haushofer's geopolitics represents the effort at an ethnocentric imperialist scientization of international politics. Necessarily denying the universal nature of world society and assessing *Raum*—after an initial defensive
stance as a basis for revision of the Versailles treaty—from the vantage of
blatantly particular interests in a "natural right" to expansion, the discipline's bias was toward expansion and conquest.[145] In its scientific theoretical self-definition as a "propaedeutic for foreign policy"[146]—meant to steer
practical decisions and directed against developed Western capitalism's abstract and formalized understanding of state and law (hence against a world
society led by Anglo-Saxon principles and values)—it was, explicitly, an
"antipolitical science."[147] The world order announced through geopolitical
planning was an imperialism that did not claim legitimacy in *economic*
terms—that is, through the abstraction of exchange and the hierarchy of
productivity—but in terms of the world's *political* repartition: a repartition
granting imperial control to a *Großraum* led by the German Reich. Force
alone could execute this project. In the end it mobilized a world coalition
against it.

THREE

Norms for Domination

Nazi Legal Concepts of World Order

Racism biologizes the social. By conceptually naturalizing social phenomena, making them seen unchangeable, it renders them eternal.[1] Projections of nature-like duration have a utopian character. Nazism was an effort to enact such a utopia, its biological fiction extending over nearly all societal realms.[2] Law and legal regulation were part and parcel of such a process—both inside Germany and beyond. Where, owing to the traditional principles of sovereignty and noninterference, the enactment of domestic law had a quasi-legitimate formal status, the consistent mutation of international law and its foundations was of far greater import. For by regulating the cosmos of legal subjects in the external sphere, international law represents the quintessential form of international political intercourse. Consequently, the Nazi transformation of *jus gentium* was meant to revolutionize the international system: a system predicated on a universal consensus drawn from long-evolving legal precedents and their consequent general legal axioms. This transformation, antiuniversalistic and anchored in racial theory, necessarily reduced the universal legal system to ruins, in order to reconstruct it biologically. To this extent, the National Socialist theory of international law is a "conceptualized," scientized version of the Third Reich's vision of world order.

The following discussion does not posit a direct link between the theoretical structure of Nazi international law and Nazism's practical foreign policy. Nor, inversely, does it derive the Nazi effort at constructing international law from various plans of action in the external sphere, always subject to the rule of expediency. At the same time, the discussion's focus will not

49

center on a fixed connection between, on the one hand, Nazi foreign policy and the strategy of conquest and, on the other, the formation of a Nazi
theory of international law—though the glaring opportunism of its syn-
cretic and eclectic theory makes its function in the everyday business of politics only too apparent. The instrumental significance of Nazi international
law for the Third Reich's foreign policy has already been the subject of much
learned study; if not conclusively, it at least covers the theme's essential aspects.[3] The following will demonstrate the unmistakable presence of the
utopian project for a biologically constituted world society in Nazi international law.

As we observed in the work of Carl Schmitt—and in the geopolitical writings of Karl Haushofer discussed earlier—the destruction of abstract legal
form was of central concern to the Nazis. Both in international and domestic law, they substituted concepts of a "concrete order" (*konkretes Ordnungs-
denken*) that adhered to the conceptual schema Schmitt described as "suiting the given situation." In this destructive enterprise, they consigned to
oblivion other accomplishments of civilized modernity that touched on
universal abstractions. So, for instance, they replaced the well-defined idea
of the territorial state with the vague idea of a Reich; dissolved contractual
principles in favor of an archaic Germanic notion of loyalty; substituted for
the formal, horizontally conceived equality of states a spuriously concrete,
vertical, and in the end racial hierarchy; and—as a negation of the idea of
universal unity implied by states linked into a world community of law—set
up a self-contained cosmos of extraterritorial spheres led by dominating
powers. Once the dam was opened, it was easy to construct an international
law based on the principle of *Volk*, and on that of *Großraum*—the "wider" delimited realm of domination.[4]

As is the case with Nazism's legal theory in general, its international law
fixed on the theoretically vapid, yet politically forceful dictum that law must
help "preserve the *Volk*," protect its unique (*völkisch*) character.[5] Anything
that seemed to threaten the biological substance or the race was considered
damaging. The struggle against a formal abstract concept of law had its
source, above all, in its neglect of the individual's putatively "concrete" affiliation with people and race, hence in its assimilative effect: such law, we
read, was not concerned with a "specific content, but only with a particular
form—legal form"; not with a specific goal, "but only with a single means—
law as a universal means for any social end one chooses."[6] The National So-

cialist critique thus targeted any law that was "not the expression of a communal entity [*Gemeinschaft*] but is only the reasoned contractual regulation of a human multitude."[7] The only justification for such contemptible "juridical formalism" was the expulsion of "culturally based organic law" (*Kulturrecht*) to a private sphere outside the state: a consigning to the state of "neutral civilizational tasks" alone.[8]

This perspective requires the replacement of law accessible only to "logical dialectical" activity—not to activity harmonizing with "laws of nature"[9] —by law that no longer can be "devised," but only "revealed" or "discovered."[10] The law's essence is thus not to be explained through "a formal act of legislation or its enforceability," but in relation to its "political, hence *völkisch* and racial grounding."[11] For this reason, in place of "abstract principles, the concrete political reality itself must be raised to a legal position and legal idea."[12] In turn, the incarnation of Nazi "political reality" lies in the notion of the *Urvolk* (primal people), a notion conceived as directly combating that of the *Staatsvolk* (state people), based on citizenship. Together, *Urvolk* and *Staatsvolk* "constitute the two key political ideas that offer access to two opposing legal worlds": the world of form and the world of concrete regulative thinking, grounded in *völkisch* values.[13]

The idea of organic order traces its roots back to the tradition of the "historical legal school" (*historische Rechtsschule*) and the fiction of the *Volk* spirit, *Volksgeist*, in order to thus elevate the "authentic people" (*völkisches Volk*) to a category of international law.[14] In contrast, it defines the *abstract* idea of the people—the people as nation—as emerging from the French Revolution.[15] The abstract idea becomes a condition of the formal state, which in turn breaks down the distinction between race and *Volkstum*, in the sense of national identity.[16] In the past, according to the National Socialist critique, "the racial-cultural-historical essence of the people was not recognized: what constitutes a people was determined by the state."[17] Under the Nazi regime the "completely new, racially determined concept of the people," that of the organic *Urvolk*, takes the place of the abstract and formal concept of state. As a biological "foundational fact" (*Grundtatbestand*), it supplants the "derivatory fact" represented by the *Staatsvolk*.[18]

National Socialist law does not assert its *völkisch* foundations solely through the opposition of authentic people and formal state. It also confirms the law's *völkisch* character by subordinating abstract form to its own organic substance, tracing abstract law back to a Jewish racial disposition. The state as an abstract sphere of competence—the heatedly attacked formal construction of Hans Kelsen's influential "pure theory of law"—is attributed to the particularities of Jewish existence, which "has lost every natural relation to the concrete soil [konkreten Boden]." Concrete elements of territory and soil, still present in earlier legal thinking as well as in the concept of state, then evaporated into abstract form. From such an "evisceration of the concept of territory [Gebietsbegriff]," its transformation into a merely normative complex, a vantage antithetical to concrete ideas of territory has emerged: "without distinction, soil, territorium, state region [were] conceived of as Raum in the sense of an empty dimension of surfaces and depths with linear borders."[19] For Nazi legal theorists, this "mathematically neutral, empty concept of territory" needs to be replaced by a geographically and politically concrete "wider" spatial concept, a Großraum.[20] To this end, they deem it appropriate to evoke the interpenetration of corporate body and region called for by Otto von Gierke, and their fusion into an organic unit or corporate region, as was the case for the medieval state.[21]

For those sharing a völkisch notion of the state, the aims of state and international law cannot be severed. In this respect, the universalistic world principle corresponds to the abstract state, hence to the opposite of concrete territory. It is an expression of the "imperialist rule of the abstract norm." That norm's highest embodiment is the "amorphous civitas maxima";[22] its dissolution through the Nazi concept of "concrete order"—through Lebensraum and Großraum, "ethnarchy" and "autarchy"—prepares the way for a transhistorical "notion of Reich respecting folkish life."

Considered in total, the Nazi legal cosmos centers on the structural opposition between abstract legal form and concrete law. This does not mean, however, that all the underlying currents of Nazi international law move in harmony with this opposition. We thus find an effort to arrive at compromise formulas, weakening the central thesis that abstract norms are only apparently of a general character, their actual purpose being simply to "mask concrete states of power." For many skeptical Nazi international jurists, in the face of the desire to raise "'concrete order' to a general formative principle of international law," such a basically correct position would overshoot its mark. As a result, they argue for a distinction between authentic, "unconcealed" general norms and those impossible to grasp in their abstract generalization, the first sort taking on a rationalizing sense where matters regularly repeat themselves with a certain uniformity.[23]

But even such reservations are not to weaken the attack of "concrete regulative thinking" on international law's formal and abstract dimension— above all, on the attribution of universal validity to international legal norms. The attack begins at the locus where international law is, in fact, at its weakest: the realm of its theoretical construction.

To appreciate the thrust of National Socialism's critique, we do not need to describe in detail the traditions of historical construction behind the Nazi demolition of international law.[24] Instead, we focus on the argumentative strand that led it to replace a horizontally oriented international law of states by a vertically oriented, racially based hierarchy of peoples. The transition points between antiuniversalist origins and biological, National Socialist unfolding are not distinct. A critique of the historical construct of *jus gentium*, grounded in the putative anti-German or "anti-Reich" tenor of international legal norms, consolidates itself around the form and concept of the territorial state, on that basis taking aim at the formalized fiction of a *civitas maxima*.

Nazi theory links this claimed hostility to Germany with the collapse of the Holy Roman Empire (*Heiliges römisches Reich deutscher Nation*). It assumes that a universal international law is at work, balancing its weak European center by playing off many middling and smaller states one against another. In a process of inverse causality, the emergence of the resuscitated Reich defines the center of Europe's political power by unsettling the international legal construction:[25] it sets up "the order of the medieval world" against the "thinking in general concepts" that resulted from the collapse of the *sacrum imperium*.[26] The "general concepts" derive from the 1648 Treaty of Westphalia and its introduction of a political order based on the territorial state, itself corresponding to the principle of *droit public européen*. From then on— so runs the argument—international law had a pronouncedly French bent.

Translated into structure, the onset of the formal state's universalization marked the triumph of the territorial state over the sacral formation of the Reich. But concentrating on the historical limits of an international law based on a territorial notion of the state, the Nazi theorists speculate on the notion's datedness—its "merely time-bound" appearance in legal history, in the sense that we can speak of a law "between states in the true sense" only starting with the Westphalia treaty. The connection between the idea of an all-encompassing *civitas maxima* and that of the territorial state—a connection peculiar to this sort of law—already makes manifest the collaboration against the Reich of a universalistic, Anglo-Saxon claim to rule and a state-centered, French awareness of territorial limits.[27]

According to this schema, the ideas of the French Revolution—freedom, equality, the secular sovereign nation—signify another phase in the development of an international law aimed against the idea of a Reich. And, despite their postulation of many different sovereign states, they also signify a conceptual thrust in the direction of legal norms that are universalistically oriented. With the French Revolution, or with the transformation of "formal democratic thought" into political reality, originally "interdynastic" law becomes "international."[28] Emerging from this development, the "democratization of states is the basis of a legal, intrastate order" and influences the further development of international law: in particular, the creation of the international alliance.[29] The Nazi critics of international law establish an unabashedly causal link between the Declaration of Human Rights and "France's continental dominion"[30]—as well as between the principles of Wilsonian democracy and the Anglo-Saxon "1919 Versailles *Diktat.*"[31] In this manner, they reach a radical conclusion, one writing off the entire development of international law since early modernity: the fundamental elements of such law emerged during periods of influence through ideas "that robbed the German people of its self-determination. . . . For a system of international law in which the German people finds its possibility for life cannot emerge from the spirit of the Westphalia treaty, nor from the ideas of 1789, and least of all from the ideals and power politics of Versailles."[32]

If this fundamental critique of the real and imagined roots of an international law based on the territorial nation-state applies to the French archenemy and the civilizational form attributed to him, the confrontation with ruling "Anglo-Saxonism" has a deeper, more theoretical origin. Its target is general, universally oriented legal form—the supportive pillar of abstract international legal norms. The purpose of its destruction emerges from the assertion that standing behind the "general norm"—a simple facade—is not only the "European power system, carried forward from the eighteenth and nineteenth centuries," but also, and above all, the "system of Anglo-Saxon world imperialism":[33] a system that has laid claim to something like "world constitutional sovereignty."[34] Such a world law—negating the concept of territory and state sovereignty—complies with the terms of free trade and is interventionist in nature. It differs from French striving for the status quo on the Continent. It is simply not of "European dimensions."[35] The critique exposes the universalistic claim of this "territory-annulling world law" as a front for particular interests and traces them back to the special character of the British empire. We thus read that behind the universalist concept, "the specially ordered interests of a geographically discontinuous *Weltreich* are discernible," its "strewn possessions" encouraging a corresponding juridical way of thinking.[36] The concept of freedom accompanying this "territory-annulling world law" has its origin here as well: what is actually at stake is freedom of trade, corresponding to freedom of transport and communication. From this perspective, the abstract idea of territory has its counterpart in the Western democratic and liberal idea of freedom.

In their inveighing against the principles of a "universalistic imperialistic" world order, the Nazi international legal theorists propose a parallel between the situation of the contemporary Western democracies and the European powers of the Holy Alliance: from a "monarchic dynastic principle of legitimacy, a liberal democratic capitalist principle has developed."[37] As "the planetary descendants of Christian-European international law," we are informed, the Western democracies have sought to organize this "liberal democratic universalism."[38] Hence on a universal scale, liberalism and democracy amount to mere secularized forms of an eternal *civitas maxima*— a sense of the world's connectedness postulating a united humanity. From the *völkisch* vantage, these ideas must be combated.

The combat's object is not only a "principle of *homo oeconomicus*, staking a claim to universal validity," through which England justifies "the profits and maintenance of its empire." The critique of universalism's origins (real or imagined) moves into a realm of the transhistorical grotesque. In regard to the idea of the world state, the National Socialist critics of universalism find evidence even in Seneca, who cynically made "cosmopolitan lack of a *Vaterland* into a replacement for healthy political feelings."[39] Likewise, the Augustinian doctrine of *civitas dei*, opposed as it is to *civitas terrana*, assigns the universal church primacy over the particular state.[40] Beyond this, the universalism of the world state takes on a variety of historical forms for the Nazi theorists: what finally emerges as secular and imperialist *homo oeconomicus*, in the form of British world rule, finds its sacral transition in the *homo catholicus* of Spain's universal empire.[41] The constructs extend from the "international proletariat" or "French bourgeoisie" to that of a "proletarian world imperialism." To this extent, modern pacifism's *civitas maxima* is at heart the virtually unmodified ideal of Augustine's *civitas dei*.[42] All that is still needed to attain a direct "denial of particular *völkisch* grouping," we are informed, is the theoretical transformation of the world state idea into a monistic international legal construct.[43]

In order to preserve the *völkisch*-organic identity from this threatening assimilation, Nazi legal theorists spurn all universalistic monistic constructions of international law.[44] Since for "world-law monism," only "the individual or the totality of individuals" upholds the international legal order,[45] which thus does not emerge from "independent, law-structuring communities" (*Völkergemeinschaften*), it cannot be the basis of any such regulation that is authentic: "The difference between the races, the foundation for the formation of popular communities and thus of intercorporative international legal regulation, is sacrificed to a normative and individualistic leveling process. The *civitas maxima* rising up behind this monistic universal regulation is the consequential expression of such a denaturalized and secret imperialism."[46] For the sake of protecting the *völkisch* community, in order to fend off an interventionist imperialism—that is, "international West-fancying [*westlerisch*] world democracy"[47]—that takes the guise of a world-monistic construction of international law, the people's defenders must maintain the state: otherwise the state form exists only as barrier, as "merely exterior wrapping."[48] To be sure, this outcome goes against the National Socialist concept of law, which foregrounds not the state but "the people as original community";[49] nevertheless on opportune "anti-interventionist" grounds, we still find adherence to the position that the international legal order is valid only "when it protects the states."

In any event, the Nazi theorists postulate a radical opposition between the monistic construct, grounded in "humanitarian collective individualism," and National Socialism's organic concept of international law, based on the people.[50] The organic element in Nazism also renders it impossible to accept other antiuniversalist international legal constructs that are not organically grounded. Such is the case, for instance, in respect to Erich Kaufmann's monistic theory of state law, rejected on account of its positivist, non-*völkisch* character.[51] "Statist legal positivism," and the nonracial criteria of its construction, were also the grounds for rejecting Ludwig Schlecher's revisionist effort in the 1930s to develop a German *Aussenstaatsrecht* (extraterritorial state law), its center consisting of the strong national state.[52] Still, in line with the above argument, as the biological basis for a new normative structure, the Nazi legal doctrine was not yet being aimed at the state form's destruction. Only later, at the apogee of a nationalist politics of conquest, can we observe efforts to amalgamate elements of "extraterritorial state law" with racially motivated arguments rooted in "concrete order."

At the center of the Nazi legal critique, we find the normative "pure theory of law" (*Reine Rechtsschule*), as represented, above all, by Hans Kelsen. The Nazis denounced the turn, in the Great War's aftermath, toward this theoretical school—it stands against the power-based state principle (*Machtstaat*) and for international cooperation—as an expression of the "rule of a specific weltanschauung that blesses Versailles imperialism, as well as the corresponding pacifist, liberal democratic disposition."[53] The *Reine Rechtsschule* is the juridical incarnation of what the National Socialists struggled to destroy, for the sake of the creation or preservation of an organic community of the *Volk:* for after all, the school severs "the communal law" from its socioracial origins and reinterprets it "within the open structural space [*Raum*] of hovering normologic, hierarchically graded injunctive value."[54] Its antiorganic impact aside, such nomologism is understood to rob the sovereignty problem of its political existential meaning. The fundamental question concerning the upholder of the highest power of decision, the "final source of any legal order," "is falsified into a question of purely logical normative hierarchy." The school, we are told, makes it easy "to turn aside from all political and *völkisch*-racial cardinal problems of an existential nature"—from the substance, in the end, of every legal decision. Such a process signifies a withdrawal to the "intellectually [*geistlich*] superior watchtower of pure objectivity." The same theorist comments, "it is not astonishing that the Jewish spirit [*Geist*] took up this method of struggle."[55]

For the Nazi critics of the pure theory of law, its Jewish advocates wished to sever both law and state from their "historical-*völkisch*-racial" determinants: to confirm, all the better, the law's status as an independent logical and formal science and render it "an ideational construct of the Jewish intellect."[56] For the same critics, this act suits the transterritorial Jewish life form, which holds a purely functional idea of state and society—as a "practical unit meant to be equated with economic activity."[57] In its adaptation to societal function, legal form attaches directly to the citizen, thus reducing the state's people to the sum of those possessing citizenship;[58] the state itself becomes simply a concept. In this way, the equation of state and law characterizing the pure theory of law transforms people and territory to mere legal fictions.[59]

Similarly, these critics considered the asserted universalistic "unity of the legal world picture" to be based on a view of law as an ordered system that realizes itself in a sequence of organized stages.[60] But with such a view, putative organic or *völkisch* differences are blended: *Volk*, law, state, society, work, community—all are hollowed out and transformed by the Jewish understanding of law; correspondingly, "as a normative discipline [*Wissenschaft*] adapted to Jewish thinking, the scholarly study of law [*Rechtswissenschaft*] *estranges* the German *Volk*."[61] But the critique goes further: according to the Nazi international legal theorists, in the end, the construction of an international law grounded in a superior and abstract norm has the goal "of furthering Jewish control of the world."[62] As one theorist summarized this Jewish claim to world dominion: "A new societal order had to be invented—a world order no longer involving division into territorial units but rather meant to bring about eternal peace."[63]

In the same vein the League of Nations, taking over sovereignty from the state, is seen to serve "the Jews as a realization of their striving."[64] To defend itself from this plot cast in a legal molding, the international legal construct must not be "founded on a base of abstract normative, rule-determined thinking, but only developed as a concrete order of states and peoples distinct in nature and recognized in their concrete particularity."[65] Within such an international legal counterorder, neither an "abstract humanity nor the single individual would appear on the scene as upholders of the law . . . but only peoples organized in the framework of states."[66] What the critics here decisively rejected is an individualist liberal concept of law as the "rational contractual regulation of a human multitude."[67]

Ideally, universalistic international law transcends the particular, sovereign existence of states. It presumes a vertical structure of norms located beneath the horizontal state order, originating in a higher norm. In opposition to this, the Nazi concept of international law provisionally posits a vertically composed and territorially demarcated, side-by-side conjunction of states: this so long as the state is still needed defensively, as "politically and legally requisite clothing for the authentic people, the actual upholder of the law."[68] A side-by-side system (*Nebenordnung*) rules, in which states mutually confer equality of status (*Gleichordnung*) that is still determined by form. In contrast, the world-monistic construct of universal international law—also termed "liberal constitutionalism"—is condemned for eradicating the territorial borders—for having the (now otherwise defined) "demarcation lines pass through the various peoples."[69] To counteract this vertical ordering principle, the Nazi theorists call for a pluralistic structure of order, and a recognition of "the intercorporative character of an international legal order based on communities organized in the framework of states":[70] a goal they suggest can be achieved, already, through a reduction in the number of norms within international law that have a general or even a universalistic nature. The fewer general norms the better. In turn, such a reduction is realizable once international law is grasped, above all, as contractual law.

"In the technical legal sense custom and contract are the most important sources of international law," is the laconic Nazi pronouncement.[71] This seemingly innocent observation narrows such law's range of applicability, in order, finally, to determine the biologistic conditions for the contract. Biologistic reservations are manifest in the assertion that mutually complementary wills—the condition for the contract—can only be assumed in the presence of "complementary legal viewpoints." These, to be sure, are "racially and culturally" determined—meaning that only between "racially related peoples" can common legal structures settle into the customary international legal practice on which the contract system finally rests.[72]

In the foundation of Nazi international law, the finding that such law is "at the most possible between peoples of the same racial origin" marks a new high point of theoretical radicalization: the assertion that international law is in fact an outcome of race.[73] This pseudo-anthropological approach adopts the premise that identical racial types produce identical feelings, hence identical concepts: "As a rule, for every descendant of the northern Germanic race, honor and fidelity, truth, and morality signify the same, whereas it is a scientifically established fact that people of other races (in particular the Hamitic and Oriental races) often endow these for us settled ideas with a different content."[74] The premise's theoretical limitation on contractual capacity has direct consequences for the problem of contractual trustworthiness. For if international law is valid only between peoples of similar stock, then it is questionable that "forms of international legal exchange can arise between peoples of completely different racial composition."[75] Granted the basic premise, contracts may be unilaterally broken. In fact, they lack legal force to begin with. The consequent reduction of the international legal community to a few subjects capable of forming contracts, and the annulment of universal international law itself, takes direct aim at the founding principle of an entire civilizational complex: at the principle of equality—here that between states. Stemming from racial doctrine, the opposite, biological principle of immutable inequality rises on equality's ruins.

Paradoxically, racism appears historically only as the hierarchical order of the medieval estate disappears. The biologistic declaration of human inequality is a reaction to the principle of equality. It represents a false reflex, embedded in the perception of social differences enduring despite all declared equality, and a resulting pseudo-explanation for the differences. In turn, differences seek out their mystification in the biological: people are irrevocably unequal and indeed are so from "nature." Beyond this, racism is a product of the secularization of life worlds. Sacral inequality understood as God-given needs no naturalistic grounding. In our present context, these two factors are significant, since what acquires racist validity for the problem of human equality and inequality was meant to apply also to the state.

Criticism of a legally founded principle of equality between states comes rather easy, since the real rule of inequality in this realm is apparent. Here the critics take formal equality, which *strictu sensu* has a regulatory function, at face value and hold it up to the reality that vitiates the principle. In playing off the formal—the shape of abstract possibility—against the real, the Nazis touched on the utopian desire to transcend the opposition, constitutive for bourgeois society, between *homme* and *citoyen*. In place of the opposition, they offered the negative utopia of a hierarchically arranged order of states and peoples, with race constituting the order's measure.

The destruction of law's axiom of formal equality thus produced a hierarchization at once political and biological. At the same time, in Nazi international legal doctrine, formal equality serves as the regulating instance for ever-changing inequality. The medium for generally accepted, "substantial" inequality, regulated through formal, "political pseudo-equality" is the economy.[76] The trivial fact that equality before the law signifies "mere freedom from formal caprice" and is thus thoroughly compatible with "substantial caprice" serves chiefly to set in play a total elimination of the equality axiom, in a move toward a material principle of hierarchization.[77] In its turn, this erosive process proceeds step by step—a transition facilitated by a newly introduced principle of "equal privilege" (*Gleichberechtigung*). Since the principle calls for endowing comparison with a concrete shape, it can be understood as striving for an elimination of form. *Gleichberechtigung* is seen as still a "consequence" stemming from equality. But it is inclined, already, in the direction of "reciprocity": a principle itself based on a quantificatory "equitable equal treatment" (*gerechte Gleichbehandlung*).[78]

In the judgment of its champions, the introduction of terms with international legal cachet such as "equal treatment" and "justice" or "equitability" (*Gerechtigkeit*) in the context of a provisionally maintained principle of equality between states represents a "combination of the ideas of absolute and relative equality."[79] Such a "combination" might give the impression that the regulatory substance of objective law still remains intact. But this is no longer the case. The procedure involved here appears in the guise of a "step by step enrichment of the formal right to equality between states, and therefore as the establishing of concrete rights to be granted states if the notion of international justice is to maintain some meaning."[80] In reality, it is a further step in the liquidation of abstract legal form. We can observe its effect in the approach taken to the quasi-legal concept of *Gerechtigkeit:* it is now deemed legitimate to consider any "contract felt as unjust" (*ungerecht*), meaning not "in harmony with one's particular principles of honor and justice," to be null and void from the start.[81]

The emphasis on "one's particular principles of honor and justice" points to an additional element in the destruction of international law's principle of equality: ethnic conformity as a condition for common legal tenets, hence for equality. This limitation follows from an analogy with domestic equality, consisting of belonging to a specific nation or, as one author puts it, to a "national homogeneity": equality can pass for politically relevant only as long as it "has a substance, with at least the possibility and risk of inequality thus being in play."[82] Consequently, the stranger, the other, furnishes the basis for equality among the nation's members. An absolute equality, applicable to "every person simply by virtue of birth or age," would rob equality of its value and substance, thereby of its sense. An absolute human equality would, then, lack the necessary correlative of inequality, becoming "a conceptually and practically indifferent equality—one that says nothing."[83]

Such observations do not yet stipulate the criteria for equality or inequality. The substance of "belongingness" might yet exist fully as form, say as state citizenship. Nevertheless it is already apparent that as soon as racist ideas of homogeneity—corresponding to the Nazi axiom: whoever is not part of the people has no equality—prevail on an inner-state level, the construct of state equality, analogous to the relation between citizens within the state, will shift toward a deformalized equality of "equal" peoples. One author, for example, emphasizes that "according to Article 109 of the Weimar Constitution, not all *people*, but only *Germans*, are equal before the law. The shared community of race forms the substance of equality here. It thus follows that no Jew can be part of the people (Law of Reich Citizenship paragraph 2, September 19, 1935)."[84]

To turn racist ideas of homogeneity outward means limiting the conditions of eligibility for international law to a select group of subjects— namely, those who have membership on the grounds of their racial substance. State equality would then exist in "word and substance," since "those having equal privilege [those who are *gleichberechtigt*] can only be factually equal." In certain situations, the need could spring up to emphasize "the substantial homogeneity" of subjects of international law under state form of rule, through a sharp demarcation of borders against the *andersgeartet*— everyone "of a different type."[85] Both on the state's inside and its outside, what we observe here are plans—running counter to the universal understanding that stems from the French Revolution and its ideal of equality— for a homogeneous utopia, one based on a principle of *Gleichartigkeit* (identical racial stock).[86]

In order to set *Gleichartigkeit* against simple equality, or *Gleichheit*, it was worthwhile to reject *Gleichheit* on intellectual historical grounds as well. We thus read that among the classical philosophers—Aristotle, for instance— the thought of "natural equality had not yet undergone legal precise formulation." Rather, equality was understood as an "absolutely substantively equal distribution of goods or an equal human capacity for virtue and purity, as well as for possession of natural rights." The ideal of natural equality was only transformed into that of equal legal status—"advanced through *naturalis ratio*"—by the Roman jurists: the opposition between "actual inequality" and an "ideal condition" defined by such access "thus served as the source of an idea that dragged forward, like an eternal disease, from Cicero and Seneca to the medieval legal theorists, and onward to the most modern systems."[87] And further: in analogy to the principle of human equality, the French Revolution inferred a principle of state equality into the bargain.[88] Abbé Grégoire's declaration that a dwarf is as human as a giant, sovereignty does not result from strength, might, or wealth, a small republic is no less a sovereign state than the mightiest kingdom, points to that absolute equality on which the normative principle of legality rests—and through which it reduces the sovereign state's existence to rubble.[89] For the National Socialist theorists of international law, such "free-hovering jurisprudence," based on the principle of absolute equality before the law, turns away from reality—hence from real, merely "metajuridical," inequality.[90] It acknowledges neither the concept of dominant power nor the legal concept of hegemony and denies, to boot, the legal character of the differences in rank among the various states.[91]

The theorists reinforce their intellectual historical struggle against the idea of equality by tracing the plurality of formally like-ranked states, and the denial connected to it of a "higher, overarching organizational power, as represented by the Reich at its historical high point in Europe," solely and strictly back to French power politics.[92] They denounce the equality principle as the effective weapon of that politics:[93] as a "masterfully manipulated intellectual instrument in the hands of the Western power, which was ready to introduce its secret claim to primacy in suitable legal form."[94] Now, they explain, National Socialism can convert formal equality into a hierarchical ranking of communal entities and grant equality and equal privilege only those entities that in fact have the capacity to be sovereign states.[95] What they call for is the establishment of an "authentic order of rank" based on such criteria, until now "systematically ignored in international legal studies."[96]

Roughly speaking, in this effort to define the relative (superior and inferior) status of international legal subjects, we can distinguish two legitimatory currents: geopolitical and racial political. A geopolitical assessment of subjects uses the "vibrant value, determined through number and historical significance, of peoples that through such factors have achieved a configuration of power."[97] Let us note that such assessment, antinormative in stance, does not, however, furnish an objective standard for the "higher and lower valuation" of states embedded in "the laws of nature" to which it lays claim.[98] It is incapable of specifying how "state-oriented thinking" can free itself "from fateful isolation" (*verhängnisvollen Vereinsamung*) in the form of free-hovering "pure intellect" (*nichts-als-Geistigkeit*).[99] It is content with the theoretically unsupported assertion that the concrete principle of "natural territory" renders defunct the abstract principle of absolute equality between states. In any event, with the later expression of hope that "the idea of Central Europe"—Mitteleuropa—might be realized "under Germanic leadership," we see clearly that what this legitimatory current in fact conveys is hegemonic political craving.[100]

In the beginning the Mitteleuropa idea—or that of territorial predestination—did not have biological foundations. For this reason, continental imperialists who privileged racial theory rejected the geopolitical delegitimization of the principle of state equality, defining it as "assimilative," and "in the end oriented toward prehistoric, elementary criteria."[101] Otherwise—so we are told—with *völkisch* thinking: in its "positive acknowledgment" of a differentiation based on "the identity or dissimilarity of racial stock" (*Artgleichheit* or *Artverschiedenheit*), such thinking has elevated "legal autonomization" into its structural principle—as the only way of securing the endurance of the integral *völkisch* life as a positive value in its own right, worthy of protection. In place of a condemned egalitarian leveling, a graded hierarchy will now prevail. For the time, it is still described in restrained fashion, as "autonomization within the law."[102] But promptly, the replacement for the formal equality principle's severed, invisible hand makes itself known: the "historical enactment" of the new order necessarily requires placing trust in a concrete power, responsible for executing the principle of dominance and submission. "In conformance to nature," such claims to leadership "are the lot of the *Urvolk*, arrived on the political stage as the creators of the *völkisch* idea."[103]

What began as a "national and *völkisch* revolution" against formal equality and for "real justice" in international relations, realizing itself through the destruction of a principle of equality between states "borrowed from the edifice of general abstract law," now moved toward the establishment of a new international order based on a "recognition of the inherent differences between races and peoples as historical reality."[104] Henceforth, equality is to convert to its opposite: the negative utopia of a putative biological *Gleichartigkeit*.[105]

The Nazi destruction of international law's universal principle of equality was not without consequence, particularly for the question of the validity of international contractual settlements. And let us note that, far from representing a minor realm of international law, contractual law in fact has twofold import: namely, within such law, the binding clause *pacta sunt servanda* is both a principle of construction and a fundamental norm. A chain of foundational elements, obligatory in their valence, extends from the contract as such to the contractually configured deduction of international law in general. For this reason, in all its gradients—that is, as both abstract form and concrete substantive obligation—the contract lies at the core of the legal form of international exchange.

National Socialist theorists of international law did not take a uniform approach to the problem of contractual obligation. As in other realms of international legal theory, we rather find a range of extremes, culminating in biological radicalization. It was of advantage to such theorists that in rejecting the self-binding principle of *pacta sunt servanda* they were not exactly treading on new soil: the principle had always systematically opposed that of political sovereignty, the prerequisite for participation in legally regulated international commerce. The political sovereignty of the state, an original *lack* of bounds manifest, above all, in the ability to decide between war and peace, finds its own expression in the contractual proviso *clausula rebus sic standibus.* The proviso's reading—broad or narrow—reveals the stance taken by the body politic toward limitations on its political sovereignty or the primacy of contractual obligation. The readier a political body is to define itself in terms of state power, hence to question the binding nature of international law—in the end to abandon its universalism for "extraterritorial state law"—all the more does it tend to resolve the tension between *pacta sunt servanda* and the *clausula rebus sic standibus* in favor of the latter. The state's legal monism and the primacy of the circumstantial clause both point in the direction of the strong state and imperialist dominance. Because of the great weight it places on precisely that clause, the doctrine of international law formulated by Erich Kaufmann at the start of the century has, in truth, abandoned the realm of international legality. The doctrine's ultimate legitimation resides in the simple application of power. The criterion or final "norm" for determining which state is "right" is victory in war. This identity of might and right is well articulated in the formula "only he who can, may."[106]

In the beginning, a number of the Nazi theorists gratefully accepted the circumstantial clause as a supportive pillar of international legal thinking. They were above all entranced by the authority to one-sidedly break contracts if these turned out incompatible—according to "one's own judgment"—with the "right to self-preservation."[107] This clause naturally accommodated revisionist intentions, and from such direct intentions, basic definitions of position soon emerged. We read, for instance:

> new legal circumstances of duration and force [*Dauer und Macht*] only emerge from the actions of a state that, owing to its right to self-preservation, one-sidedly alters extant treaties, borders, and legal circumstances, when it has been able to exert the force and might [*Kraft und Macht*] necessary to overcome all opposition, and when it has found the right proportion at the right moment. Success has consistently determined the historical right [*historisches Recht*] of such a procedure and produces new, formal law [*formelles Recht*] accordingly.[108]

Before the "majesty of life," every treaty is no more than a "scrap of paper," concluded for the sake of peace.[109] Such observations, it is clear, lie fully within the tradition of power politics identifying might with right: it is in "weapons that lies a resolution to the struggle [*Kampf*] over use of the circumstantial clause."[110]

Alongside this clause, the Nazi theorists proposed other element restricting or modifying the legal principle of *pact sunt servanda:* for instance, the principles of "mutuality" (*Gegenseitigkeit*) and "rightfulness" or "justice" (*Gerechtigkeit*). *Gegenseitigkeit* is connected with a narrow interpretation of the principle of *do ut des*—the demand for an "adequate reconciliation of interests."[111] Through its very nature, it leans in the direction of the circumstantial clause. In contrast, *Gerechtigkeit* sets about completely overcoming legal form—indeed, along with law, or *Recht*, it inevitably signifies an extralegal qualification of legal principles. The demand for *Gerechtigkeit* applies to such contracts not corresponding to "basic legal principles" (*die Grundanforderungen des Rechts*), for instance when a state has exploited its superior power in concluding a contract. Being in disharmony with the principles of "honor and rightfulness" (*Ehre und Gerechtigkeit*), the contract is thus null and void.[112]

The principle of *Gerechtigkeit* reveals the notion that things higher than abstract legal form and contractual fidelity are present within international law. The contract loses its position as sovereign ruler of legal order; in the name of *Gerechtigkeit*, it is demoted to that order's "servant."[113] In the process, a subjective ideal of justice replaces the basic form of international law, embodied in the proposition *pacta sunt servanda*. Such an inversion of principles is confirmed as follows:

> Clearly, willed or otherwise, a theory of international law that has made *pacta sunt servanda* into a basic norm—into the popular community's constitution —embraces inertial tendencies. Logical uniformity and normative continuity

can be arrived at in this manner. In such a static normative system, there would be no room left for the problem of *Gerechtigkeit*—for the thought of a dynamic development of international law accommodating the needs of life [*Lebensnotwendigkeiten*].[114]

The extensively glossed circumstantial clause and principle of *Gerechtigkeit* are not necessarily National Socialist in their basic implications. To the contrary: frequently the *clausula* is even rejected as incompatible with the "German concept of honor and fidelity"[115]—in the absence of its completion through the Nazi idea of race. An international legal distinction between "functional" and "substantive" contract—*Zweckvertrag* and *Gemeinschaftsvertrag*—here serves as a connecting link. The two contractual forms, the theorists suggest, require essentially different legal treatment: the *Gemeinschaftsvertrag*'s applicability is naturally limited, presuming a "certain minimal measure" of *Artgleichheit* between states joining in contractual community; the *Zweckvertrag*'s applicability, to the contrary, is virtually unlimited.[116] This sundering of the contract's form shatters its character as the universal participatory mode for international legal intercourse. Each sort of contract, along with its respective contractual party, has a different value.

In its particular character and construction, the *Zweckvertrag* becomes the remnant of a functionalist utilitarian way of thinking. For its part, the *Gemeinschaftsvertrag*'s character is National Socialist. It is grounded in an idea of organicity, and in a racist principle of loyalty (*Treue*). What is in force here is not the universally obligatory principle of contractual fidelity, hence the principle of mutuality—this being what the Nazi theorists denigrate as "pacta-sunt-servandism"—but rather the (literally one-sidedly) obligatory "loyalty to one's own *Volkstum*, the first principle of National Socialist international legal thinking": a racially obligatory self-limitation.[117] All contractual law is thus subject to an organic loyalty principle.[118] Its premise is a "racially and culturally" determined harmony of legal viewpoint, condensed into international legal prescription.[119] Only an identity of "racial stock" (*rassische Artung*) produces identical feelings, hence identical concepts.[120]

When racially grounded "honor and loyalty" rise to become the contract's underlying premises, thereby annulling the force of the fundamental international legal norm *pacta sunt servanda*, extensive interpretation of the norm's antithetical pole *clausula rebus sic standibus* also systematically falls by the wayside. The demarcational specification of the circumstantial clause's legal force, "self-preservation" (Erich Kaufmann) yields to "determinations of essence" on the part of folkishly determined "evaluative units," vitiating the contract and typologizing by race.[121] Moreover, in the face of an organically derived loyalty principle, the circumstantial clause falls into discredit.

At the same time, a contract settled on the basis of "racial *Gleichartigkeit*" has more force, by virtue of blood-determined "honor and loyalty," than a contract subordinate to constant shifts of interest and complying with utilitarian, functionalist criteria.[122] In the process, however, the legal community dwindles to a few political bodies considered *gleichartig*. In such a schema, then, international law would be "never possible between all peoples, but at most between those of the same racial origin."[123]

The destruction of universal contractual form, or the reduction of those subjects interacting within international legal bounds to a few political bodies satisfying racial criteria, necessarily affects the generalizing form of international legal subjectivity, the state, at its very core. Despite initial declarations of the intent to preserve state sovereignty from the international social order—an order conceived universally, hence vertically undermining the state system—it lay in the logic of Nazi international law's development to undermine the form of the state itself. This not only because the state form represents the prerequisite for participation in international legal commerce, but because, in the abstract, it is the expression of a body politic that disregards the ethnic or "organic" composition of its members. In the abstract form of the state, no concrete structures have an impact. Neither the state's size, nor its power, nor the international weight it is capable of exerting, and certainly not the "racial" composition of its populace has expression here. The form of the state implies that all states are equal. This form was now meant to change: with "the National Socialist movement's victory, a push toward overcoming the concept of the state has been successful,"[124] insofar as within the Nazi idea of law, the "people [stands] in the forefront as the original community, not the state."

In the best of cases, the state can serve as the "outer cover for an original community of the people"[125]—for "a people grown powerful in its earthly realm [*Erdraum*]."[126] But even then, the state has nothing to do with a legal entity's structural substance—that specifically "liberalist" version of what, in any case, National Socialist theorists cast aside as "statism" and identify with the rejected notions of "sovereignty" and "equality."[127] The attack thus focuses on scorned, "unpolitical" nineteenth- and twentieth-century liberal state doctrine, characterizing it—so we are informed—by its identification of the state with state power.[128] Only such a "formalistic state concept" can lead to the assumption that the state alone creates law, and that the state's law alone is valid. To expand an earlier citation, "Every political doctrine that does not explain the essence of law solely in terms of a formal legislative act or its enforcement, that discovers in law a value emerging from communal life, cannot be satisfied with the confirmation that law is the state's prerogative." National Socialist doctrine chooses rather to explain state law in terms of "its political—hence *völkisch* and racial—basis." For this reason, it spurns classical fascism as representing "a purely state-centered, formal idea of sovereignty in the Hegelian sense":[129] a "statist total order" presiding over each individual.[130] In Italy, theorists observe, the problem of race, "core of the National Socialist idea of law," is ignored in favor of the state.[131]

The primacy of race annuls abstract concepts like a state's people or territory. Even formalized political space, that is *Raum* as territory, the demarcated realm in which a state's political power unfolds, takes second place in National Socialist doctrine to that privileged "value[:] . . . the unity between partners of the same stock [*Artgenossen*]."[132] We thus see that what is at stake in liquidating the notion of the state, replacing it with an organically defined, quasi-legal notion of *Reich*, is a dissolution both of the abstract unity of the *Staatsvolk*, or that which can be understood statistically as a population, and of formalized territorial abstraction.[133]

As with other abstractions, Nazi theorists of international law trace the concept of the *Staatsvolk* back to 1789. They fiercely oppose the revolution's civilizational influences: after all, that event engendered the French idea of nation, with its abjured assimilative thrust—the integration it offered anyone willing to declare allegiance. The rubrics of freedom and equality thus announced an "incorporation of alien people into the French nation," which now was identified with the *Staatsvolk*.[134] The consequence, they explain, was the prototype of the Western nation-state, grounded in the idea of equality, working toward steady assimilation and uniformity of its populace.[135] Against such a democratic concept of state and people, judging the entire citizenry "without distinction of estate, but also without distinction of race and *Volkstum*," a completely new notion of the people has emerged, one calling not only for linguistic singularity, but "preservation of racial purity" as well.[136]

In contrast to the Western nation, the *Urvolk* can exist in the complete absence of the state as form: it relies, naturally, on the "blood community of the *Artgleiche*."[137] Where the abstract state is the assimilative national form, the "blood community" (*Blutsgemeinschaft*) finds its proper form in the idea of Reich. Such a racial definition of the notion of Reich is not inevitable but, unlike the state, it tends to take this direction. In whatever manner individual authors may theorize about the Reich, they consistently understand it as being communal in nature, hence estranged from the state; it is "the enemy of all territorialization"—the latter process making its mark since 1648, in the course of the movement of international law against the Reich.[138]

Prevalent international law displays "enmity to the Reich": this is a constantly repeated argumentative figure of the Nazi theorists. It generally accompanies the assertion that previously, Europe lived from the "middle" and not from the "margin." Based on the above-cited "state plurality," the "anti-Reich effect" of modern international law has led to its gradual slippage into the sort of law suiting states that are marginal.[139] The Reich itself was subject to such a development: the very idea of the state—even in the form of the German state—was, as one author puts it, the "actual enemy" of the idea of the Reich;[140] it destroyed the Reich from the inside, insofar as the juridical-decisionist state concept, opposed to the traditional Reich idea, seemed superior to it.

This development naturally had wider consequences: from the idea of the state emerged the territorial theory of an abstract positivistic "administrative unit," occupying a—now rejected—merely formal sphere of competence and based on the principle of making and enacting laws.[141] But once Reichs, not states, "are recognized as bearers of international legal development and the formation of law, then the area of the state no longer represents the sole idea of territory in international law."[142] As the National Socialist theorists see it, Nazi rule brought such a retroactive development. The unification of the "victorious German people" in a closed zone of settlement revised the French decision of 1648 and destroyed the premises for the rule of Europe by France, that marginal power.[143] In actuality, the Reich idea's restoration signifies an overturning of the principles of state sovereignty and equality—indeed, of the entire state framework of international law.[144]

Within that international law formulated by the Nazis, the idea of territorial space, *Raum*, takes on a new, racial dimension. But even the prebiological variant defines the Reich as the opposite of any abstract territorial concept: as antiuniversalist, antiassimilatory, defending Europe's middle on both west and east. While the Western imperial powers indulged in "assimilationist" and melting-pot notions, the Reich championed "the holiness of a nonuniversalist order of life, both stemming from and honoring the people."[145] In this regard, we find a concession that, in contrast to the concept of the state, "the term *Deutsches Reich*" in its "concrete particularity and elevation, cannot be translated"—that is, that the Reich idea lacks concrete definition. Rather, it aims at a highly potent distinction between life worlds. Namely, as the theorists explain it, in German usage, the word *Reich* (realm) signifies, above all, an opposition—for example that between "the realm of good and evil" or "light and darkness" or "plants and animals": always, the word is concerned with a "cosmos in the sense of a concrete order."[146]

This opposition, so we learn, makes the concept untranslatable, hence not generalizable. Consequently, Reich and *imperium* and empire are not the same and, seen from the inside, not comparable. The Reich's uniqueness in turn affects the determination of its law. For one aspect of the "historical power of every genuinely great political force" is to be accompanied by "its own, not arbitrarily subsumable designation and to enforce its own, particular names."[147] As one Nazi theorist explains, only he who "is capable of determining concepts and words" is capable of exercising true power. "*Caesar dominus est supra grammaticum:* Caesar is also lord of grammar." Defeat and loss of power come only after surrender "to a strange vocabulary [and] . . . strange ideas, and to what is considered law, especially international law."[148] For this reason, the time has come to withdraw from Western and universalistic, hence imperialist international law—to furnish it with a new foundation through the concept of Reich. Such "international law of the Reich," finally dissolving the formal concept of the state, is, in essence, a one-sided international law. And this one-sidedness has serious consequences, particularly in regard to the law of war.[149]

Carl Schmitt had reservations about such consequences—despite, or else precisely on account of, his pathbreaking role for other Nazi international legal theorists. In contradiction to his own intentions, Schmitt recognized the link between annulling the concept of the state and ceasing to acknowledge the equality of one's opponents in war. Orderly conduct of war—*jus in bello*—is in fact inseparable from acknowledging the other as a subject of international law within the form of the state. Whoever destroys one cannot claim the other. As a result, despite his confirmation of the antistatist, antiuniversalist concept of Reich, Schmitt is tempted to preserve at least the law governing conflict between states. He thus confirms that the extant notion of the state indeed contains "a minimal measure of inwardly calculable organization and inner discipline," rendering palpable war's status as a recognized institution of order between states. Thanks to the civilizational accomplishment of the state form, within the traditional and, to be sure, otherwise proscribed international legal system, war represents a relation "of order to order and not, say, of order to disorder."[150]

Such qualifications involve an unmistakable retreat from the plans for a vertical hierarchical world order hovering behind the Reich idea—plans meant to take concrete shape in the extraterritorial principle. The retreat is justified with the explanation that the new "element of territorial order" at work in the concept of the people has not yet become sufficiently mature "for jurisprudence to convincingly invalidate the present inter-state order."[151] In other words, neither the principle of *jus ad bellum* nor that of *jus in bello* are in a position to validate the absolute validity of the Reich idea, and of the extraterritorial order connected with it. State-induced violence is no longer universally legitimate, but only so on the part of the hegemonic power: its legitimacy rests in its status as an executory quashing by the Reich of a resistance qualified as law breaking, rebellion, treason, or civil war. In this manner, precisely what Schmitt wishes to abjure on a universal level enters the space of the *Großraum:* total war.[152]

The task of the German legal scholar is thus provisionally limited to identifying "the concept of a concrete extraterritorial order," in a zone "between a merely conservative retention of inherited thinking on interstate relations and a nonstatist, non-*völkisch* encroachment into a realm of universalistic world law." This overriding concept must "escape the two [alternatives], doing justice both to the territorial measure of our present sense of the earth and our new understanding of state and people."[153] It must be a synthetic ordering concept, meant to join a notion of people aimed at continental expansion with the defensive notion of state.[154]

Such a synthesis appears syncretistic and inconsistent; politically speaking, it is clearly opportunistic. Unmistakably, the editorial insertion of a "word concerning the author's standpoint" attempts to distance these contortions from the text's real substance. As a sign of his fidelity to the regime, Schmitt casts aside the state-bound, discriminating concept of war, with its central principle of acknowledging the enemy as one's opponent, designating it as the "conservative" and "reactionary" expression of an "old-European state order."[155] At the same time, he hopes to preserve the laws of war. The synthesis represents an effort to square a circle.

In the face of all its vagueness, the term *Großraum* still seems to possess a specific semantic weight: as the general signifier of Nazism's continental imperialist "concrete order"; as a basic and systematic designation of the administrative and legal plans for racially and geopolitically based hegemonic rule over the continent. The term was an international legal neologism introduced by Carl Schmitt in a talk delivered in Kiel on April 1, 1939.[156] His terminological innovation was doubtless relevant to the occupation of the heartland of Czechoslovakia two weeks earlier, the establishment of the protectorate of Bohemia and Moravia, and the "protective rule" over an ostensibly independent Slovakia:[157] that is, the Reich's appropriation of areas inhabited by "foreign peoples" (*Fremdvölker*) while circumventing international law governing annexation. That a notion such as "protective rule" was available at the appropriate moment owed much to Schmitt's long-standing critique of the Western system of international law and its liberal capitalistic structural elements.

The critique's starting point is the liberal constitution, characterized as "agnostic." In the present context, this term signifies a displacement, based on a separation of politics and the economy, of everything important for the body politic to the free (economic) sphere of bourgeois society—a sphere uncontrolled by the constitution.[158] As Schmitt explains it, "Thus a secret political substratum emerges within the state-free sphere; it weaves the decisive political threads together, holding them firmly in hand."[159] The effects of this development inside the state sphere also have their foreign political repercussions, resulting in a "highly political denial of the political character of economic processes and ideas."[160] And Schmitt notes that Joseph Schumpeter already saw the Anglo-Saxons, in contrast to the Prussians, as engaging, "through conceptual necessity, never in imperialism, but in something essentially different, signifying strictly economic and hence peaceful expansion."[161]

In concreto, then, the liberal constitutional state and its guaranteed freedoms preserve, within state bounds, the demarcating line between a public sphere to which the state has access and a private sphere to which it has none—"trade thus naturally and inevitably occupying the state-free sphere." The process is consequently at home, as well, within the wider world market: "In this manner, passing beyond and below state boundaries, a private association and community, outside the state's purview, comes into being. It is responsible for the world's economic system, world trade, the world market. Once uncontrolled private trade comes to an end, so ends the method of British or Anglo-Saxon world domination."[162] Maintaining the separation of public and private, political and economic spheres beyond state boundaries thus guarantees the rule of the economic over the political sphere, thereby opening wide the door to outside interference. For Schmitt, such imperialism, masked as a "liberal-democratic and liberal-capitalist weltanschauung," is grounded—as in America—in a "simple possession-based argument on the part of our present contractual status quo (*pacta sunt servanda*), hence in simple contractual positivism."[163]

According to Schmitt, however, contractualism was not always the "American point of view." He refers here to an "original American" Monroe Doctrine, considered as the historical precedent for his own idea of *Großraum*. The doctrine, he indicates, "had nothing to do with the principles and methods of modern liberal capitalist imperialism," then observes that "as an authentic spatial doctrine [*Raumdoktrin*], it even stands in marked opposition to the space-disdaining [*raummißachtend*] transformation of the earth into an abstract world and capital market."[164] Through Woodrow Wilson, the ideological thinking of liberal democracy and an interconnected idea of "free world trade and a 'free' world market" has replaced an originally "authentic" principle of noninterference.[165] This change marks an exodus of imperial power from England to America—a *translatio imperii Britannici*.[166]

With this early variety of *Großraum*, we thus find an attempt to formulate an "alternate doctrine" in the face of the free, Anglo-Saxon-dominated world market.[167] In this respect *Großraum* has two meanings. The first meaning is political in the narrow sense; it involves "securing oneself, in emergencies, against Anglo-Saxon attempts to extort political submission through economic suffocation"—that is, the concept of an autarchy by necessity (*Notautarkie*).[168] It is essentially directed against the "continental politics pursued by England"—a politics of divide and rule.[169] The second, wider meaning of the idea of *Großraum* is more basic, involving a fundamental breakthrough of the "narrow framework of thinking oriented toward liberalism and the territorial state," hence a denial "in principle" of "chaotic liberal-capitalist economic axioms."[170] At the same time, the establishment of a "zone of supply [*Versorgungsraum*] safe from crisis and blockade" is meant to guarantee regulated trade and commercial exchange.[171] Politically, the hope is to bolster this idyll aimed against the world market with the ban on intervention directed at all powers considered alien to the spatial realm. The concept of intervention is related to the rights of protection granted to minorities in Eastern and Central Europe after World War I— rights considered an instrument of Western meddling, with a liberal and "economic-capitalist basis"—as well as a "Jewish influence" defined as a force that "corrupts *Volkstum*."[172] In a general manner, Schmitt's notorious "basic idea," "the distinction of friend from enemy" is essential for the principle of nonintervention.[173] In this regard, *Großraum* and *Universalismus* represent the conceptual incarnation of these conflicting principles par excellence.

The idea of *Großraum* developed by the Nazi international legal theorists represents the reactionary, utopian blueprint for a world conceived on anti-Western lines. As the antithesis of universalism, it necessarily denies the principles of political order that structure an abstract world society: above all the principle of equality between states, and that of equal exchange as the form in which either transmission of values or exploitation takes place (within the *Großraum*, such exploitation is said to be neutralized through a "positive incorporation, befitting the hierarchical order, of lesser peoples not equal to the great-power struggle").[174] A political, "constructive *Gerechtigkeit*" is to substitute for formal equality. A "concrete factually grounded order" is to replace the balancing of opposing interests by formally constructed legal rules. As we noted, within the *Großraum*, each people is to take up the position it merits on the grounds of capacity and accomplishment— an upholding of the principle "to each his due" and not, specifically, "to each the same." The above-cited "relative equality," a "proportionately graded right to influence and proportionate duty of accomplishment according to capacity," receives its political warrant from the *Großraum*'s chief hegemonic power.[175] Such "ordering proportions" thus presume a power within the *Großraum* akin to monopolistic state power within state boundaries: a power that realizes the equality of treatment considered "equitable" (*gerecht*) or that "decides the measure of equality."[176]

Nazi antiuniversalism traces its historical roots directly back to the same autarchic continental schemata hovering behind Karl Haushofer's geopolitics. The Nazi theorists in fact link their idea of *Großraum* to Friedrich Naumann's reflections on the overcoming of the "individualistic stage" of capitalist organization. The idea is described as first achieving concrete form after the Great War, in the expression *Großraumwirtschaft*[177]—signifying the special, extraterritorial economy—at that time taking on a practical, autarchic significance in the Danubian region, being directed there against the "spheres of cosmopolitanism."[178] The idea's future, however, is seen as lying in the formation of economically self-sufficient "political continents" such as Europe and East Asia.[179]

Nazi researchers into international legal history discover the ideal of a revised world order—like its universalist antithesis—rooted within distant epochs. They thus see the "form of extraterritorial political organization" manifest in a "Europe joined together" under new leadership as linked to antique legal traditions and the "renewal of the Roman Empire under the German Kaiser."[180] It is hence incumbent on both state and constitutional theory "to build upon an expanded . . . idea of history, developing its concepts, through an introduction of the new problems of the Reich's constitution and of extraterritorial order, into a unified basis for knowledge with *völkisch*-European orientation."[181]

An antistatist concept of Reich, an extraterritorial order, and a *völkisch*-racist horizon of values interconnect in extremely narrow, systematic fashion. As one of the authors of the—still geopolitically structured—extraterritorial ordering principle, Carl Schmitt confirms that the principle, representing a specific quantity within international law, "belongs to the Reich concept": hence that the concept's legal dogmatic function is implicit in the definition of *Großraum* as a foundation of the new political order. But Reich and *Großraum* are not conceptually identical:[182] rather, "each Reich *has* a *Großraum*, within which its political idea radiates, not being subject there to any foreign intervention."[183] Since the *Großraum*, in its opposition to a "neutral," "mathematical" idea of territory, does not in fact amount to an expanded state[184]—resting instead on the (distinctly nonspecific) "acknowledgment of the basic idea that very specific historical peoples bear responsibility for very specific territories"[185]—then (so goes the National Socialist conclusion) the neologism *Ausstrahlungsraum* (literally, "space of radiation") is precisely on the mark.[186] Inherent in the concept of *Großraum* is an absence of limits.

In its limitless and indeterminate, hence finally opportune essence, the *Großraum* emerges as an example of what the Nazi international legal theorists understand by a conceptual schema "suiting the given situation"—that is, the elevation of "concrete political reality itself to a legal position and legal concept."[187] Accordingly, Schmitt's doctrine of international legal *Großraum* has the goal of "acknowledging the political reality of imperialism as a legal fact and rendering it a basis for a new international legal system."[188]

What legal relations, it asks, are to prevail between the different special, extraterritorial entities—the *Großräume*—and above all within each distinct *Großraum*? The *Großräume* are not hermetically sealed blocks, and the forms of legal intercourse between them are not especially problematic. Indeed, as a result of their predetermined differences, legal formalization of their relations is not absolutely necessary.[189] Within the *Großraum* itself, the situation is quite different: here, the various communal bodies considered part of the greater entity lose any particular, state-based *jus ad bellum*, in favor of the Reich. In the process, the state loses not only sovereignty, independence, and territorial inviolability but its general political existence as well. Only the Reich exists in the sphere of the political; the status of "states" sinks to that of administrative units with certain autonomous rights.[190]

To define the legal relations prevalent in the *Großraum* as part of international law is in fact highly questionable, especially in view of the differentiation introduced between communal bodies seen as preserving a state character and those stripped of any such identity. In the latter case, relations between the hegemonial political entity, that is, the Reich, and such "destated people" (*entstaatlichtes Volk*) could not be based on international law. Rather, legal relations were regulated by the *"Führervolk's* legal act" (*staatsrechtlicher Akt*)—as, for instance, occurred in the protectorate of Bohemia and Moravia, or in the Generalgouvernement established in Po-land.[191] A "relation of leadership [*Führung*] governed by international law" did persist between the German Reich and Slovakia.[192] But even in this po-sition of circumscribed subjection, genuine international legality was aban-doned along with the *jus ad bellum*. The relation was thus still defined, at most, in terms of federation.[193]

The annulling of the distinction between international legal and state le-gal systems through the concept of a "relation of leadership"—that is, one based on hegemony and subjugation—leads in the end to the destruction of international law.[194] Consequently, "on account of its irreconcilability with the fundamental international legal perspective," the hegemony rising from the ruins of the latter system "cannot constitute an international legal institution in the authentic sense."[195] In its place, another construction was available: the above-mentioned legal monism—more specifically, the ex-traterritorial state law developed in the 1930s by Ludwig Schlecher, with its assertion that the legal ordering of external relations proceeds only from the standpoint of a *single* state.[196] As indicated, at the time of its inception, most Nazi legal theorists rejected the theory on racial grounds, considering it mere "legal positivism."[197] But now, in connection with the new "principle of leadership" (*Führungsprinzip*) and in the context of Nazi international le-gal speculation on the *Großraum,* the monistic doctrine of "German extra-territorial law" was readily accepted: it could be tied in, now, to a geopoliti-cal or racial conceptualization, with the concept of Reich at its center. Its earlier rejection was justified opportunistically, on the grounds of "con-siderations of usefulness"[198]—that is, its interference with the rhetoric of "equal treatment." But centered on the principle of *Großraum*, Nazi inter-national legal theory was free to lean in the direction of what amounted to a legal monism based on the concept of Reich. Within such a monistic con-struct, the *Großraum* could become a "superstate" (*Überstaat*), and its law that of the new state.[199]

Legal monism easily fits a vertically structured utopian rule of one people over others. In analogy to the principle of "leadership and obedience," the stronger peoples impose their will on the weaker. Now—so we read—the "relations of superiority and inferiority" are all that matters.[200] These rela-tions can materialize in two forms of association, one based on "rule," the other on "partnership."[201] "Alien peoples" (*Fremdvölkische*) are subjugated to the form based on rule; in contrast, the form based on partnership re-quires true community (*Gemeinschaft*), which postulates, in turn, a "com-mon basis in blood"—not mere shared interests. For this reason, "relations of *völkisch* leadership" are not possible between mutually "alien races."[202]

In the beginning, this sort of hierarchical gradation of peoples within a *Großraum* did not rest on race. Rather, a pair of distinct ranking notions, one geopolitical, the other racial and political, opposed each other. As the advocate of a geopolitically based *Großraum,* Carl Schmitt hoped to realize a European concept involving the "economic consolidation and political strategic isolation of the common living territory [*Lebensraum*] of various peoples."[203] The orientation of Nazi international and administrative law toward "blood" rather than *Raum* involved a rejection of this simple, functional definition of *Großraum,* and the search for a form of legitimization compatible with Nazism's biologistic and racial doctrine.[204] Before the theory of a world of "biologically connected living territories" could prevail, the geopolitical variant of *Großraum* theory had to give way.[205] The latter represented a form of dissolution of the "*völkisch* principle through imperialist universalist thought" and was thus contested;[206] it was to be replaced as an "individualistically founded great-power principle in the tradition of the classical concept of the balance of power."[207]

The construction of the *völkisch* variety of *Großraum* begins with the premise that it represents no "isolated principle" but rather validates the "*völkisch* principles of life."[208] For this reason, here as elsewhere, the "racially specified people" is the starting point of the legal system.[209] The hierarchical vertical order—that order established by the leading power—is racial because an "authentic continental extraterritorial order depends on *völkisch* organization."[210] Hence it involves the replacement of "egalitarian leveling" by "graded autonomization,"[211] and the realization—at last—of the earlier demand for a material, "relative equality," opposed to the formal equality of international law: as "racially superior or inferior value," or as the "higher and lower value" of states "according to natural laws."[212]

The biologization of international law reaches its theoretical apotheosis in a comparison that naturalizes the cosmos of interconnected states. Its metaphoric truth applies, paradoxically, to National Socialism's inverted utopia: "An equally harsh law rules over planets within the solar system and peoples within the European community of nations: neither can remove itself or proceed against its living order without destroying itself or the system."[213]

FOUR

The Catastrophe before the Catastrophe

1938 in Historical Context

We are all in favor of emigration. But through your system of deportations, you are yourself destroying the emigration process. In expelling masses over the borders, you are making any emigration to neighboring countries impossible. Because of the mass expulsions, the neighboring countries are refusing us any more visas.

HEINRICH STAHL, CHAIRMAN, JEWISH COMMUNITY, BERLIN,
TO ADOLF EICHMANN IN MARCH 1939[1]

We can contextualize *Krista llnacht* in various ways: the commonly accepted view is that the night of November 9, 1938, is an expression and apogee of Nazi anti-Semitism before the mass murder. Physical violence, plunder, and above all the burning of synagogues cast the event in the light of classic pogroms. Within this horizon of perception and experience, Kristallnacht has considerable influence on the interpretation of the events that followed. For both the contemporary and posthumous consciousness, what took place that night embodies the subsequent horror of the "final solution" and fits into a continuum of intensifying—albeit traditional—anti-Semitism.

With closer scrutiny, this picture of linear progression reveals great complexity. Overlying the mode of perception that turns the incineration and damaging of synagogues into a paradigm of the later extermination of European Jewry is a network of historical occurrences that has far less finality. The connecting thread between November 9 and the later mass murder emerges less from the National Socialist "program" than from sequels to the night of terror that until now have not received much attention.

The most important of these sequels was the forced emigration of German and Austrian Jews. In fact, it amounted to expulsion in the absence of temporary, let alone permanent, asylum for the deported. By tracing a causal connection between the November pogrom and the subsequent mass extermination, I intend to focus not on the radicalization of traditional anti-Semitism in the pogrom's wake but on the Nazi policy of expulsion. The process commencing with forced emigration, or expulsion, eventually led to and culminated in the death camps.

In order to understand this connection, we must first delineate Kristallnacht's wider context. Through such a broader perspective on the experience, we can approach the situation of the victims. In this regard, we can adequately reconstruct their sense of reality and self-awareness, along with the options for action bound up with both, only when we formally disregard the event that takes its course starting in the summer and fall of 1941: the systematic destruction of the European Jews. Both despite and on account of this historical catastrophe, self-discipline is the historian's obligation, along with an orientation toward the self-perception of witnesses to the event— in particular of the victims. In this manner, the catastrophe *before* the catastrophe can be accorded the weight truly its due in any evaluation of the later mass murder.

Let us begin by considering a statement that has often been cited in Jewish historiography. It illuminates, as does scarcely any other *before* the mass murder's horror, the historical context of the events leading toward it. On December 7, 1938 (barely a month after Kristallnacht), David Ben Gurion took stock from the vantage of the *yishuv,* the Jewish community in mandatory Palestine. He first noted that "In these terrible days marking the onset of European Jewry's downfall [in Hebrew, *churban*] as well as perhaps the termination of the [British] Mandate, I am preoccupied with the [Mapai] party elections for the Tel Aviv region. Nevertheless I do not intend to discuss the elections; the party center has made its decision, and I shall respect it."[2] Before focusing on Mapai's internal conflicts, he then offered some comments on the difficulties facing the Jews of Germany and Austria, or rather: on the problem, intensified by Kristallnacht, of the emigration of the Jewish population of Central Europe. In this context, Ben Gurion spoke of the readiness of the *yishuv,* confronting such a dramatic situation, to embrace further immigrants, above all children, in Jewish Palestine:

> The offer to bring children here from Germany does not only reflect a sense of pity for these children. Even if I knew that all [Jewish] children in Germany could be saved by bringing them to England and only half of them in the case of Palestine, I would choose the second possibility. This because we have to answer not only for the children, but for the Jewish people.[3]

These remarks, like no other stemming from the period's most prominent Zionist figure (the later founder of the Jewish state), invite (mis)interpretation in light and knowledge of the eventual European Jewish catastrophe.[4] To be sure, in subsuming the lives of many Jewish children to the actual or putative interests of the Jewish collective—above all to the interests of Palestine's Zionist project—Ben Gurion obviously articulates a nationalism of radical, indeed totalitarian, bent. But contextualized in relation to contemporary circumstances and historicized in the face of the coming *extermination,* such an apparently cold-blooded calculation of population politics on the part of the "nation builder" turns out to be dramatic yet basically inconsequential rhetoric.

Ben Gurion speaks of the *downfall* of Europe's Jewry but could in no way have been thinking of extermination: at the end of 1938 not even the Nazis knew what they would set out on several years later. Rather, his statement reflects a general expectation of catastrophe, basic to the Zionist interpretation of history.[5]

Directly after Kristallnacht, the *yishuv* leadership announced readiness to accept 10,000 children and 100,000 adults in their "productive" years. Since this possibility signified further crumbling of a Jewish-Arab power balance to which the British had aspired, they tried to counteract it by offering an alternative.[6] Let us note that at the time, the British were engaged in an effort to suppress the waning Palestinian Arab revolt against Jewish settlement and to restore their colonial authority. As compensation for the hard-handed nature of the suppression, they began negotiations with the potentates of surrounding Arab countries. A result was the May 1939 British White Paper concerning limits on Jewish immigration and land purchase.[7] From the Zionist perspective, the White Paper amounted to the de facto renunciation of the Balfour Declaration's promise of a Palestinian Jewish homeland; and indeed, at the end of the 1930s the British had other priorities. Out of need to conform with policies taken up in India, the Colonial Office especially viewed the Palestine question through an ever wider, and imperial, lens not always in harmony with the Foreign Office's viewpoint, which was more sympathetic to the Zionist case. The overriding consideration was to counter the danger of turning the Islamic world—in particular the Moslems of India—against England.[8] And this especially in light of the German and—more significantly—Italian advances toward the Arabs who inhabited the strategically important region between the Indian Ocean and the Mediterranean Sea.

Addressing a set of interests and conflicts that prevailed in the late 1930s —hence *before* the mass murder—Ben Gurion's pronouncement may well be considered cynical; it is nonetheless far less dramatic than seems the case from the perspective of later experience. His rhetorical thrusts indicate no indifference to Jewish suffering as a result of the Nazi policy of expulsion. Rather, their basic context must be seen in a British Palestine policy more and more intent on directing the stream of expelled European Jews anywhere but Palestine.[9] Thus, his nationalist demagogy denounced a threat against the entire Zionist project.

For Ben Gurion, the conflictual constellation that would decide the Jewish emigratory direction included the British Mandate and the *yishuv*. The actual dead-end situation of Europe's Jewish population in the 1930s—the need to *emigrate* from Nazi-ruled Central Europe without any adequate possibilities to *immigrate*—had an entirely different dimension. Chaim Weizmann—president of the World Zionist Organization—described the situation accurately in 1936, bitterly observing that for Jews the world was split in two: between countries hoping to get rid of their Jews and countries unwilling to accept them.[10] Weizmann was directing his observation at the plight of East-Central European Jewry; after Kristallnacht, that of the Jews in Nazi Germany completely ruptured the delicate balance between immigration and emigration.

November 9 would lead to a significant jurisdictional shift within the Reich. Through the arrest and incarceration in concentration camps of between 20,000 and 30,000 Jews, the Sicherheitsdienst (the SD, or "security services" of the SS) gained quasi-control over Jewish emigration and expulsion. Göring—who blamed and compromised his rival Joseph Goebbels, the pogrom's initiator, on account of the night's property damage—appropriated the "Jewish question" and handed it over to the SS. Final instructions to expel the Jews were formulated for the Nazi police on January 24, 1939, when Göring appointed Reinhard Heydrich organizer of the Jewish emigration.[11]

Kristallnacht thus indeed marked a qualitatively new step in the move toward a "final solution" that was gradually taking shape. The pogrom night and subsequent deportations served, in this respect, as a lever for mass expulsion; the following days saw the adoption of a procedure toward the Jews applied by the SD for some time already, in the "incorporated" Ostmark (i.e., Austria): dismissal of Jews from concentration camps followed by their immediate expulsion.[12] The Gestapo made it clear to the various organizations supervising Jewish emigration—the Palestine Bureau and the Hilfsverein (relief organization for German Jews)—but above all to German bureaus responsible for the process such as the Reichswanderungsamt (Reich bureau of emigration) that the harried, incarcerated Jews, threatened in life and limb, would be released only if transported as quickly as possible beyond the borders. If necessary, their release was to be accomplished through illegal means such as falsified documents: a policy already practiced in annexed Austria by the SD since March. The SS appeared little concerned with the resulting overextension, to the point of collapse, of the painstakingly organized emigration network. And in requiring the immediate expulsion, in particular, of those Jews hardly fitting the host countries' strict immigration requirements, the SS doomed the policy of those countries who still maintained their doors half open. The Jews were told to get out—even in direct face of the steadily decreasing emigration possibilities.

The dramatic policy shift was analyzed with penetration by Arthur Prinz, the director of the Hilfsverein's emigration section and a leading figure in the Reichsvertretung (Reich representation of the Jews in Germany).[13] Prinz recognized the narrow connection between the shift and the 1938 vitiation of the traditional state apparatus, the Nazi Party's appropriation of its functions. We learn from his account that the Interior Ministry and—more significantly—the Reichswanderungsamt had both been staffed, for the most part, with officials who during the Weimar period belonged to the political center, as well as to other non-Nazi, albeit conservative, groupings.[14] As Prinz indicates, these officials—maintaining some distance from the regime; transferred by it to a little-esteemed office—displayed considerable circumspection: in particular a readiness to cooperate with the desire of Jewish organizations to link emigration with careful preparation.[15] The Reichswanderungsamt's experts knew well that the emigration of one individual representing—on account of health or social status—a burden for the host country could endanger the chances of hundreds of other potential Jewish emigrants. With Kristallnacht and the mass incarcerations, the influence of such experts was at an end. Once steered by the SD, Jewish emigration could be replaced by mass expulsion.

The grim future was anticipated in the Gestapo's "June action" of 1938: the rounding up, arrest, and removal to concentration camps of approximately 1,500 Jews from the Altreich stigmatized as "asocial": Jews accused or convicted of petty crimes, including offenses such as illegal parking. As in the aftermath to Kristallnacht, those incarcerated in the June action were freed only when Jewish aid organizations could arrange their immediate emigration; and as with Kristallnacht, part of the Nazi apparatus—here, the Gestapo—took over responsibilities from those officials who traditionally handled emigration.

This episode, encapsulating a procedure soon to become standard, anticipated the October expulsion of Jews with Polish citizenship from the Altreich. In turn, both the proceedings of June and October were anticipated by the policies initiated in Austria, under Eichmann's direction, straight after the annexation. The four weeks following March 15, 1938, saw mass expulsions of Jews from the Burgenland province, preceded by the incarceration of other Jews, some of whom were prominent, in Dachau.[16] This period was marked by a systematic breakdown of distinctions between Jews with Austrian and non-Austrian citizenship, as well as the expulsion of those with valid Austrian papers across the Swiss border. The steadily growing tide of refugees prompted an increasingly restrictive Swiss reaction: also in March, efforts of a group of 400 Jews to cross the border led to the Swiss demand (at the month's end) for transit visas, until then a highly unusual practice. But the visa question was itself soon superseded, as under the cover of darkness, the SS and SA drove 2,000 refugees—now indeed lacking travel documents and completely penniless—from Austria.[17] (In addition, as a later augury of the June action it is worth noting the expulsion at the end of May of hundreds of Viennese Jews born in adjacent countries, hence still formally classified as foreigners.)

Starting in October, the Gestapo's expulsion of Jews toward countries bordering the Ostmark had its follow-up within the Altreich in relation to France, Luxembourg, Belgium, and (again) Switzerland. The expulsions even proceeded over rivers and—later—lakes. Here too, this policy elicited countermeasures: anticipating the expanded limits on possible immigration, a Swiss requirement of October 5 specified that the passports of German Jews be marked by a discriminatory "J." Henceforth, the compulsory—now illegal—emigration qua expulsion would prompt procedures destined to make *any* emigration impossible. Following the November pogrom—and after Yugoslavia, Italy, and Czechoslovakia closed their borders (March and April) on the grounds of growing emigration pressure from Austria— additional countries adjacent to Germany hardened their immigration policies.[18]

We see, then, a connection between the policies initiated in the Ostmark as part of the events preceding Kristallnacht and the Nazi regime's radicalization in the course of its move toward the organized extermination of European Jewry: namely, the suppression of the old elites as both basis and result of an aggressive, ideologically propelled politics of *outward expansion* on the part of Reich and regime. In the face of the euphoria displayed by those who were being "annexed," Austria represented the first fruits of this expansionist politics. Still hampered in March by the extant authority of the Reichswanderungsamt in the Altreich, the Nazis—that is, Eichmann and his apparatus—could proceed as zealously as they pleased in the Ostmark.[19] Furthermore, the direct use of the SS, functioning as the regime's police force, could have more direct effects in Austria. In the Altreich, as well, the year 1938 signified a qualitative leap in the Nazification of the ruling apparatus. It is thus not astonishing that the *Anschluss* as a specific form of Nazi occupation made state and government authority far easier to ignore in Austria than in the Altreich itself.[20]

The connection between the German Nazis' outward expansion and the radicalizing of their approach to the "Jewish problem" is clearly evident. The deeper they penetrated eastward, the harsher their procedure. With no more possibilities for emigration or immigration, and with the steady increase of the Jewish population through further conquests, the process beginning in March 1938 in the Ostmark as expulsion in the guise of compulsory emigration shifted to the *internal* expulsion and ghettoization of the Jews. While the Jews in Poland were isolated in ghettoes, the attack on the Soviet Union inaugurated direct mass killings; geographically reversed, the scale of killings intensified westward—into the heart of Nazi dominion—as organized mass extermination set it and extended into a death-camp system located in Poland. Paradoxically, the Jews living in the Reich were among the last Jewish groups in Europe forced to wear the stigmatizing "yellow star" (starting September 19, 1941).

In the interwar period the non-German Jews of Europe (along with many non-Jews) essentially viewed Germany's anti-Semitic reality in terms of the classically anti-Jewish policies of ethnically heterogeneous Eastern European states like Poland, Rumania, and Hungary: that is, in terms of a tradition of religiously based, now nationalistically charged anti-Semitic pogroms. When, for instance, Vladimir Jabotinsky—leader of the Zionist Revisionists, with a markedly pessimistic perspective—spoke of evacuating the Jews from Europe, he had in mind the dangers facing Polish Jews within their country's political context.[21] In contrast, as the (largely assimilated) German Jews observed the Nazi anti-Semitic policies at their inception, their reaction was primarily one of shock. Even for German Zionists, laying as they did great weight on a particular Jewish identity, the early Nazi policies of separation were in no way acceptable: German Zionism had always understood itself as a cultural movement, concerned more with the crisis of Jewish self-identity sparked by secularization than with actual plans to emigrate to Palestine.[22] The turn to Zionism of previous members of the Centralverein (central organization of German citizens of Jewish faith) was entirely a reflection of their shock at the new exclusion.[23]

The shift thus catalyzed in German Jewish self-definition from religion to ethnicity, and the connected rise in estimation for a previously marginalized Zionist perspective, did not lead to any sudden flight from Germany, but rather to a new sense of the need to emigrate *in the long term*.[24] Above all the Zionists—for whom Palestine, the historic homeland, was the only sensible destination—showed little inclination to rashly abandon Germany. But as indicated above, Palestine's absorptive capacity dictated its rate of immigration; a careful selection among potential immigrants was necessary, along with their preparation and retraining. Whatever the wider implications of such a "political" emigration policy, it is certain that it was motivated by a long-range perspective and hence was most unsuitable for the rapidly worsening situation of the German Jews.[25]

Considered from the viewpoint of a formal, universal principle of equality, the Nazis' racially grounded Nuremberg laws, put into effect in September 1935, represent a thorough, qualitative intensification of their anti-Jewish measures. Nonetheless, the reaction of German Jews to the racial legislation was pronouncedly restrained, sometimes even affirmative—for which there were a number of reasons. In the first place, the discriminatory laws seemed above all else to offer the guarantee of a certain legal security, desired all the more urgently in light of the increasingly incalculable nature of daily circumstances.[26] Beyond this, the Nuremberg laws appeared to offer Jewish existence in Germany something like minority status, in analogy with the Eastern European Jewish experience—an assessment that was specifically stressed in Zionist ranks.[27] With assimilated German Jews thus appearing to return to an ethnic identity similar to the Jews of Poland, it was deemed both realistic and responsible to do everything to salvage that community, waiting out the period of the Nazis, rather than work toward mass emigration.[28]

Starting in the summer of 1938, the activity of the Reichsvertretung shifted entirely to emigration. But the project's pressing nature conflicted, paradoxically, with the caution required for its execution. The situation was exacerbated by a realignment of balance between the different Jewish organizations: it is fairly obvious that the Nazis would favor the Zionist organizations, both on account of their ideological disposition to leave Germany and their possession of the infrastructure and experience needed for emigration.[29] But such favoritism often contributed to self-delusion, for instance when, to the astonishment of members of the Zionist Hechaluz organization, the German authorities allowed five of its emissaries to visit the Reich from Palestine in the summer of 1938, for the sake of bolstering the morale of emigration candidates.[30]

The long-term planning of Jewish emigration from Germany could not keep pace with the reality of the Nazis' anti-Jewish measures. Evaluated retrospectively, what the measures called for was straightforward evacuation—

something that at the time, to be sure, was out of the question. Even at the conference devoted to the question of aid for the Jews of Austria and Germany, arranged by Franklin D. Roosevelt and held at Evian in July 1938 (as I will elaborate below), discussions focused on long-term possibilities for Jewish emigration. This line was in harmony with the policies of the Jewish organizations. At the same time, such discussions reflected the background presence of specific social and historical constellations, themselves bound up closely with Kristallnacht's fundamental meaning. One of the constellations was defined by the set of draconian immigration laws introduced in America in the 1920s: laws ending decades in which the nation's doors were open, above all, to the mass immigration of Eastern European Jews. Connected to this was a second constellation, defined by the dramatic migratory movements unleashed in Europe after the Great War, in the wake of dynastic collapse, the Russian civil war, and the formation of East-Central European nation-states with ethnically heterogeneous populations.[31] In turn, the new political demographic reality was closely connected with a third constellation, which we now need to consider more closely: that defined by the particular situation of Polish Jewry—by far the largest Jewish community in Europe, constituting some 10 percent of the Polish population— and by the Polish government's anti-Semitic stance toward them.

Along with other national minorities, the Jews in the Polish nation-state founded after World War I were subject to considerable pressure.[32] To a large extent, the state's energies were focused on safeguarding the country's ethnic Polish character through a policy of increasing "Polonization"; it undermined both the originally intended federalist character of the state's body politic and the obligations undertaken toward the League of Nations to protect minority rights.[33] In 1934 these obligations were further neutralized through a growing rapprochement between a nationalist and military-dominated Polish government and Hitler's Germany—a process that was initiated by the signing of a nonaggression pact.[34]

The pact was an expression of a revisionist bilateralism directed against the league's multilateralism and France's standing in Central Europe; one of its main functions was to help destroy the postwar status quo, itself serving as a guarantee of Poland's sovereign status between Germany and Russia. To be sure, Poland's alignment with Hitler's antipathy toward the status quo did not signify a shared ideological program—though a common note was touched on through shared hostility to the Soviet Union and, more notably, through a virulent anti-Semitism sponsored, albeit differently, by each of the states. Likewise, despite all the glaring differences between the two regimes, authoritarian Poland introduced measures coming close to Nazi anti-Jewish measures, for instance, the exclusion of Jews from various professional organizations on grounds scarcely distinguishable from the German "Aryan" clauses.[35] This sort of anti-Semitism was both embedded in and heightened by a context of interethnic conflict that had corroded the state since its inception. Fierce fighting broke out between the Polish state and Polish Ukrainians in Galicia in the 1920s, and there was unabated conflict between Poles and Germans in Upper Silesia. Starting in 1937, the tension between ethnic Germans and their Polish polity would deepen, serving as an excuse for Hitler's 1939 invasion.

Unmistakably, the aim of the policy of "Polonization" in regard to the Jews was emigration. In this period, the idea of divesting Poland of its Jewish population led to the famous plan for transforming Madagascar into a Jewish colonial project.[36] In the framework of such a population politics, the Polish government also tried to maintain its links to those Jewish groups that had elevated Polish Jewry's emigration or evacuation into a political program—for instance, Jabotinsky's revisionists.[37] The vast majority of Poland's Jews, however, favored the struggle for full equality as Polish citizens and against discrimination. For them, rather than suppressing its plurality of nations, Poland's task was to constitutionally acknowledge them as part of a wider body politic.[38]

Not surprisingly, the demographic centrality of Poland's Jews and their experience with the increasingly discriminatory regimes in East-Central Europe led them and much of world Jewry to view Nazi anti-Semitism as a project to strip the Jews of their legal status as equal citizens and to force the emigration of most of the Jewish population. For this reason, the basic response to events in Germany taken by international Jewish organizations in 1933 was the same as that of the German Jews: to preserve Jewish legal status and Jewish existence within Germany.[39] By the same token, with the founding of the World Jewish Congress in 1936, its president Nahum Goldmann pressed for an effort to preserve the remaining rights of Germany's Jews— no thought was to be given the possibility of dissolving the Jewish communities there.[40] For its part, the desire of Polish Jews to see Jews stay in Germany was not wholly selfless: against the backdrop of the discriminatory stance of the Polish regime, they feared, quite understandably, that a mass exodus of German Jews would prompt more drastic discrimination on the regime's part, or even dramatic measures to rid Poland of its Jews.[41]

We thus find the Jewish press in Poland speaking out strongly against advocates of German Jewish emigration.[42] Steps already taken toward organized emigration and partial transfer of wealth—the transfer agreement (*ha'avara*)—drew their criticism. The arrangement not only broke the Jewish trade boycott against Germany; it based emigration to Palestine on capital transfer in the form of goods. Only those individuals with enough capital would have a chance to emigrate. The process split German Jews into the fortunate and unfortunate, those Jews not able to leave being more and more vulnerable and having increasingly fewer rights.[43] From the Polish Jewish perspective, the regimes in Berlin and Warsaw were distinctly similar. Beyond mutual encouragement and legislation (which we examine below), the Polish authorities did their best not to endanger their relations with Nazi Germany, apparently solid enough in any case as a result of the non-aggression treaty. They thus took measures against the Jewish press—for instance against the newspaper *Haint,* which had criticized the anti-Semitic campaign in the period leading up to Kristallnacht.[44]

The simultaneous affinity and distinction between Polish and Nazi German anti-Semitism is manifest in an episode that—pointing toward the process that culminated in Kristallnacht—brought the two discriminatory modes together. To appreciate the episode's significance, we need to keep in mind the wider context outlined in these pages: the triumph of the Nazi party's apparatus over the traditional elites; and—more directly—the Austrian Anschluss, reflecting that interior radicalization and bearing such enormous consequences for the Jews. From the present perspective, the Anschluss did not spark the sort of fear in Poland that the event truly merited. By the same token, the Polish government took no offense from the Reich's incorporation of the Sudetenland into its territory, despite the parallelism in the genesis of Poland and Czechoslovakia, both being products of the post-Great War order. On the contrary: it saw here an opportunity to regain the Olsa region, largely inhabited by Poles but lost to the Czechs in 1920, in the course of the Polish-Soviet war. Nevertheless, Poland recognized the dangers posed by the Anschluss in relation to its own "Jewish question": a mass flight or expulsion of Jews from the Ostmark could sabotage Poland's emigration-oriented policies, particularly if the 20,000 Polish Jewish citizens living in Austria were forced back to their legal homeland.

Soon after the Anschluss—more precisely, on March 31, 1938—the Polish authorities prepared a "passport law" aimed at precluding the latter possibility.[45] Since such a law could not be directed overtly against Jews, it applied officially to all Poles living outside the country for more than five years. As explained in an interior ministry decree of October 6, 1938, such citizens were to report to the suitable Polish consulate to renew their papers, a privilege that, to be sure, could readily be denied, in a gesture equivalent to deprivation of citizenship. Transparently aimed at Austria's Polish Jews, this measure's full force would be felt by those Jew from Poland who were living in the Altreich, approximately 50,000 in total.[46] For the time, however, the new law was not put into effect. This delay had solid motives: the government was waiting for the results of an occasion with deep implications for its anti-Jewish policies—the July gathering of the international conference on refugees at Evian.[47]

Here too, the Anschluss served as principal event behind the scene. In view of the rigorous policy of expulsion at play in Austria, officials in the U.S. State Department had anticipated a similar development being initiated throughout the Reich, a huge wave of refugees thus rolling forth from both Austria and Germany. This outcome—so the officials feared—would place Roosevelt under great pressure to loosen the nation's now-restrictive emigration laws.[48] Far more desirable would be an arrangement dispersing the refugee wave among many countries. Perhaps predictably, once preparations for the Evian conference got underway, the anti-Semitic regimes in both Poland and Rumania recognized the opportunity to articulate their own inclinations: for an organized, internationally legitimized resettlement of large portions of their Jewish population.

Such hopes were no secret to the American authorities. They understood very well that an open acceptance—no matter what the mode or who the agent—of large groups of refugees, and a rendering of Europe's Jewish emigration problem into a concern of the world community, would lead directly to increased emigration pressure by the Polish and Rumanian regimes on their Jewish citizenry. The refugee pressure on the Western hemisphere's countries of immigration would then increase proportionally, cutting off any remaining willingness to maintain open doors. Consequently, the preemptive isolation of the East-Central European "Jewish problem" from that of Germany and Austria became an urgent task: the American officials reflected the concern in a systematic and euphemistic reference to "political refugees from Germany and Austria," avoiding the term "Jews."[49]

In light of the isolationist and nativist mood prevalent in America during the 1920s and 1930s—a disengagement from the Old World and its problems—the administration's initiative at Evian appears extraordinary. It seemed to mark a step back into Europe—one greeted with enthusiasm by both England and France (more so by France, on account of wider-ranging considerations).[50] But what, in fact, were the basic American intentions in arranging the conference? Did they signify the country's first, hesitant, effort to take up its international responsibilities, or rather a simple reaction, within the domain of domestic politics, to external circumstances? Whatever the correct answer to such questions, it seems fairly certain that the State Department viewed the conference as a chance for Roosevelt to move in an apparently paradoxical direction: by placing himself at the head of efforts to find new homes in Europe and America for the Austrian and German "political refugees," the president could more easily circumvent liberal demands at home for a substantial raising of the restrictive refugee quotas, and for a broad change in immigration policies.[51] The particular legislation to which liberal critics objected was the Emigration Act of 1924, meant to check the influx of both Jews and Italians onto American shores, for the sake of preserving the Anglo-Saxon "racial stock."[52] The legislation reflected an anti-immigrant atmosphere sparked by depression and unemployment, and characterized by ideological rationalizations couched in economic utilitarian terms. (To be sure, following the Anschluss, the American authorities decided to exhaust the legally prescribed quotas—anything but a self-evident measure, in that the consulates had until then steadily undercut the quotas, on Washington's orders.)[53]

The precise date of the Evian conference was July 6–14, 1938. On March 22, both governmental and international—primarily Jewish—aid organizations received invitations. The choice of locus was unusual and eloquent in its implications, casting a shadow on the conference's prospects for success. For Switzerland had refused to place Geneva—site of the League of Nations; city of international conferences and cooperation—at the international community's disposal. The Swiss feared that the simple choice of the city could imply onerous obligations for the swell of "political refugees." French Evian was close to Geneva, thus offering practical access to the American consulate's infrastructure.[54]

The conference's dominant figure was the head of the American delegation, Myron G. Taylor, the retired chairman of United States Steel and a close friend of Roosevelt. In the conference's preliminary stages, Taylor already had two absolute "essentials" in mind: first, to fend off the question of Eastern European—in other words, Polish—Jews lurking in the background; second, at all costs to avoid linking the refugee problem with Palestine as a possible place of refuge. The tactics reflected consideration for Great Britain's policies regarding the Middle East and the Arabs and a specific request from the British government—a request that was not to be disregarded.[55] In order to suppress the Polish Jewish complex, Taylor, who had officially contacted virtually all the Jewish organizations before the conference, simply ignored the representatives of Polish Zionism.[56]

In the end, the Evian conference could not help even the Jews from Germany and Austria. It finished on a disappointing note: none of the thirty-two delegations besides that of the Dominican Republic declared themselves ready to accept the burden of Austrian and German "political" refugees. One factor weighing heavily behind the scene was the stipulation by otherwise willing countries that "involuntary emigrants" possess the financial means to support their integration.[57] Added to the general reluctance of America and other countries to take in Jewish masses from Central Europe, the restrictions that the Nazis set before the Jews they expelled from the Altreich and Ostmark—making them leave practically penniless—caused the conference to fail. The fantastic Nazi "flight tax" (*Reichsfluchtsteuer*) alone totally wiped out the savings of those willing to leave, before they had even taken a single step beyond the borders.[58] According to the undersecretary, Ernst von Weizsäcker, it was Ribbentrop, the Reich's new foreign minister, who was behind many of the financial obstacles to emigration.[59]

The stance taken by the Western countries at Evian was a good reflection of their self-centered policies during the 1930s. That this national egoism reinforced the Nazis' anti-Semitic campaign is clear. With scorn and mockery, the German Reich observed the conference's course, the pusillanimity and wavering of its participants. France, for instance, one of Europe's great lands of immigration, cited the burden it had borne since World War I, indicating that over 200,000 refugees had been accepted.[60] Other lands offered complaints bordering on rampant nationalism and xenophobia. Even America—despite its democratic traditions and resistance to extremist temptations—was not free of such currents, sometimes emerging as fierce anti-Semitism.[61] Aware of this atmosphere, the Jewish aid organizations acted cautiously on behalf of those Jewish refugees knocking on the gates of the land of freedom. When it came to direct interventions, they preferred to rely on the activities of non-Jewish institutions, in order not to aggravate an impression of primarily ethnocentric concerns.[62]

At Evian, Taylor seems to have succeeded in protecting the president from domestic pressures feared in the wake of the Anschluss—so, at least, runs the gist of his own resumé of the conference.[63] It is true that an "intergovernmental committee" was established to undertake a dialogue over emigration questions with the German authorities. By and large, the conference initiative dissolved into dust or at least was swallowed up by the ever-worsening situation in Europe. But it would be clearly mistaken to translate this failure of Western immigration policy—the refusal to take in Jewish refugees—into acquiescence with the later extermination of the European Jews. At the time, the authorities and experts dealt with the refugee problem in light of their experience with mass migration from the 1920s and 1930s. They oriented all plans and proposals toward the long term, not to-

ward the dramatic evacuation that, considered post factum, was truly necessary. The problem of historically bound perception is perhaps most readily apparent in the approach taken to the refugee question by the Jewish
Agency, the Zionist executive body for Palestine.

In a meeting of the agency held to discuss the implications of the Evian
conference, Zionist immigration experts such as the eminent sociologist
and economist Arthur Ruppin stressed that Palestine was hardly suitable
as a site for mass immigration. Citing the land's highly limited absorptive
capacity and the certain British veto of a mass influx, Ruppin appealed for
a solution on the lines of what Max Nordau termed *Nachtasyl* (night shelter)—the sojourn of Jewish refugees in other lands. He urged Zionists present at Evian to work in this direction.[64] But Ben Gurion harshly rejected
such a policy of regional diversification. His fear was that to split the problem of Jewish refugees from the political program of a Jewish homeland in
Palestine would remove the pressure on England over the immigration
question and damage Zionism's historical claims. The sole responsible option for the Zionist side was to link the refugee question to that of Palestine.
At the same time, as we can gather from Ben Gurion's words, he himself
knew that Palestine (where, let us recall, the Arab revolt had been raging
since 1936) was not ready for Jewish refugees. As a matter of principle, he
was rejecting a purely philanthropic approach to the problem.[65] Offering
what amounts to a de facto countergesture to Taylor's snubbing of the Polish Zionists, the directorship of the Jewish Agency proposed sending only a
second-rank delegation to Evian, since Palestine was excluded a priori from
the chosen rescue options. Chaim Weizmann, it was decided, would not
come to the conference.[66]

The Zionist Organization itself approached the problem of Jewish emigration from Germany and Austria in light of precedents set in the interwar
period; great haste, let alone evacuation planning, did not seem called for.
The response to such precedents—pogroms and related expressions of
anti-Semitism—had been to strengthen the project of founding a Jewish
state in Palestine, regardless of historical circumstances. The Zionists, as
well as others, stood with their backs turned to a horrific future they could
not anticipate.

Evian's failure did more than disappoint those who had hoped to see a
more liberal emigration policy emerge from the conference. It embittered
the traditional anti-Semites in Poland and Rumania, whose own hopes
attached to the conference have already been outlined. And even the Nazis
apparently vented their disappointment through a speeding up of expul-

sions.[67] At the same time, the ongoing Sudetenland crisis led to a further increase in emigration: it may have determined the Swiss authorities' choice of October 5 as the date they requested the Germans to start stamping "J" in German passports held by Jews.

The following day, on October 6, the Polish authorities made their own response, issuing the decree that the Interior Ministry had planned in March, with its passport measures bordering on loss of citizenship. Possessing no more hopes for easier emigration of Jews from Poland, the government now intended at least to thwart the feared expulsion of Polish Jewish citizens from Germany.[68] But the decree did not take immediate effect, being pushed forward to November 15. Meanwhile, the Nazis proceeded to set the expulsion process in motion.

The sadly notorious "Zbacin affair" encapsulated the process. The German authorities expelled thousands of Jews with Polish citizenship who were living in Germany and chased them beyond the German-Polish border. The Polish authorities on their part tried to block their way into Poland. The Jews became trapped in the no-man's-land between the two countries. Among the expelled Polish Jews was the family of Hershel Grynspan, a sixteen-year-old boy, who revenged his parents' and sisters' misery by shooting at von Rath, the German consular official in Paris. His attempt and the later death of von Rath unleashed Goebbels's initiative of the Kristallnacht, through which the propaganda minister hoped to gain advantage over competitors in party, state, and security apparatus who had increased their power at his expense.

As I have argued above, far less emphasis has been placed than called for on the particular nature of the pogrom night's consequences for the further radicalizing of policies toward the Jews: the appropriation in the Altreich, after November, of a practice of expulsion first tried and tested in the Ostmark has remained largely obscured by the night's broken glass and flames. On account of the centrality of the "Jewish question" for Nazi ideology, the SS would gain a monopoly on the "solution" through "emigration." In this manner, the illegal crossing of borders became a practical form of escape and a reflection of the Jewish plight. Such illegality, and *only* the illegality, led to a brief collaboration between the SD and the Mossad le-aliya bet—the *yishuv*'s secret organization responsible for circumventing British immigration restrictions in order to bring Jews to Palestine from Europe.[69] Yet because of ever fewer immigration possibilities for the majority of those Jews who had remained within the Reich, Göring's directive of May 1941 (can-celed in October) that even during the war "Jewish emigration . . . be rein-forced" was of no consequence. Over several years, the Nazi policy of ex-pulsion had thus sealed off all still-extant emigration options. In a world of egoistic nation-states, the pressure exerted by the expulsions on the denat-uralized Jews, deprived of all state protection, led to the emergence of that "option" culminating in industrial mass murder.

PART II

Perceptions of the Holocaust

FIVE

The Limits of Reason

Max Horkheimer on Anti-Semitism and Extermination *

Max Horkheimer has drawn reproach for not having devoted—before, during, and even after the Nazi annihilation of the Jews—the kind of attention to anti-Semitism called for by its historical import and, above all, by his own Jewish origin.[1] In light of this alleged "indifference," his later studies on the fate of the Jews and reflections on anti-Semitism become in his critics' eyes mere "compensation" for his previous attitudes.[2] But to judge Horkheimer's position on anti-Semitism in this way is to take up a critical position outside history, outside the times, experiences, and sense of life crucial not only for Horkheimer and the original Frankfurt School, but for German Jews in general: the belief that the civil emancipation of the Jews in Germany had already been accomplished and their equality as Germans actually and irreversibly established.[3] For those dedicated to emancipation, the task at hand was to overcome further barriers and socially discriminatory distinctions. The irruption of unimaginable barbarism, which went far beyond any mere retraction of the achievements of emancipation and enlightenment, profoundly contradicted their originally optimistic schemes. And in light of this optimism, their early views of German National Socialism should not surprise us. They did not regard it as a phenomenon specifically concerning the Jews but rather as a single aspect of a general social threat, to which one reacted first and foremost as a political being, and only secondarily as a Jew.[4] Why should Horkheimer have seen things differently, imagining the unimaginable before it occurred? And is his change of attitude in light of the destruction of the Jews—an event, moreover, that qualitatively exceeds anti-Semitism—grounds for criticism? Gauged against the hope of emancipation and the significance of the historical rupture represented by Nazism and the destruction of the Jews, it could hardly have been otherwise.

Horkheimer could not help but devote his attention to anti-Semitism during these terrible years. The way he went about it led to some annoyance, particularly concerning his essay "Die Juden und Europa." Opinion about his "Elemente des Antisemitismus," written with Adorno and Löwenthal as part of *Dialektik der Aufklärung,* was quite different. Both texts are essential theoretical sources for analyzing a historic transformation of anti-Semitism. In addition, Horkheimer works the theme of anti-Semitism into other theoretical reflections in a dispersed, unsystematic fashion and interweaves it with critical remarks on current affairs and biographical notes. The observations concerning anti-Semitism reveal a striking duality: they are both an element in the phenomenology of Horkheimer's critique of reason and the secret, biographical impetus behind the theoretical endeavor; mere material for explicating his critique of civilization, they are yet one of its subliminal motives as well. This duality corresponds to the significance attached to the Jews as the primary victims of Nazism: in being murdered *as* Jews, an event afflicting the Jewish people as a specific collective, their particularity seems to be confirmed. In addition, a universal break in civilization simultaneously manifested itself. This break lies in the fact that an arbitrary and unfathomable annihilation of human beings became possible—and actually took place.

The tension arising from such an ambiguous duality is characteristic of the mass annihilation. It recurs as a leitmotif in Horkheimer's writings and notes on anti-Semitism, making an unequivocal judgment difficult. Heightening the tension between universal stance and particular concern is the question of what the term "Jew" means: it can signify both the concrete Jewish person and a social metaphor composed in the fantasy world of the anti-Semite. This metaphor has little to do with real Jews, although the fatality of a newly spun reality decreed that real Jews became its first victims. It is not surprising that for Horkheimer, as for other critics of anti-Semitism, the social metaphorical significance of the Jews blends together with that of concrete Jewish persons. Of course, a mixing of social meaning with real fates is difficult to avoid. But claims for the validity of such a conflation were plausible only before Auschwitz. On this point, the bureaucratically administered, industrial annihilation of the Jews necessarily brought in its wake a caesura in linguistic usage and conceptualization. For Horkheimer as for Marx in "Zur Judenfrage," writing before the mass annihilation that (as Horkheimer himself would come to define it) put an end to optimistic schemata of historical progress, "the Jews" did not stand for actual Jewish persons. The term bore above all an extended social meaning. After Auschwitz—after the actual destruction of the European Jews—the term's extended metaphorical and conceptual understanding receded. Since Auschwitz, common linguistic usages such as the description of phenomena from the sphere of circulation as Jewish have forfeited their dubious claim to reality.[5]

The perception and assessment of anti-Semitism necessarily take different forms from a universalistically oriented Jewish standpoint than from one of Jewish particularism. Neither perspective was immune to errors and misjudgments in dealing with Nazism. To criticize Horkheimer for failure to recognize the true significance of anti-Semitism at the decisive moment is to suggest that, faced with the evident significance of Nazism, he obstinately refused to acknowledge the particularity of the problem it posed, as a result of a distorted sense of reality and an exclusively theoretical treatment of the problem's universal aspects. Whatever biographical truth may lie in such a suggestion, it nonetheless has the ring of retrospective valuation—a process we would do well to avoid, considering the monstrosity and inconceivability of the destruction of the Jews.[6] The fact that the inconceivable came to be a thoroughly personal experience for Horkheimer does not lessen its impact.[7]

Moreover, critiques that base their reproaches of Horkheimer's texts on the problem of anti-Semitism and the situation of the Jews before and during the process of mass annihilation presume, without acknowledging it, the accomplished fact of genocide. The latent implication of such critiques is that the mass annihilation was foreseeable. They imply that anti-Semitism necessarily led to Auschwitz. If that were close to the truth, then the laxity with which Horkheimer and the predominantly Jewish members of the Frankfurt School considered (or failed to consider) the phenomenon would be incomprehensible. But if we reject this negative historical teleology—an alleged determinism leading from anti-Semitism to the destruction of the Jews—than it may be possible to shed light on those ambiguous mixtures of (undoubtedly eclectic) conceptual experiments and biographically conditioned perceptions in a way that does more justice to a tragic conjunction of political defeat, biographical suffering, and theoretically articulated pessimism. With the mass annihilation, the particular fate of the Jews had become a universal historical event, with a standing all its own in the realm of theory. Horkheimer and Adorno rightly spoke of a "turning point in history" (DA, 5:230 [200]), but only in retrospect. Few minds equipped with Western reason could have ventured to formulate that caesura before its occurrence.

No statement, no passage of Horkheimer's has been worn out more than the dictum that individuals who do not wish to speak of capitalism should keep quiet about fascism ("JE," 4:308–9 [78]). Facile postfascist recipients read out of it what Horkheimer in fact put into it—at that time, before Auschwitz. Alongside its claim for truth, the statement suggestively formulates a claim to correct political action: no opponent who does not aim to overthrow the social relationships that spawned fascism, as an authoritarian form of bourgeois political domination, can fight fascism effectively. The statement contains a latent attack on liberalism; that, too, was part of its intention.

Behind this statement, which has meanwhile been reduced to an empty phrase, stands the idea that the phenomenon of anti-Semitism is not something independent but rather the particular expression of an underlying, more comprehensive context. As if sounding a gong, the piece thus begins with the statement: "Whoever wants to explain anti-Semitism must speak of National Socialism" ("JE," 4:308 [77]). To dwell on the phenomenon of anti-Semitism would be as pointless as to remain fixated on fascism. Critique must detach itself from the phenomena and take aim at the origins of the prevailing order—at capitalism. This is the central claim of Horkheimer's essay on the Jews and Europe. Apart from the broader implications of the piece—which as indicated, ultimately has no more and no less to do with the Jews than Marx's notorious essay[8]—Horkheimer concerns himself exclusively with the altered form of political domination represented by the figure of the "authoritarian" or fascist state. The Jews and anti-Semitism serve him as shibboleths of social reality, as a litmus test of that political transformation. Yet there is more to it than that. In portraying the transition from the liberal state to the authoritarian, fascist state, Horkheimer makes statements about the Jews entirely in accord with the sentiments and convictions predominant on the left at the time.[9] These statements indicate Horkheimer's intention of denying any particularity to the fate of the Jews at the hands of Nazism. Beyond that, puzzlingly, the piece has a sardonic undertone. This tone reflects Horkheimer's orientation at the time despite his later attempts to distance himself from this text and despite the pains taken by some interpreters to explain away his attitude.

Against the background of the Nazis' anti-Jewish measures before the war—a policy of discrimination and expatriation but not of organized physical destruction, which began only later—Horkheimer can still sustain the speculative core of his thesis: with the liquidation of the market by the "authoritarian state," the putative agents of that market, the Jews, had lost their social significance. Horkheimer thereby maintains the premise that the

THE LIMITS OF REASON   *101*

Jews in fact constituted a leading element in the sphere of circulation. In so doing, he remains thoroughly bound up in the tradition of economistic interpretations, sociological and Marxist, of the Jewish question.[10] At the same time, he conflates the entirely relevant presence *of* the Jews in circulation with the significance of the Jews *for* the sphere of circulation. From the perspective of critical theory, we see in this reasoning the holdovers of traditional theory—above all, a rigorous economism. This regression may be an expression of Horkheimer's attempt to keep his distance from the Jewish problem as an existential issue by making claims to universality.[11] In the context of expectations whose basic tenor, despite all despair, was an optimistic hope for an emancipatory resolution, anti-Semitic politics in Nazi Germany became a mere ornament of the crisis. No peculiar status was to attach to it.

The construing of antipathy toward the Jews in Nazi Germany as an immediate expression of a decline in market relationships, above all of the sphere of circulation and the liberal world bound up with it, makes it possible to assign the events a theorizable sense within the paradigm of competitive capitalism. At any rate, when seen as an epiphenomenon of competition, anti-Semitism seems still to fit within structures of reason, if only those of instrumental reason. In this way, the events still serve as material for a traditional critique of the intrinsic limitations of civil emancipation. Thus, Horkheimer comments that the emancipation of the Jews, a direct result of the ambiguous character of the French Revolution, of freedom and equality, was burdened from the start with the curse of its contrary. In fact, "The order which set out as the progressive one in 1789 carried the germs of National Socialism from the beginning" ("JE," 4:325 [90]). But because emancipation proceeds as a mere function of the market economy, with the turn from the anonymous market to naked power that lies at the core of National Socialism comes the overthrow of those who have been emancipated only by means of the attributes of circulation. Their fall results from the rivalry between the market and power—or, in his later more precise formulation, between the spheres of circulation and production. At that point Horkheimer draws the conclusion so irritating today: "The result is bad for the Jews. They are being run over. Others are the most capable today: the leaders of the new order in the economy and the state" ("JE," 4:325 [89]).

The significance Horkheimer ascribes to the decline of the sphere of circulation as an explanatory framework for anti-Semitism in Nazi Germany does not stand up to scrutiny. Of course, it is striking that the Jews' loss of civil rights went together with their expulsion from the sphere of circulation, which until then had seemed a source of security. But to conclude that this double shift meant the neutralization of circulation as such, amounting to a real primacy of political domination over the economy, does not accord with reality.[12] Rather, the conclusion emerges from Horkheimer's identification of the Jews with the sphere of circulation. In explaining the identification, he argues that the economy "no longer has an independent dynamic." It has lost "its power to the economically powerful," who now achieve their goals by noneconomic means. "Exploitation no longer reproduces itself aimlessly via the market, but rather in the conscious exercise of domination" ("JE," 4:316 [83]). This finding is remarkably insensitive to the plight of Nazism's Jewish victims in the 1930s. Horkheimer assumes that the liberal state's market economy and the fascist state's economy of power have a common rationality. And since the Jews ground their existence as agents of circulation on this same rationality, their condemnation derives from the same justice on which their emancipation and prosperity depended. Indeed, when the Jews "glorify the prehistory of the totalitarian state, monopoly capitalism, and the Weimar Republic, with an understandable homesickness, then the fascists are in the right against them." Everything thus stands and falls with the "type of rationality" inherent in the specific conditions of exploitation. Previously, it had accrued to the benefit of the Jews, or rather, of Jewish entrepreneurs. Now this "kind of rationality" turns against them ("JE," 4:330 [93]). For weighed by the standards of this morality, the "morality of economic power," the Jews are "found to be too light." And "this same rationality . . . has now pronounced judgment on the Jews as well" ("JE," 4:324 [89]).

Two moments stand out in "The Jews and Europe"—moments of little significance for Horkheimer's theoretical concern with explaining fascism in the 1930s through the undermining of the economy, as a liquidation of the market, and through the political expropriation of the Jews as prominent agents of circulation. One of these is the conspicuously smug tone, bordering (clearly against his intent) on satisfaction. The smugness inflects a criticism of the Jews and goes beyond the needs of Horkheimer's analysis, which sets them up as personifications of capitalism. Tone and critique would seem to have something in common, touching on something intimate in Horkheimer, an antipathy he deflects into social criticism.[13] Thus he comments on the decline of liberalism and of the democratic forms of rule and commerce as if he cared less about the actual consequences of a dismal reality than about proving himself right. Somewhat triumphantly, he hold up fascism as the "truth of modern society, which theory realized from the beginning" ("JE," 4:309 [78]). He deplores the obduracy of liberal citizens still not ready to concede that the cause of their political ruin lies in themselves—a truth that, after all, had long been known to them as a warning in the guise of theoretical knowledge. And the Jews? "They shed many a tear for their past." But the fact "that they fared better under liberalism does not vouch for its justice" ("JE," 4:323 [88]).[14] "Leniency toward the flaws of bourgeois democracy, flirting with the forces of reaction as long as they were not too openly anti-Semitic, arranging themselves with the status quo—the refugees of today already incurred guilt back then" ("JE," 4:330 [93]). Moreover, Horkheimer indicates, it would be idle to expect that misery in general, and the fate of the Jews in Germany in particular, could lead to a change of insight into their deeper causes, which lay in capitalism and its costs; in short, that the rise of fascism could cause the abandonment of capitalism. In this way, he suggests, the victims are not entirely innocent of their own fate. "How should nouveaux riches Jews or Aryans abroad, who have always acquiesced in the impoverishment of other social and national groups, in mass poverty in home countries and colonies, in 'well-managed' prisons and insane asylums, how should they come to their senses in light of what is happening to the German Jews?" ("JE," 4:326 [90–91]).

This sort of moral appeal to the better insight and the goodwill of citizens, and particularly the Jews, rests above all on the universalistic assumption that though they were the first, the Jews would not be the particular victims of Nazism, the German form of the fascist domination spreading across Europe. In retrospect, when Horkheimer voices the expectation that the oncoming universalization of barbarism will put an end to the singling out of the Jews, it seems a kind of plea that the discrimination between Jews and non-Jews should cease. "Perhaps in the initial terror the Jews will not be noticed, but in the long run they must tremble along with everyone else at what is now coming over the earth." The longing that the Jews be spared their particular victimization is also universalistic in the way it adopts the idiom of condemning the particular. "As agents of circulation, the Jews have no future. They will not be able to live as human beings until human beings finally put an end to prehistory" ("JE," 4:328 [92]). Such desperate optimism in the face of defeat recalls the content of an incriminating aphorism in the earlier *Dämmerung*. There Horkheimer, implying that the Nazis' anti-Semitism was socially selective, reproached Jewish capitalists who were in a "blazing uproar" over anti-Jewish measures with being unable to detach themselves from the hierarchy of goods, a hierarchy that "for bourgeois Jews is neither Jewish, nor Christian, but bourgeois." Against this formal equality of Jews and non-Jews he set an emancipatory equality, which subsequent events did not realize. "The Jewish revolutionary in Germany puts his own life on the line, just as the 'Aryan' does, for the liberation of humanity."[15]

The universalism Horkheimer called for so emphatically was made universally untrue by the Nazis' singling out of the Jews and their annihilation for the sake of annihilation. We would appear to face here something like a *civilizational rupture:* a practical refutation of Western reason operating at a deeper level than what we can reach by considering anti-Semitism alone. In this regard, it would be unfair to reproach Horkheimer or the other members of the Frankfurt School for not having recognized fascism in Germany in the 1930s as what it turned out to be: Nazism on the road to Auschwitz.

In his analysis of fascism or the "authoritarian state," Horkheimer tentatively links the critique of liberalism as a political expression of capitalism to a critique of the kind of rationality he would later call "instrumental reason." The theme of the decay of reason in Western civilization takes shape as the core of Horkheimer's social criticism during and after the war. In the process, "anti-Semitism" and "the Jews" acquire a different significance. In "The Jews and Europe," he still traces the "authoritarian state" and the social expulsion of the Jews back to the logic of a market-transcendent, monopolistic undermining of competition. At the same time, however, he adumbrates his later leitmotiv by evoking "a kind of rationality" that once entailed the civil emancipation of the Jews but is now turning against the Jewish entrepreneurs. Like the Jews in general, they counted on the "utilitarian character" of political arrangements that promised calculability, predictability, and the spread of free commerce ("JE," 4:325 [78]). But these are expressions of the same origin as that of fascism or the authoritarian state: the purposive rational logic of capitalism. From this Horkheimer also concludes that anti-Semitism has utilitarian functions, as both a competitive device and a diversion from class struggle;[16] here he remains bound up in the traditional, indeed orthodox, Marxist conception of anti-Semitism. Only with the annihilation of the Jews, to which no utilitarian relation of means and ends whatsoever attaches, did that historical turning point arrive at which rationality, reason, and Enlightenment reverse into their opposites. The Nazis' annihilation of the Jews undoubtedly has categorical significance for this dialectic. Accordingly, the critique of reason and Auschwitz also stand in an epistemological context for Horkheimer,[17] even if he does not make this explicit (apart from a cautious suggestion in the introduction to *Dialectic of Enlightenment,* which makes it clear that the theses on "Elements of Anti-Semitism" address the general phenomenon of the relapse of enlightened civilization into barbarism). Anti-Semitism and the history of civilization are interwoven; anti-Semitism is the central metaphor of Western civilization. And because a practical tendency for self-destruction was inherent in that rationality from the very beginning, not only during the phase in which it emerged undisguised, a philosophical Ur-history of anti-Semitism became necessary (*DA*, 5:22 [xvii]).

In view of the triumph of fascism in Europe in 1941 and 1942—that is, at a time when the annihilation of the Jews was still heading toward its inconceivable climax in industrialized mass murder, and when the connection between the persecution and executions taking place in the east and the events of the war was still difficult to grasp—Horkheimer pronounces the "collapse of the root concepts of Western civilization." The central concept at stake here is that of reason ("VS," 5:320 [28]). Horkheimer links the destruction of reason to reason itself. His central thesis is that the origins of the decay of reason lie in the particular, dominant form of reason : a rationality that serves as a means to attain ends and thereby dissociates itself from a more encompassing reason grounded in being.

Horkheimer sees fascism as already latent in subjective or "goal-positing" reason. Bourgeois society came into its own above all in its moment of absolute "self-preservation," the egoistic assertion of particular interests. Fascism is no exception but rather the intensification of the rule. As a "leap" in the process of "transformation of bourgeois domination into immediate domination," in which the bourgeois form is perpetuated and perfected, Horkheimer conceives "the new order" as the legitimate expression of a class-bound form of reason; and "the National Socialists did not depart from this course of development" ("VS," 5:332 [34]). The essence of the social order remains, even when the transactional form of exchange is replaced by the use of brute force—the form that Neville Chamberlain tried to uphold when he characterized Hitler's demands at Bad Godesberg as "unreasonable." As Horkheimer puts it, "an equivalence of give and take should be observed. Such reason is modeled on exchange. Goals should be attained only mediately, as it were via the market, by virtue of the slight advantage which power is able to obtain by respecting the rules of the game and trading off concessions" (*DA*, 5:239–40 [209–10]). And because in exchange "each gets his own and yet social injustice comes of it, so too the reflexive form of the exchange economy, the dominant unreason, is just, universal, and yet particularistic, the instrument of privilege in equality. The fascist settles accounts with it. He openly represents the particular and in doing so exposes the ratio itself, which unjustly boasts of its universality, as partial" (*DA*, 5:240 [210]).

Both forms of appropriation—by exchange and by force—are expressions of bourgeois society. Both rest on "subjective reason" and are manifestations of self-preservation. A relationship of ends and means inheres in both—and in Nazism as well, which Horkheimer, in the Marxist tradition of the 1930s, still conceives of as fascism. But, says he, we no longer discern a total rationality of economic power at the center of a fully realized Nazism, which enacts, instead, an utterly different totality—the total annihilation of the Jews.[18] From the perspective of Auschwitz, "subjective reason," which arose from the principle of asserting particular interests and realized itself in the form of brute self-preservation, reversed into its opposite, from the fascist form of purposive unity to the comparatively manifest irrationality or, better, antirationality of Nazism. Thus any reaction by the total victim to the totalitarian order, any response to the Nazis governed by the cognitive forms of means and ends and of self-preservation, was doomed to certain failure. Nazism was indeed "reason, in which reason reveals itself as unreason"("VS," 5:348 [46]).

The opposition between forms of reason set up by Horkheimer has various dimensions—for instance, the opposition between objective reason, which grounds being, and subjective reason oriented toward particular goals and directed at self-preservation. In addition, there is also a regressive moment, the throwback produced by disenchanted, civilizing rationality ("BV," 7:28). In their atrocity toward the Jews and others, the Nazis had long since dispensed with all attributes of subjective reason, casting off the rationality of self-preservation whose utility constantly tempts even the devil, such as making deals for the sake of personal advantage. Through the industrial mass destruction of the Jews, carried out in the shadow of the war, the Nazis succeeded in horribly refuting even the principles of subjective reason and self-preservation that determine Western civilization. The fact that in a technical sense they rationally organized their irrational aims only confirms the instrumental madness of reason. The goal once imputed to the "economically powerful" in fascism had long since lost any ostensible economic rationality. Annihilation no longer had any purpose but itself.

When subjective, purposive rational reason destroys the objective reason that grounds being; when the goal-positing reason rooted in the principle of exchange forfeits even that origin; when disenchantment results in its opposite, so that the world of calculability and predictability careens to destruction as the fulfillment of senselessness—then the vital question becomes how reason could split into its contrary, component parts of mere purposive rationality and mythos. In light of such a dialectic of enlightenment, anti-Semitism, which henceforth harbors the annihilation of the European Jews at its center, acquires a more fundamental significance than the essentially functional sense previously attributed to it. Anti-Semitism and the fate of the Jews become constitutive elements of a realized totality. They become identified with an "historical turning point" where they once again await explanation.

Both the purposive moment in the explanation of purposelessness and the foundering of purposive rationality on itself remain issues in "Elements of Anti-Semitism." Utilitarian interpretations of the sort predominant in "The Jews and Europe" continue to turn up. But they are holdovers that illustrate the difficulty of making the transition to a new analysis of anti-Semitism capable both of capturing the phenomenon of hostility toward the Jews in the narrow sense and of going beyond this to a critique of civilization. Thus, we still read of the obvious utility of anti-Semitism for purposes of domination: "It serves as a diversion, a cheap means of corruption, and an example of terror" (*DA,* 5:197 [168]). An instrumental character also attaches to anti-Semitism with the statement that the individuals "who give the orders from above" know "the real reasons" and that they neither hate the Jews nor love their "own followers" (*DA,* 5:201 [171]). But the pursuit of such reflections leads to a decisive turn—seeing through mere utility as a camouflage for motives that lie deeper. The allegedly rational motive for the outburst of those followers, the anti-Semitic mobs—the ostensible desire to feast on the property of the Jews—misses its target. Gain could be the motive. The "pitifully thin rational motive, plunder, adduced for purposes of rationalization," falls away. That motive serves to veil its own purposelessness, for gauged by its proposed benefits, anti-Semitism is "a luxury" for the people. The senseless deed became honest despite itself when it "became a true, autonomous end in itself" (*DA,* 5:201 [172]).

With the turn to the view that irrational, purposeless action makes use of rational motives to justify itself, that delusions take shape in images with a rational form, Horkheimer takes leave of "conclusive rational, economic, and political explanations and counterarguments" in interpreting the hostility toward the Jews. The true grounds for anti-Semitism lie in the rationality involved in domination and social control. The "blind rage" produced by the unrecognized link between domination and rationality calls forth reactions that, for those involved, are deadly and "devoid of sense," when measured against their ostensible reason and purposive rationality (*DA,* 5:200 [171]). The senselessness of anti-Semitism in turn immunizes it against arguments that its rationality is deficient.[19] At this point in his analysis Horkheimer does not simply drop the traditional, functional interpretation of anti-Semitism. But he now classifies its exclusively instrumental character as an irrational reflex: "Only the blindness of anti-Semitism, its lack of purpose, lends the explanation of it as a safety valve its proper measure and

truth." A blinding caused by social abstraction, anti-Semitism has no meaning. It is "an ingrained scheme, indeed a ritual murder of civilization. The
pogroms are the true ritual murders" (*DA*, 5:200 [171]).

With the departure from the paradigm of economic utility and means-ends
rationality in interpreting the hostility toward the Jews, Horkheimer and
Adorno begin to develop the alternative explanation of anti-Semitism as
projection. The preparation of the anti-Semitic consciousness does not lie
in projection in itself, since "in a certain sense all perception is projection."
"What is pathological about anti-Semitism is not projective behavior as
such, but the absence of reflection in it." Anti-Semitism therefore rests on
"false projection" (*DA*, 5:217 [187])—to the point of paranoia.

The paranoiac perceives the outside world only in accordance with his
blind sense of purpose. He "seizes on whatever presents itself to him and fits
it into his mythic web, utterly indifferent to its own characteristics." Through
practical insistence, the anti-Semite models the surrounding world—the
reality in which his notions can find no firm hold—on his own truth, his
ideé fixe, an inner image (*DA*, 5:220 [190]). Fascism elevates such behavior to the level of politics. Those who, as Jews, fall under its decrees must
"first be located by means of complicated questionnaires. . . . Fascist anti-
Semitism must first, in a sense, go about finding its object" (*DA*, 5:237
[206–7]). To "call someone a Jew amounts to an instigation to work him
over until he resembles the image" (*DA*, 5:216 [186]). And once the anti-
Semite forms the Jew according to his own image, he persecutes him on account of his own fantasies, which he does not admit to himself. Instead, he
attributes them to the prospective victim. In his "blind lust for murder," the
anti-Semite constantly "sees the victim as a persecutor who drives him to
desperate acts of self-defense." Such a rationalization is "at once both a ruse
and a compulsion" (*DA*, 5:217 [187]). Instead of looking into himself "in
order to record the protocol of his own lust for power, he attributes the
'Protocols of the Elders of Zion' to others" (*DA*, 5:219 [189–90]). "The
völkisch fantasies of Jewish crimes, child murder, and sadistic excesses, of
poisoning the nation and of international conspiracies, precisely define the
anti-Semitic wish-fulfilling dream." Once projections reach the point of
potential political realization, the psychic latency of anti-Semitism becomes
a social force; fantasy converts to reality. In the process, the "execution of
evil" surpasses "even the evil content of the projection" (*DA*, 5:216 [186]).[20]
Anti-Semites transform the world into the hell "as which they have always
seen it" (*DA*, 5:229 [199]).

In *Dialectic of Enlightenment,* the conversion of the "psychic energy" of anti-Semitism into political reality emerges as "rationalized idiosyncrasy" (*DA,* 5:213 [183]). What in turn underlies idiosyncrasy, as a virtually congenital loathing, is something particular, a difference, which acquires singular significance and concrete content by means of the Jews (*DA,* 5:209 [179–80]). This difference reaches the public via the sphere of circulation and the "artificially increased visibility of the Jews." Through which the reactions of populist, anti-Semitic rebels are diverted from the domination that is the true object of the "rebellion of oppressed nature." The rebels produce a semblance of emancipation by organizing themselves as equals against the particular. In this way "anti-Semitism as a popular movement" is always also "leveling" (*DA,* 5:199 [170])—though, of course, it is the kind of leveling that finds perverted fulfillment in a racially defined national community. By means of anti-Semitism, therefore, the rebellion originally directed against domination ultimately accrues to its benefit (*DA,* 5:215 [185]).

Demonstrating the relationship between equality and anti-Semitism is an essential concern of the critique of progress and rationality that Horkheimer carries out with Adorno. Elements of the critique of liberalism and the internal limitations of civil emancipation already present in "The Jews and Europe" carry over into it, only now a pessimistic general statement on the philosophy of history replaces the earlier polemical, political cutting edge. Equality and emancipation, with their assimilatory tendencies—"in effect, a second circumcision" (*DA,* 5:198 [169])—made the Jews politically visible in the first place. From then on they existed, unprotected, in a homogeneous world shaped by others. Their particular attributes did not dissolve into the sphere of the new generality. They could belong to that generality only as German (or French or British) citizens, denying their Jewish particularity. Moreover, liberalism put the Jews in an even more exposed position inasmuch as it granted them possessions by guaranteeing property and allowed them equality before the law as human beings but as Jews denied them collective political rights and thereby "sovereign authority." Thus, from the very beginning it was the unhappy "meaning of human rights to promise happiness where there is no power" (*DA,* 5:201 [172]).

Paradoxically, the emancipation of the Jews, which accorded them equal status as human beings, was accompanied by the emergence of political anti-Semitism in the bourgeois national state. This simultaneity was no mere accident or caprice but an expression of formal equality despite persisting, unacknowledged difference. In fact, formal equality, which made comparison possible, first forced existing differences out into the open. With the formal fulfillment of emancipation, therefore, the appearance of political anti-Semitism heralded the end of the Jews' civil equality. Inasmuch as the Jews stood out from the anonymity of the general public and from that "which fits into the purposive nexus of society" (*DA*, 5:209 [180]), their existence compromised "the existing generality by their lack of adjustment." This dubious triumph of the particular—not to yield to social rationalization in the form of the predominant attributes of universality—attracts the hostility of those who, as bearers of universality, no longer possess any particularity. They believe they can secure a particularity of their own solely by constituting themselves as a mythic counterimage to the Jews. And to constitute themselves as a hypostasized particular through racial fictions, they model the Jews into a "counterrace" by means of a projective reversal. What results is by no means "natural," but rather "that reduction to the nature-like, to naked violence, to the obdurate particular which, under the prevailing order, is precisely the general." It is general insofar as the fictive racial affiliation becomes an attribute of the "self-assertion of the bourgeois individual integrated into the barbaric collective," proceeding irresistibly forward on the way "to naked oppression and to reorganization as the hundred-percent pure race" (*DA*, 5:198 [169]).

Horkheimer and Adorno attempt to interpret the fact that precisely the Jews had become the preferred object of persecution, and the counterimage for purposes of self-definition, by means of the element of idiosyncrasy: "violence was ignited endlessly by the mark which violence had left on them." The Jews are persecuted because they bear the stigma of persecution. There is no more substantial motive than the compulsion to persecute. Thus, for instance, the "desecration of cemeteries is not an excess of anti-Semitism; it is anti-Semitism itself" (*DA*, 5:213 [183]). So, too, the projection onto the Jews of "all the horrors of primeval times, which civilization has overlaid" (*DA*, 5:215 [186]) represents only a rationalization of the repetitive compulsion to confirm the idiosyncrasy through continued persecution.

The particular, the nonidentical, which eludes assimilation to the universal, highlights historically accumulated idiosyncratic features by means of equality and comparability. In the eyes of the compulsive persecutor, it comes to acquire attributes seemingly free of the grim mastery of nature—"happiness without power, earnings without work, a homeland without boundaries, religion without myth" (*DA*, 5:229 [199]). The paradox of representing the helplessly persecuted and powerless as both keepers of the grail of happiness and virtuosos of concealed domination finds expression in the phantasmic certainty that a "conspiracy of lecherous Jewish bankers finances Bolshevism," a conspiracy joined to "the image of the intellectual":

"the intellectual seems to think about what others begrudge themselves, and his brow does not pour with the sweat of toil and physical strength. The banker and the intellectual, money and mind, the exponents of circulation, are the denied wish images of those mutilated by domination, whom domination uses to perpetuate itself" (*DA*, 5:202 [172]). And through this projective burdening of the Jews as the embodiment of the nonidentical, the biblical myth of the chosen people finds dreadful fulfillment in their destruction to the extent that "fascism made it come true" (*DA*, 5:197 [168]).

In their assessment of what constitutes the nonidentical in Western civilization and what attaches to the Jews as an anti-Semitic perception, Horkheimer and Adorno oscillate between features projectively attributed to the Jews alone, which direct hatred toward them, and to the Jews as the incarnation of particularity as such. They thereby generalize anti-Semitism as prejudice against any bearers of difference whatsoever. In line with this extended interpretation of anti-Semitism, at the end of their essay they define it as a mere technique that domination makes use of to secure its hold. It is the "ticket mentality" that, as the enemy of all difference, directs itself against the nonidentical particular in order to shore up the generality. Thus, not only the anti-Semitic ticket as such would be anti-Semitic but the ticket mentality per se. "The rage against difference, a *ressentiment* on the part of the mastered subjects against the mastery of nature—a *ressentiment* teleologically inherent in the ticket mentality—is always ready to strike out at the natural minority, even when for the moment this threatens the social minority" (*DA*, 5:238 [207]).

The idiosyncrasy that adheres to the particular, performing manipulative services that help to secure domination, looms out of the depths of the past into those social formations for which Horkheimer and Adorno describe the significance of anti-Semitism. It stems from a source that secularization and disenchantment only seem to have overcome—Christian religion. To assert its ongoing efficacy as a source of hostility toward the Jews is to undercut the classical distinction, stemming from the Enlightenment, between religious anti-Semitism and its political or racial varieties. Insisting on such continuity, however, does not mean endorsing the thesis of the transhistorical character of anti-Semitism. Rather, what Horkheimer and Adorno point out is the stubborn persistence of myths that merely dye their vestments in worldly colors but otherwise retain their magical significance. Such myths recur as a secularized, rationalized idiosyncrasy whose origins lie in the relationship of the Christian religion to the Jews. Horkheimer and Adorno believe that "the religious animosity which propelled the persecution of the Jews for two thousand years" could hardly have been extinguished completely. "The zeal with which anti-Semitism denies its religious tradition testifies, instead, that the religious tradition secretly lives on within—no less deeply than profane idiosyncrasy was once inherent in religious zeal" (*DA,* 5:206 [176]).

The secularizing of occidental civilization in fact amounts to Christianity made worldly. For all the efforts at enlightenment, the culture that results remains Christian in its form and its conceptions of value. Enlightenment brought about the transformation of a religious, universally oriented nexus of civilization into national cultures supported by national states in which Christianity, secularized and rationalized, remains the underlay—altered, warped, and concealed.

The modern state in which the Jews were emancipated was an avowedly Christian state. Thus, it is not surprising that religion "was not liquidated, but incorporated as a cultural asset" (*DA,* 5:206 [176]). In the process, the anti-Judaic effect of Christianity, the resentment against the Jews from which the religion draws inspiration, was also preserved.[21] While it found expression in political form, its psychic energies continued to receive nurture from an older source.

The origin of the opposition between the Jews and Christianity is Christianity's unfulfilled claim that Jesus, the human being, was God (*DA,* 5:207 [177]).[22] According to this claim, the redemption of the world, which depends on the arrival of the Messiah, has already been accomplished. But since the world has not changed despite his arrival, it becomes obvious that Christianity rests on "a nonbinding promise of spiritual salvation" (*DA,* 5:208 [178]). That which was represented as spiritual being proves, in the face of spirit, to have been natural being. Christ, the spirit become flesh, would thus be no more than an idolized shaman, and Christianity itself exposed as a "spiritualization of magic" (*DA,* 5:207 [177]). Christianity thus splits off into a special cultural realm, and by contrast with Judaism, a belief hardly distinct from general and rational self-assertion, it becomes a religion—"in a certain sense, the only one." "Christianity's claim to represent progress beyond Judaism" thereby proves to be a relapse behind Judaism (*DA,* 5:206 [176]).

The religious origins of anti-Semitism lie in the Christians' feeling that their eschatological expectations have been disappointed, so that they must begin, with a bad conscience, to talk themselves into Christian belief. They find constant reminders that the redemption they claim has not arrived in the presence of those who have denied it from the start. "The adherents of the religion of the father are hated, as those who know better, by the adherents of the religion of the son. It is the antipathy toward spirit of a spirit that is rigidifying as salvation. The thorn in the side of the Christian enemies of the Jews is the truth that withstands calamity without rationalizing it, holding fast to the idea of unearned blessedness against the course of the world and the order of salvation, which are actually supposed to bring it about." Thus, the Christian promise of redemption can be made true only in its inversion—through the calamity of the Jewish adversaries. "Anti-Semitism is supposed to confirm the truth of the ritual of belief and history by inflicting it on those who reject its truth" (*DA*, 5:209 [179]). Secularized traces of Christian anti-Judaism thus mingle, idiosyncratically, within the cultural warp and woof of Western civilization; the ill will toward the nonidentical persists.

In the end, the "Elements of Anti-Semitism" remains what its title suggests : arguments and approaches not synthesized into a theory but serving, for the most part, as material for the overarching theme marking this phase of Horkheimer's thought: the theme of the "limits of enlightenment." The individual arguments, scarcely organized, express diverse perspectives.[23] They remain—despite the essay's own best intentions—marked by an economistic interpretation of anti-Semitism, balanced off by psychoanalytic interpretations.[24] And yet on occasion the elements cohere in a way that goes far beyond mere preliminary reflections.

One such high point is the thesis that the specifically economic motive for bourgeois anti-Semitism is "to disguise domination in production" (*DA*, 5:202 [173]). Underlying this definition of anti-Semitism is the Nazi defamation, seemingly confirmed by appearances, built on a distinction between "grabbing" and "producing" capital. "Grabbing" capital, identified with the sphere of circulation, is ascribed to the Jews, whereas "producing" capital stands for the incarnation of supposedly pure production and is equated with Aryanism. Horkheimer and Adorno demonstrate the extent to which such a perception is socially conditioned. Industrialists, who pass off their economic operations in the sphere of production as productive labor, thus posing as "producers," turn out to be the concealed exploiters. The swindle succeeds because the employer does not rake in his profit on the open market, where appropriation takes place visible to all, but at the very "source" of the creation of wealth—in production. "As a functionary of the class," the employer, whether industrialist of bureaucrat, sees to it that "he does not get the short end of the stick when his labor force works." The labor contract conceals the "exploitive nature of the economic system," the appropriation of surplus value (*DA*, 5:203 [174]). "The industrialist has his debtors, the workers, in the factory where he watches over them and checks their services before advancing them their money. They notice what has really happened only when they find out what they can buy for it. . . . The merchant presents the workers with the promissory note they signed for the industrialist. He plays the bailiff for the whole system, taking on himself the odium for the others. The accountability of the sphere of circulation for exploitation is a socially necessary appearance" (*DA,* 5:204 [174]). Once the market has revealed how few goods are allotted to the value of labor, the plundering gets thrown into an even harsher light when the merchant—with all supposedly being equal—publicly promotes goods those who are in fact unequal cannot afford. "The guilty party for the entire system is easy to find. One not merely for individual maneuvers and machinations, but in the comprehensive sense that the economic injustice of the entire class gets blamed on him" (*DA,* 5:203 [174]).

This theory of bourgeois anti-Semitism differs considerably from the sort of economistic explanation characteristic of "The Jews and Europe." The latter piece traces hostility to the Jews back to a fascist undermining of the economy: to a literal decline in the significance of the sphere of circulation. Reflecting an immediate, sociological, and empirical conception of competition, Horkheimer thus interprets the Nazis' anti-Semitic policies as a result of the Jews' loss of their economic position. In "Elements of Anti-Semitism," the motif of the sphere of circulation recurs, but with a completely different function. No longer are the Jews simply equated with that sphere. The fact that they do not have a monopoly on circulation is acknowledged; nonetheless, the public image of social exploitation, which arises from the circulatory sphere, becomes attached to the Jews "because they remained confined in it for too long" (*DA,* 5:204 [174]). As a consequence, the Jews became the sphere's metaphorical concretization. Only this translation of apparent social realities into social metaphors saves the comprehensively economic approach from the narrow economicism that leads it astray. To be sure, traces of the earlier interpretation subsist. "Elements of Anti-Semitism" does, for instance, continue to suggest that the Jews occupied positions of economic power, only lost with the undermining of the economy and the decline of "liberalist forms of enterprise" (*DA,* 5:229 [199]). A historical survey of the significance of the Jews as "colonizers of progress" (*DA,* 5:204 [175])—however accurate it may appear to be—strays from the essay's analytical intention when it becomes evidence for a history of the supposedly rational origins of anti-Semitism. At the essay's end, the authors relapse behind both their focus on the inconceivable in the annihilation of the Jews and their own critique of reason—above all, Horkheimer's critique of reason. The historical logic dictated by economic rationality, invoked now once again, is entirely in line with "The Jews and Europe." They once again speak of the "administration of totalitarian states" as mere "executors of economic verdicts long since decreed," which "consign untimely segments of the population to extermination" (*DA*, 5:237 [206]).

In the postwar years and until his death in 1973, Max Horkheimer addressed the question of anti-Semitism in basically aphoristic form. A strong personal identification with the Jewish victims of the National Socialists' mass annihilation is evident in these writings; notably, they make no direct attempt to seek relief by generalizing the experience. Insofar as they *do* raise theoretical concerns, the universalizing approach to anti-Semitism already accorded primacy in *Dialectic of Enlightenment* predominates—the moment of the socially "nonidentical" embodied in the Jews. The nonidentical expresses itself, for instance, in the will to justice, thus becoming the "enemy of all things totalitarian."[25] Horkheimer associates "justice" with two things: a fundamental, moral justice and the justice constituted by fair exchange. This contradiction is seen as "one of the roots of worldwide anti-Semitism."[26] The entire existence of the Jews points toward a "society of the free and equal, but not a national community."[27] And because the Jews are bound to trade and liberalism, to relationships between individuals, and to the bourgeoisie, they also incarnate the justice of fair exchange. Anti-Semitism would thus arise because the Jews, with every one of their gestures, serve as reminders of the henceforth general mode of existence to all those who seek to deny their own participation in the forms of a society founded on exchange. They "compromise the lie which pervades society" and are therefore in danger everywhere.[28] Both forms of justice, moral justice and the justice of fair exchange, contradict "state capitalism in the East" no less than "Western monopolistic society."[29]

Along with the stigmata of exchange, which attach to the Jews as the "hated mirror image" of society as such, and in which an antitotalitarian moment also finds expression, it is the particularity of the Jews—and even more, an "essentiality" that others imagine them to possess—that contributes to the hatred of them. Their mere existence as "God's chosen people" gives offense, because in bearing witness to a spiritual God they relativize everything "that parades as absolute." Perceiving the Jew essentially as Jews "arouses a lust for revenge which not even death can appease."[30]

Whereas the religious metaphor stand for one side of the origins of anti-Semitism—for the nonidentical, for sublimated nature—the psychoanalytic interpretation points to the other side: the psychic representation of domination embodied by the Jews as an expression of the abstract, of civilization. "Unconsciously," this representation serves "as the quintessence of unmastered, hated prohibitions"; it is part of the "suppressed, negative side of ambivalent sexuality, of unsublimated, barbaric promiscuity." In these respects, anti-Semitism belongs "essentially to the primitive instincts negated by civilization."[31]

We must read Horkheimer's political remarks about the past's ongoing effects on the present in Germany in the context of this systematics of projective reversal as a moment in the origins of anti-Semitism. Horror in the face of the occurrence of mass annihilation might not lead, as we would wish, to a moral integration and working through of guilt; instead, paradoxically, it can lead to an anti-Semitic form of release from guilt. This release would result from the fact that although (or because) the Jews were victims, the thought of the catastrophe intimately involves them. The violence committed by Germans is converted into one committed against Germans. The unconscious switches their roles: "Not the murderer, but the victim is guilty"[32]—guilty because he represents the atrocities and testifies to the reality of what happened. To rid oneself of him would be to free oneself of the inner representation of guilt as well. "Overcoming a narcissistic insult is infinitely more difficult, and even the generation that was not involved still suffers from a wound it does not know of."[33]

Anti-Semitism is not a thing of the past; the climax of mass annihilation was not the end of it. "It has not spent its force but only shown its horrifying effects. The belief that it has passed is naively optimistic."[34] By contrast with such pessimism, the practical and pedagogical gestures of assistance against anti-Semitism expected of Horkheimer have the ring of enlightened helplessness.[35] More candid is his despairing biographical confession, "After Auschwitz":

> We Jewish intellectuals who escaped death by torture under Hitler have only one task: to help see to it that such horrors never recur and are never forgotten, in solidarity with those who died under unspeakable torments. Our thought, our work belongs to them; that we escaped by accident should make our solidarity with them not doubtful, but more certain. Whatever we experience must stand under the sign of the horrors intended for us as for them. Their death is the truth of our life; to express their despair and their longing, we are there.[36]

Until the end, Horkheimer remained committed to the compelling longing that runs like a guiding thread through his life: to make sure "that the murderer not triumph over the innocent victim."[37]

SIX

Beyond the Conceivable

The Judenrat as Borderline Experience

In the decades following World War II, hardly any question has been the source of so much controversy for Jews as that of Jewish self-government in the ghettos, the "Jewish councils" (*Judenräte*) set up by the Nazis as a crucial mechanism of the Final Solution. Indeed, the question centers on a group of motifs basic to the postwar Jewish self-understanding: the problem of how to behave in the face of mass destruction; the dead-end choice between a resistance that is clear-cut and a resistance that is problematic, emerging from that strategy of putative compliance represented—at least in the collective consciousness—by the Judenrat. For the Jewish world after the Holocaust, the indistinct, schematic image of the Jewish councils has largely served, in fact, as a threat to precisely that moral orientation and psychic ballast furnished by the evocation of armed struggle against the Nazis in woods and ghettos.

To a great extent the threat is not surprising, since the very dynamic set in play by the Nazi instrumentalization of "self government" for mass extermination involves a breakdown of the normally distinct line between perpetrators and victims. Both in Eastern and Western Europe, the strategy of the German occupants thus achieved an apogee of imaginable horror: an implication of the victims in the perpetrators' deeds. But the Nazi manipulation of their victims' cooperative behavior—the victims' participation in the complex planning and execution of their own murder by the Germans —has consequences going beyond the concrete event or the historical experience of the victims.

The theme of the Judenrat has a double dimension: on the one hand, it represents that real history of Jewish individuals responsible for the survival of a community faced with destruction and thereby participating against their expressed will in the Nazi exterminatory project. On the other hand, it represents the most concrete historical material for gaining a radical vantage on the phenomenon of the Final Solution. At the phenomenon's center, the Jewish councils hovered between self-preservation and self-destruction; or put otherwise, at its center lay self-destruction *by means* of self-preservation. We face here a specific and terrible instance of a universally applicable borderline experience; it addresses basic assumptions about human nature and human behavior, bringing us to the fragile, outer limits of reason and rationality. As Isaiah Trunk stresses, only in the ghetto could a tragic struggle for survival reach such degrees of inextricability.[1] Approaching the position of the Jewish councils discursively, we consider the institution both as a particular Jewish response to Nazism and its genocidal intention as well as a universal experience of a human situation in extremity.

By and large, historical treatments of the Judenrat reflect the effort by survivors to come to terms with the Nazi horror. When courts of honor were set up in displaced persons' camps after the war, what was stake was not only meting out justice to those who had become culpable in the context of "Jewish self government," but also aiding those blamed unfairly for collaboration with the Nazis. Through clarification of the events in camps and ghettos, such false charges were to be laid to rest. In Israel, where a large portion of the survivors found shelter and a homeland, ensuing controversies over guilt and complicity continued unabated—often becoming entangled in party political feuding. The notorious "Kastner affair" is exemplary in this respect, remaining until now a focal point of Jewish discourse on the Jewish councils' character and the dilemmas they faced.[2] Such discourse gained public attention through the 1961 Eichmann trial, that central event in the judicial effort to come to terms with the Final Solution. The trial also served as a spur for increasingly systematic research into the councils, a historiographical effort with meanwhile substantial results. But more than the trial itself, the source for the growing interest in the Jewish councils was the reception history of a book that brought heated controversy—particularly in the Jewish world—in its wake: Hannah Arendt's *Eichmann in Jerusalem: A Report on the Banality of the Evil.*[3]

In apodictic—albeit somewhat ambivalent—fashion, Arendt raises very serious accusations against the councils. The political philosopher thus maintains that without the cooperation of Jewish functionaries, and without the existence of well organized Jewish communal structures, a form of chaos would have ensued posing grave impediments to the Nazis' industrial-bureaucratic machinery of murder. "Recognized Jewish leaders," she indicates, not only behaved complicitly under Nazi rule but actually arrived at a form of absolute rule from which they were not reluctant to profit. "To a Jew, this role of the Jewish leaders in the destruction of their own people is undoubtedly the darkest chapter of the whole dark history," she then observes.[4] While Arendt thus appears to in the end condemn—at least equivocally—the Judenrat, she expresses sheer admiration for the militant Jewish resistance. It was, she indicates, a distinct boon to encounter "the appearance in the witness box of the former Jewish resistance fighters. It dissipated the haunting specter of universal cooperation, the stifling, poisoned atmosphere which had surrounded the Final Solution."[5] Arendt's unlimited enthusiasm goes, above all, to the testimony of the ghetto fighters Zivia Lubetkin and Abba Kovner, who coined in Vilna the well-known reference to sheep led to their slaughter.[6] Armed resistance in woods and ghettos, evaluated in absolutely positive terms, versus the Judenrat's disdained strategy of delay through self-selection, in the interest of the survival of ever fewer Jews: dominating Jewish consciousness since the war, such a dichotomy is manifest in Arendt's succumbing to an all-too-easy reverence for the ghetto's youthful heroes.

Clearly offered for the sake of psychic relief, that admiration taints a distinguished political philosopher's formidable faculty of judgment.[7] Meanwhile, underscoring a revision of the paradigmatic dichotomy, the recent publication in Israel of diary entries written in the 1950s by the Hebrew poet Nathan Alterman casts a far different, far more differentiated light on the Judenrat and those who led it. Both in the period of the state's foundation and after, Alterman represented the militancy and heroism of the Palmach generation as few other Israeli writer have.[8] At one point in the diary excerpts, he describes a conversation with the aforementioned Abba Kovner and Zivia Lubetkin in which he casts doubt on the exalted nature of armed struggle—advocating instead the approach of the Judenrat; survival at any price is more important than the ghetto fighter's dignity in death.[9] Retrospectively, we can see Alterman's remarks as anticipating a general shift in stance over the past few decades—from easy denunciation to far-reaching sympathy for the Judenrat—a shift itself reflected in the belated appearance of the diary excerpt. We should note that such a development is not only a result of advances in historical research. It is also the result of greater distance within the Jewish collective consciousness from the cult of militancy promoted since 1948 both inside and outside Israel: a cult grounded in a long-held negative differentiation of the modern state from a putatively compliant Jewish diaspora.

If we are to base our definition of the Judenrat on the impossible position in which representatives of the Jewish community in German-occupied Poland found themselves, it would seem appropriate to include other Central and Western European institutions of "Jewish self government" within the definition's purview.[10] For all these institutions found themselves in the same situation of compulsory, incriminatory cooperation with Nazi rule— this even when working toward the still-tenable goal of emigration. In fact, Jewish institutions already in existence before the inception of the mass-murder process became deeply entangled in its unfolding: Vienna's Central Bureau for Jewish Emigration, for instance, established in August 1938 on Jewish initiative for the sake of Jewish welfare, saw the emigration lists it had painstakingly assembled transformed, covertly, into death-camp deportation lists.[11] This slippage from steps meant to preserve life to those facilitating its destruction, scarcely perceptible to the Jewish authorities at the start, marks the tragic situation of the Jewish councils throughout occupied Europe.

As with the Viennese example, the Jewish councils in German-occupied Poland did not at first confront exterminatory measures that, once put in motion, they would try their best to delay, and that would finally lead to forced self-selection. Starting in the autumn and winter of 1939, the newly established councils concerned themselves above all with Jewish social welfare in the widest sense—a thoroughly sensible response, it seemed, to the Nazi concentration of Jews into demarcated, soon to be sealed-off areas, and to the ensuing loss of sources of normal sustenance (that is, work and property). The subsequent outbreak of disease and death throughout the ghettos—the result of malnourishment and disastrous hygienic conditions —pointed, already, toward the Nazi campaign of mass extermination; the Jewish councils' decision to ask the German authorities for work, the Germans being their only remaining source, should be thus reconsidered in light of the terrible circumstances of seclusion.[12] It was an effort to cope with the plight facing those for whom they bore responsibility: to slow down, at least, the steady worsening of their circumstances. But above all—as with the Warsaw Judenrat's proviso in its offer of labor at the end of 1939[13]—it was an effort to end the brutally executed and unpredictable seizure of Jews by the Germans for the sake of forced labor, to render the German actions relatively predictable instead. Such an approach by the councils must be distinguished from their later strategy of "rescue through labor" in the face of extermination. Nevertheless, it is evident that the earlier procedure facilitated the later one to a considerable degree. Blinded by anti-Semitic contempt, the Nazis decided to systematically use Jewish artisanal and industrial workers only in the middle of 1940. What followed had its precedent in the shift of organized Jewish emigration in prewar Central Europe to eventual enforced cooperation with the Nazis: in Eastern Europe, the representatives of the Jewish ghettos ended up, by way of their approach to labor, in a relation of dependency that would turn against themselves.

The horrible form taken by this turn involved a constant exchange of the lives of those capable of work for the death of those no longer "useful": an exchange that, in its steady decimation of the Jewish population, reveals the drastic hopelessness of the Jewish situation. Different responses to the situation were possible, ranging from clear-cut gestures of resistance to undertaking something like a Faustian contest with the Nazis: an effort to salvage the life of some through a controlled and limited fulfillment of the Nazi need for Jewish deaths, always in the hope of the behemoth's imminent military defeat. In face of the variety of individual responses, generalization is difficult. To a considerable degree responses depended on the identity and personality of the different Jewish elders, as well as on specificities of location, as was the case with the Lodz ghetto: lying in the Warthegau region annexed to the Reich, it owed its relatively long survival to conflicts of responsibility between Gauleiter Greiser and the SS.[14] At the same time, the degree of community organization was an important factor. In Poland, the Jewish communities to a large extent remained intact corporate entities; as prolonged instances of Nazi will, they were thus subject to instrumentalization via the Jewish councils. The circumstances were very different in conquered areas of the Soviet Union, where the authorities had dissolved Jewish communal structures more than twenty years before. The Jews here were also put in ghettos, unless they were not immediately seized by the mobile firing squads of the various *Einsatzgruppen*. But in the absence of such traditional structures, the selections imposed by the Germans on the Jewish councils in these areas were far more arbitrary in nature.

Once burdened with knowledge of the deportations' end goal, and confronted with the demand for self-selection, the Jewish councils displayed a range of defiant responses, described in detail by the Israeli historian Aharon Weiss in his work on the councils in eastern Galicia and eastern Upper Silesia.[15] Such responses ranged from open refusal to deliver up Jews entrusted to the councils—a decision promptly punished by the Nazis with death for those responsible—to suicides like that of Adam Czerniaków—he declared the delivery of children to their murder a border he could not cross[16]—to the decision to join the resistance (as far as this was possible). There were also the many elders who gave up their functions: the stand taken by the Jewish elder Weiler from Vladzimierz, who abstained from a selection with the words "I am not God and will not pass judgment over who shall live and who shall die" was far from an exception.[17] In view of the historical evidence, the generally over-sharp line of demarcation—particularly in the collective Jewish memory—between Judenrat and resistance is scarcely tenable.[18] Tensions and conflicts between the two only emerged, in any event, with the onset of deportations in the autumn of 1941.[19] Cooperation between the councils and the armed resistance, including supplying the latter with money, material, and information, was commonplace.

In the Bialystok ghetto, for instance, contacts and arrangements between the Judenrat led by Efraim Barasz and the resistance were routine.[20] Until the rebellion broke out in August 1943, the resistance saw itself compelled —just like the Jewish council—to wait for a moment judged propitious, that is, to play for time, meanwhile complying with the draconian principle of sacrificing *some* for the sake of those who remained. It is important to recognize that because of the partisan activity in the Soviet territory captured by the Germans in 1941, effective armed Jewish resistance such as that in Bialystok—forming a sharp contrast to the hopeless Warsaw revolt, with its essential motive of salvaging historical honor—was far more likely, across the board, than in the Generalgouvernement established in Poland in 1939. To be sure, not all partisan groups were ready to accept Jews into their ranks. Hostility to the Germans did not necessarily translate into friendly feelings for the Jews, and many who managed to escape from the enforced community of camp or ghetto found their death at the hands of anti-Semitic partisans.

In a comparison of the strategy of reluctant compliance for which the Judenrat generally stands with that of armed Jewish struggle, the latter emerges more ambivalently than is commonly assumed. For a start, the imperatives of military organization undermined the family structure—hence survival in the ghetto. Whoever managed to reach the partisans left behind old people, children, the weak, in circumstances making death very likely. For most people, the factor of family loyalty thus constituted an unassailable barrier—or in the words of a contemporary witness: "the feelings for one's own family were far stronger than fear of death."[21] Those most firmly opposing flight from the ghetto to the armed bands were Jewish elders who had now set upon the clearly demarcated and terrible path they termed "rescue through labor," its reverse side being constant self-selection for destruction. In Vilna, for instance, Jakob Gens spoke up against youths who joined the partisans by pointing to the ghetto's loss of productive workers and subsequent reduced chances for survival.[22] The feeling was that such resistors threatened the ghetto with reprisals; and as suggested, although standing up for themselves, by the very nature of armed resistance, they were abandoning those left behind to their fates.[23] In contrast to those joining the partisans, the Judenrat—such was the feeling—had a sense of responsibility for the collective.[24] The only tenable strategy involved becoming indispensable to the Germans—through labor.

In Poland, as mentioned above, the Jews offered labor to the Germans in the early phase of the ghetto's formation (the fall and winter of 1939), the offer having, however a different character than "rescue through labor." The latter procedure came into force only with the onset of the Nazis' organized, industrial mass-murder project. And let us note the low likelihood— then or later, during the mass murder—that the Jewish elders who had decided to embark on "rescue through labor" (in particular Chaim Rumkowski in Lodz, Jakob Gens in Vilna, Mosche Merin in Upper Silesia, and Efraim Barasz in Bialystok), along with the Jewish councils they headed, would recognize something more than a local or regional phenomenon behind the murder operations. The various German agencies offered ample grounds for such a limited perspective. Not all of them, for example, adhered to the instructions handed down from the Reich's ministry for the conquered eastern territories to the Reich commissioner for what was termed Ostland—comprising Lithuania, Latvia, Estonia, and the greater part of White Russia—upon the latter's query (November 15, 1941): to exterminate all the Jews in the region, regardless of economic priorities. This drive toward total extinction ran into countervailing policies on a local level in December. We thus find Karl Jäger, the head of Einsatzkommando 3, responsible for murder operations in the Baltic region, complaining of being forced by the Wehrmacht and civil authorities to refrain from exterminating 15 percent of Lithuania's Jews, since they were needed for labor.[25]

By means of their strategy of "rescue through labor," the Jewish councils did their best to exploit this tension within the Nazi administration between a will toward absolute extinction and the war-determined interest in exploiting Jewish labor capacity. In however limited a sense, the councils would thus maintain an ability to act, for the sake of gaining time: time worth struggling for in the expectation of a turn in the war's course and—most concretely—the arrival of the Soviet army. The possibility of gaining time was hence made available, paradoxically, by the requirements of the German war effort. Crucially, underlying the councils' apparently compliant adaptation to such requirements—that is, underlying their postponement of total extinction by means of labor and the self-selection of those really or supposedly incapable of labor—were presumptions of purpose-oriented rationality on the part of the enemy: of an overriding interest by the Nazis in their own self-preservation. In this respect, it is striking that such presumptions were frequently confirmed by information gleaned on emerging conflicts between the different Nazi agencies, and on their real divergent interests. In his monumental study of the Jewish councils, Isaiah Trunk indicates that Barasz, Gens, and Rumkowski, in particular, were informed about policy conflicts by "good" Germans in the administration—a favor, by the way, that often had a steep price.

In essence, there was a built-in conflict between organs of the SS and police, who took their orders from Berlin, and agencies of the Wehrmacht and civil administration, located on site. In his diary of February 14 and 18, 1943, Mordechai Tenenbaum-Tamaroff—one of the central figures in the Bialystok resistance—notes the surfacing of heated differences in the office of Königsberg's armament inspector regarding the planned murder operation in Bialystok, causing its postponement: "Our fate is supposed to be settled on Friday, when General Constantin Canaris [commander of East Prussia's security police and security services] will be back. . . . Klein [administrative director for the head of the civil administration], our generous protector, has become lord of the ghetto. We see in this a victory for moderate circles in the Gestapo. He maintains that 'there'll always be time to exterminate the Bialystok Jews, even at the end—meantime they can slave for us.'"[26]

Indeed, behind the admonishment of Jakob Gens in Vilna, "Jewish woman, remember: labor spares blood!" lay the assumption that the Germans desired above all else to win the war.[27] In that case, its material requirements, hence the war economy, would necessarily have absolute priority. It is this basic assumption of the Jewish councils, grounded in sound common sense, that Raul Hilberg sees as the first step into the trap laid by the Nazis: for Hilberg, such work amounted to cognitive bait, meant to keep the Jews calm so the extermination could proceed as planned.[28] And yet no remotely plausible alternative seemed available to the exchange of labor for time and life. For this reason, it became a principle around which all generally accepted norms and values centered. It is manifest in Efraim Barasz's criticism, in October 1942, of the Bialystok ghetto doctors for maintaining an ethos befitting normal circumstances, trying to free patients with TB from work: "the doctors don't understand that today people are not dying from tuberculosis, but because they do not work."[29]

The strategy of "rescue through labor" hardly ever succeeded. But in many places Jews would certainly not have survived without such a strategy—for instance in Czestochowa, where several thousand Jewish workers, including many from Lodz, made it through the war in the Hasag factory complex. The same can be said for Radom, where 4,700 out of 30,000 Jews survived—one of the highest Jewish survival rates in Poland, as Yehuda Bauer stresses—and for the ghettos of Bialystok and Siauliai.[30] But the most controversial and remarkable example certainly remains the Lodz ghetto under Rumkowski's leadership.[31] In many respects it was a special case, but it defines, better than any other historical example, what the Judenrat truly signified as a situation. Granted the self-aggrandizing, autocratic nature of the elder Rumkowski's policies: under the stewardship of his Jewish council, the Lodz ghetto could survive until July 1944, not only the largest, but also the last of the Polish Jewish ghettos. Had the Soviets not stopped their advance that very month, had they begun it again earlier than January 1945, the 70,000 Jews remaining in the ghetto would certainly have remained alive thanks to "rescue through labor" and the accompanying self-selections.[32] And yet if the ghetto had chosen a strategy of direct armed struggle, the Nazis would doubtless have followed through with their deportations in a speedier and more horrible manner. Adam Czerniaków has in fact been criticized for not mobilizing the Warsaw ghetto's work potential at an early point, as Rumkowski was doing in Lodz.[33] To be sure, it would be sheer speculation to suggest that a total deportation could then have been avoided. Nevertheless, many survivors of the Lodz ghetto asserted that they owed their lives precisely to the absence of an armed revolt in the city.[34]

Whereas work was the sole available key to winning time against the German collective death sentence, the self-selections posed an irresolvable ethical dilemma for the Jewish councils. In the context of the ghettos, the phrase *mi lechaim ve mi lamavet* (who receives life and who receives death [referring to God's will]) denoted forced decisions that rarely confront human beings. It is clear that the Jewish elders were well aware of the burden's weight. Even though in the end they lacked free will and were condemned to act as instruments of an executioner, they constantly tried to move, by means of this compulsory function, in a reverse direction. The resulting movement in two directions, along with attacks on the part of the resistance and corrosive self-doubt drove these very ordinary men to a discourse with themselves and others reflecting well their Faustian dilemma. Jakob Gans laid out its shattering terms before an assembly of Jewish writers and journalists who— so, at least, he believed—scorned him as a traitor. Defending himself with the assertion that he gave life priority over death, he indicated that if ordered by the Nazis to hand over a thousand Jews, he would do it: otherwise, the Germans would themselves arrive in the ghetto and seize not a thousand, but many thousands. In sacrificing a hundred, he saved a thousand; in sacrificing a thousand, he saved ten thousand: "Should I, Jakob Gans, survive, I will leave the ghetto soiled, blood on my hands. But I will go before a Jewish court and declare: I have done everything to save more and more of the ghetto's Jews and bring them to freedom."[35]

Rudolf Kastner described the situation of the Jewish councils with penetration: if they fulfilled their functions, they contributed substantially to the smooth unfolding of the liquidation process. If they refused, they called down sanctions on the community and abandoned the possibility of slowing down the mass-murder process. Almost all of Europe's Jewish councils found themselves caught between these extremes and incapable of escaping their deadly logic. And yet the logic's nature was not so clear-cut at the beginning: relatively "insignificant" demands for precious objects, for money, and apartments. But finally, what was desired was life; and the Judenrat decided who went sooner, who later:

> In sacrificing to Moloch, horrible criteria came to prevail, such as age, accomplishment, general reputation. Personal considerations pressed to the forefront: degree of kinship, predilection, even interests. The way taken by the *Judenrat* was tortuous, ending inevitably in an abyss. Everywhere, the Jews were confronted with the same problem: shall I, whoever I am, become a traitor in order to help or even save others; or shall I leave the community to its fate—pass on my wavering responsibility to others? But is flight from responsibility not something akin to treachery?[36]

This reproach was in fact leveled at the Warsaw ghetto's Jewish elder Czerniaków, who ended his life, hence his responsibilities. According to a report of the underground, he had offered far more support to the penned-up Jews of Warsaw than his successor, Marek Lichtenbaum.[37]

In respect to the dilemma of the Jewish councils, the words of Leon Rosenblatt are still terrible to read, despite all we now know concerning the monstrous nature of the Final Solution. Rosenblatt was head of the Jewish police in the Lodz ghetto, responsible, on pain of death by shooting, for delivering contingents of Jews to the Nazis—hence presiding over life and death against his will. The words were transmitted by a sympathetic German interlocutor:

> That [=Rosenblatt's own execution] is hence the simplest solution for me. But what happens then? The SS has already explained: then they select. That means the unbroken, the pregnant, the rabbis, the scholars, the professors, the poets, pass first to the ovens. But if I remain, I can take the volunteers. Often they press themselves on me. And sometimes I have the number I need to hand over. Sometimes there are fewer than I need. Then I can take those who are dying, reported to me by the Jewish doctors, and if they don't suffice, then the deathly ill. But if they don't suffice—what then? Then I can take the criminals: but God know—who here is not a criminal? Using our ghetto money,

which we have to print according to German exchange rates, a loaf of bread costs three hundred to five hundred marks. I know mothers who inform against their neighbors to procure a piece of bread so their children won't die of hunger. Who can judge that? And yet: if I *still* haven't reached the full number? Often I manage without the criminals. But not always. And sometimes even they aren't sufficient. Then I can take those in advanced old age. But what sort of criterion is that? Herr Hielscher, I'm a poor Jew from Lemberg; I learned my trade and could also lead my battery [Rosenblatt commanded an Austrian motorized mortar battery in World War I]. But I haven't learned what I'm supposed to do here. I've asked the communal elders, the rabbis, the scholars. They've all said to me: you're doing the right thing, stay and select in the way you've arranged it. I've asked the different communal groups into which we've divided the ghetto, I've asked the old people, the condemned, the deathly ill: they've all assented. And still, Herr Hielscher, I'm no longer content with my life. I implore you on the God in whom you believe: if you know of a better way than what I've chosen, please let me know and I'll bless you day and night. And if you know of none, please tell me: shall I remain, or have myself shot?

The German interlocutor gave this answer: "With God's grace, proceed as you have—there is no other path, and when you choose it, you are justified before God. I myself would do nothing different."[38]

Burdened with a demand such as self-selection, enforced at pain of death and challenging the capacities of human reason, religious Jews or those relying on tradition as the basis of their actions often sought out rabbis and scholars for advice. But the extremity of the Jewish councils' situation exceeded even their capacities, sharpened as they were through deep intellectual labor. As found in the codex of Maimonides (*Halikhot yessodai hatora*, chap. 5, par. 5), the basic rule had always been that in situations where Jews are forced by Gentiles to deliver one of their own to death on account of being Jewish, the others thus remaining alive, all should rather opt for self-sacrifice.[39] But what force could such a principle have when the delivery unto death represented, not an exception, but a *universal rule*—one that the Nazis were determined to apply to every living Jew? In Vilna, Jakob Gans was confronted with Maimonides's rule. But the rabbi of Kovno, Abraham Duber Cahan Schapiro, ruled that when the entire community is threatened with physical destruction, and when a chance exists to save a portion of it, the community leaders had a paramount duty to save as many Jews as possible from death, by whatever means at their disposal.[40] Even the traditional, sacramental preference for death over complying with one's persecutors and accepting baptism—the principle of *kiddush hashem*, the sanctification of God's name—was vitiated by the totality of the Nazi extermination project. As Rabbi Issak Nissenbaum, a revered representative of

Polish Judaism in Warsaw, explained it, now was the time of *kiddush hachaim,* the sanctification of life and not of the martyr's death. So long as the enemy laid claim to one's soul, it made sense to refuse the claim by sacrificing one's body, that is, life; but now that the enemy wished to simply extinguish Jewish life, the duty was to hold on to it, at every price.[41] Or in the words of Rabbi Zamba, "When conversion can no longer save one's life, the martyrdom of a Jew can no longer be considered a sanctification of the name of God . . . [but] his struggle to live."[42] *Kiddush hachaim* was elevated to a *mitzvah*—a religious duty.

In light of the absolute nature of the Nazis' exterminatory planning, and the accompanying overthrow of all inherited values, the problem of continued Jewish existence could no longer be couched in traditionally conceivable terms: that is, the death of one Jew for the sake of another's survival. The ghetto's leaders understood perfectly the extreme situation they were facing: either total annihilation—or the survival of a fragment.[43]

However varied the councils' circumstances may have been, together they shared the experience of a borderline situation that renders null and void all anticipations of human behavior ordinarily deemed to be universally valid. It is only through the situation of the Jewish councils that we can start to fathom the extent of the civilizational break represented by Nazism: the denial of all commonly valid—hence action-steering—forms of thought based on usefulness and utilitarianism—indeed on the enemy's interest in self-preservation. The heads of the councils made themselves clear: "I act economically, ergo I exist."[44] The Nazis negated this basic assumption when—all ethics and morals long since cast aside—they broke through any abiding scruples, placing the extermination of the Jews above all economic interests and the war's demands.

The Jewish councils' assumption was a response to what they considered a form of *traditional evil:* limitless material egoism and unfettered satisfaction of one's drives. A desire to economically exploit those one has subjugated would fall entirely within the purview of such traditional evil, conforming to basic criteria of rationality. Such criteria had—perhaps they still have today—cultural roots so deep that even when the Nazis had long since revealed as false the belief that work would preserve life, the Jewish councils clung to it, lacking an alternative: in the hope that the enemy's self-interest would help grant work and productivity their civilizational due and place a check on a process of extermination perceived, according to these criteria, as lacking all sense.[45] Such long-trusted, universally internalized forms of thought and action would, however, turn out a trap, since the Nazis transformed them into their opposite. An anticipatory rationality of action, commonly presumed to be life-preserving, ended up as a practical paralysis—extending to cooperation with one's own destruction.[46] The councils did not fall into the trap through attributing to the Nazis a morality that the latter did not acknowledge but because their only choice was a final appeal to socially based behavior: that of furthering one's own, *amoral* interests.

Since the Nazis did not even maintain this final barrier, from a German perspective their behavior may well be considered irrational. From the perspective of the victims, it would appear—far more radically—as *counter-rational.* The situation into which the Jewish councils were forced, without an exit, draws us into those vortexes for which Nazism historically stands: into a profound crisis for a moral consciousness based, necessarily, on the fundamental cognitive building blocks of our ordinary world—that is, on be*havior perceived as rational, sustaining, even in the most extreme of cases, faith in the enemy's ultimate interest in self-preservation.

SEVEN

Historical Understanding and Counterrationality

The Judenrat as Epistemological Vantage

The difficulty inherent in describing Nazism—or, more precisely, in representing the mass extermination in historiographical terms—reflects the basic unimaginability of the event itself. Such an observation would be trivial if this problem of describability and representation did not have a powerful epistemic dimension: one directly bound up with the entire question of understanding Nazism. Moreover, the remarkable debate between Martin Broszat and Saul Friedländer on the historization of the Nazi era has underscored just how narrow the boundaries indeed are of a descriptive mode aimed at achieving historiographical understanding, *Verstehen:*[1] a considerable theoretical and analytic effort is necessary before any effort to historicize Nazism can begin.

Beginning with Droysen if not sooner, historical research has proceeded on the assumption that a *Verstehen*-oriented reconstruction of a historical, hence social, context is possible only under one condition: when the reconstruction can be subjectively meaningful for the observer;[2] when he or she can rely on what is familiar from previous experience. Moreover, this project of experientially based comprehension must not be in conflict with the dictates of reason.[3] Such a notion of *Verstehen* as a process in which conclusions are drawn about an internal motive on the basis of external evidence relies on the assumption that the historian proceeds in the same way as the agent making history.[4] Or to formulate it differently, that both historical reconstruction and the action of the historical subject rely, in similar fashion, on reason.[5] In short, we have an assumption that the anticipated, logical connection between *explanans* and *explanandum* is fully functional in the process of understanding.[6] From this perspective, the meaningfulness of a dialogue between past and present is based on an intersubjectively *generalizable*, hence *objective* mode of communication—namely, what is frequently termed "rational discourse."[7] Consequently, what we are attempting to discover in the historical object through an approach aimed at *Verstehen* is always and only its interpretable core: what is accessible to reason and amenable to experiential verification. This approach applies also when historians find before them a subject appearing to them to be etiologically irrational.[8]

Despite all assertions to the contrary—namely, that what faces them is an incomprehensible set of events—historians approach Nazism and the mass extermination in terms of just such premises, that is, they view the catastrophe as accessible to a process of *Verstehen* guided by rational principles. Such an assumption is manifest, for example, when historians note an extreme disparity between ends and means, between the necessities of the conduct of war and the mass extermination: a disparity that dissolves a relation generally assumed to be socially operative. The assumption informs treatment of the Nazis' ideologically motivated aims: by dint of their inaccessibility to the judgmental standards of the rational personality, those aims are classified as "irrational." They are hence *disqualified* as incomprehensible—to be sure, according to those very standards.

And yet, this commonly advanced postulate of "irrationality" is deeply questionable. It raises two historiographical problems that, in their epistemological resonance, merit some scrutiny. To begin, the postulate serves as an impediment to analysis, blocking, by its very nature, any approach *oriented* toward a "rational" comprehension (*Verstehen*) of a process of pure destruction that remains past understanding. At the same time, and just as problematically, the postulate is in turn predicated on a highly particularistic vantage—that of a specific collective experience. For it amounts to an assertion that Nazi German conduct was not in keeping with a "rational" pursuit of Germany's *own* interests, that Nazi behavior caused intolerable injury and harm to the collective whose leadership it commandeered and whose fate it had been presumptuous enough to try to control.

The particularism becomes evident if we attempt to view the Nazi anti-Jewish campaign from the perspective of its victims. From such a perspective, the notion of the mass extermination's "irrationality" emerges as something akin to a mocking euphemism within the total context of Nazi anti-Jewish policy—as if we might classify measures such as mass expulsion, graded below the critical threshold of the Final Solution and evaluated in its terms, as being "rational" by contrast. It is the case that almost by default, owing to the sheer mass and horror of the extermination, all Nazi measures anterior to that event would, in the eyes of the victims, seem to claim the attribute of rationality. Indeed, such attribution might well be regarded as itself reflecting a specific experiential vantage: that of the Jewish victims. And in turn, this vantage emerges from a dimension of historical consciousness addressing a familiar complex of anti-Semitic traditions—the old, in their own way virulent forms of anti-Jewish enmity. To the extent that the Nazi measures *before* the Einsatz squads and gas chambers can be understood as familiar phenomena—as a sort of historical repetition—these measures, in their relative calculability and familiarity, may thus well have appeared reassuringly "rational" to the desperate victims of impending collective murder.

Significantly, both Hannah Arendt and the sociologist Norbert Elias, motivated by biographical existential concerns, commented on the Final Solution along these lines. Elias even ascribed a "strong element of realism and rationality" to Nazi anti-Jewish policies that stopped short of extermination.[9] Arendt, in focusing on deeds that tax all conceivable limits of common reason—acts neither "committed due to passion nor for one's own advantage"[10]—claimed that the anti-Semitic suppression and expulsion of the Jews was an "atrocious and criminal act, yet one that was completely rational and purposeful [*zweckrational*]." What provokes such discourse on rationality concerning events that preceded the mass extermination is only the inability to grasp the Holocaust itself in rational terms. In other words, we need a thorough evaluation of the actual meaning of "rational" and "rationality" in such situations.

Articulated within the context of "decision theory"—an assessment of the character of the social relations at work in processes of intersubjective communication—George Shackle's argument that "rationality means something only for the outside observer" has clear meaning: it is impossible to determine the rational content of a given action from the internal perspective of an actor.[11] The argument points, for a start, to the impossibility of a credible evaluation of the "rational" content of Nazi actions being offered by the Nazis themselves. In this regard, we need only note that however problematic the "irrationality" thesis for Nazism and the Holocaust may be, ascribing "rationality" to actions on the grounds of their accordance with Nazism's own criteria and objectives is all the more problematic. Shackle's argument thus also points, albeit less directly, to the possibility of such evaluation emerging from the perspective of the Nazis' victims—that is, within an "outside" framework supplied by historians struggling toward a reconstructive *Verstehen*. For within such a framework, the perceptions and forms of behavior of the victims, reflecting the existential urgency of their predicament, can serve to some extent as a practical vantage point—an epistemological grounding. It is from such a vantage that the Nazi system, and its annihilative purpose, emerges as neither rational nor irrational, but rather *counterrational*.

As Isaiah Trunk first stressed, within the ghetto, confined in a condition characterized by seeming, albeit specious, self-determination, the Jews were able to contemplate options for action—hence to reflect on their predicament. They were allowed just enough social normality, and just enough semblance of political autonomy, to retain an illusion of their capacity to further their own long-term survival. Within what thus amounts to a *boundary locus* —trapped between total subjugation and a modicum of self-organization— the victims were nonetheless furnished with socially viable time: a period between the sentence of collective death and postponement of the execution, hence time to assess their relation with the executioner. In this respect, the situation of Jews in Eastern European ghettos differed fundamentally from that of individuals in *death camps*. There the victims possessed virtually no options for action or volition—no alternatives, however aporetic. And by virtue of the presumption of such alternatives—in the interests of survival both for others who had entrusted themselves to their care and for themselves—the Jewish councils struggled to anticipate Nazi actions, and to exert a moderating influence on them: to *think* the Nazis.

We can move toward a deeper understanding of the counterrational nature of Nazi policies with some closer consideration of the concept of labor within the ghettos.[12] Three different meanings of labor are in fact involved here. First of all, there is labor in its immediate role as a *practical activity*, aimed at survival and based on material reproduction. As a result of ghettoization, the Jews had been torn, of course, from a social context that had previously functioned to guarantee material existence. As discussed in the previous chapter, expropriation measures, loss of jobs, and resulting pauperization meant that the only potential work was in the framework of domination and servitude: work offered by the Nazis themselves. In addition to the role of work as the only value that Jews could exchange for food, it had a meaning and function bound up with the role of the Jewish councils: as we noted, it provided the Germans with Jewish labor for production in an organized manner. This second role meant, for the Jews, a "rationalizing" of the Nazis—a rendering of their arbitrary and unpredictable behavior more transparent and amenable to calculation. Such an apparently viable option presumed, in turn, certain skills and a social context with some complexity. In this manner, work became both a means of rationalization and a medium for *social communication:* for "civilizing" the Germans through the obligations and ties the work relation engendered. The Jewish survival strategy thus involved an assumption preshaped by social forms of exchange—an assumption of reciprocity on the part of one's deadly enemies for behavior demonstrated toward them. To this extent, the councils acted in accordance with the following, socially self-evident stipulation: an organization of human cooperative endeavor and a self-rationalizing structure of interreferential behavior modes are possible only if they make use of an external fact.[13] And work was such an external, self-objectifying fact.

A third role of labor for the ghetto's Jews was linked to Nazi use of Jewish trust in the exchange act as a trap—the shift of an offer of labor at the ghetto's own initiative to a demand for labor by the Nazis themselves. As a result of knowledge, or at least premonition, of the ultimately annihilatory aims of deportation, the Jewish councils no longer tried simply to "rationalize" the Nazis in a communicative context; rather, they now used the value-creating function of human work as a means of postponing the death sentence. For in light of the war effort, it was of obvious benefit to the Nazis to give priority to the practical exploitation of Jewish labor over the ideologically motivated desire for Jewish death.

Proceeding on the basis of rationally structured forms of everyday social behavior, the strategy of "rescue through labor" pursued by the Jewish councils thus appeared well founded, at least to some degree. The economicizing veneer to the Jewish labor, visible for all to see, suggested to the Jews that an economic relation was now predominant: hence that a social process was now operative with a certain rough normality. The very form of work demanded from the Jews—productivity and efficiency—suggested such a process.[14] It generated a blinding effect, masking the extermination project from its intended victims. And in fact, under conditions of radical oppression, individuals particularly adhere to assumptions of rationality on the part of their oppressors. Such oppression does not, in other words, negate the traditional, socially rational meaning of labor, but only the otherwise voluntary nature of the exchange. In its form, such compulsory labor became a kind of *material rationality.*

The Jewish councils' presumption—all signals to the contrary—of utilitarian motives on the part of the Nazis was tied to a more broadly operative civilizing logic: that of *homo oeconomicus.* Ultimately, their reliance on rationality had its source within this logic.[15] But the operational system of *homo oeconomicus* does not simply aim to maximize utility and minimize costs; rather, it proceeds on the supposition that acting subjects are indeed reasonable. *Homo oeconomicus* transposes the maxims of reason of economic life to the sphere of social action in general.[16] To this extent, such action relies on utilitarian ethics—especially since decisions that are truly economically reasonable appear, in general, correct in an ethical sense.[17] At the same time, we need to note that economicizing criteria occur immediately to individuals who face a decision.[18] Every decision-making process meant to be rational relies on calculations of utility, since no human activity assumes greater rationality than the effort to engage in gainful pursuits. When individuals facing a decision receive contrafactual input, they give greater credence to information that appears in keeping with the utilitarian character of economy as a form of social intercourse.

In other words, the only information they allow into consciousness is information pointing to alternatives relevant for action. When, for example, skilled Jewish workers in Czestochowa received word about the deportation of similarly qualified workers in Warsaw, they failed to draw any conclusions from this about their own fate. Owing to its absolutely negative valence, news concerning the industrial annihilation was blocked out and the principle of rationality, materialized in the form of labor, preserved. Here it is useful to once more recall Uriel Tal's terse formulation of the Jewish councils' strategy of survival: "I act economically, ergo I exist." Given the situation of the councils, this strategy constituted a plausible effort to draw conclusions from the means—namely, labor—about the ends—namely, the production of value. In this way, the councils fell victim to a fundamental, yet necessary, misperception, since for the Nazis the form of labor did not possess any *systemic* meaning.

Yet here too, when judged on the basis of a generally valid relation between means and ends, the Jewish councils' behavior possessed a high degree of rationality, since it is not only the ends that follow a value determination, but the means as well. In respect to value scales, means cannot be indifferent or neutral.[19] The determination of an ethical action's value refers to the entire sequence of an event, and not just its anticipated final result. Consequently, the councils had virtually no other choice than to constantly nurture the hope that labor would, somehow, lose its exceptional character and transmute, after all, to life-sustaining regularity—to normal routine. Or, viewed differently, that the form (labor) would finally shift from its meaning as a mere means to encompass the ends as well, paradoxically negating the very nature of annihilation as a negation of any rational pursuit of interests.

In retrospect, faced with the Nazi intention to destroy the Jews, the Jewish councils tried to defend themselves through forms of thought and action unsuitable in their indebtedness to criteria of rationality. Labor, as the materialized form of communicative social rationality, was not isolated in this context but rather interlinked with a key strategic fact that concerned the councils: protraction, forestalling, the struggle for "time."

Where for the Jewish councils, labor thus represented a form of concretized rationality, first oriented toward presumably utilitarian motives on the part of the Germans, later functioning as a psychological denial filter to block out the ever more obvious hopelessness of the ghetto dwellers' plight, the category of *time* here represents, in contrast, a strategic element to which everything else is subordinate. As we saw, the councils tried to gain more time, or to protract the period of "borrowed time," by expending their sole asset: the physical labor at their disposal. In the early phase, the councils hoped that through time gained, some miracle might happen; later they harbored, as indicated, illusory hopes that the front would soon be approaching or that, for whatever reason, there would be some saving shift in German policy. Yet the struggle to gain time by labor was bound up with a further factor: *terror,* as a reversal of the formal ethical proportionality of ends and means. The strategy aimed at gaining time forced the councils to make decisions in keeping with the logic of utilitarian considerations. However, the originally rational aspect of that forestalling logic—warding off the worst by means of the lesser evil—successively shifted and then reversed.

We now arrive at the ultimate consequence of the process of forced self-selection that the Jewish councils themselves implemented: the program of participatory self-destruction by means of self-preservation. Because the Nazis continued to control time—owing, for example, to the fact that the front was not approaching with the expected rapidity—the process of weighing options, using an ethics of ends and means, turned back on itself. The small numbers of those consigned to death as a result of the self-selection had, in the course of events, long since become multitudes. The upshot was that the councils, bereft of any alternative, directed the Nazi-engendered reversal of all values—the ethics of ends and means and the associated assumptions of rationality—against themselves, and against the Jewish communities entrusted to their care.

This absolutely radical value reversal does not only inform the specificity of Jewish historical experience; it also represents, more generally, a historical negation of the basic faith in the civilizing power of rational judgment per se. Under this analytic light the logic of the mass extermination no longer appears *irrational* but takes on decidedly *counterrational* significance —one experienced existentially by the Jewish councils. The Nazis' counterrationality is the key, in turn, to identifying the deep-seated problem facing historiography of the Holocaust, the problem tied to the basic, rational links between *explanans* and *explanandum:* guided by a desire to understand inherently attached to rational epistemological premises, historians tend, intuitively or self-consciously, to read such premises into the structures of Nazi behavior—structures that nevertheless can hardly be seen as rational when measured by the imperatives of Nazi self-preservation. As suggested, the ensuing frustration can lead to a retreat—in some cases, into evocations of incomprehensibility, or of impenetrability to rational scrutiny.

For historians, awareness of the Jewish councils' situation can offer an epistemological alternative to such impenetrability. To begin on a practical level: that situation relates to a number of precious *proleptic* historical insights—insights emerging from the need to anticipate Nazi behavior by penetrating as "participant players" into the Nazi bureaucratic administrative apparatus. In a double sense, the strategy, noted in the previous chapter, of trying to influence this apparatus by offering support to various factional interests more concerned, apparently, with the exploitation of Jewish ghetto labor than with immediate annihilation makes the Judenrat an epistemologically relevant indicator for assessing the adequacy of a given theoretical methodological approach. Hence perceptions taking the Judenrat as point of departure reveal just how closely the structuralist explanatory paradigm for Nazism, with its stress on the chaos of conflicting authorities and power, indeed adheres to an underlying reality. Furthermore, the practical failure of Judenrat strategy reflects a salient fact: despite such chaos, the plan of the Nazis to destroy the Jews was highly successful.

On a more theoretical level, reconstruction of the councils' situation demonstrates that if "rationality" was ever involved in the Nazi enterprise, it was a very fractured rationality—one embedded in the overriding logic of the mass-exterminatory project. Posing its own problem for the process of rational, historical *Verstehen,* the reality of the Nazi project makes its logic of bureaucratic administrative action inherently impossible to follow: it demolishes such rationality, as the object of *Verstehen.* In this manner, the endeavor to describe Nazism and the Final Solution requires what we can term a *negative historical cognition* because historians must accept a cancellation of basic principles of rationality before venturing on their enterprise. Auschwitz must be *thought* before it can be written about historically.

EIGHT

On Rationality and Rationalization

An Economistic Explanation of the Final Solution

Representation and historical evaluation of the Holocaust have always assumed a far wider significance than the simple facts defining the event. In this regard, the event is not unique. Indeed, if there actually is such a thing as history *pure et simple,* radical historical moments never seem to embody it. They are historical eclipses: they rupture both individual remembrance and collective memory.

Consciousness thus tends to seize on such moments as a springboard for engaging in a process of assessment and diagnosis that, though always unavoidable, is equally problematic. In the case of research on the Holocaust, what makes the process particularly unavoidable is the crushing magnitude of the facts: facts from which consciousness both recoils and extrapolates. What makes it at the same time problematic is a tendency to shift the focal point from the historical character of the facts in question—to appropriate and mobilize them as a material arsenal in support of an ultimate rationale in some weltanschauung, overrunning, in the end, their proper perimeters.

Basing their work on a demographic template of population economics, Götz Aly and Susanne Heim attempt to explain the Final Solution in terms of ultimate causes, and to discover a single source for its occurrence.[1] The attempt is striking and, initially considered, at some remove from currently accepted methods of research on the Holocaust. Their general approach is in deep debt to a covering *principle of intentionality:* the authors both base their argument on the postulate of a programmatic intention underpinning the mass annihilation and presume a linearly executed National Socialist plan, carried out to the most minute details. But at the same time the authors stand remarkably opposed to the central element in most intentionalist approaches to their subject, since they flatly reject a racial-political or anti-Semitic motive for the destruction of the Jews. Their thesis proceeds from a notion of strictly economic Nazi interests: a utilitarian impulse leading directly to the Final Solution.

Through such a "political economy," the thesis epistemically levels out social and political phenomena preceding and following the rise of Nazism —flattening these phenomena in their relevance to the central phenomenon they frame. What is ultimately at stake here is not a fuller understanding of the Final Solution. Rather, it *instrumentalizes* the event and conscripts it in service of a drastic civilization critique: a dogmatic rejection of what Heim and Aly conceive of as modernity and rationality.

The following observations focus on the methodological approach taken by these two authors, examining the logic of their interpretation's central axes and the solidity of the historical evidence mustered in its support. Naturally, the choice of extracts from their writing are selective; but the extracts reflect their centrality for the total argument advanced by the authors.

At the heart of the authors' thesis is a presumption of the "rational" character of Nazi mass annihilation—especially the mass annihilation of the Jews. In this context, "rational" essentially means "economic": an operative economic rationality, guided by a set of specific interests.[2] Steered by utilitarian motives, as if directed by an invisible hand, its thrust ultimately resulted in genocidal policies.[3] In their argument, the systematic liquidation of human beings was essentially a modernization program, geared to a population policy within a European economic sphere (*Großraumwirtschaft*) dominated by Germany. Correspondingly, the liquidation is to be charged to the account of such a policy—and of the expertocracy entrusted with its execution.

Aly and Heim pointedly reject explanations of the Final Solution that stress mere racial or eugenic motives. Summing up their own position, they explain that the population policy resulting in the mass killings was not "carried out for its own sake," its aim rather being "to reduce the 'dead costs' and to boost total social productivity" (*VdV*, 483). The "annihilation of the Jews," they assert, "was part of a large-scale social-political attack aimed at a new ordering of the entire complex of class relations" (*SuJ*, 16)—in a sense, a grand-scale project of demographic social engineering.

In order to support such pivotal assertions, the authors rely on a corpus of documents they themselves have uncovered and made accessible for research. To a large extent, this material consists of working and position papers drafted by young academics in various Nazi German research institutes and offices, for the most part within the eastern occupation zone, and predominantly in the Generalgouvernement. From these papers, Aly and Heim derive various core concepts understood as the ultimate basis for eventual mass destruction—blueprint ideas seen as both guided by practical interest and based on arguments of economic and social policy.

Among the documents Aly and Heim have discovered, a considerable number do indeed propose, in one manner or another, an economic justification for the mass killing and its antecedent measures; the evidential character of such documentation, its usefulness for reconstructing the Final Solution in its entirety, is nevertheless extremely doubtful. This holds true particularly for material "affirmatively" appropriated by the authors: an adaptation of its vantage accompanied by utter disregard of the historian's constant need for critical distance from his or her sources. Virtually without exception, Aly and Heim take the arguments of Nazi academic subalterns—stylized by the authors as *Vordenker* (forethinkers, or brain trusters) —literally.

The ideas put forward by this "brain trust of annihilation" are derived from economic and social scientific conceptual models; Aly and Heim thus deem them "rational." In doing so, they take the arguments offered by such harbingers of destruction at their word—their quasi-expert analysis, couched in social scientific terminology, as a bona fide reflection of social reality. It was precisely that distorted interpretation of social reality that was National Socialist development policy, involving a "modernization" that fit the vision of a European economic sphere dominated by Germany. In this manner, seemingly unmindful of the historiographical hazards, Aly and Heim adopt the tendentious social diagnosis culled from their sources. Put somewhat more bluntly: they offer a description of empirical social-historical reality tainted by National Socialist reasoning, particularly, and egregiously, in regard to the social evaluation of Jews and Poles as targets of Nazi policy in the east.

Aly and Heim award a special bonus of authenticity to the *economic* terminology of their sources, implying that—in quasi-magical fashion—the more materialist a motive claims to be, the more credible its stated significance. They place much stock in the apparent absence of "racial" reasoning in the sources—an absence understood to corroborate the overall validity of their own, economic rationalistic thesis. It is thus only natural that no attention whatsoever focuses on the possibility of a weltanschauung grounded in racial hatred being hidden under a veil of social semantics: an obvious possibility, in fact, and one confirmed by the sources themselves—but only from a vantage of ideological distance. Racist metaphors do not necessarily involve a biologizing imagery.

The writings of Peter-Heinz Seraphim, a Nazi research expert on Eastern Europe, are symptomatic of just such a racist encoding process. His study *Das Judentum im osteuropäischen Raum*, published in 1938, is presented by Aly and Heim as a credible analysis of Eastern European Jewry's social situation. For Seraphim, the Eastern European Jews were an "urban poverty-stricken proletariat . . . poor artisans, the bottom rung of small merchants and jobless *Luftmenschen*"; for Aly and Heim, it was precisely these Jews who, by dint of their social structure, were "the first group standing in the way of plans for rationalizing the economy" (*SuJ,* 7). Yet the basis of Seraphim's social diagnosis and its rationalizing conclusions is a blatant and classic form of anti-Semitic stereotyping. It seeks the reason for Jewish poverty in their "rejection of physical labor, especially work in factories" (*SuJ,* 47)—a core metaphor of modern anti-Semitism, to the effect that the Jews were "underproductivized."[4] At the same time, confirming the true nature of Seraphim's motives, it disregards the presence throughout Eastern Europe of a large and educated urban Jewish bourgeoisie in the 1930s: a "productive" Jewish population that—together with its proletarian Eastern and more assimilated, bourgeois Western counterparts—would also be ghettoized, then murdered industrially in Auschwitz.

The biologizing of social attributions is generally recognized to be a recurrent and idiosyncratic component of racist thinking. And racist thinking leads to a circle of projective causality: the Jews are paupers because they are Jews. The findings of the "brain trust" of *Vordenker* in the Nazified east are compatible with such a biologizing reversal. We find such a reversal, for instance, in the statement, earnestly cited by Aly and Heim, that "social stratification of the population of the Generalgouvernement is . . . at the same time, a racial stratification" (*VdV,* 209). The distinction between such a statement and their own assertion that "genocide here was the form for solving the social question" (*SuJ,* 15) involves what is, unmistakably, a process of slippage.

As one step in such a process, Aly and Heim argue that the use of the term "restratification" (*Umschichtung*) in "brain-trust" blueprints refers to a "sociological" context—not a "racial" one (*VdV,* 42). In the same literalizing vein, they stress that important guidelines, used to decide the death by starvation of millions, do not contain "a single remark based on race ideology" (*VdV,* 373). All in all, no testimony is too suspect for the authors. Thus, they call Heinrich Himmler to the historical witness stand, in his capacity as political economist. As Himmler—the racial fanatic par excellence—explains it, neither social class nor extraction is decisive for him: what matters is the "value of a person's performance" (*VdV*, 167). Satisfied with such a "discovery," Aly and Heim pass over the highly circumscribed nature of Himmler's remark: exercising a necessary critical distance from the sources, we recognize readily enough its restriction to an *internal* ("Aryan") context. Himmler was referring to ethnic Germans, not to "inferior" races.

As an important step in their "rationalizations" thesis, Heim and Aly propose that the National Socialist population project, at first limited to the eastern occupation zone, was later extended to all of German-dominated Europe. There, too, we read, the Jews were utilized as a "stopgap" population of victims—for after all, the costs of the huge demographic political restructuring could be shifted to them with relative political ease (*VdV*, 488).

Whatever the shreds of validity adhering to the economistic reductionism of Aly and Heim when applied to the eastern situation, the argument that the expulsion and destruction of the Jews in the *west* was a function of "rational" economic interest lacks all historical credibility. The truth is rather that the evolving murder process, fueled by political ideological motives grounded in hate, was then—and is here, again—economistically rationalized *post factum*. It is, for example, an incontrovertible fact that in the territory of the Reich, a Jewish population vegetating in terrible poverty such as Seraphim postulates for prewar Poland—a population that had to be removed for reasons of socioeconomic rationalization—did not exist. For this reason, Aly and Heim cannot present any meaningful evidence of such a linkage.

As a matter of fact, their general attempt at reconstruction avoids laying out connections between the hypothesized underlying economic rationale and subsequent anti-Jewish measures. Rather, they elucidate the steps leading to the destruction of the Jews in the east through a sweeping demographic notion of "negative population policy." In light of such a policy, Heim and Aly argue that the National Socialists basically regarded the Jews as superfluous mouths to feed, occupying what were at best "bogus jobs" in the ghettos (*VdV*, 472)—and that a process of genuine rationalization, based on principles of sound management such as workforce downsizing, operated in the east as a causal factor for deportation and death (*VdV*, 452–53). Yet when applied to the prewar period, with its transparent policies of discrimination and deprivation of rights directed at the Jewish population of the Reich (including annexed Austria), such a line of reasoning is clearly untenable.

Aly and Heim stake the claim to having discovered proof, in the "Protocol of the Meeting in the Interior Ministry on December 16, 1938, dealing with the Jewish Question," that the new anti-Jewish policy formulated in the meeting was based on cost-benefit calculations (*BuM,* 14). There is no mention of such calculations in the protocol, the only policy specifically formulated being organized emigration, and its administrative facilitation, as the expressed "wish of the *Führer.*" It is possible that in interpreting the protocol, the authors were influenced by an exchange (also documented) between Nazi leaders immediately after Kristallnacht. In the exchange, Göring decries the senseless destruction of Jewish property, complaining cogently about the damage this had inflicted on the German economy. But Göring's complaint and the "expiation tax" levied on the Reich's Jewish population do not justify extrapolation into an economic rationalization strategy, or even broader considerations of population economics, as the "blueprint" of a persecution of the Jews—their community in Germany had meanwhile dwindled to far less than one percent of the total population in the Reich—and the theft (or "Aryanization") of their assets. (Let us note *en passant,* as historians of National Socialism are aware, that Göring, the commissioner plenipotentiary for the Four-Year Plan, was never at a loss for trotting out economic arguments if he could use them to expand his powers.)

Doubtless, it is worthwhile to investigate the possibility that tendencies toward economic rationalization emerged from the consequences of anti-Jewish policy or even guided that policy into channels meant to serve the "structural changes" to which the regime aspired. But to posit an imperative for rationalization cannot etiologically explain the policy itself. The methodological weakness clearly emerges in regard to the great weight Heim and Aly place on Nazi measures to rationalize the retail shoe trade in Vienna. Put simply, it leaves unclear the reason for singling out Jewish businessmen for rationalization if the policy's base was economic motives. There are two theoretical possibilities. There may have been a governing assumption that only Jewish businesses were highly undercapitalized, hence natural candidates for rationalization. But far more likely, these retail firms, along with other Jewish enterprises such as banks, were "rationalized" because they were owned by Jews, their owners thus being stripped of normal legal protection.

In place of talk of "rationalization," it would have been be more appropriate for Aly and Heim to use the term *Aryanization*—meaning robbery pure and simple. This robbery, the dispossession of a specific group within the population solely because of their origin, was disguised by a great deal of double-talk, which also facilitated the necessary administrative bureaucratic procedures. Who precisely carried out the plunder, and how, and with what far-reaching structural conceptions, are questions that merit serious research. But in the etiology of the Final Solution, they are of relatively minor importance.

Since Heim and Aly are unable to locate a foundation of convincing "rational" economic reasons for the dense network of anti-Jewish measures taken inside Germany, they resort to the general argument that the Nazis wished to consolidate their overall hold on power by means of economic redistribution. As they explain it, such redistribution helped diminish the "political resistance of a broad majority" of the German population (*SuJ*, 80). In a similarly fuzzy manner, they explain the policy of "de-Judaization" in Holland as "combined," somehow, with a policy of capital concentration (*VdV*, 276). The theme of rationalization takes on a tenor both absurd and galling when the authors clearly invoke it for the sake of maintaining their economistic thesis. We are offered, for instance, the case of alleged black-market activity by the Jewish population of the Warsaw ghetto, with the responsible German authorities deciding to "deal with these 'abuses' . . . by a new wave of rationalization" (*VdV*, 473/74)—in other words, by stepping up the transports to Treblinka.

The material Aly and Heim themselves present points to motives in the decision-making process leading to deportation and annihilation very different from those linked to economic expediency. They cite, for example, the mid-1943 report by an SS and police chief in Galicia explaining why the "craft trades sector" in the area of his jurisdiction, consisting of 90 percent Jewish craftsmen, could not be immediately dissolved: precisely because of the war economy (*VdV*, 452). Again, arguing "economic expediency" as the rationale for efforts by German offices in the Generalgouvernement to replace the traditionally far better qualified Jewish workers in the clothing industry by unskilled Polish trainees would appear drastically counter-intuitive. Such efforts would in fact seem much more likely motivated by the single, fiercely held desire to be able to proclaim, "Tarnow ist judenfrei" (*VdV*, 242).[5]

Still, Aly and Heim would doubtless muster a "rational" explanation for such examples in their writing: an explanation responding to the charge of a "narrow" focus on macroeconomics and sound management by evoking "broad" considerations of population policy. In this respect the two authors do, indeed, claim the existence of blueprints demonstrating that the National Socialists wished to replace Jewish workers in order to create a stable

Polish middle class: a project meant, we learn, to have a "pacifying effect," forestalling a social revolution in Poland. In view of the euphemistic reference by Aly and Heim to the "often undifferentiated violence of the Germans" (*SuJ*, 64)—the violence in fact amounted to "undifferentiated" bestiality—such pacification strategies themselves add up to little more than mere euphemism: marginal plans at best, with a status that remained almost entirely theoretical.

Aly and Heim are, in any event, often inexact in their reading of sources, playing fast and loose with both content and purport. Consistently, the documents they reproduce in toto as "key sources" invite an opposite reading to what they offer. The protocol from the auditor general's office (*Rechnungshof des Deutschen Reiches*), for instance, flies in the face of the very thesis of insufficient Jewish productivity they are striving to establish. As this document's authors explain it (their context is, in fact, the Lodz ghetto, with its mass of weakened and starving dwellers): aside from the "monetary advantage" for the Reich, "given the existing shortage of manpower, the most complete exploitation possible of Jewish labor is also in the interest of the war economy" (*BuM*, 72).

An even more glaring instance of such misreading emerges in connection with the "Economic Balance Sheet on the Jewish Residential District in Warsaw" issued by the Reich committee on economic efficiency (*Reichskuratorium für Wirtschaftlichkeit*), a body that the authors credit with distinct professionalism. This report defines the underlying causes for the pauperization of Warsaw's Jewish population with a clarity that serves, many decades after its writing, as a rebuff to the economistic interpretation of Heim and Aly. At an important juncture, the report's authors speak of an ultimate intention to "exclude" the Jews "from economic life for political reasons. Thus, the measures taken," they inform us, "were determined primarily by politics, and not by the economy" (*BuM*, 90).

These political measures took the following form: grind down the Jewish population by stigmatization, exploit them to the point of physical exhaustion, and reduce them deliberately to a state of starvation—to the point where they can, indeed, be of no possible use. Pauperized and superfluous, the Jews were thus made ready for annihilation. "Lack of utility" was a subterfuge for the Nazi planners—and for those historians who now take their word for it. There was no "rational" economic concept at the *etiologic base* of the annihilatory process.

In their reduction of the Nazi German crime against the Jews to an act propelled by radical utilitarianism, Aly and Heim display willful ignorance of one, central tenet of any historically sophisticated economically focused analysis: "pure" economics does not exist.[6] Adam Smith, for example, conceives "economy" to be an integral component of moral philosophy. Along with ethics and politics, it is a structural part of an overarching whole.[7]

Once acknowledged, Smith's insight has substantial epistemic implications for an understanding of the Nazi project's true nature. His insight underscores, for example, the complete absence from the calculations at work in Nazi "economic planning" of the ethical delimitations informing classical economic discourse. As epiphenomenal products of the Nazi weltanschauung, such planning merely served, from the start, as a rationale for ideology. In the Nazi framework, the planning reflected a process of ideological "unbounding" (*Entgrenzung*), replacing the ethical provisos immanent even in utilitarian cost-benefit calculations.

In fact, National Socialism spawned an amalgamation of esoteric, biologico-racist, pseudo-rational concepts with traditional technocratic calculations geared toward cost and benefit. The eradication of distinctions between various spheres maintained within civilized polities—including distinctions between the "economic" realm and realms beyond its perimeter—was typical for Nazism. It was integral to the National Socialist "greater economic sphere": a sphere conceptualized, we noted, in terms of an ideal of autarchy itself representing the specific, ideological manifestation of a centralized command economy. An interpretive model that attempts to reconcile the Nazi economic system, extending far beyond the borders of the Reich and based on plunder and pillage, with the categories of equivalent exchange at work in classical economics, as well as with the liberal conception of social order presupposing those categories, is in the end not only totally inappropriate. It also simply and fundamentally misses the point.[8]

The sort of negative "cancellation of the economy" (*Aufhebung*) taking place under Nazism opens the door to many "economic" possibilities, as it dismantles normal ideological boundaries of material interest and utilitarian pursuit.[9] Such ideological unbounding extends far beyond the economically beneficial manipulation of things and relations; it deems even the materiality of the human body an object for limitless exploitation. On the basis of racial precepts, it changes the ethically taboo economic constant of the "human being" into an exploitable "economic" variable. This particular form of transgression of ethical boundaries ordinarily considered universal is roughly equivalent to, say, a view of human flesh as a tasty delicacy well worth eating. It is no accident that cannibalism, by and large, is considered as an *ethical* problem, only secondarily involving culinary concerns.

Quite clearly, the same priority prevails in considerations of the deliberate mass murder of human beings: it prevails in the face of their labeling as "superfluous," first from a purportedly economic but actually biologistic perspective, then through retrospective application of a familiar social semantics.[10] For this reason, the neat distinction Aly and Heim claim to discover within the demographic economic analyses of their Nazi "brain trusters," between "economic" or "sociological" semantics and racial semantics is, in the end, an unconvincing distinction. In offering the distinction, the two authors must constantly acknowledge the phenomena of admixture, or "amalgamations" (*SuJ*, 30); but they nonetheless insist on the primacy of the economic factor. The confusion manifest here reflects, precisely, the failure to acknowledge the collapse of ethical delimitations inherent in Nazi ideology and its biologistic weltanschauung.

As time went on, the Nazi regime tended more and more toward a successive erosion of institutional responsibilities, along with an undermining of associated divisions of competence, authority, and function. It is difficult to ascertain whether a decision was made in the interest of a specific issue or whether it was instrumental, meant to help consolidate and extend power. The Wannsee Conference remains a notorious example of this process.[11] Of analogous infamy are the results of the definitions arrived at the conference, in response to administrative imperatives regarding categorization: who was and was not to be singled out for victimizing by the regime?

Yet despite all polycratically generated arbitrariness within Nazism, the eugenic and racist template for defining groups of victims was not altered arbitrarily, and certainly not on the basis of general notions of utility. No one was put to death simply, or even mainly, for economic reasons. No German worker who did not perform to expected production levels was sent to the gas chambers on the grounds of "deficient utility" or in order to reduce the number of mouths to feed. In this regard, the regime remained quite firm in its principles.[12]

Aly and Heim display awareness of the fragility of their economistic demographic thesis on the *Endlösung* (see for example *BuM*, 8), admitting many provisos obviously meant to dampen doubts bound to arise. They do not claim, for instance, to be able, in each individual case, to "explain convincingly in an economic sense" why "for example, in June 1944, 2,200 Jews were sent from Rhodes over a distance of 2,000 kilometers to Auschwitz" (*SuJ*, 14)—and this at the cost of leaving heavy military equipment behind.

Through this sort of concession, Aly and Heim attempt to shore up their economistic thesis by presenting what it defines, implicitly, as an extreme exception to the rule. But in actuality, the Rhodes tragedy is anything but an exception in its suggestion that the presence of a "rationality of self-preservation" on the part of the regime in the war's final phase is hard to discover. In its basic meaning, the tragedy relates to a phenomenon often cited by researchers: the massive mobilization, at the war's end, of the limited Nazi transportation capacities, in order to bring Jews to the death camps. Not accidentally, Heim and Aly invest considerable resources trying to diminish the enormous symbolic weight of this phenomenon—a weight directly connected to the patently counterrational nature of the frantic Nazi efforts. By necessity, their thesis bypasses the argumentative meaning of the historical image it presents here: endless rolling freight trains loaded with human victims, silhouetted against a backdrop of German military chaos. In place of reflections on this meaning, it uses detailed calculations claimed to prove that the Reichsbahn had to mobilize far less transport capacity to move persons a single time over a given stretch (namely, to their liquidation) than was necessary if it constantly deployed the railway to bring the victims essential supplies on a regular basis (*VdV*, 296–97); in other words, we learn, the one-way trip to oblivion was cost-efficient.

But again, such cost-benefit accountancy does not grasp the point: that the rational content of social communication cannot be determined from the *internal* vantage of the actor alone.[13] By means of a particularistic, quasi-autistic interior view—the sort of view formulated by the Nazi "brain trust" relied on by Aly and Heim—we can certainly manage to arrive at the conclusion that economic criteria were being fulfilled here in a rational way. The Nazi demographic experts share one chief objective: establishing administrative measures for a "gigantic, short-term spurt in concentration and investment" (*VdV*, 297). This project was supposedly designed to serve the rapid industrialization and agrarian rationalization of the Generalgouvernement—which the authors, using contemporary development parlance, dub a *Schwellenland,* a "country at the takeoff stage" (ibid.). But such optimistic planning, aimed at a still-open future, was formulated in the 1941–42 post-blitzkrieg phase of Nazi success and exuberance; and the epistemic questions about National Socialist rationality of action take on their clarity in the face of a considerably later phase, that of Nazi decline and defeat: the evaporation, not just of grandiose imperialist plans for conquered

Lebensraum, but of the existence of the Reich itself. Accountancy cannot take from the deportation of the Jews of Rhodes in 1944 its terrible symbolic meaning.

The determination Aly and Heim demonstrate to evade this meaning— their quite forthright overriding of historiographical common sense for the sake of an untenable thesis—draws on their vague and overgeneralizing critique of "modernity." This critique informs their argument that the putatively rational nature of the mass murder of the Jews must be viewed in the context of a strategy of modernization, aimed at rendering individuals both "highly mobile and available" and "adaptable to the rapid changes in an industrial society" (*VdV,* 166). The critique appears in both relatively bland pronouncements such as that "placing minorities at social disadvantage, an enterprise with a lethal outcome" functioned "to provide the majority of the population with advantages or guarantee its social status quo" (*SuJ,* 12) and less benign pronouncements reflecting a radical and antiquated approach to capitalist society and economics. It offers us, for instance, haphazardly earnest assertions that "the murder of a segment of the European population" was attributable to an interest-based intervention by "German firms and corporations" (*SuJ,* 8), and that the "genocide brought the German Reich economic gain and commercial advantages" (*VdV,* 378)—assertions tending to reduce the Final Solution to a bid at gaining improved terms of trade. The source of such a tendency is not hard to fathom: Aly and Heim wish to perceive the Nazi regime as not differing in principle from antecedent or successive regimes. To that extent they must attribute murderous effects to the very rationale of economy and demography, without any historical distinctions. Thus, the mass annihilation emerges as an innate, albeit certainly extreme, manifestation of bourgeois capitalist society. In their critique of capitalism, Heim and Aly thus make manifest a basic, troubling feature of their historical method: a detemporalization of the historically specific phenomenon of Nazism and its "normalization"—its transformation into a variant of garden-variety capitalism.

Aly and Heim deserve credit for uncovering new sources for the wider context of the Final Solution—sources whose historical meaning they largely misinterpret. These sources—culled, as indicated, from Nazi research institutes and offices connected to population policy—offers important insight into the "seepage processes" of the Nazi weltanschauung, particularly in the middle and lower levels of applied scholarship and administration. Many valuable nuggets can be extracted here—though hardly what the authors are basically concerned with, namely, evidence about the origins of and direct responsibility for the Holocaust.

In light of their drastically reductive historical thesis, it becomes evident again that the Final Solution cannot be explained monodimensionally, but only in terms of a complex intermeshing of highly diverse tendencies. Granted the activity of die-hard anti-Semites, the "Jewish problem" served many functionaries primarily as political currency. In the struggle for sinecures and bureaucratic power, careerists even completely indifferent to Jews took an initiating and active role in the enterprise of the mass annihilation.

A methodologically well founded reconstruction of the developments leading to the annihilation, directly tapping the sources and tracing direct chains of causality, focusing on minute details and investigating specific, circumscribed events, remains a challenge for research. We owe its absence less to an abundance of source material than to the very logic and form of Nazi power and the Nazi polity, with its disastrous mesh of institutional chaos—a tangle of bureaucratic competencies amounting to organized irresponsibility—and rational bureaucratic action.[14] The nature of this evidence is highly sobering. It acts to curb all claims and aspirations to finality, to holistic explanations and talk of ultimate causes.

Aly and Heim try to skirt such impassable terrain through a rigid, literalist focus on their source material and an exploitation of its suggestive effects. It is a short step from acknowledging that the drafts and blueprints in the research papers of the Nazi "brain trusters" appear to strive directly toward the Final Solution to concluding that the blueprints *caused* the act: a conclusion that, as we have seen, Heim and Aly render into a methodological principle. A basic tool at their disposal in the process is *rhetorical:* an extensive use of the subjunctive mood that helps to compensate for weaknesses of a *methodological* nature—that is, the lack of demonstrable causal connections between that Nazi academic theorizing and the concrete history of events. Through such rhetoric the Final Solution emerges as a function of an economistic armature: of the exigencies of food-supply economics.

Amply using the subjunctive, Aly and Heim construct a closed chain of evidence stretching from initial euthanasia (1939–41) down to the last major act in the destruction of Europe's Jews, the deportation of the Hungarian Jews to Auschwitz in the early summer of 1944. In line with their overarching thesis, the authors speculate here on a "need to save on social outlays and foodstuffs"—"if the Aryanization and liquidation of Jewish businesses brought economic and personal advantages, the murder of the incurably sick resulted in what tended to be a better level of care for the curable" (*VdV,* 270)—the same sort of speculation being repeated in various modalities (the "euthanasia action"—Aktion T4—we are informed, *may* well have "been at the initiative of the Agency for the Four-Year Plan and its administrative group for nutrition" [*Geschäftsgruppe Ernährung*] [*VdV,* 271]).

It is through an alignment of such *possible* sources for the mass euthanasia with similar sources for the mass murder of the Jews that Aly and Heim arrive—again, through copious use of the subjunctive—at the proposed common origin of food-supply economics: more specifically, at a concern on the part of the general Agency for the Four-Year Plan about the securing of a solid basis for German meat supplies—a concern leading to far-reaching plans for annihilation of a superfluous population. Those plans—so runs the speculation—pointed in the direction of the Final Solution, and to even more gargantuan murder schemes. There was talk, we learn, of approximately 30 million potential victims (*VdV,* 369). The weight of actual developments then being added catalytically to the plans and blueprints, a ferment finally "may have culminated" in the decision to annihilate the Jews.

Playing the "food-supply" thesis to the hilt, Aly and Heim enter sweeping speculative terrain on the basis of statements by Assistant Secretary Hermann Backe (general councillor of the Four-Year Plan office):

> If one reads against this backdrop what he [Backe] said to Hitler in the spring of 1941 about an imminent crop failure for all of occupied Europe, then it is possible that in 1941, the theory of overpopulation, with its arguments geared to the medium term, was now supplemented by the massive anxiety of the Nazis over impending hunger revolts, jointly feeding into the causation of the *Endlösung*. (*SuJ,* 44)

Later, the two authors formulate this notion in a more restrained, albeit no less approximate, manner: "Taken together, both arguments [i.e., those of hunger and overpopulation] acted to spur planning for mass resettlement and genocide." Although not proven, the connection, they contend, is in any case a "plausible" one (*VdV,* 370).

Now it is quite possible that a quasi-Malthusian population policy had an impact on the political decision-making process of the Nazi regime.[15] It may have had an importance analogous, for example, to Hitler's desire, against the background of the World War I experience, to accord the highest wartime priority to supplying the population with essential foods. But here, such conjecture is the material of a monocausal explanation, presented in willfully ignorance of previous historiographical spadework. (Let us note, in passing, the complete omission by Aly and Heim of any attention to "anti-Bolshevist factors"—and to the effect of the heinous "commissar order" signed by General Warlimont on June 6, 1941, demonstrably implemented via the chain of command.)[16] The methodological problem at work here becomes blatantly evident in the explanation Heim and Aly offer for the deportation of the Hungarian Jews to Auschwitz—an explanation, steeped both in subjunctivity and in neglect of the empirical circumstances of the Hungarian situation, which they bring in as they ask whether, viewed against the "backdrop of Backe's conception of guaranteeing food supplies for Central and Western Europe . . . the deportation and murder of a large segment of Hungarian Jewry in 1944 is not perhaps linked with precisely these very considerations" (*VdV,* 390/91).

The scheme for mass deportation Hitler discussed with Horthy, the Hungarian head of state, in 1943—which the authors remarked on earlier in a quite different vein, using Hitler's verbatim comments[17]—now connects up with the loss of the Ukraine, and of the food supplies that had been extracted from the region. According to Aly and Heim, the required food replacement corresponds "rather exactly to the nutritional minimum for one million persons, almost precisely the same number as the Jewish minority in Hungary, according to German estimates." The authors thus consider a policy link based on food supply "conceivable." They admit an inability to "prove" causality here but think "that the connection between these deportations and food-supply policy also constitutes a plausible hypothesis" (*VdV,* 391).

In light of the broad documentation available about the fate of the Hungarian Jews, the attempt by Heim and Aly to trace their deportation to Auschwitz back to food-supply calculations is especially remarkable. The documentation leaves scarcely any latitude for such a thesis. The deportation occurred at the eleventh hour, from a country that had up to then been a German ally. The position of Hungary in the final phase of the war, vacillating between Germany and the Allies, is unmistakably a relevant factor in grasping what would occur: here as in other contexts, the treatment of Hungarian Jewry took on the function of a political currency, exchanged in both directions.[18] This function underscores, once more, the spatial and temporal diversity of the specific circumstances that led to the *Endlösung.*

Let us now focus on Aly and Heim's use of subjunctivity: their interpretation of past occurrences through an evocation of *historical possibility.*

Fundamental here is the thesis that the Nazi population-policy blueprints were aimed at encompassing all of Europe and were meant to apply indiscriminately to all imaginable population groups within the framework of a "rationality" based on specific economic criteria (*BuM*, 11). To that extent, they argue, it is not productive to proceed only from the actual, historical victims. To do so, they contend, leads to an inadmissible narrowing and distortion of perspective in research on motives.

It may well be that an approach using future possibilities to interpret real events—or put otherwise, one contextualizing real events against the backdrop of their potential spatiotemporal expansion—can be quite profitable. Such extrapolation is, in fact, convincing in this context. Since Nazi Germany was destroyed from the outside in 1945, no definitive statements can be made about the murderous potential the dictatorship *might* have unleashed had it lasted longer—or even emerged victorious. Conceptualization of a *possible* Nazi future, derived from the documents, can thus be fruitful, increasing our historical understanding insofar as it views what has come about as the product of intentions implemented according to a set of plans.

If we follow such a strict intentionalism—the assumption of an immediate causal link between conception and practical implementation—then the material Aly and Heim uncovered, as well as other similar material, provides a convincing basis for postulating that what actually occurred represented only a segment, an extract, of what was in fact intended. As an example, we might cite the plans that were part of the Generalplan Ost to "Germanize" (*eindeutschen*) segments of the Polish population (*VdV*, 409), subjugate and plunder some as slaves, while liquidating the remaining segment. As the authors note, such a project would have resulted in the death of 20 percent of the Polish population "based on considerations of economics and technicalities for domination" (*BuM*, 139).

The realization of future Nazi projections would indeed have considerably expanded the total number of victims. At the same time, the sources tapped clearly indicate that such an end was not planned for *all* Poles. The Generalplan Ost, as said, envisaged both a racial selection and one guided by the interest of plunder. Such a distinction was not contemplated in the case of the Jewish population.

The lack of a distinction between victims meant for plunder and victims meant for murder in the framework of the Final Solution offers its own comment on the utility-centered thesis of Heim and Aly. For at the heart of this thesis is the premise of an absence of *specificity* in the murderous plan's victims (*BuM*, 11): an absence inherent in the "universalistic" nature of economic and population policy.[19] In a statement underscoring the premise's centrality to their argument—and possessing an almost self-congratulatory tenor—Aly and Heim confirm that Section IV B4 in the RSHA (Reich main security office) did not function just as a *Judenreferat,* that is, a 'Jewish section,' but was also responsible for *all* population expulsions according to the official plan for division of competencies (*VdV,* 43). They assert, to boot, that the "liquidation camps were supposed to continue working even after the murder of the European Jews had been completed." It remains unclear how we are to reconcile this assertion with the razing and leveling of the death camps in which Polish Jewry met its end—straight after the deed had been accomplished (*BuM,* 139).

In the course of formulating such future-centered arguments, all pointing, in one or another manner, to the negative universality for the Nazi annihilatory project, Heim and Aly offer disturbing misjudgments of logic and semantics. Detailing, for example, what they consider the likely levels of intensified mass terror, they suggest that the prevalent policy in a National Socialist future would "no longer have been to murder individual ethnic groups as a whole [*sic*], but rather populations of Eastern Europe, who 'are without any value for us Germans,'" meaning the sick and those unable to work, as well as the "political fanatics" (*BuM,* 139). On the one hand, what the two authors define here as a qualitative intensification of the mass murder and a further extension of the regime's terror would in fact *also* maintain the earlier selective policy of eugenic "eradication"; on the other hand, without wishing to set up some sort of hierarchical ordering of the *individual* victims—in any event an ethically inadmissible procedure—we can note that Aly and Heim see no conceptual difference between the total, bureaucratically planned destruction of "individual ethnic groups" (in other words, the Nazi form of genocide) and the murder of individuals, even if such murder occurs on a colossal scale.[20] They consequently have no reservations about hierarchizing in quantitative terms, in respect to a fictive future. In view of the "far greater projects for murder" on the drawing boards, the "murder of the European Jews" was only a first segment (*VdV,* 299)—albeit one given priority "under conditions of war" (*VdV,* 492) and "implemented to a very extensive degree" (*VdV,* 299).

In proposing such a reading of reality, Aly and Heim confront the same, profoundly serious methodological and epistemic problem touched on above—that the annihilation of the Jewish population fails, inherently, to correspond with an economistic rationale indifferent to the specific, collective identity of the victims. It also fails, of course, to correspond with their entire thesis of "utilitarian thinking" on the part of the Nazis. As a reflection of the problem, at one point in their effort to make the Nazi plans for future murder fit their thesis of economic exploitation Aly and Heim stumble, logically and historically, into a telling trap:

> If one ignores the linkage between Auschwitz and German projections at the time for a modernized and pacified Europe, the German crimes appear to be a reversion to barbarism, a rupture with Western civilization—and not a possibility inherent in that civilization. In the light of such a short-sighted assessment, the German annihilation policies of that period appear to be the product of an exceptional historical situation, disjointed, inexplicable. (*VdV,* 491–92)

The trap is that if the assumption about the arbitrariness of the selection of victims should prove untenable, or if the economistic final causation for the mass annihilation should lead nowhere, the inverse would have to be correct—Auschwitz would remain inexplicable.

We note that the "subjunctivist" approach of Aly and Heim involves a propensity for drawing conclusions about past events from future-oriented planning documents of the Nazi expertocracy. In the process, the two authors lose contact with their temporally delimited object of inquiry, the Final Solution as actually implemented. What they consider epistemically relevant for that event they shift to time periods either antecedent or subsequent to the event itself—at the cost of disregarding explanatory connections that are empirically germane.

In respect to the Nazi period, the approaches of social history and the history of science present an analogous picture, even if it is not as extreme. Though historical efforts geared to the *longue durée* have certainly shed light on ideological and structural aspects of the Nazi period, they have shed less light on the immediate history of events.[21] And in research on a short-lived phenomenon like the Final Solution, it is precisely the specific history of crucial events that is pivotal, the conditions prior to Nazism being of lesser importance.

The extremely short historical span involved in the study of Nazism tends, paradoxically, to deflect researchers' scrutiny from the concrete phenomenon to its antecedents. In place of a history of the specific events linked to the phenomenon, along with a clarification of associated questions of immediate causation, responsibility, and, ultimately, guilt, it encourages more abstract etiologic speculation. But at the same time, in raising questions of ultimate philosophical rationale—and urgency, when comprehension of the phenomenon's nature makes it relevant to the present—such speculation points back to more pragmatic problems (such as how to prevent a possible return of the terror and horror). In the playing out of this process, research on the Final Solution becomes a heavily politicized discipline. It offers historians an ethical opportunity or lends itself to dubious methodology.

As we noted in the context of their implicit anticapitalist polemic, Aly and Heim propose exaggerated paths of continuity between past and present and instrumentalize the past for the present: quite obviously ideology and structure are a powerful general motive for their historical research. They aggravate their detemporalization of the Final Solution through an extensive inclusion of biographical information derived from research on the careers of diverse social scientists. This focus on continuity of personal careers is deceptive, insofar as it suggests the existence of a political continuity.[22] It necessarily obscures the substantial differences between the Third Reich and the Federal Republic of Germany, fuzzing the sharp caesura marked by the year 1945. Yet no one in their right minds would dare to allege that people are being systematically murdered in the Federal Republic.

The same eradication of temporal and political distinctions is apparent, painfully, in the use by Heim and Aly of the term "European economic community" (*BuM,* 13), cited in Nazi literature from about 1942 on in the context of planning related to *Lebensraum,* to denote the present-day European Community (*BuM,* 8). In their candid declaration that, to the extent that the Nazis were interested in acquiring cheap food and raw materials in southeastern Europe, "their plans bear similarities to today's EC structure" (*SuJ,* 40), they would appear to be aligning the current structure with the Nazi program of plunder and murder, while simultaneously suggesting that such activities are hardly what really matters. A similarly obscurantist manner affects the Nazi rationalization plans for agriculture. The plans were meant, we are told, to bring about a change in agrarian structure "in the direction of larger production units; that later occurred in the postwar period with the closing down of hundreds of thousands of farms not only in West Germany, but throughout Western Europe—and, by the way, actually led to a situation where Europe became an agricultural surplus area" (*BuM,* 22).

There are additional examples of such conflation of liberal capitalistic present and (Nazi) past throughout the two authors' writing. Their repeated reference to the Generalgouvernement as a "country at the takeoff stage" has already been noted (they in fact apply the term to other areas in German-occupied Eastern Europe as well). Another example is the use of the concept of the "two-thirds society"—a contemporary concept, aimed at neoconservative policies of welfare cutting that remove one-third of the population from the productive economy (*VdV,* 289).

Meant to scandalize and shock, these casual semantics in the context of a process Aly and Heim themselves define in terms of 30 to 50 million projected victims have, in the end, an opposite effect: they trivialize the past. They do not merely reflect a polemical effort to forge discursive links with the present. Rather, for the two authors, the equation of Nazi policy with current political configurations is a deadly serious matter.

It is a curious fact that despite the grave methodological problems involved in their analysis, and despite the innovational gestures accompanying it, the arguments of Heim and Aly often conform closely to commonplace historical assumptions. For example, the policies on minorities and nationalities in East-Central Europe during the interwar period have always provided a popular springboard for comparisons with the present—as did efforts in the more distant past aimed at national homogenization.

It was precisely in the period between the two world wars, in the wake of the dissolution of dynastically legitimated multinational empires, that a variety of options were proposed for the nationalities question—and some implemented, at least in part. They ranged from the radical solution of a "transfer" of groups within the wider population for purposes of national homogenization to measures in national and international law for the protection of minorities. In general, extreme solutions such as the "exchange" of Greeks and Turks on the basis of the 1923 Lausanne accords—in that instance, in the aftermath of a war fought between the two nations—tended to be the exception.

Against this complex and equivocal background, Aly and Heim assert that the "forced resettlement of persons and entire peoples was not taboo in the first half of this century, but rather a widespread practice" (*VdV,* 483). They also point out, correctly, that successive Polish governments were interested in getting rid of large segments of their Jewish population through emigration (*VdV,* 88)—that indeed the "Madagascar Plan," later appropriated by the Nazis, had its origin here. Thus, they conclude,

all the main arguments in economic and social policy that later also determined the decision-making processes of the German occupying power in Poland had already been thrown into the debate by 1939 in the Polish and international discussion on migration, overpopulation and forcible displacement of persons. (*VdV,* 91)

The authors seem strangely unaware of the world of difference between a repressive minority policy, as practiced by the Polish state between the wars, centered on possible emigration and cultural homogenization measures, and the genocidal practices of the Nazis, based as they were on eugenic and racial tenets.

Certainly, the Nazi policy of *Heim ins Reich* (back home to the Reich) and the resettlement measures in the region of Wartheland (western Poland) may in the beginning have been partly motivated by traditional, national-territorial objectives, aimed at *homogenization.* But as a result of the "deportation" of Poles and Jews to Lodz and into the territory of the Generalgouvernement, these measures were the prelude to a systematic *extermination*—a conceptually separate development. And yet Aly and Heim regard their quasi-historical paradigm as having extensive—even universal—validity. Their contention that the fundamental Nazi objective was "relief from 'population pressure'" (*BuM,* 24) is broad enough to cover an array of phenomena: the policy of "Germanizing" the Poles, as practiced "75 years earlier in the Ruhr" and placed here in the context of national homogenization (*SuJ,* 56); the expulsions and resettlement actions after World War II.[23] By a genetic linking of the Final Solution with disparate measures of national homogenization in Europe, the paradigm levels the decisive difference between the two processes —and detemporalizes the actual historical object to the point where it crumbles and then disappears.

Years ago Götz Aly and Susanne Heim set about on an ambitious venture: to ferret out the fundamental factors responsible for the Final Solution. They wanted to balance the scales, so to speak; to make up historiographically for what the judicial system had failed to do over the recent past. But increasingly, their initial aspiration vaporized, turning into an exercise within an untenable realm of universal ideas and structures. They speak of a "planning, praxis-oriented rationalism" (*VdV,* 485)—in short, of a "specifically German contribution to the development of European modernity" (*BuM,* 12). The truly specific question of why "modernity" (as indicated, a substitute for "capitalism") reached its negative apotheosis in Germany and not elsewhere is no longer, it seems, of epistemic interest. Or—and perhaps more in line with the authors' real intentions—all the world's injustice is ultimately one and the same because any historical distinction implies an ethically intolerable hierarchization of suffering.

Such generalizations and commonplaces inimical to the founding principles of Western civilization reflect an approach bent on obscuring the historical object, along with its moral and epistemological challenges. Aly and Heim adopt the stance of marginalized outsiders but, deplorably enough, actually represent a trend increasingly gaining acceptance—the deconstruction of the historical event by historiographical means.

NINE

Historical Experience and Cognition
Juxtaposing Perspectives on National Socialism

It would be a truism to qualify Nazism and its core event, the Holocaust, as "historical." No one seriously denies the capacity of historical cognition to integrate this catastrophic era of the German and European past into the stream of history. However, as I suggested in the previous chapter, it is primarily a descriptive approach to the period that makes the phase amenable to processing by historiography. The interpretive, *verstehende* perspective on the era, no less pressing in its importance, gives rise to a number of complications. A historian wishing to "understand"—rather than merely describe —Nazism rapidly comes up against an analytic impasse, that is, a dimension appearing to elude the usual modes of human comprehension. As secular consciousness grapples with the enigma of the Nazi era, it must deal with a paradox that presents a number of diverging views about the universal historical significance of Nazism. Becoming *historical*, the phenomenon has taken on a *suprahistorical* meaning. Yet the historian can address this meaning only by putting the reality of industrial mass extermination—the most radical act of the regime—at the center of efforts to reconstruct the era.

The historian's decision to study National Socialism with the mass extermination as its focus is not arbitrary. Although such a perspective may orient itself, empirically and experientially, toward the victims, the meaning that emerges has a universal character. The radical perspective appropriate to the deed's radical nature makes cognitive use of the experience of the victims for theoretical and interpretive purposes, namely, to penetrate to the universal historical significance of the mass extermination.[1] To this extent, the question of the historical locus and meaning of Nazism depends on the choice of historiographical perspective.

In the present essay I probe a number of epistemological questions on the character and historical significance of Nazism and the Holocaust. I endeavor to demonstrate the limits of the usual methodological approaches toward their history and its universal significance.

The historical picture of Nazism's core event, the mass extermination, is characterized by an extreme polarity: the juxtaposition of banality and monstrosity. The banality underlies the perspective of those reconstructing events from the angle of the perpetrators, of the Nazi bureaucratic apparatus. Insofar as this perspective reaches out to include societal phenomena beyond the more narrow confines of the Nazi era, it obscures the exceptional character of the period within the perspective of the victims; in doing so, it focuses on continuities reaching through and beyond the era, emphasizing elements of abiding "normalcy." In contrast, owing to its psychological impact, the element of monstrosity experienced by the victims becomes the principal pillar for their attempts at explanation. At times, this focus on monstrosity as Nazism's core element leads to suprahistorical interpretations. More generally, perspectives concentrating on the mass extermination as Nazism's focal event tend toward finalistic interpretations.

The use of different historiographical approaches thus reflects a marked divergence of historical experience. In a conclusion to this chapter, I propose a historical perspective that may illuminate the counterrational behavior that lies at the universal core of the Holocaust.

The characterization of Nazism and the Holocaust as a "historical crisis" makes them comparable with watersheds as significant for the universal process of civilization as the Reformation or the French Revolution.[2] Yet the Reformation radically altered the Occidental word's relationship with God, and the French Revolution transformed the relationship of the individual to authority and dominance. With the mass murder of millions and the depths of its depravity, the Nazi period is surely a cause for moral shock. But the notion of a "historical crisis" seems inappropriate at first sight: that chapter in history has left no visible changes in the secularly grounded and rationally organized structures of civilization. Consequently the period has not even gained the status of a fundamental watershed in historical consciousness—in distinct contrast, for example, to World War I.

In order to grasp why Nazism nevertheless marks the onset of a "historical crisis," we must confront basic issues of historiographical presentation and representation, of the sort referred to above. Let us note, for a start, the generally accepted historical practice of approaching an era principally along the avenue of description. But any approach also contains, a priori, a number of suppositions shaping the perspective, thus predetermining the description.[3] Such is the case even when the historian is content with nothing more than the modest aim of reconstruction. Implicit value judgments can, for example, underlie questions articulated in a pretheoretical, intuitive form, but categorizable as specific to both the era and the object. Thus, we understand Ranke's classic dictum of admonishing historians to present the past *wie es eigentlich gewesen,*[4] articulating his ideal of the past's objective "mirroring," as an expression of the profound Prussian faith in the veracity of the governmental document (especially in the field of foreign policy), seen as a fundamental and trustworthy source in the narrative hermeneutic reconstruction of assumed reality.[5] Furthermore, the epistemologically oriented query as to "how it really was" identifies the objects at issue with societal normalcy.

The extent to which the historian's epistemologically oriented question implicates the particular features of a given epoch or specific object of investigation becomes clear with consideration of the historiography of the Weimar Republic. Heinrich August Winkler has pointed out that the historian of Weimar approaches his object—in general, of course, not consciously so—with a quite different purpose from the one expressed in Ranke's dictum. His curiosity directs another query to his data: namely, *Mußte es so kommen?* (was it inevitable?).[6] Was the surging of the National Socialist tide societally preprogrammed, or preordained by events? Was the transfer of power to Hitler politically inevitable?

These historians would thus appear to have their sights fixed constantly on the history of the Republic as the *pre*history of National Socialism. To that extent, the historiography of the Weimar era is engulfed, *nolens volens,* in the vortex of the subsequent Nazi period. Moreover, the question "was it inevitable?" ranges beyond a reconstruction of past reality as an object of research. Rather, the question implies a need to explore various possibilities —the alternatives to Hitler and the degree of their feasibility at the time.

In respect to Weimar, the Rankean dictum becomes a mere preliminary to the necessary enterprise of ferreting out political alternatives within the framework of societal possibilities. Dominating that historiography on Weimar are largely politically oriented questions. Controversies over commission, omission, and responsibility are quite "appropriate," and in close keeping with the historical significance of Weimar as the *political* prehistory of National Socialism. This holds true even when those questions reach into the realm of *social* history.

Where historical cognition of the Weimar Republic reflects the influence of the National Socialist period that succeeded it, we can observe a closely related and striking historiographical phenomenon in the case of Nazism proper. The historian of Nazism, in short, will direct the historian of Weimar's fundamental question, *Wie war es eigentlich möglich?* (how was it actually possible?), straight back at the central event of National Socialist rule: the mass crimes perpetrated by the regime. In both cases, that spontaneous, pretheoretical query for historiographical comprehension presupposes, in an intuitive and methodologically still unreflected fashion, a judgmental key position: namely, that crimes of such a nature and magnitude are "actually" not possible in our civilization and exceed its bounds.[7] Empirically, the events did occur, yet they elude our powers of comprehension, imagination, judgment—and, in the final analysis, even the civilizational shaping of the era's consciousness and the forms of thought that constitute it. The historian thus faces new, previously little-pondered problems of depiction and understanding. These problems cluster, in the form of omissions and distortions, around the core of the event labeled a "historical crisis." The crisis, in turn, becomes a crisis of historiography itself.

This crisis is visible in the antithetical collective perspectives that dominate historiography on the Holocaust—in the unresolvable dichotomy of perspectives between victim and perpetrator. In order to understand its nature, we must explore the specific character of the bureaucratically organized mass murder.

The specificity of this particular crime against humanity appears to lie in its radically abstract character, that is, the above-mentioned phenomenon of a project of industrial mass extermination organized along lines of highly differentiated division of labor. The historian encounters a social collective enterprise enlisting virtually every member of the *Volksgemeinschaft,* no matter how indirectly, as a participant—all those involved in the social, economic, administrative or military spheres. Or put somewhat differently, the project comprised myriad fragments of societally divided labor, often quite nonspecific, and capable of serving a wide range of possible purposes. To this extent, it was possible to be a part of the annihilation without necessarily being aware of one's participation in the overall deed.

Of central importance for the deed's historiographical reconstruction is the reality of implication in a capital crime, by means of socialization into the *Volksgemeinschaft,* in varying degrees of passive segmentation. Confronted at a later point with the deed's accomplishment, those abstractly implicated in it will not be aware of having been involved. Analogies to the production processes of highly differentiated societies immediately come to mind here. Just as the producer is alienated from his product through the division of labor, socially segmented perpetrators are alienated from their sense of political responsibility and their criminally relevant guilt—aside, of course, from those immediately and sadistically involved in the mass murder. One of the most outstanding examples of the phenomenon is the smooth functioning of the Reichsbahn within the mass-extermination process. And remarkably, the more closely the historian focuses on the abstract and labor-divided structure of the overall process of extermination, the further he moves from the horror of the deed.[8]

Efforts to approach Nazi mass murder in terms of division of labor are relatively recent. In the 1940s and 1950s historiography was so strongly marked by compelling problems of ideological criminality, and of the event's sheer horror, that no approach was possible other than one shaped by *juridical* questions—questions of crime and punishment. Reconstruction of the events was guided principally by moral and ethical motives. Epistemologically directed interest centered on questions closely bound up with the complex of individually traceable responsibility and guilt. The Nuremberg trials were not the only impetus for this approach or the basis for ensuing treatments of the phenomenon of Nazism, in terms of both documentary data and the juridically oriented perspective. Rather, the issue of guilt had such weight on its own that the corpus of Nazi documentation served more as incrimination evidence for a real tribunal of justice than as historical source material for the reconstruction and evaluation of history as such.

In the 1960s and 1970s there was a marked change in historiographical perspective. A structural approach, based on concepts drawn from sociology and political science, increasingly took precedent over the juridical perspective, focusing on individual action and responsibility. This fundamental shift in analytical angle may well have been linked to the adoption of theoretically oriented methods, centered on the work of social scientist émigrés like Franz Neumann.[9] Nonetheless, it cannot be accounted for solely in terms of the reception of specific theories—even though Hans Mommsen, in direct reference to Hannah Arendt, has elevated the formula of the "banality of evil" to a founding concept in the structural approach to Holocaust research.[10] And yet the predominantly juridical inclination of Arendt's book on Eichmann does represent a thematic milestone in the transition from a perspective seeking its historical object in individual responsibility to one focusing on an essentially depersonalized structure.

Though Arendt's Eichmann book has become a cipher for the historical and moral evaluation of Nazi crimes, as well as for the possibility of systematic mass murder in the modern era, it was not Arendt alone who inaugurated the new historiographical direction. A number of historians who offered their knowledge and expertise to the criminal courts in the 1960s and 1970s underwent a similar shift of perspective: a growing sense, while pursuing the traditional question of individual guilt, that the mass annihilation was based essentially on depersonalized, functional participation, despite numerous instances of direct individual complicity. Estrangement between criminal deed and criminal awareness formed the context in which historians took up Arendt's thesis of the "banality of evil," incorporating it into their historiographical approach.

The thesis in no way mitigated the harshness of a reality marked by massive cruelty and sadism. Such savagery was in fact not necessary for the smooth functioning of the industrial machinery of murder. On the contrary, it often proved a hindrance. The result was that *indirectly* implicated persons, despite their actions being central to the implementation of the mass extermination, were seldom charged with major criminal offenses, let alone with murder—an act requiring morally despicable qualities few wished to attach to "normal" cogs in the machine. Hence there were hardly any *murderers* in the formal juridical sense of the term, though there were excessive numbers of accomplices (*Helfershelfer*) to various degrees of segmented involvement.[11] Raul Hilberg for instance has pointed out that not a single employee of the Reichsbahn was convicted for his indispensable participation in the abstract bureaucracy of death.[12] It is also important to note that the totalitarian fog of the regime, which enveloped a political system contradicting general forms of rational bureaucratic behavior, contributed to obfuscating individual responsibility, hence any relevant guilt in a criminal sense. The opaque character of this system could not fail to have an impact on the historical reconstruction of National Socialism: reflected, as I have described it, in a methodological retreat into the description of structures.[13] In turn, this tendency reinforced a growing awareness that the governmental administrative document had forfeited part of its function as a reliable source. With the mass extermination being regarded by its administrative perpetrators as a "sensitive" area requiring bureaucratic reticence, the documentation of its planning had been concerned less with any direct record of actual decisions than, ultimately, with concealing those decisions by way of a reign of "organized chaos."[14] As a result, the instruction or order, the unauthorized personal initiative, opportunistic omission, and failure to act, entered into a barely reconstructible, obfuscated alliance, with the legitimating racial ideology looming in the background.

This historiographical perspective on National Socialist rule in general,

and the mass extermination in particular, finds itself in quite clear-cut harmony with a German collective memory inclined to play down any causal
connection between the Nazi weltanschauung (which had infected many)
and the mass extermination. Where the quasi-judicial perspective, directly
linking ideology and action, is in close harmony with the victims' picture of
experience, the perspective of the collective involved in the deed, using an
impersonal division of labor, tends to dissolve even the last remainder of
identifiable culpability into exculpatory structures. Through the use of psychological selection, it gives certain elements excessive emphasis. Doubtless,
such elements are relevant for reconstructing the total picture; but in a kind
of "subjective objectivity," they isolate components of banality inevitably
present in the division of labor necessary for the extermination process.

In its own way, the overriding monstrosity of the murder project con-
denses within the perspective of the victims into a form of complementary
objectification. And in the historiographical realm, the obvious dichotomy
between (functional, labor-divided) banality in implementation and monstrosity in individually experienced victimization reflects the fundamental
divide between two different approaches to, and presentations of, the Final
Solution. This dichotomy is doubtless one principal source for the fury of
the criticism that has been leveled at Hannah Arendt, principally by her
Jewish opponents. By coining the expression "the banality of evil," Arendt
seemingly adopted the perspective of the perpetrators, with its emphasis
on functionalities.[15] Yet in the eyes of the victims, evil was by no means limited to "banalities"—for them, in plain and simple terms, it was an absolute
monstrosity.

In a certain manner, we can understand approaches generally classified
under the rubric of social history as offering an additional mode of presentation for the period of National Socialism—but not for the mass extermination. This approach, it would appear, is more in harmony with the
specific collective experience of the German *Volksgemeinschaft*. It focuses,
necessarily, on social and economic phenomena that—though here tied up
with National Socialism—readily occur in periods before and after, thereby
neutralizing the human subject's relation to the event—hence its specific
political history. Conversely, concentration on the political implications of
Nazism as a historical rupture leads, again, to a historiography in proximity
with the perspective of Nazism's victims. For the effort to understand and
represent Nazism's meaning cannot rest content with a focus on continuity—that is, on the normal conditions through and beyond the incriminated
area—but must also consider the exceptional character of that epoch, and
its universal implications. As Fernand Braudel has indicated, social and eco-

nomic history, the history of mentalities and institutions, are oriented toward a different time span than a history centered on political developments and the unfolding of major events.[16] The former approach, extending by its very nature beyond the life spans of history's individual actors, is obliged to abstract itself from the circumstances of a historical period: from the existential experience of the historical subject. Submerged in a complex of "continuities," and mainly rooted in a subjective experience of normalcy, such an approach is, in the end, unable to grasp the extreme and exceptional phenomenon of the mass extermination.

Historians utilizing techniques of "oral history" have observed that Germans rarely frame the Nazi era within the key years 1933 and 1945 but rather make a fundamental distinction between "good times" and "bad."[17] In such periodization, the Stalingrad debacle is the watershed between "good" and "bad times," the latter continuing, significantly, beyond the end of the war until the 1948 currency reform. Such an approach has found apt scholarly expression in the scope and focus of *From Stalingrad to Currency Reform.*[18]

However little this periodization fits one based on a political history of key events, it reflects the lived experience of Germany's World War II generation. Inversely, since the *victims'* experience of suffering apparently corresponds to the political duration of the Nazi regime, their sense of historical sequence would rather accord with the standard political periodization. It is striking, however, that the historical memory of those destined to die—to great extent because they were Jewish or of Jewish ancestry—creates a periodization that, owing to the monstrosity of the intended and executed deed, will often extend beyond the twelve years of the regime, thus assuming a suprahistorical character—a phenomenon that I explore below.

Weighed down by the nightmare of the deed, consciousness desires explanations—those reconciling a collective inner world with an external world that—measured in secular rational terms—is radically incomprehensible: a reconciliation that is, of memory and history. The monstrosity of a suffering experienced individually, yet determined by belonging to a collective, leads to a transposing of the mass extermination into a context of *collective historicity:* it becomes the seemingly paradoxical phenomenon of suprahistorical consciousness. In this regard, we find the emergence of different explanatory topoi. The most frequent and striking topos is the recurrence of anti-Jewish and anti-Semitic outbreaks in Occidental history. When religiously grounded, it contributes to the formation of a liturgical memory, and to that of a *negative teleology* of the catastrophe: a teleology reverberating, already, in the words "Shoah" and "Holocaust."[19] Such a negative teleological perspective naturally lays considerable stress on a causal linkage between anti-Semitism and the mass extermination. It grants to the connection between ideology and deed a finality that, measured against the complexity of the implementation of the Final Solution, inevitably results in distorting reductions.

There can be no doubt that anti-Semitism lies at the heart of the Nazi weltanschauung, and of the Nazi genocide. But for the Jewish victims, the latter not only reflects an ideological context but follows a practical program—the outcome of a causal chain stretching from the anti-Semitic measures of 1933 to the Nuremberg laws of 1935 and *Reichskristallnacht*—and intensifies the pattern of traditional pogroms in a qualitative jump to mass extermination in 1941. But in the end, despite its apparently clear-cut nature, the Holocaust historian can hardly rest with such a schema, which fails to fully and specifically explain how *human beings* as such, regardless of their cultural-ethnic or "racial" origin, could in fact be sent like freight for systematic mass annihilation. With anti-Semitism as cultural-historical matrix, the ground for the shift from "normal" anti-Jewish measures to extermination was prepared by another motif in its syncretistic ideology: the motif of euthanasia.[20] The Nazi policy of ending "life not worthy of living" (*lebensunwertes Leben*) can be viewed as an ideologically blinkered effort to use biology to resolve social problems. At a time when the Jewish question was considered "solvable" within the framework of a policy of emigration and expulsion, a large number of citizens of the Reich had already been forcibly sterilized in the framework of legal programs; it was only a small step from such eugenics to the medical murder of tens of thousands of individuals defined, in one way or another, as handicapped or retarded.

In turn, mechanized mass murder can be understood as a continuation of such eugenically based extermination. There is, in fact, ample evidence of such a continuum, most obviously in the transfer of the personnel of Aktion T4 from the Reich eastward in the framework of Aktion Reinhard. It reveals an anti-Semitism originally geared toward expulsion fused with the perverted medical ethos of the euthanasia program.[21] Yet we would be misguided to argue that the annihilation of the Jews was an *inevitable* consequence of "practical" eugenics, despite all the Nazi rhetoric about *Schädlinge* (human pests) and *Untermenschen*.[22] "Science" and biological racist ideology had a preparatory function, lowering the threshold of what was considered permissible to a crucial degree; the deed itself, however, evolved much more from conditions established by the Nazis for *anti-Semitic* reasons, that is, the barbaric concentration of Jews in the east, conditions that—as we noted in the previous chapter—they "rectified" using measures grounded in social and racial "hygienics": factory-like murder on a mass scale. Nonetheless, even acknowledging this crucial juncture between traditional anti-Semitism and radical eugenics, we would be misguided here, as well, to grant it a "final" causal status. We need only note the absence of any murder program in a number of countries where anti-Semitism was sometimes as virulent as in Germany—these countries also having many doctors and scientists who believed fervently in "racial hygiene." Moreover, it is enough to point to the notorious tradition of eugenics that evolved in both Scandinavia and North America to show the limits of any linkage between Auschwitz and the spirit of social and racial hygienics. After all, in the United States during the 1920s and 1930s, some 30,000 persons were forcibly sterilized for "eugenic" reasons, without this culminating in any mass extermination of life "not worthy of living." In order, then, to grasp the historical *specificity* of Nazi mass murder, we need in the end to return to a sphere of political action and personal accountability: to a specificity resting within the political-historical constellation at the time.

To recall our preliminary point, the intuitive historiographical query directed toward National Socialism is not "how it really was" but rather "how was it actually possible?" This is the motif shaping historical cognition: it stresses the universal historical crisis that indeed was marked by the advent of National Socialism, though without the presence of major changes in society and consciousness such as were engendered by the Reformation and the French Revolution. What characterizes the crisis must be decoded through a specific, though simultaneously universalizing, context of experience.[23]

As I argue at length in chapter 6, we have such a context, paradoxically, in an eminently particularistic historical empirical phenomenon: that of the Judenrat. For in our close look at that institution as defining a particular situation we saw that it encapsulated the experience of perpetrator *and* victim, as well as making manifest a dynamic charged with both banality *and* monstrosity. Although the official Jewish representative body in dealings with the Nazis, the Judenrat was likewise a mediating agency of National Socialist will—one that utilized Jews in its dealings with Jews. Here, in the interlinked opposing wills, in the Jewish elders' need to *think* the Nazis, and through its very specificity, the council brings us to the center of the phenomenology of mass extermination. In this manner, by examining the reactions and behavior of Jewish councils, we approach the content of a "historical crisis" that has remained invisible. This is what has been referred to as a crisis of universally valid, action-guiding forms of thought—in this case, forms based on a ruthless enemy's presumed utility orientation and desire for self-preservation, or *traditional evil.*

The "historical crisis" represented by National Socialism nullifies that rationality of action—a rationality on which society and its functioning continues to be based. Precisely because such rationality is the cognitive building block of our *Lebenswelt*, our world of lived experience, the crisis is scarcely comprehensible—and then only through the psyche of the victims. Beyond this, the indispensability of rationality produces in its wake a persistent phenomenon of denial: a relegation of industrialized extermination, and the radical boundary experience of its victims, to mnemonic oblivion. Such forgetting underscores the function, for our post-Auschwitz culture, of a historiography that in its particularity and universalism, strives to adequately confront the radically negative deed.

PART III

Holocaust Narratives

TEN

Varieties of Narration

The Holocaust in Historical Memory

History and memory are commonly viewed as antithetical. Historical research is rightly skeptical about evidence recycled, as a purported reflection of reality, by memory. After all, sciences base their claims to verity on time-tested instruments of knowing and proof, a gamut ranging from source criticism to the densely aggregated fields of discourse and debate on method and epistemology. Nonetheless, historiography cannot escape the confrontation with memory, which represents a world that relativizes, and hence undermines, scholarship's claims to universal validity. The present chapter offers some reflections on the interrelationship of historiography and memory within an event still struggling to find its proper locus in historical research: the Holocaust.

In his major work on Europe from 1815 to the present, the American doyen of German history, Gordon A. Craig, makes no mention whatsoever of the Nazi Final Solution, the destruction of the Jews of Europe.[1] Such an omission cries out for explanation. After all, Craig is certainly not one of those historians who deliberately bypass the Holocaust, denying it any serious significance. In his many publications, he has often given ample space to such topics as Jewish emancipation and the contortions of anti-Semitism; and elsewhere he has written about the Nazi Final Solution, even though he does not claim any special expertise on the topic.

How, then, can we account for this seemingly anomalous omission in his comprehensive study of European history in modern times? Is this a simple oversight, sheer neglect, a moment of scholarly laxity of no further import?

By asking this, I do not intend to treat the omission as scandalous or even to hint at some deeper, unconscious motivations. Rather, my query precedes from what would seem to be a plausible assumption: namely, that Craig's neglect of the Holocaust in this book is rooted in the far more fundamental factors that shape research—the systematic preliminary decisions a historian makes; the perspective and periodization, the preferred method and narrative structures that he or she chooses to stand by.

Historiography is always "situated." And there are various contextual clues suggesting that the omission of the mass murder of European Jewry in Craig's work reflects its overall layout and structure. It can be argued that his perspective on European history of the nineteenth and twentieth centuries, and the closely linked periodization that such a perspective entails, necessarily predisposed him to sidestep the Holocaust. The fact is that in his presentation of European history over the last two centuries, he develops a historical systematization that is thoroughly Anglo-American in stamp and stance.

An inveterately "Anglo-American" perspective on German and Continental history does not somehow necessarily omit the Holocaust or give short shrift to the Jewish catastrophe. Nonetheless, considerable evidence supports the assumption that, in reconstructing historical events, an Anglo-centered historiography of German and European history in modern times tends to proceed from a set of preliminary "blueprinting" tendencies that seriously impede the integration of the Holocaust into its thematic framework.[2] A case in point is the preference for a scheme of periodization that conjoins the nineteenth and twentieth centuries into a single epoch.

Historians reared in a Continental tradition are far less likely to splice the two centuries into a conjunct age. After all, seen from their shared perspective, the centuries appear quite dissimilar. In the light of the succeeding catastrophic era, the nineteenth century seems like a veritable epitome of optimism, a promise of the forward march of history. The contrast is clear, even stark: on the one hand, the age of industrialization and the emergence of nation-states, democratization and the genesis of parliamentary government, positivism and the belief in progress; on the other, that dark concatenation of events encompassing two world wars, mass murder, and totalitarian experimentation with human nature.[3]

Of course, what can be characterized vaguely as an Anglo-American periodization does not profess agnosticism in the face of the cataclysms of European history—in any event, not when it comes to an assessment of their moral dimension. But its perspective is likely to generate a slew of distinct emphases. For example, the distance from the Continental vortex of events that is scrupulously maintained by the historical naval nation and manifested in the principle of the *balance of power* also has implications for historiography, informing analogous patterns of interpretation. It holds in particular for the characteristic approach to political, diplomatic, and military history that pervades classical British historiography. In turn, associated images of history mold perceptions that increasingly have their own logical consequences, producing a context of interpretation manifest in method as well as in topic selection. And it is in this choice of both methodology and theme that the distant stance of the imperial sea power toward the Continent and its convulsions exerts its influence. In short, the high-relief distinction between the optimism of the nineteenth century and the catastrophes of our own age, consonant with Continental memory, tends in the British perception to be flattened down, abraded to relative inconsequence.

Thus, it should not be surprising if Craig's oeuvre is geared to historical preconceptions of a type quite different from those predominating among Continental historians. After all, the design of any historical project is always linked to some paradigmatic perspective. And to a significant degree, that very perspective is shaped by the primacy of power politics, that is, the primacy of the principle of balance. Such a perception has a long reach, stretching at least from the Napoleonic wars and the subsequent reorganization of Europe by the 1815 Congress of Vienna, to the foundation of the Second (Wilhelminian) Reich, the ravages of the Great War, and Hitler's totalitarian claim to continental hegemony. It thus catalyzes and constructs an image of history with massive implications for the analysis of political behavior, especially that concerning Nazi Germany. True, the British image of Germany was imbued with a view of Prussia that originated in the nineteenth century, but it was then also projected onto the Third Reich—as though that polity were a hegemonic power of the traditional type, albeit an inordinately aggressive variant.[4]

Craig's image of history does not simply follow these lines. Nonetheless, the interpretive scheme that he employs to analyze the history of political events does follow the general thrust of such a paradigmatic mode. To that extent, the structure of his historical narrative participates in a culturally biased view of Prussia—and hence of Nazi Germany—as, above all, a fundamental threat to the principle of the balance of power. Seen from such an angle, a conflation of the nineteenth and twentieth centuries into a single epoch in European history hardly requires revision.

A perspective so tilted toward the history of power politics and the centrality of balance does provide a useful lens in the sense that it can meaningfully interpret and give a congruent treatment to diverse chains of events in European history. Yet there is a major drawback specifically pertaining to Nazi Germany: if, in view of the enormity of its crimes, Nazism holds a specific significance in the universal history of mankind, a perspective founded merely on the concept of power relations becomes exceedingly problematic. At the very least, the view of Nazi rule as a culmination of Prussian history vitiates the explanatory meaning of long lines of continuity. Through such a contorting aperture, the specifics of Nazism blur and disappear. Examples of such a sharply angled perception are legion, among them Britain's tragic underestimation—on various occasions—of the extent of Prussian-German military opposition to Hitler. Attempts to establish contact with that opposition foundered in some measure as a result of Britain's blinkered and negative image of Prussia.[5]

Easy acceptance of such continuities could only have a dramatic impact on views of the Holocaust, both during and since the Second World War— whose very designation suggests a straight continuation of the Great War, a further phase in the traditional struggle for hegemony in Europe. Perceptions of this sort contributed to the tendency, then as now, to marginalize events, such as the mass killing at Auschwitz and elsewhere, that took place beyond the frame of military action. Industrialized mass extermination was covered up by the images of warfare; that Auschwitz was not bombed by the Allies in 1944 reflected in part the fact that the fate of European Jewry remained hidden behind the filters of the logic of war.[6]

Again in the Allied judiciary's treatment of Nazi crimes and criminals after the war, the Anglo-American view of Nazi Germany as an extension and apotheosis of Prussia pointed in a similar direction. From the outset at the Nuremberg tribunal, the overriding concern was far more to punish those Germans held responsible for a war of aggression as well as for war crimes and crimes against humanity committed *during* the war proper, rather than to examine the genocide against the Jews and other victims of systematic atrocities perpetrated *beyond* those parameters. The breakup of Prussia by Allied decree in February 1947 also dovetailed with that anachronistic tradition that views Nazi Germany as the caretaker of the Borussian *Machtstaat*.

Thus, the design of historical surveys such as Craig's *Europe Since 1815*, based on a peculiarly British periodization, points to the fact that longstanding narrative traditions are intricately woven into the web of historiography. It becomes clear that memory and history should be seen not as outright antitheses but rather as variant expressions—differing in density —of a narrative structure that is common and antecedent to both.

The primary focus here is not on British memory and historiography. I note their striking distance from the Holocaust mainly in order to stress one basic point: the proximity of collective memories and popular images of history to their congruous types of historiography. By elaborating on the previous chapter's distinction between German experience and Jewish suffering, I now intend to explore the meaning of this linkage for political cultures far more directly affected by the Holocaust. It is doubtless insufficient to claim that historiographical narratives derive solely from the historian's rootedness in a given "ethnic," national, or other collective belonging. The precepts of historical methodology and the criteria imposed by the discipline cannot, with all their complexity and universality, simply be shaped by the demands of collective memory. Yet the opposite claim is no less problematic; it would be excessively rationalistic to ignore the impress of traditional and group memories on historiography. Especially at those critical junctures where mere empirical evidence, the putative historical facts, enter the flow of the narrative, variant experience tends to produce critical divergencies in historical interpretation. And in questions of cause and causality, this tendency becomes still more acute. The historian works by and large under the impact of group remembrances that generally differ in terms of their duration and rates of decay. Their impact strongly influences the way in which the historian represents the events and circumstances of the past.[7]

As far as the narratives termed "German" or "Jewish" are concerned, there is much evidence for the claim that the different approaches are molded along the patterns of a courtroom discourse. True, the thrust toward justificatory narratives is not confined to the issue of the Holocaust: it lies at the basis of most historical writing. Yet this tendency becomes accentuated in the face of such an extreme event as the Holocaust and its moral backdrop.

Courtroom discourse is generally characterized by a juxtaposition of long- and short-term recollections. The fact that the plaintiff's memory usually reaches further back in time than the more modest recollections of the defendant is taken into due account, as is reflected by certain procedural structures of the trial. Peter Burke stresses the judicial character of patterns of historical memory by recalling that, in England in the early modern period, there was an official (known as the "remembrancer") whose job it was to repeatedly remind a debtor of the necessity to pay his debt. His function was to assure that, for the sake of social peace, the still-outstanding claims would not be forgotten.[8]

Collective memory is similarly marked by differing degrees of durability. Peter Burke distinguishes between nations with a long, as opposed to a short, memory span. The Irish, Poles, Serbs, and Jews are generally assigned to the former category, with the British, French, and Germans being placed in the latter. Despite all differences between the individual and the collective, it is evident that even on the level of shared sentiments, the creditor's claims clash with the defensiveness of the debtor. This discrepancy is clearly evident for historiography in general, and for the Holocaust in particular.

Indeed, at the earliest stage of the confrontation with the mass crimes of the Nazis, there stood a *trial*. And the Nuremberg tribunal probably influenced the later historiography of Nazism more than any other postwar event, its judicial structure exerting a tremendous impact on the collection and systematic sorting of materials, and later, on the basic patterns of historical argument. To be sure, the parallel with trial discourse requires careful nuancing. After all, those who write history must conform to the rules of a discipline; they are expected to offer a rational analysis that tempers the influence of collective biographical experience. Hence it would be inaccurate to simply posit an adversarial polarity between "German" and "Jewish" memory.

Nonetheless, the basic outlines of a courtroom-like structure emerge quite clearly when we pursue a lurking suspicion: namely, that the intentionalist school of research on Nazism and the Holocaust is ultimately claiming culpability. Which is to say, as I defined it at several earlier points, that this tendency in research is more consonant with the memory of the victims, whereas the structuralist or functionalist approach seems more in harmony with German memory. Such recollection tends toward a certain leniency, befitting a behavior more in the realm of negligence than culpability.[9]

By dint of its negative "radicality," generating an exceptional divergence in the choice of perspectives, the Holocaust seems to differ fundamentally from other historical events. This radicality emanates from various elements in the cataclysm: the relative swiftness of the mass murder; the large number of victims; the special modes of killing, and, above all, the locus of the murder in a zone beyond warfare and lacking any apparent meaning when measured by previous historical experience. Such characteristics cannot help but have an impact on historical narration. At first glance it may appear a paradox, but gauged in terms of the victims' experience, Auschwitz *has* no appropriate narrative, only a set of statistics. And this fact is consonant with an entire complex of phenomena centered on its negative radicality. One such phenomenon is the extreme relationship between *time* and *number*. The singular slaughter of millions took place in an extremely short period of less than four years; and if the industrial mass destruction is taken as the actual core of Auschwitz—leaving to one side such events as the mass killings by the Einsatzgruppen in the early phase and the death marches

toward the end of the war—then the actual span of the Holocaust is con-
tracted still more, to the period from the spring or summer 1942 to the autumn of 1944.

Characterizing Auschwitz as an administrative and industrial event entails far more than just condemning it as particularly reprehensible. To classify the mass murder in this way is to emphasize the *standardized* nature of
death, a repetition of one and the same action for weeks, months, and years.
The metaphor of statistics thus becomes cauterized into the negative icon
of the six million. Beyond its mere empirical meaning, this figure symbol-
izes the appropriate narrative, which the event itself lacks.

Given Auschwitz's *un*narratability, the vacuum fills with surrogate tales
possessing an epic structure. This epic form evokes a reversal to what seem
familiar, historical images and recollections, those pointing to an antecedent remembrance. Thus, the history of the Warsaw ghetto uprising, although peripheral in its importance when measured against the atrocious-
ness and scope of the administrative and industrial mass murder, takes on
the meaning of a narrative that substitutes for what cannot be properly re-
counted. In view of the statistical vacuum that Auschwitz creates for posterity, the uprising provides a compensatory tale.

Moreover, for Jewish memory, the absence of a narrative appropriate to
the event leads to the historical phenomenon or mode of consciousness
that can be termed *compressed time*.[10] In other words, in place of a historical
representation of the Holocaust comes a narrative that concentrates mostly
on its real or supposed prehistory, that is, on the history of anti-Semitism.
That narrative is as long as it is ramified. Analogous to a negative teleology,
it is able to shift the enormous, unnarratable weight of the Holocaust back
to a temporal continuum emerging from the distant past. It can, however
interpreted, imbue the event with meaning. Among the various Jewish narratives of anti-Semitism, one stands out in particular: that of Jewry in the
Polish lands. The Polish-Jewish relationship has such particular salience because its patterns became, by and large, the dominant form of narration for
Jews in general after 1945. Its principal distinguishing mark is that everyday
Polish anti-Semitism, experienced historically in *concrete* terms over longer
periods of time, comes to represent the basically *abstract* and short-term
phenomenon of Nazi mass murder. In the interests of continuity and narrativity, the historical experience of Eastern European Jewry becomes the
common narrative providing the images that illustrate the Holocaust.[11] A
strange conflation results. The Holocaust committed by Nazi Germany becomes somehow placed in a framework of narration that is clearly outside

its causal scope and empirical explication. In short, the history of the Holocaust becomes largely integrated into the history of experienced everyday anti-Semitism.

Though structured along substantially different lines, the motif of anti-Semitism is also salient in the attempts characteristic of non-Jewish memory to represent the Holocaust and come to terms with it. Beyond all other specificities, the event assumes a special importance because of the fact that its main victims were persons of *Jewish* descent. This fact does not automatically assign the Jewish victims some kind of superior moral standing, as compared with other victims of Nazism. Rather, it holds an important psychological and cultural fact: namely that the Jews continue to occupy a special place in Western consciousness. And no matter how secular its external configuration, it still largely attaches to layers of perception with a sacral and Christian content. Partly for this reason the mass murder of the Jews appears to touch deeper emotional and psychological cords than the victimization of others by the Nazi machinery of destruction. The "significance of the Jews" still poses an urgent existential problem for Western self-understanding.

In its own turn, this deeper dimension calls forth Gentile memories located far before the concrete historical event. Imbued with quasi-mythical, suprahistorical images, these memories form a subliminal source for endowing the Holocaust with powerfully symbolic meaning. Such mythic interpretations have their own validity, acknowledging the reality of anti-Semitism as a major aspect of European history. In this fashion, a sense of guilt pervades the process of coping with the enormity of the mass annihilation. Its articulation follows the form of confession, or of mere defense.

A deed such as the Nazi mass extermination, implemented with bureaucratic and industrial efficiency, and thus based on a high degree of division of labor, induces a massive sense of distance in the perspective of the perpetrators—a dissociation from any adequate sense of personal responsibility. Yet this dissociation is repudiated—massively so—by the existential experience of the victims. For them, the effect of the extermination, based on a mobilization of an entire society, takes on an immediate concrete form, absolutely monstrous both in its intrinsic enormity and in terms of individual personal suffering.[12] After all, as we observed, the purpose and meaning of the administrative and industrial annihilation was precisely to interpose emotional distance between perpetrators and victims, in order to make it easier for the former to kill indiscriminately. And such an organizational form of mass murder had its intended results, those implicated in the collective outrages remaining relatively well shielded from any *individual* sense of guilt. However, in a compensatory shift mediated by collective memory and belonging, that guilt has come to be felt all the more by later generations. In Germany today, it is a conspicuous component of public culture and public ritual.

Historiography must thus acknowledge a split between what I described in the previous chapter as antipodal worlds of experience: banality on the side of the perpetrators and monstrosity on the side of the victims. It is unlikely there will soon be any reconstruction of Auschwitz that can splice the two worlds of experience together. As suggested, Hannah Arendt's apparent choice of the world of banality over that of monstrosity was cause for the accusation leveled against her of having betrayed the Jewish people. In her report on the Eichmann trial, Arendt was intent on repudiating the Jewish historical narrative as developed by Gideon Hausner, the Israeli chief prosecutor: a narrative grounded in a bleak and fatalistic perception of Jewish history in the diaspora, and in a conception of anti-Semitism as virtually suprahistorical in character and scope—indeed, a negative teleology of Jewish experience. What provoked the anger of Arendt's Jewish critics was the fact that in addressing such a historical interpretation, she offered a historical narrative of her own that universalized the crime by marginalizing anti-Semitism.

Anti-Semitism as the pivotal factor behind the Holocaust is undoubtedly at the core of the historical narrative most attuned to the experience of the victims. The *longue durée* in the Jewish experience of anti-Jewish sentiment is congruent with a view of the Holocaust as premeditated. And this focus clearly gives rise to a narrative in the form of a prosecutor's brief. The most prominent recent version of such a narrative is the controversial and much discussed work by Daniel Goldhagen, *Hitler's Willing Executioners.*[13] Goldhagen constructs the history of the Holocaust as springing from a deeply ingrained and long-existent German anti-Semitism—an anti-Semitism of an annihilistic nature. In order to emphasize an extreme hatred that supposedly animated the perpetrators, Goldhagen focuses selectively on specific events involving an immediate physical proximity of the murderer to their victims. These include the massacres committed by police reserve battalions, which he describes in copious detail, and the death marches in the final phase of the war. But for the same reason, Goldhagen refrains from presenting a description of the Final Solution in its more narrow sense:

namely, the assembly-line gassing of millions of Jews, based on division of labor and on technical rationalization; the kind of industrial killing that does not require any emotional involvement.

Seen against the backdrop of an evolving historiography, his theses invite a reading in counterpoint to Arendt's in *Eichmann in Jerusalem*. Where Arendt underscores the banality of the events—semantically proximate, already, to the zone of assembly-line murder—Goldhagen shifts the spotlight back to purported anti-Semitic motives of the perpetrators. To that extent, his narrative of the past draws close to that shaped by Jewish memory. It is, of course, questionable whether anti-Semitism in itself offers a sufficient explanation of the perpetrators' motives. Indeed, the approach exemplified by Goldhagen blurs distinctions between the diverse layers of motivation behind the anti-Jewish actions. Some agents of mass murder doubtless acted according to traditional anti-Jewish revulsions, others—regardless of their innermost convictions—according to Nazi ideology in which the Jews loomed large as the very epitome of the enemy. But a great many others made natural use of the Jews or the Jewish question, and its ideological importance for the regime, as a ticket to advancement—an opportunism or careerism that, in any society, is always amoral. The anti-Semitism of conviction that Goldhagen musters for his argumentative onslaught is far too erratic to be serviceable as a unitary mapping of the road to Auschwitz. Such reservations notwithstanding, Goldhagen offers a valuable contribution to the further course of Holocaust research, challenging readers and researchers to a long overdue reorientation of perspective. His book represents one response to a dominant, antithetical tendency in Holocaust historiography: a tendency to vault past the Holocaust's Jewish victims in their existential and historical status as victims chosen for death only because they were Jews.

In lieu of anti-Semitism, various possibilities attempt to explain the path to genocide. Götz Aly, for instance, seems now to have moved away from his earlier "economistic" approach that (as we saw it) defines the Jews as victims of totally blind processes geared to rationalization and maximization of gain. His new interpretive framework is, in fact, the almost precise reverse of Goldhagen's. Where Goldhagen focuses on anti-Jewish hatred, on the police battalions and the death marches, Aly takes up the Nazi policy of *Flurbereinigung* as executed in the Warthegau region of Posen and the contiguous parts of Poland that were incorporated into the Reich.[14] Here again, we find a careful shift of emphasis away from a specific anti-Jewish policy executed by the Nazis. Aly now highlights, properly, not only the expulsion of Poles into the Generalgouvernement but also the "resettlement" of ethnic

Germans into the vacated areas. In order to place Nazi policy in the context of "ethnic cleansing" and define genocide as the ultimate consequence of such actions, Aly underplays the broader context surrounding his key year of 1940: namely, the German anti-Jewish measures in the 1930s—the systematic exclusion and forced emigration from Germany and Austria—as well as the murderous actions begun in summer 1941 against the Jews on Soviet territory. It is crucial to note that the massacre and genocide of Jews here *preceded* the mass murder of Polish Jewry. In any event, an immediate linkage—insinuating direct causation—between the early "ethnic cleansing," the subsequent ghettoization, and the later annihilation of Jews in the Polish areas not connected to "Barbarossa" is in the end unconvincing. In order to paper over the apparent lack of causal elements, Aly offers his readers a kind of chronology in each chapter, lumping together sundry developments of the time, whatever their proximity might actually signify. Such a surrogate for causality is meant to disguise an inability to prove what Aly's thesis asserts: the centrality of the early "ethnic cleansing" operations for the Final Solution.

A closer look at Aly's work reveals a particularly troubling thesis. As he sees it, Germans brought in from the Sovietized Baltic and Bessarabia and resettled *into* the Warthegau were just as much victims of population politics as the Poles and Jews resettled *out* of the region. In the logistics of the resettlement policy, Aly finds an overriding uniformity: the trains rumbled on indifferently, transporting Poles, Jews, and ethnic Germans to and fro. From there he need take only a short step to include the problem of the expulsions of the Germans from vast areas of East-Central and Eastern Europe at the end of the war within this same syndrome. And however real and terrible the suffering of Germans who were driven from their homes, to link their fate conceptually with the evolution of policies of mass annihilation so significant for European Jewry is rather problematic. In the context of Aly's own, hidden narrative, there is a suggestion of covert rivalry between victims' recollections—a rivalry challenging the historical memory of the Jews as central victims of the Holocaust.[15] And such a rivalry touches on the problem of German *guilt*.

Conflict in Holocaust interpretation and representation arises principally from questions of *continuity* and *causality*. In the historical construction, an approach embracing the perspective of the victims will stress an immediate connection between an intention to destroy expressed long before the act, and the measures that actually led to the destruction. Generally, such an interpretation will find support in key documents—most notably, the corpus of German archives, consisting in large part of the materials amassed at Nuremberg—that dramatize the judicial character of the historical discourse. Such documents may be especially suitable in proving deliberate, criminal intent or culpability. Yet in the light of present-day research, they appear to have only limited value in the reconstruction of the historical *circumstances* that led to the Holocaust. Among the fundamental documents suggesting a direct link between intention, decision, and realization are, for example, the Euthanasia Decree issued by Hitler in September 1939; Hermann Göring's note to Reinhard Heydrich dated July 31, 1941, empowering him to execute the Final Solution in the territories occupied by Germany; and the minutes of the Wannsee Conference on January 20, 1942.

In actuality, these documents pose interpretive difficulties not entirely dissimilar to the blueprints of the Nazi "brain trusters." The theories propounding a direct link between the intention expressed in the documents and the mass murder proceed from a supposition that the actions of decision makers in the Nazi Reich were consonant with rational administrative behavior. If such rationality occupies the foreground, the question of personal responsibility becomes irrelevant. By its very nature, however, such an approach fails to take into account the fragmented, polycratic reality of Nazi rule. Thus, the Euthanasia Decree was not only written on Hitler's private stationery but was actually backdated to the beginning of the war on September 1, apparently for the sake of intervention in a dispute between the führer's subordinates over the spheres of their authority.[16] Similarly, the memo from Göring to Heydrich bears a dubious date (July 31)—one that, like September 1 on the Euthanasia Decree, does not reflect any particular conjunction of events; it was prepared by Eichmann on Heydrich's order, to be endorsed by Göring. Finally, the Wannsee Conference was originally planned for December 9, 1941, but was postponed and finally rescheduled for six weeks later, in order to take place, not in Heydrich's office, but in an unofficial site, the Wannsee Villa, and not during usual working hours, but at noon. All of the carefully choreographed details had their purpose: to impress upon the assembled bureaucrats, representing party and state officials, that Heydrich was empowered with special authority over the Final Solution to the Jewish question in all parts of Europe under German control—that he was entitled to intervene at will wherever he desired. For Heydrich, the Jewish issue had metamorphosed into a currency of power and influence within the region's framework. Indeed, it sounds convincing that no decision had to be taken in regard to the execution of the Final Solution; the extermination of the Jews was long underway when the bureaucrats met in Berlin. The mass slaughter seems, in short, hardly a process reconstructible by reference to planned, rational bureaucratic action by a central agency or government. It seems rather the result of continuous radicalization, nourished by different sources at the periphery as well as at the center of power. And the decision to exterminate seems even more plausibly the outcome of the Nazi agencies' practical inability to find a way out of the dead ends into which they had maneuvered themselves.[17]

And yet. Even in the absence of unambiguous causality, to interpret the destruction of Europe's Jews exclusively as a consequence of mere negligence, of unpremeditated action, is unacceptable to Jewish memory. The testimony of experience is too insistent. Jewish consciousness profoundly opposes any tendency to situate the Jewish victims in some locus beyond the fact of their being Jews. After all, they were murdered arbitrarily not as human beings, but as Jews, and the survivors often owed their lives to a deception about their ethnic origin. How, then, can we account for the trend toward "universalization" of the Holocaust, toward its sanitizing through "humanization"?[18] For a start, we note that the desire at work here is less to explore and illuminate the murder of the Jews, so burdensome to consciousness, than to develop a far less binding critique of civilization and its discontents, framed largely in anthropological, not historical, terms. And that critique centers on a historiographically misconceived universalization of what transpired in the Holocaust: misconceived insofar as it appropriates the event not so much for the sake of understanding past reality, as for that of discovering potentialities for mass murder in the present and the future.

Such an approach amounts to a strategy of avoidance. Its triggers, so it seems, are subliminal narrative structures, bearing, in fact, a strong similarity to classic structures familiar from the tradition of theological disputation between Christians and Jews—between a Judaism universalized into Christianity, on the one hand, and the particularistic self-understanding embodied in the concept of God's chosen people, on the other. The concept of God's elect stands in stark opposition to the Christologic repudiation of that conception.[19]

These anterior structures of remembrance and narrative are manifest in the now notorious antagonism between Jewish and Polish memory, reflected with cyclical regularity in both recurrent rituals of remembering and Holocaust historiography. The Poles view themselves within a deep-seated mnemonic framework—that of the chosen people of Christ—a martyrologic tradition clashing with the even longer-term memory of the Jews. This contrast spills over into historiography and even into book titles. Thus, we find the standard work by the Israeli historians Israel Gutman and Shmuel Krakowski on Poles and Jews during World War II entitled *Unequal Victims: Poles and Jews During World War Two,* and Richard C. Lucas's work *The Forgotten Holocaust: Poles Under German Occupation 1939–1944* is obviously an attempt to redress a perceived imbalance.[20]

In the end, the "Jewish" and "German" approaches to the historiographical reconstruction of the Holocaust differ as much as do the memories of Germans and Jews with regard to the actual historical events. Jewish historiographical memory tends to view the mass murder from a certain telescopic distance, in order to set it against the backdrop of major political developments and ideological commitments: to view it from, so to speak, the perspective of *intention.* A reconstruction congruent with the German experience will largely focus on everyday life, on images leaning toward the trivial and accidental—in other words, on *negligence.* Put more bluntly: reeling from the enormity of the event, Jewish memory feels more adequately reflected by a *macro*perspective in its representation of the Holocaust. And indeed, it is far more plausible to symbolize the complex process that led to the disaster by consideration of the great historical ruptures, the incisive political shifts, and the overt ideological programs than by recourse to contingent circumstance. The "German" *micro*perspective tends to dissolve the total picture into its seemingly trivial constituent parts.[21]

Memory and historical method, then, interconnect—in any event, more so than most Holocaust historiography cares to admit. There may be a link between this fact and the meaning of Auschwitz for the present and future: an event of veritable *supra*historical importance whose impact does not weaken as time passes. Yet the linkage does not relieve historians of their obligation to utilize conscientiously all tools available to reconstruct the past. After all, this is the homage that history owes to memory.

ELEVEN

Nazism and Stalinism

On Memory, Arbitrariness, Labor, and Death

In his book on the origins, progress, and effects of the forced collectivization and mass starvation inflicted on the Soviet Union in the early 1930s, Robert Conquest frequently resorts to images and metaphors generally reserved for Nazi mass atrocities to open his account of the widespread suffering in the Ukraine.[1] He writes, for instance, that over the Ukrainian expanses "a vast Belsen" extended in all directions: one fourth of the Ukraine's population—men, women, children—displaced there; wasted figures, merely distorted shadows of their former selves. As in Belsen, we read, well-nourished policemen and special units of the Party ruled over their victims. And the parallel extends from such suffering to its consequences: decades later, the author encountered individuals who, having haphazardly escaped the Ukraine's horror, were ridden with the same "survivor's guilt" familiar in the context of the Nazi death camps.

On methodological grounds alone, the equivalence Conquest proposes between Nazi and Stalinist mass murder is highly interesting. We find, for example, the use of a later event to evaluate an earlier one—something quite unusual in historiographical praxis. Such an approach points to the transhistorical and iconic meaning of the Nazi crimes for the Western, which is to say secular Christian, consciousness. The image at the center of Conquest's analogy, endowed with historical authenticity, is rather misleading. For a start, his effort to view the Nazi mass-murder project through the lens of "Belsen" is based on an illusion. As authentic as it was, the image British cameras captured with the liberation of the Bergen-Belsen concentration camp in April 1945 did not reflect what had occurred on location, in the Nazi camps on German soil. By and large, the wasted, expiring figures captured on celluloid were in fact individuals who had been driven, in brutal death marches, from the east—including Auschwitz—into the German Reich in the war's final weeks and days. The camera's image thus fuses separate complexes of Nazi criminality: the world of the concentration camp and that of the various death camps in the east. But the universe of Nazi horror has become iconized in the metaphor of liberated Bergen-Belsen. Since the site of Auschwitz lacks equivalent representation, the images from Bergen-Belsen have come to be identified with the cipher "Auschwitz."

The iconographic inscription of historical images, its grip on consciousness, influences the nature of historical interpretation. The distinction eradicated in Conquest's image of Belsen, between concentration camp and death camp, is profoundly relevant for establishing criteria of difference between the twentieth century's most significant crimes against humanity, those of National Socialism and of Stalinism. For this reason, it is not so much the inevitable error, captured in celluloid, of the "Belsen" image that merits our attention, as, in fact, the theoretical implications of the equivalency implied by the error—implications emerging from the image's metaphysical meaning. The import of his historical glance back at Belsen as a displaced reference to Auschwitz lies, for Conquest, precisely in a postulated equivalency between such crimes against humanity: the author's interest glides over the starved faces peering over a German concentration camp's barbed wire—Hitler's deed; the faces serve as a stigmatizing reference to other barbarities—here, those of Stalin.

Beyond any specific assessment of Conquest's study, the idea of an analogy between Nazi and Stalinist crimes would seem by no means invalid—rather called for. And yet a sense of doubt accompanies all willingness to grant the analogy. On the one hand, such doubt reflects a general awareness of the inflationary dimensions that have come to distinguish the rhetorical appropriation of Nazism's horror to define all kinds of political evil, with "Auschwitz" achieving major success as their standard metaphor. On the other, the doubt stubbornly gravitates around more concrete questions like the following: what is the goal of historical consciousness in formulating such an analogy? Is there not more at stake than mere empirical curiosity—a narrative whose significance lies elsewhere than the bare facts on which the analogy is based? The evaluation of *each* crime in relation to the other appears to link them to a deep-seated, complex network of presumptions about the Nazis' principal victims, the Jews. The premise, embedded within such analogical discourse, that Stalin's crimes were, if not worse than

Hitler's, at least as bad, points to another, buried connection, one defining any empirical comparison of mass murders as mere material for a profoundly anchored historical *theological* subtext: the juxtaposition of Judaism and Christianity.

From this perspective we recognize that once instrumentalized and universalized, the Nazi mass murder is robbed of the historical meaning specifically its own: a meaning that emerges—like the universal "Auschwitz" citation itself—from a particular, secularized Christian cultural backdrop. For clearly, by virtue of the significance held by Judaism in the long-term historical memory of the secular Christian West, the implications of the crime represented by "Auschwitz" cannot be equated with, say, the number of victims alone. Rather, something akin to a transhistorical stigma is being defined here. To this extent, beyond its own empirical claims, the project of analogizing and contrasting two monstrous crimes against humanity can be considered an effort, marked by a pronounced paucity of self-awareness, to offer some relief for the universal Christian consciousness in relation to the Jews. At the same time, through the image it makes use of, the project carries forward the form of Christian-Jewish counteraction: as if what is at stake in the analogy is sweeping the Jews away from their pedestal of *negative election,* a pedestal so constitutive for the Christian self-understanding.

To be sure, through this citation of historical-cultural context, we do not exhaust possible misgivings. Both in Germany's contemporary political culture and elsewhere, such comparative discourse has taken on the significance of a national historical *exculpation,* grounded in an effort, morally dubious in nature, to empirically weigh suffering and death. In the forty years of the Cold War, the comparison also had the benefit of mutual delegitimization in the struggle between the two German states. The opposition between National Socialism and Bolshevism settled into the tenor of everyday consciousness to the same degree as it sharpened historical-philosophical perspectives. Against the backdrop of such a constellation, willingly or not, a whiff of partisanship clings to the comparison.

For various reasons, the project of comparing Nazi and Stalinist mass criminality thus takes on an aura of disrepute. Nevertheless, we need to engage in such comparison, cutting through the culturally superimposed images and metaphors. But what, in fact, are we meant to compare here—the total of victims, perhaps, or else technique and procedures of mass killing? Is it appropriate to factor in the regime's duration with the quantity of those murdered, in search of a vector of time and number? Should the comparative researcher's approach be quantitative or qualitative, in both cases for the sake, in the end, of passing judgment on who or what was "worse"?

The following remarks do not address these research possibilities: in light of the always singular or individual nature of the death experience, and an accompanying principle of equality in (unjustly inflicted) death, a hierarchization of mass murder based on empirical substance would seem to lack any clear ethical import. At the same time, for both survivors and later generations, urgent questions regarding the sense and significance of that murder need answers. In fact, only through a retrospective vision focused on understanding can the historical consciousness begin to take the murder's measure. A basic methodological problem faces us here: the need to grasp the very nature of a massive crime on the basis of such posthumous awareness. To this extent, the various belated reactions to the crime take on *epistemological* meaning. In turn, each distinct reaction formation serves as material for historical understanding: material ranging from concrete experiences and perceptions of contemporaries to the different ways of processing and overcoming the crime shown by posterity. As a result, the category of memory itself takes on epistemological import.

Indeed, acknowledging the imperatives of memory, as opening a belated prospect on the past's shadowy silhouette, enable our longer contemplation and hence more precise scrutiny of the crime than an approach claiming immediate access to—or a direct view of—its unfolding. The latter approach incurs, in the end, a risk of conceptual blindness, whereas its alternative allows a more measured approximation. Hence in the case of both Nazism and Stalinism, the historical material of such subjective experiences, perceptions, and forms of overcoming serve as the mnemonic foundation for objectifiable concepts and criteria—those located beyond both exculpation and blame. Likewise, within the dynamic of memory and overcoming, we find the epistemological criteria for drawing analogies and distinctions between Nazi and Stalinist mass murder. There is, for instance, clear epistemological significance to the fact that in Germany, despite all the references to "fascism" (*Faschismus*), the *nation* is the focus of perception and judgment for dealing with Nazi crimes. In contrast, the *regime* serves as the focal point for dealing with Stalinist crimes in the former Soviet Union. The mnemonic distinction between nation and regime reflects a real historical distinction, the National Socialist project representing a fateful fusion of the nation with the regime.

In this respect, it is important to note that the Nazi regime's arch-victims were, above all, those whom the German *Volksgemeinschaft* considered part of a culturally and historically different collective—that is, whom they approached as the "other." Thus marked, they entered the ethnicized memory of the national collective from whom the crime emanated. In this manner, reflecting the Nazi fusion of regime and nation, within both that memory (despite all differences in degree of individual guilt and responsibility) and—above all—within the collective memory of the victims, the crime acquired the status of a specifically *German* crime. But for a German body politic engaged in coming to terms with the past, the crucial element in grasping this specificity has not only been the crime's perpetuation against *others,* but also its consequent direction toward a zone *apart,* as it were, from one's own mnemonic collective. Quite different the task of coming to terms with the mass crimes of the Soviet Union's Stalinist regime. In a political structure defining victims and perpetrators, on a real and virtual social basis, as part of the same historical mnemonic collective, the process of overcoming the evil past naturally becomes a wrestling with oneself.

We can test this thesis of a fundamental difference between the memory of crimes understood as either committed inside or outside specific national, ethnic, and religious collectives—hence between vertical "national" (outwardly directed) and horizontal "social" (inwardly directed) declarations of enmity—by proposing a hypothetical historical scenario: a transferal of phenomena linked with Stalin's tyrannical rule to the German context. What form, in fact, would German memory's confrontation with Nazism take if that regime's victims had represented, for the most part, ethnic Germans, "Aryans"—members of the *Volksgemeinschaft?* What would the psychic constitution of the following generations be like if—in analogy to the Soviet situation—after successfully completing their crimes, parents belonging to the regime's elite organizations had found themselves in turn murdered en masse by the regime? If, for instance, after serving their purpose, SS units devoted to extermination were themselves liquidated, as was the case with murder squads of the NKVD, the People's Commissariat of Internal Affairs? Doubtless we would not be wrong to assume that overcoming such crimes against one's "own" population would involve an entirely other mnemonic discourse than that linked to crimes against the "other." In any event, such a distinction appears manifest in the recent East German confrontation with Stasi, as opposed to Nazi, rule, that is, in the yawning gap between 1949 and 1989.

As a result of the unique fusion of the crimes committed by the Nazi regime with those of the nation, a restrained solidarity with the perpetrators was evident in Germany during the Nuremberg trials. The prevalent talk, tinged with the bitter tones of a national discourse, was of "conqueror's justice." In sharp contrast, the post-1989 years have been marked by a prosecutorial zeal against crimes committed under the East German regime—a zeal in complete harmony with the logic of a civil war, party against party and not nation against nation. Nevertheless, within this constellation of civil strife, the national motif is also at play, albeit now both subdued and socially encoded: the shadow of treason—the nation's sundering; collaboration with the Soviet Union—rests on the loser in the ideological struggle.

It is in any case evident that whatever phenomenological proximity may have existed between the Nazi and East German regimes, these hardly serve as a basis for a convincing correlation. The usual, broader parallels between Nazism and Stalinism—say those based on a perceived elective affinity between two totalitarian projects—carry equally little conviction. Ubiquitous cites of the "Röhm" and "Kirov" affairs as evidence of such affinity notwithstanding, all the two really have in common is the year they occurred. For the Nazi regime, the liquidation of the SA leadership in the summer of 1934, with its undertone of civil war, was an exceptional development, reflecting force of circumstance: Hitler's need to choose between the Reichswehr and the Brownshirts. In contrast, the purges that followed Kirov's murder were a strikingly recurrent expression of the Stalin regime's internal political program.[2]

In a posthumously published study, Maurice Halbwachs argues that only particular groups, nations for instance, possess a memory that is historically transmittable.[3] He also observes that the notion of a memory extending beyond that of a particular collective is fundamentally implausible—that, at least as a historiographical construct, there is no such thing as a *universally* grounded memory. The same might be said for groups constituted along social or political lines, as well as for institutional entities. They are equally incapable of producing something such as an identity-forming *transgenerational* memory. We could cite numerous convincing examples—for instance, that of the great effort invested, over many decades, in ideologically furnishing an international collective like the "working class" with a universal, transnational, historically transmittable *social* identity. This and other such efforts have proved basically unsuccessful, to one or another degree smacking of the artificial. The dynamic of social mobility alone assures the futility of attempting to transmit socially connotative group identities across several generations. We can in any rate observe a pronounced paucity of enduring "mnemonic investment" in such group identities: their rate of decay is simply too short.

A similar distinction of capacities exists within the *passive* memory of tyranny and mass murder. Even in their distortion through suppression, crimes inflicted on other historical collectives reveal themselves as far more mnemonically durable than deeds suffered by those stigmatized on strictly "social" grounds. Let us note, for a start, that in Germany, the Jewish victims of Nazism do not dominate the mnemonic hierarchy of the Holocaust because of a view that Jewish lives have more inherent worth than those of the Romany or victims of euthanasia. Rather, along with the reality of sheer numbers of victims, such ranking reflects, in the end, a longer presence and deeper impact of the Jews within the collective German memory. Formed over centuries, Christian Europe's troubled relation to the Jews and Judaism has furnished an imagistic arsenal for coming to terms with the post-Holocaust present. Contrary to widely held assumptions, the name "Auschwitz" thus not only evokes the Holocaust's most profound horror but actualizes deeply set mnemonic traces conveying Germany's own—Christologically rooted—historical relation to the Jews. In contrast, the Romany's more recent occupation of a place within Germany's collective memory, stemming from the seventeenth century, makes less claims on the nation's self-understanding; not being grounded in the religious juxtaposition at work in the cultural memory of the Jews and Judaism, it is, from this German perspective, relatively superficial. And in turn, as a socially stigmatized group of *individuals* belonging to their *own* collective, those the Germans murdered on "medical" grounds have left few traces within Germany's collective memory, when again compared with both the Jews and the Romany. The euthanasia victims' fate, though it calls for recollection and description with greatest empathy, simply cannot produce the grounded mnemonic resonance needed for that sort of historical transmission.

Focused on the differences and affinities between Stalinist and Nazi mass murder, such reflections on (either assumed or experienced) collective historical memory suggest the following problem: can a "socially" motivated crime like the "extermination of the kulak class" be remembered in just that capacity? Putting aside the dubious nature of references to an actual, socially and cognitively formed "class" of Soviet landed peasants: could the putative class of kulaks have been in any position to form some sort of collective memory—one grounded in the mass crimes connected with the Stalinist forced collectivization and famine of the early 1930s, transmitted onward as part of an historical group identity? Apparently, the answer would have to be in the negative. Nevertheless, such crimes are clearly accessible to long-term memory—albeit to a somehow displaced memory—in their appropriation by a *national* collective: here, that of the Ukrainians.

Although it was by no means exclusively Ukrainian peasants who fell victim to Stalin's policies, the crime of "exterminating the kulaks as a class" has been remembered as a crime against the Ukrainian people, hence as a form of genocide. There are, to be sure, socially grounded objections to viewing the crimes in the Ukraine from such an angle, namely that the Ukraine in fact experienced the greatest toll from forced collectivization because it was the most important Soviet agricultural region. Within this collective mnemonic framework, such objections represent apologetic evasions of a genocidal crime. In general, both the "passive" collective memory and the national historiography are inclined to view the "socially" motivated policy of "intensified class struggle in the country"—a form of "social cleansing"—as the expression of Stalin's deliberately anti-Ukrainian national program: a view bolstered by the fact that parallel to the policy's unfolding, the Ukrainian intelligentsia (among other social strata) was also subject to murderous repression.

In the case of Poland, as well as of the Baltic peoples, we can discern a similar transformation, for the sake of collective memory, of a mass crime whose motives were primarily political and social, into a nationally connotative event of genocidal implications. The perception of atrocities systematically committed against the Polish people is a constituent element of Poland's historical experience, as well as of its national self-understanding—delivered to a tragic fate, caught between Germany and Russia. Correspondingly, whatever the true determining factors at work in the former Polish-Soviet relationship, the Polish collective memory experiences it as a direct followup to the traditional, conflict-laden relationship between Russia and the Poles. Hence Polish collective memory converts crimes committed by communism from crimes of the regime to ones committed by Russia against Poland.

Such a reorientation is perhaps most dramatically evident in the case of the slaughter of 15,000 Polish officers by the Soviet NKVD at Katyn in 1940: this notorious event, deeply etched in the Poles' collective memory, is memorialized as an exemplary act of martyrdom on the part of the modern Polish *nation,* that is, precisely as a chapter in the inherited continuum of Russia's enmity toward the Poles. The durability of this interpretation found confirmation in the early 1990s when Polish nationalists refused to support ratification of the Polish-Russian treaty in the Polish parliament, the Sejem, on the grounds that the Russian *people*—many of whom, let us recall, were themselves murdered by Stalin, which is to say by a *regime*—have not atoned sufficiently for the crime at Katyn.

And yet, though the mass crime perpetrated by the Nazis at Auschwitz far exceeds that of Katyn in both quantity and, in fact, significance, Auschwitz has been assimilated into Poland's national consciousness, and hence remembered, to a strikingly lesser degree. Because *ethnic* Poles were not the sole or principal victims of Auschwitz's industrial mass murder, perhaps memory of the horror cannot be effectively Polanized. Still, in "Catholicized" form, the universally negative event defined by Auschwitz occupies considerable space in Polish memory.

Selective remembrance is the necessary expression of the rationalizing effect of collective memory. By no means does the reduced form of perception involved here equate with historical falsification: quite to the contrary, it enables reflection on the particular character of a given crime—for instance, on the qualitative distinction between the act of genocide and mass crimes that may extract a far greater toll of individual victims. When in 1949 Stalin ordered the prosecution and liquidation of Soviet Jewish writers, the act was, not unjustly, interpreted as signaling the systematic persecution of the wider Jewish population; the event is now remembered in this very fashion—as an act of genocidal inclination. At the same time, the far greater number of Soviet Jewish citizens who lost their lives as individuals alone, and not as Jews, in the course of the Stalinist purges and other mass crimes have received no such memorialization. Evidently the murder of particular individuals, collectively unspecified, has very little mnemonic impact on a memory-bound collective—this even when far more members of that particular collective lose their lives than in a separate attack on the collective as such. To this extent, such crimes resemble the crime of Nazi euthanasia: certainly historically describable but hardly mnemonically transmissible. And to a great extent, the specific manner in which different historical realities are perceived, remembered, and evaluated by individuals is itself linked intimately to different possible modes of historical experience: to the phenomenon of collective memory.

Against this backdrop of arbitrariness, so specific to the Stalinist regime, Ernst Nolte's observation—that compared with Stalinism, Nazism represents a *Rechtsstaat,* a "state acting according to legal forms and procedures" —may even sound convincing.[4] If we leave aside for now the question of the extent to which such an observation emerges from a *Volksgemeinschaft*'s experience of the Nazi system, Nolte's unique understanding of "legality" points to a significant difference between Nazism and Stalinism. Under Stalin's rule, every individual was a potential target of the regime's unpredictable behavior. Under the Nazis, the identity of the victims was thoroughly predictable. In contrast to the blind caprice that distinguished the Stalinist system—in other words, a form of *negative equality,* where *everyone* could become victim, the Nazi system employed the negative certainty of stigmatization based on origin.

Arbitrariness is the basis of rule by fear. Under Stalin, fear and terror were constitutive and endemic, serving as the primary means of political subjugation—the glue holding the Soviet entity together. Asked which form of consensus with his policies he preferred, that based on fear or that based on political conviction, Stalin chose fear, since convictions were subject, in the end, to change. To an extreme degree, his rule was totalitarian in nature: a qualification hardly applicable to the Nazi system, precisely on account of the enviable calculability of action enjoyed by those Germans possessing the required racial attributes and not inclined to defy the regime. Nothing interfered with their prospects for happily living out their lives under the Nazis, and most proceeded to do exactly that. Whereas for those whom the regime stigmatized on the grounds of origin—those excluded from the communal entity, the *Volksgemeinschaft*—the principle of calculability implied a very different fate: the certainty of being delivered to extinction.

To repeat: we must indeed agree with Ernst Nolte that, compared with Stalin's absolutely arbitrary rule—a rule in which no one, and put to the extreme, not even Stalin himself, could be free of fear—the Nazi regime appears a model of just and calculable state power. Nolte's brazen adoption of a German *Volksgemeinschaft* perspective—one centered, as it happens, on the principle that "Aryan" Germans enjoy life and stigmatized "others" suffer death—is quite apparent here; the extension of this perspective, through praise of the *Rechtsstaatlichkeit* of the Nazi state, so that it emerges as a standard of historical interpretation, is quite remarkable. In any event, what is most important in our context is that the specificity of the victims' deaths determines the distinct natures of the Nazi and the Stalinist regimes. As opposed to the high degree of certainty with which death struck the Nazi regime's victims, it overtook them capriciously in Stalin's empire—hence according to individual chance. To be sure (and in quite different fashion), chance also had its role in the unfolding of Nazi mass murder. Within a framework of death's certainty, or extermination's normativity, survival resulted from chance alone. It is true that among those who faced certain death under the Nazis, many might well have not survived Stalin—but this primarily as a result of caprice, and not by virtue of belonging to a condemned *collective.*

In contemporary discourse over Nazism and Stalinism, the distinct dispositions of historical perception and experience can produce paradoxical points of convergence. We thus find Nolte's stance corresponding well to that of ex-Communists from the former Soviet Union, leading to the suggestion of a universal consensus in the comparative evaluation of regimes. From the perspective of ex-Communists *and* the German *Volksgemeinschaft,* benefiting under the Nazis from a relatively chartered legal security, the comprehensive arbitrariness of Stalinism is "much worse" than the partial repression inflicted by the Nazis on political opponents of the regime. The sentiment informing ex- and post-Communist discourse classifying Stalinism as more barbaric than Nazism is that by persecution of opponents and advocates *alike,* the Stalinist regime robbed its victims' deaths of any political meaning. In the face of such arbitrary incoherence, Fascism, its putative antithesis, gains—at least in the eyes of former Communists—a residue of meaning. In its essential definition as anti-Bolshevism, Nazism represents a deadly juxtaposition of great portent in the 1920s and 1930s; but the discourse simply screens out the Nazis' biologistic weltanschauung as beyond the realm of political anti-Bolshevism. Thus fixed—despite all distancing from the "antifascist" discourse of the Communist past—on the old polarity, such thinking both privileges one nation's history and suffering and plays down the deeper meaning of Nazism's crimes.

Conveyed through the distinction between caprice and certainty, crime inflicted on a multiplicity of individuals and crime inflicted on a collective, characteristic differences emerge between Nazism and Stalinism, perceptible in their condensation within collective memories. In order to scrutinize these differences at a remove from opposing cognitive perspectives—to universalize them and endow them with precision—it is useful to introduce an additional interpretive category: that of *labor.* This category has a double meaning. On the one hand, we need to consider the significance of work as a value-generating activity, in the context of the distinct use made of work by the Nazis and the Stalinists in connection with their respective mass murders. On the other, we need to consider the significance of work as an expression of completed, tangible activity per se: the objectified expression of societal rationality.

In respect to the connection of work with mass murder, one distinction comes immediately to mind: where the Nazis used work as a means of extermination, in the Stalinist system of forced labor the death of innumerable individuals through an exceeding of physical capacity formed an essential element of the planning equation. The goal of such enslavement was labor—the individual simply a means, one ruled over violently and absolutely. Matters were otherwise with the Nazis: in their extreme yet standard policy of extermination beyond all economics, work served as a mere masquerade of usefulness, camouflaging the literal purposelessness of the murder. Such rationalizing served less to mislead victims, who in any event had been robbed of all free will, than to protect the agents' own civilizational consciousness, exposed to the deed's offense. In this manner, the death camp is a fitting symbol of Nazism's underlying nature, as is the slave-labor camp for the Stalinist system.

Beyond this opposition, justified doubts have been raised concerning the economic rationality of Stalinist slave labor. Certainly, the system understood itself as oriented toward the exploitation of value-producing labor: it is evidence of a civilizational immanence that the Nazis did not even think of maintaining. But in the face of a regime like Stalin's, resting on arbitrariness, fear, and terror, work appears very plausibly indeed as more a rationalization of total rule than anything with real economic purpose. The Leninist and (even more so) the Stalinist systems held to a sense of historical telos: a faith in the acceleration of historical time—a leap over epochal stages of development—by means of a rigorous productiveness exploiting "living labor." And such temporal acceleration implied a justification of concomitant human suffering, understood as a mere making up for lost time: precisely that pseudohistorical legitimation of a "primary accumulation" post tempore.

Rather than serving social development and the common good, this teleological vision indeed amounted to justifying a limitless power understood to be the motor of economic progress. Nevertheless, forced labor can in no way fit comfortably into an economically rational framework. Already in his *Wealth of Nations* (1776), Adam Smith indicates that despite all appearances of only costing a minimum, slave labor is the dearest labor: an individual not allowed to own goods or sell his services can have no other purpose than eating as much as possible, and working as little. As Smith puts it, "Whatever work he does beyond what is sufficient to purchase his own maintenance, can be squeezed out of him by violence only, and not by any interest of his own."[5] This anthropological principle is thoroughly supported by what took place within the Soviet Union's organized labor system at its Stalinist height: it appears that in the 1930s and 1940s, the productivity of Soviet slave labor was around 50 percent below labor that was "free."[6]

Still, whatever the real figures here, it is apparent that any carefully weighed doubt as to the rationality of Stalin's economic project is fundamentally at a remove from the basic problem posed by the Nazi extermination project, operating as it did beyond all economic factors. Accepting the premise that work represents concrete rationality, we can infer that in the death camps epitomizing their regime, the Nazis did not engage in a production of *value*—the process being anything but rational, yet still ultimately economical—but rather in a production of *death*.

We can gain insight into the categorical difference between the mass crimes of Nazism and Stalinism by gauging the responses to each system on the part of its victims: their acts of resistance resemble a silent speech with epistemological significance. Both firsthand and other accounts from the Soviet camps refer to denial of work as the primary form of resistance. One effective means of such denial was *self-mutilation:* the collectivized, enslaved subject's negative reappropriation of the work potential expropriated by the state monopoly, hence a withdrawal from its caprice and terror. Such a gesture underscores the economic purpose of Stalinist rule, the state's will to exploit, to the point of breaking through all barriers of physical self-preservation, the full work capacity of those it controls, making them work's material instrument until their death. In the absence of all moral or institutional impediments, the utterly powerful Stalinist regime thus had a limitless supply of human material at its disposal.

Entirely different the defiant gestures of withdrawal in Nazi death camps. Strikingly, these did not involve the (negative) reappropriation of work capacity characterizing the gulag system. True, much use was also made of—to be sure, non-German—slave labor by the Nazis. But it would be difficult to consider such labor as a defining feature of the Nazi regime, since beyond any exploitation of human material, in the end what mattered was simple extermination. In camps that *also* incorporated forced labor, and in which individuals were not necessarily killed on arrival—a policy that in any case left them with no options—they often reacted to the approaching loss of work capacity through hunger, weakness, and disease by suicide in the camp's electrified barbed wire. Such a response points to the individual's "freedom" in the face of systematic murder for its own sake as consisting in a choice of form of death (and not, say, in that between death and life).

Even in the Jewish ghettos, where the suggestion of normal life seemed to imply a degree of free will, the Jewish resistance in fact itself disposed only of such a choice. In the context of a collective and certain death sentence passed on all Jews with no exceptions, armed rebellion could never really aim, in the end, to maintain life. For the ghetto's prisoners, work only represented a means to stave off certain death—a medium to gain already forfeited time. In the despair of the head of the Bialystok ghetto at the insistence of the ghetto's doctors in upholding fundamental medical ethics, and shielding desperately ill patients from work, we noted the absolute nature of the break with norms of behavior based on purposive rationality and defined by the Nazi production of death. In the ghetto's context, squeezed-out work could no longer serve as a utilitarian alternative to death. Its sole purpose was to delay the executioner.

TWELVE

Cumulative Contingency

Historicizing Legitimacy in Israeli Discourse

> The Zionist movement, which no longer trusts in the prospects of plural-
> ism and the culture of the autonomous individual in Europe, constitutes
> the radical, yet resigned reaction of the Jews to the possibilities opened up
> during the past century. It is a sad aspect of the history which has since
> transpired—sad both for the Jews and for Europe—that Zionism was
> proven right.
>
> MAX HORKHEIMER, "THE GERMAN JEWS" (1961)

The appearance of the so-called new historians on the stage of Israeli historiography has given rise to considerable conjecture. What are the well-
springs of this phenomenon? What future repercussions does its emergence
forebode? The answers are many, ranging from the hypothesis of cyclical
generational conflict in academe to possible reverberations of the peace
process. Some suggest that the underlying cause of the shift in historical orientation may lie in the recent access to new documentary sources on the
early formative years of the state, so heavily mantled by foundation myths.
For its part, the group of new historians is also involved in the public interpretation of its own significance. It increasingly lays claim to something like
a paradigm shift in research on contemporary Israeli history.

Adversaries seize on such preening to accuse the new historians of a
thoughtless embrace of modish methods, of scholarship's fickle, trendy
winds. Yet that charge reveals just how unfamiliar the traditionalists themselves are with the methodological approaches they claim to criticize. Some
have also trotted out classic juxtapositions to diagnose the controversy's syndrome, styling it as a clash between positivists and relativists, facticity and
interpretation. Those unpersuaded by such methodological explanations
take recourse to political readings considered long since outmoded: Zionist versus anti-Zionists, the latter evasively donning the cloak of "post-
Zionism."

Post-Zionism—there may be something to that. The label designates
a milieu of discourse that breaks free from traditional ideological entice-

ments, pursuing a decidedly individualistic stance. This phenomenon is far from peripheral in Israel today. Emanating from modernistic Tel Aviv, it bounds over the metropolitan area's cultural perimeters with postmodern ease, expanding across the country's length and breadth. And the radiation of this counterculture, directed specifically against the lingering residue of a now defunct collectivist self-identity, proceeds seemingly unimpeded. Increasingly, it molds the intellectual tastes of everyday *haute culture* in Israel. In its wake, certitudes of the national past find themselves labeled as mythical—marginalized.[1] This is the soil that breeds the *public* phenomenon of the new historians.

In this manner, the phenomenon is more the symptom of a changing Israeli self-identity than the harbinger of a trailblazing new historiography. Not that the works of these historians, alternately lauded or damned, depending on one's position, are devoid of significance. On the contrary, each makes its own contribution to illuminating the Israeli past, Israeli reality, especially those studies that, over and beyond any innovative importance they may have, open up new documentary ground, exploring neglected topics and corners. Yet it would be premature to see the formation of a new and distinctive school here, or even the genesis of a new historiography.

In any case, the vehement public reaction that the phenomenon has provoked reflects its importance. Considerable public attention in Israel goes, almost de rigueur, to history and historical interpretation. Whereas other symptoms of change in Israel tend to elude the spotlight of public perception, historiography—by dint of its ever present and seminal importance for the legitimation of the Jewish state—is subjected to an intense, even sensational, scrutiny. More than the discursive and interpretive social sciences that are also caught up in the dispute, history is central to the Israeli "civil religion," the polity's desire for legitimation, and thus its self-identity. Owing to its special and particular genesis, Israel's legitimacy remains in doubt, challenged not only from without, but also from within. Thus, by the mere fact of history's immediate practical importance, any enterprise of Israeli historiography finds itself embroiled, ineluctably and unintentionally, in abrasive discourses of justification.

Indeed, history and legitimacy remain heavily intermeshed in the Jewish nation-state. Despite all temporal distance, the past still stubbornly retains its immediacy and contemporaneity, resists becoming history. It is thus no surprise that all discourse on history in Israel is ipso facto discourse on legitimacy. This fact helps explain both the pitch of emotion accompanying the debate on the new historians and its locus outside the walls of academe,

in the widely accessible spaces of the public arena. Its forum and participants underscore what the dispute in fact is: a debate on the legitimacy and
self-identity of the state extending far beyond the professional perimeter of
the historians' guild; a debate in which one and all feel entitled to partici-
pate—an ongoing open national colloquium.[2]

For Israeli historical discourse, both the nagging question of legitimation
and the validity of a homogeneous, nationalizing image of history are absolutely central. The outward-oriented issue of legitimacy arises mainly from
questions of justice connected with the Arab-Israeli conflict; the inward-
oriented collective self-definition reflects the readings and representations
of the Nazi destruction of European Jewry, the Holocaust. Both elements—
questions of the polity's legitimacy and the construction of a collectively
binding historical narrative—are as closely interlinked mentally as are the
mass annihilation and founding of the state temporally. The oppressive
proximity of disparate spatial and temporal planes of historical experience
generates a clustering of causalities and moralities in collective memory.
These reach deep into historiography's terrain, created by a specific, all-
embracing tension: to be *of* Europe, but not *in* Europe. Such representations of history, spatially and temporally disparate yet dovetailed as a result
of concrete historical experience, lead perforce to a highly problematic
configuration of causality in public consciousness and historiography alike.
In the main, the issues are of central legitimizing salience—such as the genesis of the Arab refugee problem, or the tricky maze of casual interconnec-
tions between historical anti-Semitism, Nazi mass extermination, and establishment of the state.

Differences in the construction of Jewish history emerge between a more
conventional historiography and one that is innovative in its methods. The
more conventional approach tends to overstress causalities in constructing
a quasi-teleological national narrative, representing the historical past as an
inescapable necessity. Such linear reconstruction—reducing complexity to
an extremely narrow interlinking of cause and effect—reflects no methodological preference or deliberate political intent to manipulate. Rather, its
more likely matrix is the phenomenon of the experience of cumulative contingency that traumatized consciousness translates into a teleological perception of historical events. The conventional approach proceeds from the
premise of *Jewish history,* where the Jewish people is viewed as a quasi subject in history. The innovative approach has a methodologically less bind-

ing, more open framework as the *history of Jews,* where phenomena of contingency, fortuity, and difference all clamor for a rightful place.

Jewish history, or the history of Jews? The choice of orientation is not arbitrary. Both tendencies have their own historical experience and narrative structures in the nineteenth and twentieth centuries. Jewish history is more in keeping with the patterns of emancipation of Eastern European Jewry, which moved largely within the collective pathways of an ethnic religious understanding of nationality and nation so typical of East-Central and Eastern Europe. The history of Jews, by contrast, tends to correspond to the dynamic of the emancipatory process in the West, where, in the framework of the institutional nation-state, human rights and liberties, the individual's autonomy, was stressed. If the experiential context of Jews in Eastern Europe comes closer to the narrative form of what I define as negative teleology—a heading toward catastrophe—the self-identity of Western-rooted individuality leads historiography to view Jewish fate in the twentieth century less in causal terms of sheer negative necessity, and more as a consequence of tragic aggregation.

The Israeli historians' debate indeed appears to reflect these two paradigmatic patterns: one tends to stress the primacy of the national collective; the other underscores the value of the individual. Thus, we may view the different historical experiences of the Jews in Eastern and Western Europe as quasi-subliminal translations into historiographical approaches.[3] The distinction between the primacy of collectivity or individuality finds its source in the underlying perceptions and valuations of diverse Jewish historical experiences *there and then.* Inevitably, it also extends into the context shaping the era and arena where Jews emerge as subject in history: namely in the conflict with the Arabs or, more precisely, with the Palestinians—the *here and now.* Hence, different Jewish histories concerning the cultural and historical experiences of emancipation in Western and Eastern Europe lead to different assessments of the local conflict, its causes, trajectory, and associated value judgment. Those experiences also engender diverging historiographical preferences in respect to both choice of topic and methodological approach. Seen from such a perspective, the current debate becomes a conflict between a previously dominant historical discourse, largely of Eastern European Jewish provenance, and the structural content of historical interpretations based on other biographically filtered historical experiences, mostly the Western European one.

The Israeli historians' debate is a symptom and harbinger of a comprehensive conflict—a struggle over the plurality of representations of history in Israel. In actuality, a contest for recognition of a multiplicity of differing

Jewish experiences is taking place here, replacing the hitherto homogeneous narrative, binding for one and all.

Although participants in the historians' debate focus primarily on the question of the causes underlying the Palestinian refugee problem in 1948, the previous mass annihilation of European Jewry has far greater salience for the differentiation and revamping of Jewish history's representation. Paradoxically, an increasing significance for legitimation and self-identity is precisely what makes the understanding and interpretation of the Holocaust the focus for questions from within: its very centrality for the all-embracing national consciousness inevitably entails a hierarchization of particular sub-memories, arranged in a kind of graduated pyramid according to their proximity to that central event of collective self-identity. Thus, particularistic experiences further from the core event in real historical terms tend to accept the dominant narrative structure by mimesis. Particular histories are implicitly denied via a kind of mere retelling according to given national patterns. The narratives are reauthored, submerged, and thereby hegemonized. Sooner or later, such subjugation perforce mutates into resistance, even open opposition, through a questioning of the dominant national narrative structure, molded as it is on the formal patterns of Eastern European Jewish experience. This shift particularly affects the accepted readings of the destruction of European Jewry. The current Israeli historians' debate is its harbinger.

Again, the main difference between the more traditional Israeli historiography and that of its opponents must be sought at the fracture line between an approach of teleology or conflated causality and one of cumulative contingency. That fracture line in Europe finds its most manifest expression where the specific German Jewish experience collides with the more ethnicized self-identity of Eastern European Jewry. Against the distorting backdrop of political polemics, these diverse histories of emancipation and their respective modes of narrativity can easily be falsified and whittled down into a clash between Zionism and non-Zionism. Yet such a classificatory scheme is deceptive, especially since the internal Jewish levels of discourse and discursive battlefronts stemming from the period before the Nazi mass extermination have long since blurred. As is the case with Jews elsewhere in the world, the year 1945 constitutes a certain caesura in Israeli Jewish consciousness, dissolving the earlier contrast between the options of individual emancipation ("assimilation") and Zionism, and the multifaceted array of intermediate gradations and nuances. Signaling this rupture, the survivors immigrated as refugees, and not as ideological proponents of a historiosophic project culminating in the state of Israel. It is therefore patently misleading to view the state's establishment as some sort of "vindication" of Zionism in the sense of the defunct internal Jewish discourses from the era before 1933–39.

That teleological delusion largely stems from the fact that the *yishuv,* the Jewish community in Palestine, remained physically unscathed by the Jewish catastrophe in Europe. Yet it was not spared that disaster owing to some supposed ideological superiority or prophetic foresight. Its survival was rather the product of mere contingency.[4] Only as a result of those fortunate circumstances which brought Rommel in Egypt to a halt in autumn and winter of 1942, beyond any Zionist ability to shape and direct events, and therefore by chance, did *real time*—represented by the destruction so common to the fate of European Jewry at that very historical moment—remain at a distance from *utopia* and its locus, the *yishuv* in Palestine.

This favorable twist of events permitted the *yishuv* and later the state of Israel to adhere to a perception of time dramatically different from that imposed on Europe's Jews.[5] The periodization introduced by the *yishuv,* seemingly exochronic, ultimately gave rise to that delusion of historical superiority to which all perspectives of Jewish self-identity, apparently now refuted, willingly surrendered in self-abjection, if only to partake in that chronology and the associated victorious chronography that stood for collective freedom from harm—the *yishuv* unscathed. Here is the source of the vehemence and the profound public passion in Israel accompanying historical research on the *yishuv* during the period of World War II and the Holocaust.[6] Ultimately, what is manifest here is a clash: on the one hand the linearly calibrated chronology of national utopia that survives intact despite the Nazi assault on Jewish existence and on the other, a contingent perspective, obligated more to the catastrophic events engulfing Europe. The tragic outcome of those years induced the presumably "victorious" variant of Jewish self-identity to adopt a pose of self-righteousness toward its former ideological competitors—suggesting covert triumphalism and an appeal for humility and subordinacy.

The effects of such historiosophic triumphalism—a powerful element in political culture in Israel and among Jews in the diaspora—are not easy to brush aside as some sort of idiosyncratic oddity, a crank configuration of the time. For decades, the Zionizing memory held its superior status and its hegemony in Israeli self-identity until it began to lose ground to an alternative narrative: that based on the memories of the Holocaust victims.

These two lines of internal historical interpretation and legitimation in

Israeli self-identity—the *yishuv*-ist and the *shoah*-centric—also point to differing hierarchical pillars undergirding collective memory. They can stand
in rivalry, but need not be competitors. However, they generate a dominant
narrative structure with which all other Jewish-Israeli submemories willy-
nilly comply. Such accommodation and its associated forgetting of actual
individual experience is only understandable. After all, in the process of the
shaping of collective Israeli self-identity, the ultimate aspiration was to belong, and therefore to mold one's own biography according to the structure
of the dominant narrative.

Israeli collective memory is synthetic in its makeup. The hierarchically
structured components of Jewish self-identity correspond to historiographical preferences and choice of narrative structure—telos over contingency
—despite the fact that Israel, in marked contrast to the ideological premises of the prewar period, is more the product of mass immigration in the
aftermath of the Holocaust and the process of decolonization in the Islamic
countries. Thus, this kind of Jewish territorialism ex post facto, taking the
form of the state of Israel as a result of historical contingency, is not primarily the outcome of Zionism proper, even though its realization in Palestine was indeed indebted to the premises of prestate Zionism. Because of
such material premises and above all the philosophical weight of purported
historical superiority, the Zionizing components in Israeli and Jewish self-
identity found themselves inflated in a quasi-sacrosanct way after 1945.

This phenomenon cannot be attributed solely to social and cultural pressure. The acceptance by the survivors of European Jewry and other Jewish
communities of an interpretation of history that was tantamount to a denial
of both their own biographical experience and the lines of tradition preceding it, rests on a principle of cumulative contingency—that overwhelming
semblance of negative teleology. In addition, the telos-oriented historiosophic orientation—individual amnesia for the sake of national rebirth—
provided a certain balm for traumatized consciousness. Indeed, forgetting
and accommodating to the *yishuv*'s chronography, however problematic in
retrospect, did bring solace to the trauma-shattered generation after 1945.
By contrast, for the generations born later, historicizing the past can be a
source of relief.

Thus, the acceptance of fundamental elements of Zionist interpretation
of the past, elements seen as having survived the era's ravages intact, was a
product of psychological reaction formation to the trauma of loss. Such a
guileless desire for identification, in turn, contributed to an upgrading of

a narrative that, simply by dint of its preservation, tended to downgrade previous life worlds back *there*.[7] Nonetheless, it is wrong to assume that Zionism enjoyed some sort of total victory over its Jewish adversaries. True, Jewish consciousness after 1945 was increasingly Zionized; yet even Zionist self-perception had been deeply affected by annihilatory anti-Semitism.[8]

Indeed, after 1945 there was a melting down of various Jewish components of self-understanding in the crucible of Palestine qua *eretz Israel* (the land of Israel), which processed both Zionist components of Jewish self-identity and those formerly opposed or agnostic toward political Zionism in its pre-1933–39 historical form. The resulting amalgam—Israel—was a nationalized patchwork of differing Jewish historical experiences but can hardly be interpreted as a direct product of Zionism.

Today, displaced in time and generation, such a complex contingency of evolved national existence is becoming transparent, and thus even acceptable. That insight has certain consequences. Internal Jewish differences believed long since defunct, defuse, are reemerging: not in actuality, but on historiography's stage, as revision. The phenomenon of the new historians is symptomatic of this tendency. Although they are not consciously embracing jettisoned components of Jewish memory, their choice of topics and stance points in this direction.[9] Their flaunting oppositional pose is regrettable, since it forces them into a mirror-image acceptance of the target of their critique. In the hubbub of declamation, claim, and counterclaim, historical topics that should constitute the actual object of the controversy disappear. True, a methodological distinction between old and new historiographical approaches is reflected in teleologically molded narrative structures on the one hand, versus their contingent counterpart on the other. However, the purported new historiography remains caught up in old patterns, despite all desire for innovation. It opposes traditional historiography by negatively accepting its presuppositions, instead of overcoming this legitimizing paradigm with a historicizing perspective. If it goes no further, historiographical criticism will arrive—though by an opposite route—at the same impasse of legitimizing discourse that for so long has held Israeli historiography in its grip.[10] Rather, innovative approaches should circumvent the traditional legitimation-centered discursive structure—largely patterned on the dichotomy between Western individual and Eastern collective models of emancipation.

This basic motif recurs in virtually all constellations of modern Jewish historical experience. It lurks in the juxtaposition between Zionists and non-Zionists, the polarization between *eretz Israel* and the diaspora, the tension between resistance and Judenrat, and other situations perceived as dualistically structured. Although such a dichotomous discourse structure has relevance for Jewish history as such, it gains particular poignancy with regard to the contemporary period. Thus, the choice of topics befitting the dichotomous structure dominates simply because of its legitimizing importance for the polity, and other topics languish precisely for the same reason. Although this choice says little about the actual historical relevance of the topics chosen, an upgrading of marginalia seems to fit legitimizing needs, in the context of a dichotomously polarized interpretation of history.

In any event, the choice of topic is largely the result of a primary commitment to an ethnocentric pattern in historiography. It is highly problematic for a Jewish historical understanding that views itself first and foremost as a history of Jews because it assumes a collective consciousness, existing somehow transhistorically, even though such a broad collective perception did not emerge until after 1945. In the choice of topic, the structure and organization of the work and the more covert judgment of the historian, we can discern the effects of an anticipatory, ethnically grounded and Zionizing notion of the Jewish people: a quasi-political notion intended to unite the Jews but failing to do justice to the historical reality of the Jews in the diaspora prior to Auschwitz. Studies, for example, dealing with Jewish resistance to the Nazis or with the Jewish leadership's attitude at the time ("proper" or "improper") fall victim to the illusion of the existence of the Jews as political subject. Historiosophic perception did not correspond in any way to Jewish realities before the catastrophe; admittedly, after 1945 it matched reality to a far greater extent. Again, this phenomenon of the historical reproduction of collective patterns and behavioral premises is not merely the result of political manipulation. Rather, it is the product of that readiness after 1945 to not only internalize collective basic premises with regard to the future, but to *project* them back into the past—a readiness that is only too understandable in the light of the traumatic experience of the destruction of European Jewry. Moreover, the specific nature of the destruction has a profound effect on any perception or interpretation of it.

The administrative and industrially organized extermination of so many in such a short span (1941–44)—an extreme disparity of time and number—destroys any narrative structure appropriate to the event. Thus, as observed in different contexts throughout this book, "Auschwitz" stands for a mode of murder that standardizes, serializes, annuls individual biographies. In this sense, "Auschwitz" has a *statistic,* but—as we noted—no narrative. The figure of six million stands for this forfeiture of narrativity, and constant questioning of the figure reflects not so much a search for truth driven by a frenetic urge for exactitude as a coded interrogation of the event itself.

Mass destruction has a drastic impact on historical consciousness and historical representation, illuminated by the metaphor of *compressed time.*[11] As if blocked and deflected, time takes evasive recourse to periods that enable a plausible surrogate narrative. This substitute tale or its specific narrative structure may draw on concrete incidents during the period of the destruction—for instance, the Warsaw ghetto uprising—to symbolize the entire event. But in order to contextualize the event in its entirety, consciousness resorts to apparently relevant prehistories, constructing them in a decidedly teleological fashion.

It is thus the contextualizing prehistories that imprint their narrative pattern on the catastrophe. In such a way, they create the semblance of a historical fulfillment of the predetermined, of a radicalized return of the old and familiar history. The substitute representations are mostly congruent with the Jewish experience of traditional anti-Semitism and the patterns of conflict between nationalities in the period between the world wars, in the areas that formerly belonged to the Polish-Lithuanian empire.[12] The mass extermination ultimately acquires an interpretation, a retrogressive reading via such a narrative template. What is more, the history of conflict between Poles and Jews provides that arsenal of national Jewish remembrance in accordance with which the dominant Israeli collective narrative takes its shape. Thus, the basic patterning of representation comes into view even before the catastrophe. As a result of its enormous pressure, the narrative precedent to it mutates into that full-fledged negative teleology, one that rushes headlong, seemingly inexorably, toward the mass annihilation. The representation itself instinctively follows the siren song of historical interpretation worked out in retrospect. This process applies both to traditional historiography and the often well-intentioned, albeit mirror-reversed constructions of its critics. Such reversals, like slides viewed the wrong way round, demonstrate to what extent historical discourse still moves within patterns of the forging of self-identity, to what degree historiography and questions of legitimacy still fatefully intertwine—in short, that a genuine historicization is still on the agenda.

When it comes to the history of Jewish settlement in Palestine—that other, more empirically accessible aspect of the Israel historians' debate—the agenda is open here too. The juxtapositions and contrary modes of Jewish experience, mainly the different modes of emancipation, are evident as basic patterns of interpretation and understanding of the Arab-Israeli conflict—at least insofar as its origins are concerned, that is, the Palestinian dimension.

The "Western" sensibility, with its stress on individual emancipation and the civilizational primacy of human and civil rights recognizes an injustice: that those universal values were fundamentally violated in the process of Zionist colonization of the land and the associated exclusion of the indigenous Arab population, and that this is the origin and basic template for the conflict between Jews and Arabs in and over the land. By contrast, the "Eastern" approach, Jewish experience rooted in the paradigm of ethnic nationality, takes cognizance of those elements but subordinates them to the primacy of the collective.[13] The structure of valuation, interpretation, and narrative of those two experiential contexts necessarily differs. The perspective indebted to "Western" criteria of emancipation will regard the act of Jewish land purchase as a legal transaction yet have difficulties coming to terms with its claim of legitimacy, since it did not take place on a basis of equal and continuing exchange relations between Jews and Arabs.[14] Similarly, the principle of "Jewish labor," though cloaked in the righteous garb of socioeconomic conceptions of justice, advanced the national acquisition of the land, that is, the exclusion of the Arab population from the nascent Jewish polity not primarily by the direct use of force, but by virtue of economic forces.[15] The forms of social collectivization served one aim: ethnic homogenization. Such practices encountered a liberal critique both in the *yishuv* and later in the state of Israel. Its authors were principally groups or individuals within or even beyond Zionism's pale, who at times employed Communist discourse and, by dint of their cultural or even value-grounded context, leaned toward Western conceptions of emancipation or stemmed biographically from German-speaking Central Europe.

In terms of historical development, it was precisely the intermediate position of Mitteleuropa's emancipatory traditions that transformed the area into a conflict-ridden locus for the encounter between Eastern and Western Jewry. Moreover, this intermediate position rendered it an eminent site for potential friction between the Western project of individual civil and human rights—the state as a framework of political institutions—and the more collectivistically oriented conceptions of an ethnically founded nation-state. Indeed, Central European Zionism was notoriously ambivalent. It harbored both elements, a valorizing of individual and national emancipation, and attempted to find a compromise between them. The patterns of Central and Eastern European disputes between nations and nationalities became paradigmatic for interpreting the idea of the Jewish nation, and for the political perception of the conflict between Jews and Arabs in Palestine. What is more, the settlement of the land by Jews reveals itself largely as a transfer of modes and models forged in the struggle of nationalities in Eastern Europe. The key intellectual planners of Zionist settlement in Palestine perceived Arab-Jewish relations as analogous to those between Czechs and Germans or Germans and Poles. And they mustered corresponding intellectual armament into position in Palestine, drawn from the arsenal of the East-Central European conflict between nationalities.[16]

All in all, the confrontation of Jews and Arabs in Palestine was displaced into the Central and Eastern European context of *ethnos*—at stake were questions of nationalities and minorities. But one substantial difference prevailed in Palestine: the struggle was not between existing nationalities, but between an indigenous population and immigrants from Europe with an experience of modernity who were in the very process of constituting themselves as a nation. And above all, the aspiration of that newly constituted nationality was to change the demographic status quo in the country in order to form a political entity for itself and thus to the disadvantage of the indigenous population.[17] This national homogenizing became interlinked with the context of World War II and the Holocaust—ultimately leading to the establishment of the state of Israel and the resulting Palestinian refugee problem. For the Jews in Palestine—being morally *of,* but physically not *in,* Europe—those events *there* justified expulsion *here,* which they contextualized in a European frame.

The charge of colonialism probably points to a different interpretive context. The term colonialism generally signifies two things: a value judgment about relations of rule that entail even formal inequality; and a historiographical conception of periodization. The value judgment derived from the armory of notions of emancipation. To that extent, the perspective critical of colonialism (or of a political relationship stigmatized as such) is, in principle, indebted to Western conceptions of law and its proper institutions—ultimately, to the ethos of human and civil rights. From such a perspective, the inherent inequality between Jews and Arabs arising in the process of the Zionist enterprise deserves to be rejected. However, such a stance has a paradoxical result. By adopting the cause of an excluded collective in the name of human *individual* rights, its advocates find themselves embracing the *national* standpoint of the colonized—a nationalism in reverse they never intended. Involved here is an aporia inherent in colonial situations, an incapacity to relate to individuals on a basis other than ethnic origin.[18]

In contrast with the value-judgmental approach to a situation perceived as colonial, the concept of *colonialism* rests on a historiosophic perception of history's development and has a strong European maritime dimension. The use of this concept implies that phenomena such as migration, settlement, expropriation, and violent population transfers relate solely to a specific historical stage.

What implications does such a view have for the Zionist enterprise in Palestine? The fact that it utilized the presence of an imperial power (Britain) that was subjugating the indigenous population is probably an inadequate criterion for defining it as colonialism. It goes without saying that any entity that aspires to realize power by and in concrete situations must weigh historical circumstances and seek to exploit them to its benefit. However, not every phenomenon of colonization and settlement—including the direct subjugation of the indigenous population—need follow historiosophic lines to pose a problem within a framework of universal justice. In the case of Palestine in the late 1940s, the basic issue must take different terms: was a colonial conflict at work here or was it a conflict between nationalities?

The main Zionizing variant in historiography proceeds from the obviously interest-guided premise of a tragic conflict between nationalities. It rejects use of the term colonial for the conflict between Jews and Arabs in Palestine because, quite naturally, its approach applies historiosophic categories of universal justice. Zionism resists being associated with an era basically doomed to decline. Ensnared in the discourse of legitimation, Zionist historical explanations and exegesis thus take flight into a quibbling over terms. Philologically, philosophically, and psychologically, they endeavor to distinguish between *colonialism* (which they also castigate) and *colonization*, with its positive connotation of progress. This enterprise is fraught with difficulty—especially if its content has all the attributes of a conflict between nationalities but its form is colonial.

Such a complex historical constellation raises serious problems of legitimacy that are particularly problematic for those seeking to justify the argument of the "return" of the Jewish people to its ancient land in secular terms, in the face of the presence of an indigenous population, beyond the crude equation of might with right. After all, at stake is a fundamental and massive alteration in the status quo, involving both the ownership of land and, far more, the ethnic composition of the population. Any status quo, if simply by dint of a generally accepted aspiration to maintain peace, acquires an important cultural reality and the aspiration to change it entails a powerful compulsion to justify one's actions, both to oneself and others. The usual strategy involves establishing a historical interpretation, that is, an appropriate narrative structure or even a particular chronology, in order to justify unilateral actions and bypass the legitimizing demands of the present. In the case of Zionism, the obsessive insistence on past times appeared urgent as long as the status quo involved the unmistakable presence of an Arab majority in the land. In any event, there was a need to evade the awkward *now*ness of the place—by evoking other times, either past or future. The remote past presented itself as a conducive space to flee to since virtually all Zionist arguments underpinning even the most secular of Jewish claims to the land are based on biblical justification. Such claims necessarily involve an acrobatic feat of bridging past and future in an effort to leap over the present. The projected future beckoned in the guise of social utopias, holding out the hardly plausible hope that later on, in a better society, everything could come out right. Until that time, right collided with right, so that force would have to decide.

After 1948 (or rather 1945) patterns shifted in the discourse of legitimation, both for the Jews, who increasingly conceived themselves to be a national collective, and for the "relevant" world, which, immediately after the mass destruction of European Jewry, constituted the secularized Christian West.

Western consciousness read the event of the Holocaust against a Christian backdrop. From that perspective, the establishment of a Jewish state appeared totally justified in its reactive significance. But such legitimacy is binding almost exclusively on the West and leaves the Arabs outside the contexts of complicity. Traditional historiography in Israel has followed a quite different tack: in order to obligate the Arabs at least to accept the legitimation of Israel as anchored in contemporary history, it has exaggeratedly stressed the collaboration of some personalities in the Arab national movement with the German Nazis—such collaboration was often peripheral, at least when assessed in terms of the relevant events at the time—and even elevated it into a kind of research subfield. In the meantime, while the Arabs may have come to terms with the de facto existence of the Jewish state, the legitimacy of its genesis is still in dispute. This holds both for its biblical legitimation and for that allegedly universal legitimacy flowing from the matrix of the Holocaust.

In contrast with the legitimatory efforts directed toward the outside worlds, what is the situation regarding the internal Israeli discourse of self-justification? On the surface, it focuses on the relative impact of various historical events that in one or another combination may have led to the establishment of the state. Depending on their respective political and philosophical leanings, historians can engage in a gamut of speculations.

They can attribute the creation of the state to the sheer omnipotence of the *yishuv;* to the pressure generated by Holocaust survivors, to the benevolence of the Soviet Union; or, paradoxically, to the self-injurious defiance of the Arabs. These and analogous accounts of the state's genesis—the inclination to derive it from some supposed "final" cause—may well serve the vital needs of a teleological meaning of creation. Although they have little historical tenability, they are significant as discursive elements addressing questions of Israeli legitimacy.

Among the majority of Israelis certain preferences are clearly discernible, over and beyond all questions of historical evidence and plausibility. Thus, the matrix of legitimacy for the state is recognized far more commonly in the catastrophe of the mass annihilation than in its biblical justification, as is revealed by the reemergence of fundamental questions of legitimacy in the wake of the June 1967 war. On both the right and the left "Auschwitz" was adopted as a metaphor for the insecurity of life in Israel before the war. Menahem Begin, leader of the right-wing Likud Party, used to quote former Labor Party foreign minister Abba Eban who had described Israel's pre-1967 borders as "Auschwitz lines."[19] Beyond all polemical exaggeration, which Eban may well have later regretted, this term reveals a profound truth—one that perhaps even escaped its author—namely that Auschwitz had indeed legitimized the borders of 1948–49. Despite all rhetoric since 1967 to the contrary, after Israel gained control of the biblical heartland, and thus control of the physical material site of its historical self-legitimation, no Israeli government was able to bring itself to annex Gaza, "Samaria," and "Judea" politically, even though such a move would make state existence consistent with ideology.

Thus, although the time span from 1967 to the present is considerably longer than the period from 1948 to 1967, 1948 remains the decisive time icon. Duration, generally the determining factor in acquiring a title by prescription, would appear to be inoperative when it comes to the 1967-occupied territories. All historical claims notwithstanding, the "borders of Auschwitz" still appear to retain greater weight and saliency—in Israeli public consciousness too. Israel's self-legitimation thus oscillates between two foils of justification: biblical, and therefore Zionist, and "territorialist"—territorialist in the sense of a Jewish homeland as response to Jewish distress, without historiosophical claims a result of, and not a blueprint for, history. The paradox is that traditional territorialism, which was not directed toward Palestine, was realized in *Eretz Israel* after 1945. This insight opens up a perspective centered, again, on cumulative contingency—now resulting in a Jewish state. This contingency stands in contrast to the standard Zionist view, with its stress on historical necessity, purposefulness, telos. Zionist or territorialist: seen from the outside, from an Arab perspective, both may appear identical. However, from an internal Jewish perspective, the associated distinctions can lead to enormous differences—especially concerning future political prospects.

As already mentioned, such a distinction surfaced within the identity crisis in the wake of the conquest of the biblical heartland during the June 1967 war. The internal Israeli controversy on the future fate of those territories stirred up basic questions pertaining to the justification of Israeli existence in the land. The biblical legitimation played out against the territorialist reality in the suggestive conclusion that whosoever proposed abandoning Hebron was forfeiting his right to Tel Aviv.[20] To that extent, the wave of settlement in these territories initiated soon after served more for self-legitimation than as a response to purported necessities. The factual takeover of the soil was the expression of a newly erupted unilateralism in the *justification* of national existence, given the lack of even the most minimal agreement by the local Arab population. Connected with this, the newly added territories, representing an Arab temporal-spatial reality, posed a *threat* to the principle of biblical claim, even where it had been realized in the past, that is, before 1967.

The clash of differing temporalities that resumed in 1967—a fictional time striving to become reality, a real time shunted aside into the world of fiction—culminates in violence. In turn, the use of violence requires an additional legitimizing underpinning, especially since violence generates an inward-directed equivalent, the compulsion to formal consistency in the discourse of legitimacy. This "all-or-nothing" approach (the argument that "whosoever proposes abandoning Hebron forfeits his right to Tel Aviv") sets an argumentative trap in order to negate an Israeli existence justified on the grounds of contingency. The collective commitment to the biblical basis of self-legitimation—the commitment to a past that, though fictive, nonetheless reshapes itself into reality unilaterally, and therefore without any communication with the "other"—leads to the only mode of communication possible, the language of violence. For reasons of sheer consistency and legitimacy, what happened up to 1948–49 had to continue after 1967. In other words, the past (1948) would turn to injustice unless it continued in the present (1967).

Conceptions based on the state of Israel *or* the land of Israel imply not only divergent political options but also divergent historical memories. The collective memory that focuses on contingency perceives Jewish statehood as a result of an unanticipated and bitter experience of catastrophe, a kind of Zionized Jewish territorialism. Counterposed to this interpretive construct is the metaphysical view of history that makes the past horror almost a necessity. It is only such a teleology that must grapple with problems of formal consistency in regard to legitimacy. By contrast, the notion of contingency frees later generations from the cognitive bind of needing to base collective existence on a consistently justified legitimacy. Indeed, only those wishing to continue the historical Zionist enterprise as an ideological project feel compelled to justify its past as well.[21] Such a compulsion blocks the path to a legitimacy that can be acknowledged by the Arab "other."

The territorialist approach to Israeli history stands for a political existence devoid of eschatology or telos; it emerges from consciousness of contingency in a Jewish history conceptualized as the history of Jews. As time passes, such contingency gains greater presence and significance, overriding self-interpretations celebrating the lure of national homogeneity. It does so in particular for those who have no need to justify their presence as part of the Jewish Israel collective, for the simple reason that they were not the authors of what exists but only found it there from the beginning. For them, what is past has already become history. Their situation anticipates a point when the process that led to the establishment of the state is indeed regarded as completed. Only when 1967 ceases to be regarded as a legitimate continuation of 1948–49 will such a closure have been reached. This, of course, is something that the present must determine.

The signs appear to point in that direction. In this respect, the new historians may not be the pioneers of a new historiography—but they are certainly symptomatic of that move to uncouple history from the constrictive armature of a legitimacy discourse.

THIRTEEN

On Guilt Discourse and Other Narrations

German Questions and Universal Answers

The Holocaust has increasingly become a universal moral icon in the realm of political and historical discourse. The impact of the catastrophe can be felt in various European cultures, with their disparate legacies in regard to the diverse domains of tradition, experience, and memory. Its highly complex imprint, as enigmatic as it is ambiguous, can be observed even within the realm of collective and individual identities.

No wonder that in Germany and within the framework of its political culture the traces of the Nazi past, and of the Holocaust as its core, can be discerned at almost all layers of feeling and expression in both the private and the public spheres. Indeed the history of the Federal Republic seems to be accompanied by cyclically recurring debates and periodic outbursts in regard to the Nazi past, which are often prompted by questions concerning the Holocaust's interpretation and representation. Such a discourse appears basic to Germany's moral and historical self-awareness. Its fluctuations allow the beholder to gauge prevailing German circumstances—the formation of a specific collective consciousness, indebted to an incriminated past. By all appearances, the Holocaust might well be defined as an identity-forming foundational event.

Almost any German who has passed through the educational system of the Federal Republic can recall some sensation in the public sphere relating to the genocide. Such sensations may have been journalistic or artistic; they may have focused on historical representations, enactments on stage or for the cinema, eyewitness accounts captured on celluloid, or events such as parliamentary debates. Whatever their nature, these events take on an iconic significance, in the form of recurring rhetorical figures. Their

traces are evident in the unease that accompanied the appearance of Anne
Frank's diary in the 1950s; in the stir prompted by Rolf Hochhuth's *Deputy*
in the 1960s; or in the remorse publicly demonstrated at the end of the
1970s in response to the broadcasting of the television series *Holocaust* and
as an accompaniment to the notorious *Historikerstreit* of the mid-1980s. And
they turned up in the astonishing reaction to Daniel Goldhagen's study of
Hitler's Willing Executioners, which elicited glaringly divergent reactions, ranging from an initial brusque rejection to, eventually, a loud and broad approval possessing, as it were, a hieratic tenor.

How should these various responses be understood? What subcutaneous
currents within the consciousness of the Germans vis-à-vis Nazism and the
murder of the Jews produce such enduring consequences, repeated anew
in a decade's cycle? Many of the reactions point to profound layers of feeling that stir the Germans again and again to different degrees of intensity.
A central factor in this process seems to be what Karl Jaspers called the
"question of guilt" (*Schuldfrage*),[1] or, more precisely, the effect of a constant
sense of guilt.

The question of guilt accompanies the discourse on Nazism and the Holocaust in a markedly constant way.[2] Indeed, it becomes an abiding, collectively self-confirming motif, which has powerful cultural implications.
From this perspective, Jaspers's discussion of the theme in 1945–46 reads
like a founding text for the new (West) German collective identity, based on
the moral imperative that Jürgen Habermas later repeatedly evokes.[3] Behind such evocations lies the premise that the body politic has to be constantly reminded of the specific conditions in which it was constituted. As
was the case with Jaspers, Habermas's stance has incurred the steady hostility of those wishing to establish another, opposing approach to the past.[4]
However, their efforts have proved futile in the face of the resistance of the
subconscious. Hence despite, or perhaps, precisely because of, all inner
resistance, the question of guilt repeatedly invites renewed discussion—a
repetition compulsion based on the complex fabric of collective memory:
direct or by deferral, revealed or camouflaged, acknowledged or denied. As
an erratic backdrop for the collective self-understanding of the Germans, it
can be sensed everywhere.

What is the meaning of the notorious question of guilt? Jaspers, whose con-
fessional text acquired quasi-normative significance for the old Federal Republic, undertook what he termed a "differentiation of German guilt." He
thus distinguished *criminal* guilt of the few from *political* guilt binding all

members of the national collective, as well as asserting a distinction between *moral* and *metaphysical* guilt.[5]

The fact that the idea of moral guilt led to the greatest controversy is no coincidence. The notion of moral guilt shared by the Germans as Germans ends up in a twilight zone, somewhere between a layer of an apparently judicial nature and a collective shadow beyond juridical control. In relation to the subject of Jaspers's essay—the impact of guilt discourse on the collective consciousness of the Germans—this kind of guilt may well be the most relevant. It seems to correspond in its effect to the historical and cultural-anthropological category of *remembrance*—what the Germans call *Gedächtnis*. This "moral guilt," which Jaspers himself did not consider objectifiable, needs to be located in the context of what he characterized as *Überlieferung*—"transmission" or "tradition." He thus wrote that "it is not the liability of a nation but the concern of one who shares the life of the German spirit and soul—who is of one tongue, one stock, one fate with all the others—which causes here not tangible guilt but something analogous to co-responsibility." Jaspers could thus feel "co-responsibility" for what Germans do and have done "in a way which is rationally not conceivable, which is even rationally refutable."[6] He thereby revealed himself in the eyes of his opponents as an advocate of a legally inapplicable collective guilt: the very accusation, in effect, that the philosopher originally wanted to ward off in his essay.

In fact, the thesis of a cross-generational, predetermined collective German guilt cannot be rationally grounded. What is more, it has also been argued that to acknowledge such a collective phenomenon would be to abandon the principle of the autonomy of the individual as the bearer of freedom, responsibility, and morality, and thus to evoke obscure forces of collective identity.[7] Nevertheless—and despite all difference between individuals who were either directly responsible for crimes or belonged in varying degrees to the circle of criminals, and ones who were utterly unaware of any such complicity—a sense of guilt, traceable to the Holocaust and incapable of rational illumination, simply clings, mildew-like, to all those who feel part of Germany's collective memory. It is precisely this sense of guilt without culpability of a legal nature that has produced the cross-generational convulsions accompanying public discourse on Nazism and German mass crimes. These guilt feelings, evoked *without* individual involvement and even displaced temporally, point back to the specificity of the deed branded into the locus "Auschwitz."

To understand the phenomenon and impact of guilt on collective consciousness, it is irrelevant how many Germans were either *directly* or to various degrees *indirectly* involved in the Nazi German crime against the Jews. In the face of all historical controversy concerning the scale and character of participation, it remains obvious that, in the psyche of contemporaries and the consciousness of posterity, "administrative crimes" generate a feeling of unbearable disproportion between the individual guilt of relatively *few* perpetrators and the immeasurable suffering of *countless* victims. A huge number of victims normally leads to the expectation of an equally massive number of perpetrators. Moreover, because the victims were murdered solely because of their origins, that is, solely because of their belonging to a *collective* and not because of any individual transgression, the amount of guilt resulting from the deed rebounds onto the *entire* collective from which the deed originated. Because the crime was directed at another collective, it intuitively invites a presumption of *collective* guilt. And since such kinds of crime cannot in any way be expiated appropriately, the guilt remains unresolved, incapable of being resolved, and descends on *everyone* who, via common memory, belongs to the same collective as the perpetrators.[8] In this way the crime generates a vagabond, cross-generational sense of guilt that has mutated into a central feature of the collective consciousness of the Germans.

How does this complex of guilt affect the form of both academic and public discourse on the question of the Nazi past? It would be naive to expect a simple acceptance of an omnipresent element of guilt in consciousness and memory, for such a sense of guilt is unbearable and eventually manifests itself as resistance rather than acknowledgment. Although some acceptance of the *Schuldfrage* may be discerned in the realm of theology or moral philosophy, or even in individual psychoanalytic therapies, in other domains the question is paradoxically most present in terms of denial—a phenomenon that is particularly prominent in those fields concerned with representing the incriminated event itself, such as the discipline of history.

Historians, in their capacity for objectification and rationalization of past realities, generally believe themselves to be adequately protected from the effects of their affiliation to a specific collective memory. Professional craftsmanship, methodological polish, epistemological capacity are all part of this process of inoculation. Armed with these tools, the historian is guaranteed appropriate professional distance from the object. Thus, it is argued that the influence of the *Schuldfrage* on the collective memory should not have any critical significance for the appropriate, that is, objective, representation of the past. And this assertion is maintained even though the discipline of history itself is directed at a broad public with which, despite all claims to objectivity, it shares at least the underlying resonance of a common memory.

Indeed, in Germany, it is extremely difficult to evade the effect of the *Schuldfrage* on the depiction and interpretation of the Nazi genocide. Its effect assumes manifold features, some paradoxical, some contradictory, and fine distinctions have to be used in order to decipher its various modes of expression. This can be seen both in the *Historikerstreit* of 1986, whose fronts were finally determined in relation to the *Schuldfrage*, and, albeit in quite a different form, in the Goldhagen controversy that raged a decade later.

In the case of the *Historikerstreit*, the debate, steered below the surface by the *Schuldfrage*, rationalized itself according to the political distinction between *left* and *right*. This constellation corresponded to another distinction, one that is classically West German: namely, the distinction between those who argued in the tradition of Jaspers's *Schuldfrage*, seeing the foundations of the Federal Republic threatened by a morally agnostic approach to the Nazi past, and those who demanded historical "objectivity" in the name of scientific freedom understood in one manner or another, in order to dispense with disagreeable historical images.

Although numerous professional historians participated in the *Historikerstreit*, the controversy, as is well known, was more concerned with the moral texture of historical images than with new research findings or innovative methodological approaches. Simultaneously, this shift in perception on the part of an intellectual elite—a shift with public resonance—pointed to something more, or to something entirely different. Beyond the thematic content of the *Historikerstreit* in its narrower sense, a general shift in paradigm emerged whose broad significance for the country's political culture could not be disregarded. In retrospect, the process can be summarized in the following manner: in the old Federal Republic the social sciences, which until then had enjoyed hegemonic status in interpretation of *Lebenswelten*, were gradually displaced by history as the leading discipline. Parallel to this, a transformation was beginning to take place in the political realm that would be realized only years later, through Germany's unification. What really happened was the transformation of the Bundesrepublik into Deutschland—the displacement of the constitutive interpretive model of the body politic from *society* to *nation*.[9] Only this later event can locate the *Historikerstreit* in its rightful historical context and reveal the controversy's underlying concern—in anticipation of the political process of reunification—with the problem of German identity. The *Historikerstreit*, then, involved a debate over the past's significance in relation to a shift in Germany's sociopolitical status from a Western, that is, institutional, body politic to a veritable continental nation.

Taking place in the waning years of the old Federal Republic, the *Historikerstreit* was still conducted in the form of a struggle over political direction and was still entirely obligated to the deeply ingrained distinction between "left" and "right." As a rationalizing cipher, this distinction was meant to mask the historical discourse's own *national* texture: that is, its predominant concern with the notorious *Schuldfrage* of the Germans.

The constellation that emerged with the Goldhagen debate was very different. A decade after the *Historikerstreit,* the old Federal Republic's distinction of left and right had largely evaporated. Nonetheless, leading protagonists in the *Historikerstreit* clearly wished to direct the debate on Goldhagen's "willing executioners" along the lines of the earlier confrontation, with its now moribund political distinctions[10]—a desire aimed at concealing the paradigm shift that had meanwhile taken place in the discourse on guilt. For the semantics of public discourse on history and the past are no longer marked by an inner, political formation, but by a distinction related rather to origin, collective memory—to *ethnos.*

Indeed, Goldhagen's representation of the Holocaust focuses on the Germans as a collective and not on one or another faction—left or right— in the previous political debate. Thus the American Jewish scholar, if only unintentionally, has awakened the Germans' guilt discourse anew, something that was already evident in his use, in *Hitler's Willing Executioners,* of the language of collective association. Without hesitation Goldhagen speaks of "Germans" rather than "Nazis," as was previously both politically correct and de rigueur. Unwittingly, he links his thesis to the semantics of German guilt discourse and thereby strikes an exposed nerve.

Whereas the guilt discourse underlying the *Historikerstreit* had remained concealed behind the wide-ranging use of political terminology, in the Goldhagen controversy this discourse appears to have come into its own. For instance, the reading public took the historian's representation of the Holocaust to be what it unmistakably was, as defined by its narrative framework: a veritable writ of accusation, necessarily coming from the outside and presented to the Germans from the victims' perspective. There is a certain limited validity to the vehement reproach initially leveled at Goldhagen that his sole aim was, in fact, to renew the accusation of collective guilt previously cast at the Germans, an accusation that now took historiographical form. This reproach can be considered accurate solely to the extent that Goldhagen's type of presentation necessarily evokes the questions of guilt and of guilt's effect on the German collective memory—questions that refuse to be settled.

I argue above that we should understand the two basic, conflicting schools of Holocaust research—the intentionalist and the functionalist—as judicially shaped structures of narration with opposing orientations. The intentionalist approach attempts to interpret the mass crime more or less as an expression of culpable action; the functionalist approach appears, on the contrary, to link it to interpretive models based on a principle of negligence—a kind of *guiltless guilt*.[11]

I also assert that the form of memory bound up with the Jewish experience in the Nazi period naturally takes as its starting point the victims' universe of experience. It does so in that it places the question of *who* in the foreground: *Who* were the victims? Or more existentially "why us?" In the end, all further questions stem from such an epistemological orientation. For example, the question of the perpetrators' motives is linked, most narrowly, to that of the victims' origins: once again, "*who* were the victims?" or "why us?"

It is this question, addressing the significance of anti-Semitism as a path to the Holocaust, that introduces the basic methodological problems linked to the particular perspective of each collective. Consequently, despite similar semantics, when it comes to the Holocaust there is little agreement over what is in fact to be understood by "anti-Semitism" and anti-Semitically stamped intention. In practical terms, endowing anti-Semitism with ideological coherence is doubtless problematic, since it involves less a homogeneous weltanschauung than an accumulation of a variety of negative attitudes toward the Jews, ranging from social distance, to denigrating language, to an outburst of violence that, however momentary, extends far beyond a threat to individuals, directly implicating Jewish existence itself. To be sure, these different degrees of anti-Jewish sentiment require political circumstances in order to move from latency to virulent and murderous action.

In the present context, it may still seem somewhat trivial to make the methodological observation that the coherent, conceptual approach to anti-Semitism typifying both historians' public and private discourse bears only a slight resemblance to the varieties of anti-Jewish expression found in the real world. Any concept subject to ideal-typical coherence functions only as a superordinate symbol for differentially layered phenomena. At the same time, such conceptual abstraction has a symbolic resonance that is generally lacking in the empirical description of "fact." Beyond any factuality, the concept is imbued with an accumulated historical patina that becomes no less important to an understanding of the phenomenon than its empirical tenor.

It is in any case clear that in relation to the Holocaust, the rubric of anti-Semitism has many facets, and this complexity calls for careful differentiation. It is thus empirically hardly productive to attempt to compare different countries and cultures with regard to their greater or lesser disposition to genocide against the Jews. Such comparison may lead the historian or social scientist to the conclusion that, for instance, anti-Semitism was far more prevalent in purely Catholic lands than in Germany. However, with regard to the politics of extermination, Catholic mentality and culture might have served as a barrier to the homicidal intent that led to the implementation of eugenic tenets. Those tenets were regarded as modern, completely devoid of anti-Semitic sentiments born of a profound faith. In other words, just as anti-Semitic sentiments may be accompanied by a disapproval of anti-Semitic deeds, so—from a particular perspective—anti-Jewish deeds do not necessarily imply profound anti-Semitic convictions.

What are the consequences of such a vaguely coded understanding of anti-Semitism for research on the Holocaust and the motives that led to it? To begin, such vagueness engenders various perspectives, with the phenomenon of anti-Semitism taking on a different consistency depending on whether the research adopts a distanced perspective or one of extreme proximity. For example, close scrutiny—or a micro-oriented reconstruction—of anti-Semitic phenomena may actually detract from their significance for mass murder. The closer the inspection of a historical object, the more amorphous it appears. Thus, what from a suitable distance appears to be a homogeneous anti-Semitic motive, grounded in a weltanschauung, tends to acquire, in close-up, a syncretistic form; it loses its apparently obvious ideological features and reveals itself as a blend of all kinds of secondary motives such as opportunism, careerism, greed or various other familiar forms of baseness. Of course, those who shared these kinds of motives not only enjoyed a priori exemption from punishment for ethically repugnant behavior but were also very well aware (as a result of the political and other privileges they were being tendered) against whom such behavior could be asserted. To this extent, the grand, ideologically grounded anti-Semitic convictions may have been far less murderous than the small inducements to implement anti-Jewish measures determined by the regime.

It is surely true that almost every conceptual rationalization, when subject to close empirical scrutiny, disintegrates into a mass of disparate elements that cannot evoke the drama packed into their conceptual synthesis—into their symbolization in the form of rationalizing images. This is as true for the concept of anti-Semitism as for other concepts that rationalize complex social processes and phenomena. To a great extent, the close-range perspective robs the phenomenon of the aura accompanying the iconic symbolization embedded in the concept: an aura reflecting much more faithfully what contemporaries "truly" experienced than the mere empirical description of the so-called reality. Historical constructions of past reality are always more than just an objectified mirroring of bygone events, for a response to pressing ethical questions is part and parcel of history writing. The opposing approach, which places empiricism in the forefront of interest in order to "de-demonize" the horror of the event in a quasi-enlightened manner, through anthropological generalizations, attempts to drain the object of its specificity, hence of its historical qualities. Instead of posing the question of *who,* such an approach has recourse to *how:* how could it have happened? How could events have taken such a turn? [12] Nevertheless, its operation may be subject to intuitive reactions that draw on appropriate emotions such as guilt.

The loss of historical substance—of the aura attached to concepts that endow an event with meaning—leaves behind a mere set of vague anthropological tenets such as the existence of a regrettable iniquity allegedly embedded in human nature. Missing are concrete questions about guilt and responsibility for individual decisions, emerging from specific historical constellations and narrated against the backdrop of collective memories.

From the victims' perspective, the increasing attempts to interpret the Holocaust anthropologically, to center on human inadequacy or indeed iniquity, are suspect of organized resistance to guilt. After all, the victims find it hard to accept the premise of persecution on account of an abstract human nature. In their experience, persecution results from their belonging to a specific collective, from being *Jews.* Certainly, persecution and extermination of the Jews were more the product of the anti-Semitic disposition of the persecutors than of the blind chance that was doubtless also a factor in the Holocaust.

Nonetheless, as has been suggested, interpretations of the Holocaust that focus on real or presumed anti-Semitic motives can lead to an exaggerated and overly narrow emphasis on the Nazis' specifically anti-Jewish measures. But while this emphasis tends to obscure other motivational elements contributing to the mass murder, it does endow the horrifying event with something like historical meaning. Furthermore, a perspective that side-steps anti-Semitism would appear to carry far less conviction. For in the end, what apart from compulsive behavior, strongly informed by ideology, can account for murdering a particular group of people in the absence of any perceptible conflict, and solely on account of their origin?

For Jews, anti-Semitism justly stands at the forefront of every historical reconstruction of explanation of the Holocaust, given the lack of any other convincing motive. From the Jewish vantage, it is thus of little consequence if an extreme close-range viewpoint reveals the anti-Jewish measures introduced by Nazi German officials to be an accumulation of actions designed strictly for their career advancement, and the asserted anti-Semitic motives to be illusory. Anti-Semitism need not be defined *only* as an expression of deepest conviction.[13] From this perspective, the victimization of Jews solely because they are Jews is perfectly sufficient grounds for the attribution of anti-Semitic motives to the perpetrators.

The source of the victims' insistence on anti-Semitism as the Holocaust's ultimate cause would seem apparent. Less obvious is the source of the desire manifest in the perpetrators' memory, and in other related memories, to deny tendentiously the notion of anti-Semitic purpose, while recognizing the full horror of the extermination: as if crimes motivated by anti-Semitism were far more objectionable than those grounded in secondary motives such as opportunism or careerism. One explanation for the desire may be a judicial inclination to diminish intentionality, to argue the case for negligence or *guiltless guilt*. But however satisfactory such an explanation may appear, we must seek its source on a deeper level—in the depths of cultural memory, in the timeless figuration and rhetoric of theological argument. It is only natural that against the backdrop of a Christian-based memory, the Jewish victims of the Holocaust stand out as very special victims. For in Christian memory, the collective death of the Jews resonates—in secular self-perception as well—with the features of the timeless mythic narrative.

The relatedness of Holocaust and the features of Christian memory leads to an apparently paradoxical observation. Let us first assume that the extermination of the European Jews was *not* the direct result of a stock of late antique, medieval, and modern anti-Jewish traditions. Nevertheless, the fact that the Holocaust's principal victims were Jews evokes within Christian-grounded memory that mythic tale by which its own religious self-understanding was founded, in other words, by means of a negative demarcation from the Jews. In its turn, such a foundation myth in Christian memory engenders an apparently enigmatic resistance to acknowledging a causal link between the hatred of Jews and the Holocaust—a link that would enmesh memory in an indissoluble network of guilt. Hence reinforcing the manifest causality, the mythically charged deep dimension of Christian memory establishes a dramatic interrelation between a traditional, sacrally grounded pejorative attitude toward the Jews and their eventual extermination—a connection that reveals itself in paradoxical, refractory denial.

In interpretations of the Holocaust, the rejection of the obvious connection between culturally embedded hostility to the Jews and the actual Nazi genocide employs a strategy of universalization or "humanization" of the deed. In other words, since the Jews of Europe were fed to the extermination mills not as *Jews* but as Jewish *humans,* every effort to explain as well as historically reconstruct the events needs to start at the locus of humanity-centered phenomena, that is, the *general.* In contrast, an emphasis on the *particularity* of Jewish fate draws the charge of narcissistically loaded ethnocentrism, in the vein of the religious myth of the chosen people.

In the present context, the public theological discourse on the particularity of the destruction of the Jews is of scant interest since it follows a well-worn trail of argument and response beyond the temporal framework of the event's historical understanding. More interesting is the extension, or transposition, of structural elements from an originally theological discourse into modern historical narrative, where they exert a steady influence without being recognized for what they are. The efforts to deny the Holocaust's Jewish victims a specific fate, grounded in anti-Semitism, by means of a narrative structure aimed at universalization, or to locate the Holocaust within a long sequence of identical or similar events, represent such instances, which amount to transforming the tale of the Holocaust into a narration beyond Jewish existence and Jewish historical experience.

The universalization and "humanization" of the Holocaust thus takes a variety of forms, of which one is modern genocide studies.[14] Although this discipline casts no doubt on the Holocaust's status as a genocidal project, placing it among other mass murders in the past and present, its systematically comparative approach raises doubts in itself. Any discussion of differences and similarities clearly involves comparison, but it would seem probable that in the case of comparative genocide discourse, what is at play is precisely that theological discourse, in secular garb. Indeed, such a problematic extension of theological semantics and rhetoric occurs whenever the description, narration, and explanation of the Jewish Holocaust—as well as other genocides against other collectives that share a common memory—resort to anthropologizing planes of comparison. Here again the always particular, hence historically specific, blurs in a universalizing intent. What at first glance seems trivial and self-evident, the demand for *empirical*

comparison, turns out on closer scrutiny to be the old familiar model of jux-
taposed timeless narratives based on that primal theological rivalry. Such an
empirically oriented comparative structure lacks any differential auratic element—the only element that produces meaning.

In their endeavor to reach the most general generalities, comparative
genocide studies overlook that essential difference we considered in the
context of Nazism and Stalinism: between the extermination of an ethnic
community based on common memory—a *mnemonic entity*—on the one
hand, and the extermination of a mass of human beings who do not identify themselves as part of a collectivity based on common memory, on the
other. The principle of memory—and nothing else gives coherence to *ethnos*—has epistemological import for qualifying difference, and hence for
creating meaning. A genocidal deed also has this qualifying effect, woven
into the historical narrative of those involved in its catastrophic import. The
deed can appear to memory as something familiar—as a repetition of what
already happened. In turn, the narration of an experience that appears repeated is constitutive for collective memory. True, that memory repeatedly
reconstitutes itself to the extent that it *appears* to repeat its history in terms
of the overlaid tale.

The phenomenon of a narrative repeated either really or ostensibly is
not unusual for those forms of collective memory that are long—that is, *ethnic* in nature. In contrast, groups that have fallen victim to genocidal crime
because of "ad hoc," historically contingent and chiefly *social* circumstances
can hardly form a culture of memory to confirm the group's collective identity from generation to generation. This distinction between long and short
memories has significant implications, for without an overlaid collective
memory the incriminating event may still exist in the historical annals but
will expire as living memory.

The distinction between collectives constituting themselves ethnically
and socially—that is, through *long* and *short* memories—is essential for any
qualitative study of genocide. In the case of genocide, what is truly at stake
is not simply the number of victims, but the attempted or actual extermination of a mnemonic entity. The objects of genocidal extermination belong
not simply to an ethnic entity, but to an entity that is both bearer and subject of a historical—hence specifically collective—memory.[15]

Alongside this distinction between long and short memories, ethnically
and socially constituted groups, it is also essential to consider the different
circumstances under which one mnemonic entity perpetrates genocide on
another. Genocide can thus be the result of a conflict between two ethnic
entities in which populations themselves, rather than regular armies, wage

war, to the point of the total extirpation of the opponent-as-enemy. "Ethnic cleansing" is one form of such violence, aimed at getting rid of the very presence of the other, at removing the other from a territory claimed as exclusively one's own. But such genocidal conflicts possess a certain innate limit, for once the desired territory is free of the other, that ethnic entity loses its significance as absolute enemy.

As we remarked, the Holocaust suffered by the European Jews was fundamentally different from such forms of genocide. Not only did the persecution lack any concrete preceding conflict but Jews, including those hardly aware of their Jewish origins, were declared Jewish by the Nazis according to arbitrary criteria in order to subject them first to discriminatory and then to more drastic measures. Moreover, the Nazis did not stop with the expulsions that notoriously characterize "ethnic cleansings." Apparently inverting the principle of ethnic homogenization at the Holocaust's height, they regularly tracked Jews down in lands neither settled by Germans nor possibly ever destined for such settlement, rounded them up, and deported them for extermination.[16]

Once the Holocaust's specificity is eradicated, what remains are general and generalizable universalist insights, which have gratifying implications in that they relieve the oppressive weight of guilt. In this manner the Germans too can come to perceive themselves as victims, since they indeed suffered expulsions that resulted in a huge number of deaths.[17] They too have tales of suffering to tell—bombing victims, abducted members of the Wehrmacht, rapes at the end of the war.[18] But, they lament, this history goes unexpressed, for constant reference to "Auschwitz" denies the Germans the "right to a hearing" that befits their suffering.[19] This history still seems to await its narrators.[20] Meanwhile, displacing the different national narratives and their underlying memories, the discourse of the Holocaust negotiates endless questions of guilt, suffering, and pain.

NOTES

Frequently cited periodicals have been identified by the following abbreviations:

DJZ	Deutsche Juristen-Zeitung
GuG	Geschichte und Gesellschaft
VfZ	Vierteljahrshefte für Zeitgeschichte
YLB	Yearbook of the Leo Baeck Institute
YVS	Yad Vashem Studies
ZaöRV	Zeitschrift für ausländisches öffentliches Recht und Völkerrecht
ZfG	Zeitschrift für Geopolitik
ZgStW	Zeitschrift für die gesamte Staatswissenschaft
ZöR	Zeitschrift für öffentliches Recht
ZVR	Zeitschrift für Völkerrecht

1. ON THE BRINK OF DICTATORSHIP

1. In *Der Begriff des Politischen* (1928; Berlin, 1963), Carl Schmitt develops the theoretical concept of *Feind*. Concerning the dichotomous concept "friend and enemy," see George Schwab, "Enemy oder Foe: Der Konflikt der modernen Politik," in *Epirrhosis: Festgabe für Carl Schmitt,* ed. Hans Barion et al. (Berlin, 1968), 2:665–82.

2. Heinrich Muth, "Carl Schmitt in der deutschen Innenpolitik des Sommers 1932," *Historische Zeitschrift,* supplement 1, Beiträge zur Geschichte der Weimarer Republik (1971): 76.

3. See Christian Graf von Krockow, *Die Entscheidung: Eine Untersuchung über Ernst Jünger, Carl Schmitt, Martin Heidegger* (Stuttgart, 1958). Over the past decade there has, of course, been a great deal of attention devoted to the question of Heidegger's own relation to Nazism: a controversy already initiated, to a large extent, by Karl Löwith in the late 1940s, then reinitiated in the much more recent work of Victor Farias and Hugo Ott.

4. See Thilo Vogelsang, *Kurt von Schleicher: Ein General als Politiker* (Göttingen, 1965), 94; Joseph W. Bendersky, "Carl Schmitt in the Summer of 1932: A Reexamination," *Cahiers Vilfredo Pareto* 16 (1978): 51–52. Schmitt's programmatic proximity to Kurt von Schleicher's social and economic conceptions is probably reflected in his "Gesunde Wirtschaft im starken Staat," *Mitteilungen des Vereins zur Wahrnehmung der gemeinsamen wirtschaftlichen Interessen in Rheinland und Westfalen (»Langnamverein«)* 1, n.s., no. 21 (1932): 13–32.

5. See Nicolaus Sombart, *Jugend in Berlin, 1933–1943: Ein Bericht* (Frankfurt am Main, 1986), 247: "*Arcanum* was one of his favorite words, coming up again and again. . . . This duplicity and double dealing constitute the fascination of Carl Schmitt."

6. See Reinhard Höhn, "Großraumordnung und völkisches Rechtsdenken," *Reich, Volk, Lebensraum* 1 (1941): 269. Carl Schmitt stresses the highly political nature of each legal term in "Reich—Staat—Bund: Antrittsvorlesung, gehalten an der Kölner Universität am 20. Juni 1933," in *Positionen und Begriffe im Kampf mit Weimar—Genf—Versailles 1923–1939* (Hamburg, 1940), 190 ff., 198.

7. Concerning the ambiguous and "phenomenological" nature of Schmitt's legal and political concepts, see Joachim Schickel, ed., *Guerrilleros, Partisanen: Theorie und Praxis* (Munich, 1970), 11. See Sombart, *Jugend in Berlin*, 247: "He plays with the double meaning of words, used as signs that mobilize emotions drawn from the depths. . . . He favors the conceptual figures of Christian theology and gnosis, down to their late Hegelian form. . . . He considered himself a bearer of secrets, an 'initiated' in the gnostic sense."

8. See Carl Schmitt (hereafter C.S.), *Politische Theologie: Vier Kapitel zur Lehre von der Souveränität*, 3d ed. (1922; Berlin, 1979), 22: "the normal case . . . proves nothing, the exception everything: it does not simply confirm the rule; rather, the rule owes its very life to the exception." During Schmitt's interrogation by Robert Kempner after the German capitulation, he characterized himself as "an intellectual adventurer"; see Claus-Dietrich Wieland, "Carl Schmitt in Nürnberg (1947)," *1999—Zeitschrift für Sozialgeschichte des 20. und 21. Jahrhunderts* 2 (1987): 117.

9. See Ernst Rudolf Huber, "Verfassung und Verfassungswirklichkeit bei Carl Schmitt," *Blätter für deutsche Philosophie* 5 (1931–32): 318.

10. See C.S., "Clausewitz als politischer Denker: Bemerkungen und Hinweise," *Der Staat* 6 (1967): 479.

11. See Günter Maschke, *Der Tod des Carl Schmitt* (Vienna, 1987), particularly the first part ("Carl Schmitt in Europa: Bemerkungen zur internationalen Diskussion anläßlich seines Hingangs, 11. April 1985"), dealing with the most important obituaries.

12. See the biography by Joseph W. Bendersky, *Carl Schmitt—Theorist for the Reich* (Princeton, 1983) and the critical review by Stefan Breuer in *Kritische Justiz*, no. 1 (1984): 110–13. See also George Schwab, *The Challenge of the Exception: An Introduction to the Political Ideas of Carl Schmitt between 1921 and 1936* (Berlin, 1970). Schmitt's former pupil Otto Kirchheimer tried to block Schwab's dissertation, believing that Schmitt intended to rehabilitate himself in the United States via Schwab. See George Schwab, "Through a Glass Darkly," cited by Volker Neumann, "Verfassungstheorien politischer Antipoden: Otto Kirchheimer und Carl Schmitt," in *Der Unrechts-Staat:*

Recht und Justiz im Nationalsozialismus, Red. Kritische Justiz (Baden-Baden, 1984), 35n. 31.

13. The term is Muth's in "Carl Schmitt," 137.

14. See the organ of the SS, *Das Schwarze Korps,* December 3, 1936, 14 ("Eine peinliche Ehrenrettung") and December 10, 2 ("Es wird immer peinlicher!"); "Der Bauftragte des Führers für die Überwachung der gesamten geistigen und weltanschaulichen Erziehung der NSDAP," *Mitteilungen zur weltanschaulichen Lage* no. 1–3, Jahrgang 8, Januar 1937—Der Staatsrechtler Prof. Dr. Carl Schmitt (14 pp). See also the SS-Sicherheitsdienst files on Schmitt, Institut für Zeitgeschichte, Munich, AKZ 4062/69, Fa 503 nos. 1–2.

15. See Otto Kirchheimer's "Zur Staatslehre des Sozialismus und Bolschewismus" (Ph.D. diss., Bonn, 1928), published in part as "The Socialist and Bolshevik Theory of State," in *Politics, Law and Social Change: Selected Essays of Otto Kirchheimer,* ed. Frederic S. Burin and Kurt L. Shell (New York, 1969), 3–21. In the summer of 1931 Otto Kirchheimer and Franz Neumann attended a seminar on constitutional problems offered by Carl Schmitt at the Handelshochschule in Berlin. See Neumann, "Verfassungstheorien," 35; concerning affiliations, see Volker Neumann, "Kompromiß oder Entscheidung? Zur Rezeption der Theorie Carl Schmitts in den Weimarer Arbeiten Franz L. Neumanns," in *Recht, Demokratie und Kapitalismus,* ed. Joachim Perels (Baden-Baden, 1984), 65–78.

16. Walter Benjamin, *Schriften,* ed. Theodor W. Adorno and Gretel Adorno (Frankfurt am Main, 1955). See Michael Rumpf, "Radikale Theologie: Benjamins Beziehung zu Carl Schmitt," in *Walter Benjamin: Zeitgenosse der Moderne,* ed. Peter Gebhardt et al. (Kronberg im Taunus, 1976), 38. See the controversy over Schmitt's influence on the left: Ellen Kennedy, "Carl Schmitt und die Frankfurter Schule: Deutsche Liberalismuskritik im 20. Jahrhundert," *Geschichte und Gesellschaft* (hereafter *GuG*) 12 (1986): 380–94 and the replies by Alfons Söllner, "Jenseits von Carl Schmitt: Wissenschaftliche Richtigstellung zur politischen Theorie im Umkreis der 'Frankfurter Schule,'" *GuG* 12 (1986): 502–29; Ulrich K. Preuß, "Carl Schmitt und die Frankfurter Schule: Deutsche Liberalismuskritik im 20. Jahrhundert; Anmerkungen zu dem Aufsatz von Ellen Kennedy," *GuG* 13 (1987): 400–418; Martin Jay, "Les extrêmes ne se touchent pas: Eine Erwiderung auf Ellen Kennedy," *GuG* 13 (1987): 542–58. See Volker Neumann, "Carl Schmitt und die Linke," *Die Zeit,* July 8, 1983; Alfons Söllner, "Leftist Students of the Conservative Revolution: Neumann, Kirchheimer, and Marcuse," *Telos* 61 (1984): 55–70. Wilhelm Hennis, *Verfassung und Verfassungswirklichkeit: Ein deutsches Problem* (Tübingen, 1968), 34 f., mentions "Carl Schmitt frankfurterisch."

17. Concerning C.S.'s secularization of theological terms (here Paul, 2 Thess. 2:6), see *Der Nomos der Erde im Völkerrecht des Jus Publicum Europaeum,* 2d ed. (1950; Cologne, 1974), 29.

18. For a discussion of the Weimar constitutional assembly, see Ernst Rudolf Huber, *Deutsche Verfassungsgeschichte seit 1789: Weltkrieg, Revolution und Reichserneuerung 1914–1919* (Stuttgart, 1978), 1178–1243. For an excellent overview of the problems of the constitution, see Reinhard Rürup, "Entstehung und Grundlagen der Weimarer Verfassung," in *Vom Kaiserreich zur Weimarer Verfassung,* ed. Eberhard Kolb (Cologne, 1972), 218–43; Gerhard Schulz, "Artikel 48 in politisch-historischer

Sicht," in *Der Staatsnotstand,* ed. Ernst Fraenkel (Berlin, 1965), 39–71; Hans Boldt, "Der Artikel 48 der Weimarer Reichsvertassung: Sein historischer Hintergrund und seine politische Funktion," in *Die Weimarer Republik,* ed. Michael Stürmer (Königstein im Taunus, 1980), 288–309; Ulrich Scheuner, "Die Anwendung des Art. 48 der Weimarer Reichsverfassung unter den Präsidentschaften von Ebert und Hindenburg," in *Staat, Wirtschaft und Politik: Festschrift für Heinrich Brüning,* ed. Ferdinand A. Hermes and Theodor Schieder (Berlin, 1967), 249–86; Frederick M. Watkins, *The Failure of Constitutional Emergency Powers under the German Republic* (Cambridge, Mass., 1939).

19. See Richard Thoma's "Das Reich als Demokratie," in *Handbuch des deutschen Staatsrechts* (1930), 1:196.

20. See Heinrich Pohl, "Der Reichspräsident und die Reichsregierung," in ibid., 487; Gerhard Schulz, *Zwischen Demokratie und Diktatur: Verfassungspolitik und Reichsreform in der Weimarer Republik* (Berlin, 1963), 114–42.

21. See *Gesammelte politische Schriften,* 2d ed. (Tübingen, 1952), 455, 486.

22. See Willibald Apelt, *Geschichte der Weimarer Verfassung,* 2d ed. (1946; Munich, 1964), 370.

23. See Karl Löwenstein, *Verfassungslehre* (Tübingen, 1959), 90 ff.

24. Hugo Preuß, "Reichsverfassungsmäßige Diktatur," *Zeitschrift für Politik* 13 (1923): 105.

25. In his *Beiträge zur Staatssoziologie* (Tübingen, 1961), 388.

26. Concerning Article 48 see Gerhard Anschütz, *Die Verfassung des Deutschen Reiches vom 11. August 1919: Ein Kommentar für Wissenschaft und Praxis,* 14th ed. (Berlin, 1933), n. 8.

27. Ibid.

28. The term *Verfassungsstörung* was coined by Johannes Heckel in his article "Diktatur, Notverordnungsrecht, Verfassungsnotstand," *Archiv des öffentlichen Rechts,* n.s., 22 (1932): 257 ff., 269 f.

29. See Heinz Kreuzer, "Der Ausnahmezustand im deutschen Verfassungsrecht," in *Der Staatsnotstand,* ed. Ernst Fraenkel (Berlin, 1965), 9–38.

30. Boldt, "Der Artikel 48," 293–95.

31. Hans Boldt, "Der Ausnahmezustand in historischer Perspektive," *Der Staat* 6 (1967): 419.

32. On the distinction between "measure" and "general law," see Karl Zeidler, *Maßnahmegesetz und "klassisches" Gesetz: eine Kritik* (Karlsruhe, 1961).

33. Kreuzer, "Der Ausnahmezustand," 33–34.

34. See Boldt, "Der Artikel 48," 293 f.

35. Scheuner, "Die Anwendung des Art. 48," 257 f.

36. See C.S. and Erwin Jacobi, "Die Diktatur des Reichspräsidenten," *Veröffentlichung der Vereinigung der deutsche Staatsrechtslehrer* 1 (1924): 63–139; see Ulrich Scheuner, "50 Jahre deutsche Staatsrechtwissenschaft im Spiegel der Verhandlungen der Vereinigung der Deutschen Staatsrechtslehrer," *Archiv des öffentlichen Rechts* 97 (1972): 353 f. (along with Carl Bilfinger, Schmitt and Jacobi would represent the Reich at the Supreme Court in Leipzig in October 1932, in the context of Prussia's appeal against the von Papen government's effective "execution" of its independent social-democratic government).

37. See Scheuner, "Die Anwendung des Art. 48," 268–69.

38. The letter of the president is documented in Schulz, *Zwischen Demokratie und Diktatur,* 1:647 f.

39. C.S., "Der Hüter der Verfassung" (Tübingen, 1931). The essay is an extended version of his original article with the same title, published in the *Archiv des öffentlichen Rechts,* n.s., 16 (1929): 161. Volker Neumann, in *Der Staat im Bürgerkrieg: Kontinuität und Wandlung des Staatsbegriffs in der politischen Theorie Carl Schmitts* (Frankfurt am Main, 1980), 107, characterizes this essay as Schmitt's "shift to the antiparliamentary administrative state."

40. See the excellent description by Heinrich August Winkler, *Der Weg in die Katastrophe: Arbeiter und Arbeiterbewegung in der Weimarer Republik 1930 bis 1933* (Berlin, 1987), 207 ff.

41. See Karl Dietrich Bracher, *Die Auflösung der Weimarer Republik,* 3d ed. (Villingen, 1960), 508 and the same author's "Brünings unpolitische Politik und die Auflösung der Weimarer Republik," *Vierteljahrshefte für Zeitgeschichte* (*hereafter VfZ*) 19 (1971): 113–23; see Gerhard Schulz, "Erinnerungen an eine mißlungene Restauration: Heinrich Brüning und seine Memoiren,"*Der Staat* 11 (1975): 61–81.

42. See Ludwig Biewer, *Reichsreformbestrebungen in der Weimarer Republik* (Frankfurt am Main, 1980); Schulz, *Zwischen Demokratie und Diktatur,* 1:564 ff.

43. Bendersky, *Carl Schmitt,* 19.

44. In *Zeitschrift für die gesamte Strafrechtswissenschaft* (hereafter *ZgStW*) 38 (1916): 138–61.

45. In *ZgStW* 41 (1916): 783–97.

46. It was first published in Munich, 1921.

47. C.S., *Die Diktatur,* 3d ed. (Berlin, 1964), 97 ff., 136.

48. Georg Jellinek, *Allgemeine Staatslehre,* 3d ed. (Darmstadt, 1959), 307 ff.; C.S., *Politische Theologie,* 46. See Karl Lowith, "Der okkasionelle Dezisionismus von Carl Schmitt" (1937), in *Gesammelte Abhandlungen* (Stuttgart, 1960), 93 ff. Ingeborg Maus, *Bürgerliche Rechtstheorie und Faschismus: Zur sozialen Funktion und aktuellen Wirkung der Theorie Carl Schmitts,* 2d ed. (Munich, 1980), 81 ff.

49. Armin Mohler, "Begegnungen bei Ernst Jünger," in *Freundschaftliche Begegnungen: Festschrift fur Ernst Jünger zum 60. Geburtstag* (Frankfurt am Main, 1955), 198.

50. C.S., *Politische Theologie,* 20 f.

51. C.S., "Das Reichsgericht als Hüter der Verfassung," in *Verfassungsrechtliche Aufsätze aus den Jahren 1924–1954: Materialien zu einer Verfassungslehre* (Berlin, 1958), 16–53.

52. C.S., "Das Ausführungsgesetz zu Art. 48 der Reichsverfassung (sog. Diktaturgesetz)," *Kölnische Volkszeitung,* October 30, 1926.

53. Bendersky, *Carl Schmitt,* 82, 118–19.

54. Ibid., 113, 152.

55. Ibid., 123 f., relying on "Gutachten Dorn zu Punkt I der heutigen Ministerbesprechung (3.4.1930): Zur Frage der Anwendung des Artikels 48 der Reichsverfassung und der Auflösung des Reichstages, Reichskanzlei," R-43-1, 1870, BA, 107–10. Concerning C.S.'s "Verfassungsrechtliches Gutachten über die Frage, ob der Reichspräsident befugt ist, auf Grund des Artikels 48 Abs. 2 RV. finanzgesetzvertretende Verordnungen zu erlassen—(28.7.1930)," Reichskanzlei, R-43-1, 1870, BA, in *Weimarer Republik, Die Kabinette Brüning I und II,* ed. Akten der Reichskanzlei (Boppard am Rhein, 1982), 11 f.

56. Along with the already cited works by these authors, see Joseph Bendersky's article "Carl Schmitt and the Conservative Revolution," *Telos* 72 (1987): 27–42.

57. See Ernst Rudolf Huber, "Carl Schmitt in der Reichskrise der Weimarer Endzeit," in *Complexio Oppositorum: Über Carl Schmitt*, ed. Helmut Quaritsch (Berlin, 1988), 33–70, and discussion, 53.

58. Ibid., 37–38.

59. Niederschrift über die Ministerbesprechung am 25. Juli 1932, Reichskanzlei, R-43-1, 186f., cited in Bendersky, *Carl Schmitt*, 157.

60. See Gerhard Schulz, "'Preußenschlag' oder Staatsstreich: Neues zum 20. Juli 1932," *Der Staat* 17 (1978): 553–81; Ludwig Biewer, "Der Preußenschlag vom 20. Juli 1932: Ursachen, Ereignisse, Folgen und Wertungen," *Blätter für deutsche Landesgeschichte* 119 (1983): 159–72. For the importance of Prussia, see Gotthard Jasper, "Preußen und die deutsche Republik—Belastung oder Bollwerk?," *Deutsche Verwaltungspraxis* 32 (1981): 188–93.

61. C.S., *Legalität und Legitimität* (1932; Berlin, 1968).

62. Ibid., 40 f.

63. Gerhard Anschütz, *Die Verfassung des Deutschen Reiches*, 351 ff.

64. Ernst Fraenkel, "Verfassungsreform und Sozialdemokratie," *Die Gesellschaft* 9, no. 2 (1932): 486–500. For the context see Heinrich August Winkler, *Der Weg in die Katastrophe* (Berlin, 1987), 802–9.

65. See Huber, "Carl Schmitt in der Reichskrise," 54–55.

66. Erich Marks to C.S., September 6, 1932, cited in Bendersky, *Carl Schmitt*, 172.

67. Muth, "Carl Schmitt," 133.

68. Bendersky, *Carl Schmitt*, 173 f.; Peter Hayes, "'A Question Mark with Epaulettes'? Kurt von Schleicher and Weimar Politics," *Journal of Modern History* 52 (1980): 49 f.

69. Huber, "Carl Schmitt in der Reichskrise," 40–41.

70. See Helga Worm, "Legalität und Legitimität—Eine fast vergessene 'Vortragsnotiz' aus dem Reichswehrministerium," *Der Staat* 27 (1988): 75–92.

71. See Bendersky, *Carl Schmitt*, 176 f.; C.S., *Der Begriff des Politischen*, 59–68.

72. Muth, "Carl Schmitt," 128 f.

73. It was published in Munich, 1919.

74. Ibid., 50 ff.; see also C.S., *Donoso Cortes in gesamteuropäischer Interpretation* (Cologne, 1950).

75. See C.S., *Römischer Katholizismus und Politische Form* (Hellerau, 1923).

76. See note 4 above.

77. See Hays, "A Question Mark," 51 f.; Axel Schildt, *Militärdiktatur mit Massenbasis: Die Querfrontkonzeption der Reichswehrführung um General von Schleicher am Ende der Weimarer Republik* (Frankfurt am Main, 1981), 161–97.

78. See Huber, "Carl Schmitt in der Reichskrise," 55.

79. Radio interview by Ansgar Skriver with C.S., "Hitlers Machtergreifung vor 40 Jahren im Gedächtnis von heute: eine zeitgeschichtliche Befragung," Westdeutscher Rundfunk, Hauptabteilung Politik, January 30, 1973, 8:45 P.M.

80. Hans Meyer, *Ein Deutscher auf Widerruf: Erinnerungen* (Frankfurt am Main, 1982), 1:151.

2. KNOWLEDGE OF EXPANSION

1. See, e.g., the study by Hans-Adolf Jacobsen, *Karl Haushofer: Leben und Werk,* 2 vols. (Boppard am Rhein, 1979). Along with Haushofer's writings, I rely on Jacobsen's documentation and evaluation of Haushofer's estate and correspondence.

2. For scholarly descriptions of the relationship between geography and geopolitics, see Carl Troll, "Die geographische Wissenschaft in Deutschland in den Jahren 1933 bis 1945: Eine Kritik und Rechtfertigung," *Erdkunde* 1 (1947): 19; and Peter Schöller, "Wege und Irrwege der Politischen Geographie und Geopolitik," cited in Josef Matznetter, ed., *Politische Geographie* (Darmstadt, 1977), 248 ff., 251 f.

3. "Bio-geographische Ergänzung einseitig bodenfremder Staatslehren"; Jacobsen, *Haushofer,* 1:249. See Karl Haushofer, *Freie Wege vergleichender Erdkunde: Festgabe für Erich von Drygalski zum 60. Geburtstag* (Munich, 1925); see Jacobsen, *Haushofer,* 1:508, cited there as "Politische Erdkunde und Geopolitik" (and in my citations below).

4. Letter of Karl Haushofer (hereafter K.H.) to Hans-Otto Roth ("against the premature dogmatization of geopolitics"), June 24, 1935, in Jacobsen, *Haushofer,* 2:205 f.

5. K.H., "Politische Erdkunde und Geopolitik," n. 3, in ibid., 1:515, 509.

6. K.H., "Vergleich des Lebens-Raumes Deutschlands mit dem seiner Nachbarn unter besonderer Berücksichtigung der wehrgeographischen Lage der Vergleichs-Staaten," in ibid.,see 1:524 ff., 533.

7. K.H., "Geopolitische Grundlagen," in *Grundlagen, Aufbau und Wirtschaftsordnung des nationalsozialistischen Staate* 1, group 2, no. 14 (Berlin, 1936), 30.

8. Ibid., 26.

9. K.H., *Grenzen in ihrer geographischen und politischen Bedeutung* (Berlin, 1927), 226; "Politische Erdkunde," in Jacobsen, *Haushofer,* 1:523f.

10. K.H., "Geopolitische Grundlagen," 29.

11. Jacobsen, *Haushofer,* 1:558ff, 605, 34.

12. K.H., "Apologie der deutschen 'Geopolitik,'" November 2, 1945, in ibid., 1:639 ff.

13. Diary entry K.H., January 29, 1918, in ibid., 148 ff.

14. Diary entry K.H., January 14, 1916, in ibid., 122.

15. Karl-Heinz Harbeck, "Die *Zeitschrift für Geopolitik,* 1924–1944" (Ph.D. diss., Kiel, 1963), 39.

16. Letter of Kurt Vowinckel to K.H., March 26, 1943, in Jacobsen, *Haushofer,* 2:543 f.

17. Diary entry of K.H., January 11, 1918, in ibid., 1:123 f.

18. Halford J. Mackinder, "The Geographic Pivot of History," *Geographical Journal* 23, no. 4 (1904): 421 ff.

19. Diary entry of K.H., September 3, 1917, in Jacobsen, *Haushofer,* 1:137.

20. Ibid., 1:457.

21. Letter of K.H. to Kurt Vowinckel ("concerning the future shape of the journal *Geopolitik*"), April 1, 1943, in ibid., 2:553 f., 554.

22. K.H., *Grundlagen der Geopolitik,* 2.

23. Diary entry of K.H., March 28, 1903, in Jacobsen, *Haushofer,* 1:75.; diary entry, March 1, 1918, in ibid., 1:152.

24. K.H., "Politische Erdkunde und Geopolitik," in ibid., 1:524.

25. Letter of K.H., August 8, 1918, in ibid., 1:132.

26. On letter of Oskar von Niedermayer to K.H., November 21, 1921, in ibid., 2:5.

27. Letter of Rudolf Heß to Martha Haushofer, December 17, 1921, in ibid., 2:6–7.

28. Ibid., 2:6n. 1.

29. Letter of Rudolf Heß, November 14, 1938, in ibid., 1:384.

30. Ibid., 1:456.

31. Ibid., 1:443; also 172, where the author suggests that the American military government's withdrawal of Karl Haushofer's academic chair was the decisive reason for the suicide of Haushofer and his wife in 1946.

32. Haushofer both wrote references for Hans Kohn and worked to have him appointed professor at the Hebrew University (K.H., "Apologie der deutschen 'Geopolitik,'" in ibid, 1:458n. 33); despite his residence in Jerusalem (in 1929 he would leave Palestine, emigrating to the United States in 1931), Kohn is included in Martha Haushofer's list of Jews whom her husband helped or tried to help (ibid., 1:458). Letter of K.H. to Ernst Simon (thoughts concerning Zionism), April 9, 1927, in ibid. 2:79 f.

33. Letter of Albrecht Haushofer to his mother ("Nazi Germany: on the ship mainly ruled and steered by fools and criminals"), December 13, 1939, in ibid., 2:416: "An example: I sit at my desk with a man whose task will be to see, according to plan, to the starvation and freezing of a large portion of the German Jews who have been shipped [to the ghetto of Lublin]."

34. In an early, programmatic essay, K.H. spoke out against any order based on estate or race: K.H., "Nationaler Sozialismus und soziale Aristokratie," *Zeitschrift für Geopolitik* (hereafter *ZfG*) 1 (1924): 127 ff.

35. See Ursula Laak-Michel, *Albrecht Haushofer und der Nationalsozialismus* (Stuttgart 1974), 141. According to Laak-Michel, Albrecht Haushofer was active at this Nazi institute ("Amt Ribbentrop") for foreign policy between 1934 and 1938.

36. Letter of Albrecht Haushofer to his mother, May 7–8, 1939, cited in Laak-Michel, *Haushofer und der Nationalsozialismus*, 120.

37. Ibid., 119.

38. Ibid., 121; Albrecht Haushofer was murdered as a resister by the Gestapo during the night of April 22–23, 1945, through a shot in the nape of the neck, on a piece of wasteland in Berlin-Moabit.

39. Carl Schmitt, *Der Begriff des Politischen*, 2d ed. (Berlin, 1963), 76.

40. The geopoliticist Erich Obst, cited in Rudolf Kjéllen and Karl Haushofer, eds., *Die Großmächte vor und nach dem Weltkriege* (Leipzig, 1933), 73.

41. Jacobsen, *Haushofer*, 1:133; see also K.H.'s foreword to Scott Nearing and Joseph Freeman, *Dollar Diplomacy: A Study in American Imperialism* (London, 1969).

42. Cited in Jacobsen, *Haushofer*, 1:92.

43. K.H., *Der Kontinentalblock: Mitteleuropa-Eurasian-Japan*, ed. Reichsstudentenführer Scheel (1940), in ibid., 1:606 ff., 625.

44. Ibid., 632.

45. Kjéllen and K.H., *Die Großmächte*, 267; K.H., *Bausteine der Geopolitik* (Berlin, 1928), 41.

46. Diary entry of K.H., August 29, 1918, in Jacobsen, *Haushofer,* 1:126.

47. Diary entry of K.H., July 2, 1918, in ibid., 1:153.

48. Diary entry of K.H., appendix 1918, in ibid., 1:129.

49. Letter of K.H. ("von dem erwürgenden angelsächsischen durch 'democracy' nur verschleierten großangelsächsischen Kapitalismus"), August 8, 1918, in ibid., 1:132.

50. K.H., *Weltpolitik von heute* (Berlin, 1934), 111.

51. K.H., *Nostris ex ossibus: Gedanken eines Optimisten, Zukunftsperspektiven vom 19. 10. 1944,* cited in Jacobsen, *Haushofer,* 1:634 ff.

52. Ibid., 635.

53. Ibid., 635. In his *Land und Meer: Eine weltgeschichtliche Betrachtung* (Stuttgart, 1954), 47, Carl Schmitt describes the Thirty-Years' War as an international civil war on German soil.

54. Jacobsen, *Haushofer,* 1:267.

55. David H. Norton, "Karl Haushofer and His Influence on Nazi Ideology and German Foreign Policy, 1919–1945" (Ph.D. diss., Clark University, Worcester, 1965; University Microfilms, Ann Arbor, Mich.), 16; also Halford J. Mackinder, *Democratic Ideals and Reality: A Study in the Politics of Reconstruction* (New York, 1919), 186: "Who rules Eastern Europe Commands the Heartland, / Who rules the Heartland Commands the World's Islands, / Who rules the World's Islands Commands the World!"

56. Jacobsen, *Haushofer,* 1:267.

57. Laak-Michel, *Haushofer und der Nationalsozialismus,* 159.

58. K.H., *Japan baut sein Reich* (1941), cited in ibid.

59. Adolf Grabowski, *Raum, Staat und Geschichte: Grundlagen der Geopolitik* (Cologne, 1960), 32.

60. K.H., "Der Ferne Osten" (speech), ms., January 15, 1920, in Jacobsen, *Haushofer,* 1:498 ff.

61. Grabowski, *Raum, Staat und Geschichte,* 197.

62. Jacobsen, *Haushofer,* 1:89.

63. "Two Japans were thus evident: one that masked itself, revealing as little of itself as possible . . . and another that was voluble and in love with publicity—that of the Nisei, the Rotary people, which wished, as in similar circles elsewhere in the Occident [*sic*], to be more Western than the West itself, more American than the Americans, and was ready to give up ancient inherited values for the common, platitudinous fare of third-rate American universities and squabbling missionary sects" (K.H., cited in ibid., 1:103).

64. In conversation with Haushofer, the Japanese ambassador in Berlin sarcastically—and with delicious succinctness—pointed to the political opportunism marking the German-Japanese alliance, and to its fundamental contradiction with Nazi racial doctrine: "As long as we made lovely woodcuts and built temple parks, we were barbarians; now that we smelt iron for guns and launch battleships, we are a cultured nation, and a noble race" (cited in ibid., 1:364).

65. Laak-Michel, *Haushofer und der Nationalsozialismus,* 143.

66. Ibid., 143, which Jacobsen (*Haushofer,* 365n. 42) views as an overinterpretation.

67. Troll, "Die geographische Wissenschaft," 21; and Jacobsen, *Haushofer,* 1:412.

68. For a critical appraisal of the American turn to geopolitics see Johannes Mat-

tern, *Geopolitics: Doctrine of National Self-Sufficiency and Empire* (Baltimore, 1942), 107 ("Geopolitics meets Geopolitics").

69. Franz Neumann, *Behemoth: The Structure and Practice of National Socialism* (London, 1942), 146.

70. Laak-Michel, *Haushofer und der Nationalsozialismus,* 159.

71. This approach was reinforced by Haushofer's positive assessment of the Bolsheviks because of their anti-British policies. As he saw it, through their action they freed men "from the slavery of banks and capital" (Jacobsen, *Haushofer,* 1:133).

72. Laak-Michel, *Haushofer und der Nationalsozialismus,* 258.

73. To be sure, we also find procolonialist remarks on Haushofer's part, directed at German overseas possessions. This constant ambivalence in the concrete configuration of a politics meant to be "scientized" has, not least of all, opportunistic sources: "Fully conscious of his intentions, Father has for years treated the colonial question in such a way that final possible objectives have remained open on both sides" (letter of Albrecht Haushofer to Kurt Vowinckel, February 21, 1936, cited in Harbeck, "Die *Zeitschrift für Geopolitik,*" 16).

74. Klaus Hildebrand, *Vom Reich zum Weltreich* (Munich, 1969), 768.

75. Adolf Hitler, *Mein Kampf* (Munich, 1934), 152.

76. Troll, "Die geographische Wissenschaft," 6.

77. Hildebrand, *Vom Reich zum Weltreich,* 771.

78. Jacobsen, *Haushofer,* 1:268.

79. Ibid., 275.

80. Ibid., 272.

81. On the notion's development, see Karl Lange, "Der Terminus 'Lebensraum' in Hitlers 'Mein Kampf,'" *VfZ* 13 (1965): 426-37, in regard to Friedrich Ratzel, "Der Lebensraum: Eine biographische Studie," in *Festgabe für Albert Schäffle* (Tübingen, 1901).

82. Herman Beukena, "Geopolitics," *Encyclopedia Americana* (1965), 12:472-74.

83. According to Lange, "Der Terminus 'Lebensraum,'" 428, this metaphor stems from a programmatic statement of the All-German League on January 7, 1894, made in relation to German east-southeastern expansion into the Donau region.

84. K.H., *Weltpolitik von heute* (Berlin, 1934), 23.

85. Hans Grimm, *Volk ohne Raum* (Munich, 1933), 1286.

86. Lange, "Der Terminus 'Lebensraum,'" 430.

87. K.H., "Geopolitische Grundlagen," cited in Jacobsen, *Haushofer,* 1:585; K.H., *Weltmeere und Weltmächte* (Berlin, 1941), 15.

88. K.H., *Grenzen,* 162, 168.

89. Grabowski, *Raum, Staat und Geschichte,* 173.

90. K.H., "Vergleich des Lebens-Raumes Deutschlands mit dem seiner Nachbarn," in Jacobsen, *Haushofer,* 1:525; K.H., *Weltpolitik von heute,* 55; K.H., *Grenzen,* 162.

91. K.H., *Weltpolitik von heute,* 19.

92. K.H., *Wehrwille als Volksziel* (Stuttgart, 1934), 20 (italics outside brackets are Haushofer's).

93. Letter of K.H. to Martens, March 6, 1930, in Jacobsen, *Haushofer,* 2:101-2.

94. K.H., "Geopolitische Grundlagen," in ibid., 1:600.

95. K.H., *Erdkunde, Geopolitik und Wehrwissenschaft* (1934), in ibid., 1:249.

96. K.H., *Weltpolitik von heute,* 13-23.

97. Ibid., 60.

98. Jacobsen, *Haushofer,* 1:463.

99. On the notion of autarchy, see—along with the following discussion—the next chapter.

100. On the extension of such a policy into Nazism see Alfred Sohn-Rethel, *Ökonomie und Klassenstruktur des deutschen Faschismus* (Frankfurt am Main, 1973), 78 ff., 136 ff.

101. See Grabowski, *Raum, Staat und Geschichte,* 31.

102. See Friedrich Naumann, *Mitteleuropa* (Berlin, 1915).

103. Friedrich List, "Das nationale System der politischen Ökonomie," in *Friedrich List: Schriften, Reden, Briefe,* ed. Erwin von Beckerath et al. (Aalen, 1971), vols. 33-36.

104. Ibid., 458-76.

105. K.H., "Geopolitische Grundlagen," in Jacobsen, *Haushofer,* 1:572; Norton, "Karl Haushofer and His Influence," 15.

106. Troll, "Die geographische Wissenschaft," 5.

107. Rudolf Kjéllen, *Der Staat als Lebensform* (Berlin, 1924), 69.

108. Ibid., 142.

109. Ibid., 143.

110. Ibid., 142.

111. Ibid., 144.

112. See Jacobsen, *Haushofer,* 1:125.

113. Cited in ibid., 1:337.

114. Cited in ibid., 1:336 (parenthetical terms are Haushofer's).

115. K.H., *Grundlagen der Geopolitik,* 10.

116. Cited in ibid., 1:489-90n. 26.

117. E.g., Manfred Langhans-Ratzeburg, "Begriff und Aufgaben der geographischen Rechtswissenschaft (Geojurisprudenz)," *ZfG,* n.s., 2 (1928): 77 ff.; and Hans Offe, "Geopolitik und Naturrecht," *ZfG* 14, no. 3 (1937): 239 ff.

118. Hans Keller, "Völkerrecht von Morgen," *Zeitschrift für Völkerrecht* 17, no. 5 (1933): 366 ff.

119. Heinrich Triepel, *Die Hegemonie: Ein Buch von den führenden Staaten* (1943; Aalen, 1974), 211 ff.

120. Carl Schmitt, *Nationalsozialismus und Völkerrecht* (Berlin, 1934); Carl Schmitt, *Der Nomos der Erde im Völkerrecht des Jus Publicum Europeum* (Cologne, 1950), 256 ff.

121. On recent approaches to the question of ground rent in relation to raw materials, see Mohsen Massarrat, *Weltenergieproduktion und Neuordnung der Weltwirtschaft: Die Weltarbeitsteilung und die Neuverteilung der Reichtums in der Welt* (Frankfurt am Main, 1980), 338 ff.

122. See Mattern, *Geopolitics,* 163 ff.

123. Norton, "Karl Haushofer and His Influence," 192.

124. Letter of K.H., December 24, 1938, cited in Hildebrand, *Vom Reich zum Weltreich,* 76n. 169.

125. Letter of K.H. to N.N. ("plea for the fatherland societies"), November 29, 1926, in Jacobsen, *Haushofer,* 2:71; letter of K.H. to Alzo Alzheimer, Munich ("refusal of a leading role in the Oberland Group"), March 8, 1925, in ibid., 2:38. Haushofer attributes a tactical tendency to his post-1933 writings in general—indeed, in

the evaluation of his role under the Nazis he insists on a "sharp distinction between all texts published before and after 1933" (ibid., 1:641).

126. Ibid., 1:280.

127. Cited in ibid., 1:246n. 30.

128. Hildebrand, *Vom Reich zum Weltreich*, 75; Jacobsen, *Haushofer*, 1:252.

129. Hildebrand, *Vom Reich zum Weltreich*, 77.

130. Jacobsen, *Haushofer*, 1:452.

131. Ibid., 243.

132. Ibid., 450.

133. Norton, "Karl Haushofer and His Influence," 84.

134. Jacobsen, *Haushofer*, 1:451.

135. Ibid., 389: earlier (337) we learn from Jacobsen of Haushofer's indication that he and above all his son Albrecht played an "essential role" in the negotiations over the fleet treaty with England.

136. Ibid., 1:257, 448.

137. Ibid., 643, 257.

138. See Grabowski, *Raum, Staat und Geschichte*, 79.

139. Jacobsen, *Haushofer*, 1:451.

140. Ibid., 327.

141. Letter from Peter Hofer to K.H. ("'a cry for help' from the South Tyroleans"), June 27, 1939, in ibid., 2:375 ff., 1:237.

142. Ibid., 325; letter from Dino Odoardo Alfieris to Goebbels ("Italian critique of Karl Haushofer's *Grenzen* book"), July 4, 1939, in ibid., 2:379 f.

143. Norton, "Karl Haushofer and His Influence," 92.

144. Jacobsen, *Haushofer*, 1:273.

145. Ibid., 462 f.

146. K.H., "Geographische Grundzüge auswärtiger Politik," *Süddeutsche Monatshefte,* January 1927, cited in ibid., 1:542.

147. See letter of K.H. to Hans-Otto Roth ("geopolitical education of the people"), September 13, 1933, in ibid., 2:146 f.

3. NORMS FOR DOMINATION

1. In this regard, see Günter Altner, *Weltanschauliche Hintergründe der Rassenlehre des Dritten Reiches* (Zurich, 1968); Heinz-Georg Marten, *Sozialbiologismus: Biologische Grundpositionen der politischen Ideengeschichte* (Frankfurt am Main, 1982); George L. Mosse, *Towards the Final Solution: A History of European Racism* (London, 1978); Patrick von zur Mühlen, *Rassenideologien: Geschichte und Hintergründe* (Berlin, 1977).

2. I rely here on Hans Mommsen, "Die Realisierung des Utopischen: Die 'Endlösung der Judenfrage' im 'Dritten Reich,'" *GuG* 9 (1983): 381–420. See Ernst Krieck, "Der Wandel der Wissenschaftsidee und des Wissenschaftssystems im Bereich der nationalsozialistischen Weltanschauung," *Volk im Werden* (1936): 378 ff.

3. Among the essential literature see Lawrence Preuß, "National Socialist Conceptions of International Law," *American Political Science Review* 29 (1935): 594–609; Eduard Bristler (pseudonym of John [Hans] Herz), *Die Völkerrechtslehre des Nationalsozialismus* (Zurich, 1938); Jacques Fourier, *La conception National-Socialiste du droit*

des gens (Paris, 1938); Lothar Gruchmann, *Nationalsozialistische Großraumordnung: Die Konstruktion einer "deutschen Monroe-Doktrine"* (Stuttgart, 1962); Manfred Messerschmidt, "Revision, Neue Ordnung, Krieg: Akzente der Völkerrechtswissenschaft in Deutschland 1933–1945," *Militärwissenschaftliche Mitteilungen* 1 (1971): 61–95; Carl H. Paußmeyer, "Die Grundlagen nationalsozialistischer Völkerrechtstheorie als ideologischer Rahmen für die Geschichte des Instituts für Auswärtige Politik 1933–1945," in *Kolonialrechtswissenschaft, Kriegsursachenforschung, Internationale Angelegenheiten: Materialien und Interpretationen zur Geschichte des Instituts für Internationale Angelegenheiten der Universität Hamburg 1923–1983 im Widerstreit der Interessen*, ed. Klaus Jürgen Gantzel (Baden-Baden, 1983); Diemut Majer, "Die Perversion des Völkerrechts unter dem Nationalsozialismus," *Jahrbuch des Instituts für deutsche Geschichte* 14 (1985): 311–32.

4. Günter Küchenhoff, "Der Großraumgedanke und völkische Ideen im Recht," *Zeitschrift für ausländisches öffentliches Recht und Völkerrecht* (hereafter *ZaöRV*) 12 (1944): 46; Werner Best, "Grundfragen einer deutschen Großraumverwaltung," in *Festgabe für Heinrich Himmler, anläßlich dessen 40. Geburtstages* (Darmstadt, 1941), 33 ff.

5. C. G. Meinhof, "Rasse und Recht," *Juristische Wochenschrift* 64 (1935): 3077; Helmut Nicolai, *Die rassengesetzliche Rechtslehre: Grundzüge einer nationalsozialistischen Rechtsphilosophie* (Munich, 1932), 18.

6. A. Merkl, *Allgemeines Verwaltungsrecht* (Vienna, 1927), 294.

7. Norbert Gürke, *Volk und Völkerrecht* (Tübingen, 1935), 4.

8. Ibid.

9. Meinhof, "Rasse und Recht," 3076.

10. Gürke, *Volk und Völkerrecht*, 57.

11. Meinhof, "Rasse und Recht," 3077.

12. Ernst Rudolf Huber, "Positionen und Begriffe: Eine Auseinandersetzung mit Carl Schmitt," *ZgStW* (1941): 1–44.

13. Gustav Adolf Walz, *Völkerrechtsordnung und Nationalsozialismus* (Munich, 1942), 81.

14. Ibid.; Gürke, *Volk und Völkerrecht*, 36

15. Norbert Gürke, "Grundzüge des Völkerrechts," in *Grundlagen, Aufbau und Wirtschaftsordnung des nationalsozialistischen Staates* (Berlin, 1936), 1:6.

16. Walz, *Völkerrechtsordnung*, 85.

17. Gürke, "Grundzüge," 6.

18. Walz, *Völkerrechtsordnung*, 87.

19. Carl Schmitt, *Völkerrechtliche Großraumordnung mit Interventionsverbot für raumfremde Mächte: Ein Beitrag zum Reichsbegriff im Völkerrecht* (Berlin, 1941), 7.

20. Ibid., 6.

21. Ibid., 8.

22. Carl Schmitt, "Großraum gegen Universalismus: Der völkerrechtliche Kampf um die Monroedoktrin" (1939), in *Positionen und Begriffe im Kampf mit Weimar—Genf—Versailles 1923–1939* (Hamburg, 1940), 295.

23. Alfred Verdross, "Abstrakte und konkrete Regelungen im Völkerrecht," *Völkerbund und Völkerrecht* 4 (1937–38): 213.

24. See Gustav Adolf Walz, *Wesen des Völkerrechts und Kritik der Völkerrechtsleugner* (Stuttgart, 1930).

25. Carl Schmitt, "Der Reichsbegriff im Völkerrecht" (1939), in *Positionen und Begriffe im Kampf mit Weimar—Genf—Versailles 1932–1939* (Hamburg, 1940), 308.

26. Ernst Wolgast, "Großraum und Reich: Bemerkungen zur Schrift Carl Schmitts, 'Völkerrechtliche Großraumforschung,'" *Zeitschrift für öffentliches Recht* (hereafter *ZöR*) 21 (1941): 22–23.

27. Carl Schmitt, "Raum und Großraum im Völkerrecht," *Zeitschrift für Völkerrecht* (hereafter *ZVR*) 24 (1941): 154.

28. Gürke, *Volk und Völkerrecht*, 89; Gürke, "Grundzüge," 3; in general, see Robert Redslob, "Die völkerrechtlichen Ideen der Französischen Revolution," *Festgabe fur O. Meyer* (1916): 271 ff.

29. Gürke, *Volk und Völkerrecht*, 89.

30. Gürke, "Grundzüge," 3.

31. Ibid.

32. Ibid., 4.

33. Schmitt, "Raum und Großraum," 165.

34. Hermann Jahrreiß, "Wandel der Weltordnung: Zugleich eine Auseinandersetzung mit der Völkerrechtslehre von Carl Schmitt," *ZöR* 21 (1941): 518.

35. Schmitt, "Raum und Großraum," 162 f.

36. Schmitt, *Völkerrechtliche Großraumordnung*, 20.

37. Schmitt, "Raum und Großraum," 168; Schmitt, *Völkerrechtliche Großraumordnung*, 20.

38. Schmitt, "Raum und Großraum," 168.

39. Max Schweizer, *Eine ideengeschichtliche Grundlage der Staatengleichheit: Zugleich ein Beitrag zur Geschichte des Natur-, Staats- und Völkerrechts* (Breslau, 1936), 12.

40. Ibid., 148.

41. Walz, *Völkerrechtsordnung*, 135.

42. Schweizer, *Grundlage der Staatengleichheit*, 21.

43. Gürke, "Grundzüge," 7.

44. Walz, *Völkerrechtsordnung*, 84.

45. Gustav Adolf Walz, "Das Verhältnis von Völkerrecht und Staatlichem Recht nach nationalsozialistischer Rechtsauffassung," *ZVR* 18 (1934): 147.

46. Ibid., 148.

47. Gustav Adolf Walz, "Nationalsozialismus und Völkerrecht," *Völkerbund und Völkerrecht* 1 (1934–35): 474.

48. Walz, *Völkerrechtsordnung*, 42.

49. Walz, "Nationalsozialismus und Völkerrecht," 473.

50. Ibid., 477.

51. Ibid., 474.

52. Ernst Wolgast, "Nationalsozialismus und Völkerrecht," *ZVR* 18 (1934): 130; also Herbert Kraus, "Das zwischenstaatliche Weltbild des Nationalsozialismus," *Juristische Wochenschrift* (1933): 2419; Hans Schneider, "Kritik von Schecher, Deutsches Außenstaatsrecht," *ZVR* 21 (1937–38); E. Tatarin-Tarheyden, "Kritik von Schecher, Deutsches Außenstaatsrecht," *Völkerbund und Völkerrecht* 1 (1934–35): 295 ff.

53. Carl Schmitt, *Nationalsozialismus und Völkerrecht* (Berlin, 1934), 5.

54. Walz, *Völkerrechtsordnung*, 67 ("und deutete es in ein im freien Raume schwebendes normologisches, hierarchisch gestuftes Gefüge von Sollgeltung um").

55. Ibid.

56. Norbert Gürke, *Das Judentum in der Rechtswissenschaft: Der Einfluß jüdischer Theoretiker auf die dt. Völkerrechtslehre* (Berlin, n.d.), 9 ("Ideengebäude jüdischen Intellekts").

57. Ibid., 14.

58. Gürke, *Volk und Völkerrecht*, 11.

59. Ibid.

60. Ibid., 20.

61. Gürke, *Judentum*, 28 (emphasis mine).

62. Ibid., 15.

63. Ibid., 28.

64. Ibid., 19.

65. Schmitt, *Nationalsozialismus und Völkerrecht*, 5; Schmitt, "Die deutsche Rechtswissenschaft im Kampf gegen den jüdischen Geist: Schlußwort auf der Tagung der Reichsgruppe Hochschullehrer des NSRB vom 3. und 4. Oktober 1936," *Deutsche Juristen-Zeitung* (hereafter *DJZ*) 41 (1936): 1197.

66. Walz, "Nationalsozialismus und Völkerrecht," 475.

67. Gürke, *Volk und Völkerrecht*, 21.

68. Walz, "Nationalsozialismus und Völkerrecht," 473.

69. Schmitt, "Raum und Großraum," 162–63.

70. Walz, "Völkerrecht und Staatliches Recht," 149.

71. Gürke, "Grundzüge," 14.

72. Ibid., 10 f.

73. Günther Kranz, "Nationalsozialistisches Völkerrechtsdenken," *Reichsverwaltungsblatt* 55 (1934): 10; Gürke, *Volk und Völkerrecht*, 130.

74. Kranz, "Nationalsozialistisches Völkerrechtsdenken," 9.

75. Gürke, "Grundzüge," 9; Gürke, *Volk und Völkerrecht*, 99.

76. Carl Schmitt, "Der Gegensatz von Parlamentarismus und moderner Massendemokratie," in *Positionen und Begriffe im Kampf mit Weimar—Genf—Versailles 1932–1939* (Hamburg, 1940), 62.

77. Karl Petraschek, "Grundrecht und Völkerrecht: Grundsätzliches zur Frage der völkerrechtlichen Grundsätze," *Archiv für Rechts- und Sozialphilosophie* 27 (1933–34): 505.

78. Carl Bilfinger, "Zum Problem der Staatengleichheit im Völkerrecht," *ZaöRV* 4 (1934): 485.

79. Ibid., 494.

80. Petraschek, "Grundrecht und Völkerrecht," 506.

81. Viktor Bruns, "Rechtsgemeinschaft oder Herrschaftsgemeinschaft?," *Völkerbund und Völkerrecht* 1 (1934–35): 15 ("eigenen Grundsätzen von Ehre und Gerechtigkeit").

82. Schmitt, "Parlamentarismus und moderne Massendemokratie," 59.

83. Ibid., 61.

84. Schweizer, *Grundlage der Staatengleichheit*, 36.

85. Carl Schmitt, *Verfassungslehre*, 5th ed. (Berlin, 1970), 228 ff.; Schweizer, *Grundlage der Staatengleichheit*, 36.

86. Carl Schmitt, "Das gute Recht der deutschen Revolution," *Westdeutscher Beobachter* 31, no. 5 (1933): 1–2. In its most general possible usage, *Art* means "type or

kind," the racial significance of *Gleichartigkeit* (as well as *Artgleichheit*) thus being ideologically determined.

87. Schweizer, *Grundlage der Staatengleichheit*, 7.

88. Ibid., 96.

89. Carl Bilfinger, "Gleichheit und Gleichberechtigung der Staaten," *Nationalsozialistisches Handbuch für Recht und Gesetzgebung* (1935): 120; Schweizer, *Grundlage der Staatengleichheit*, 96.

90. Carl Schmitt, *Über die drei Arten des rechtswissenschaftlichen Denkens* (Hamburg, 1934), 20.

91. Bilfinger, "Staatengleichheit im Völkerrecht," 491.

92. Walz, *Völkerrechtsordnung*, 11.

93. Ibid.

94. Ibid., 28.

95. Bilfinger, "Gleichheit und Gleichberechtigung," 120.

96. Schmitt, "Reichsbegriff," 306.

97. E. Tatarin-Tarnheyden, "Organisches Völkerrecht," *Völkerbund und Völkerrecht* 3 (1936–37): 26 ("[die] Wertigkeit der ... zur Machtgestalt gelangten Volkstümer").

98. Schweizer, *Grundlage der Staatengleichheit*, 50.

99. Hans Offe, "Geopolitik und Naturrecht," *ZfG* 14 (1937): 245.

100. Herbert Kraus, *Die Krise zwischenstaatlichen Denkens: eine Bilanz* (Göttingen, 1933), 19.

101. Walz, *Völkerrechtsordnung*, 134.

102. Ibid., 141.

103. Ibid.

104. Carlo Costomagna, "Autarkie und Ethnarkie in der Völker- und Staatsrechtslehre der Neuordnung," *Zeitschrift der Akademie für Deutsches Recht* 8 (1944): 202; Friedrich Berber, *Sicherheit und Gerechtigkeit* (Berlin, 1934), 19.

105. The following observation by Hasso Hofmann (*Legitimität gegen Legalität: Der Weg der politischen Philosophie Carl Schmitts* [Berlin, 1964], 196) is relevant: "For his part, Karl Löwith indicated in the journal *Maß und Wert* that 'the biological equality of race' replaces theological equality before God and moral equality before the law. In the arithmetic *Volks-* and party-comrade, all the problems of the last century appear to vanish: the conflict between state and society, bourgeoisie and proletariat, *homme* and *citoyen*. But—just so—only apparently."

106. Erich Kaufmann, *Das Wesen des Völkerrechts und die Clausula rebus sic stantibus* (Tübingen, 1911), 198.

107. Graf Westarp, "Die Clausula rebus sic stantibus im heutigen Völkerrecht," *Juristische Wochenschrift* 63 (1934): 203.

108. Ibid.

109. Hans Keller, "Völkerrecht von morgen," *ZVR* 17 (1934): 366.

110. Westarp, "Die Clausula rebus sic stantibus," 155.

111. Kraus, "Weltbild," 2421.

112. Bruns, "Rechtsgemeinschaft," 15.

113. Gustav Adolf Walz, "Der Treuegedanke im Völkerrecht," *Deutsches Recht* 4 (1934): 521; Friedrich Berber, "Von der Heiligkeit der Verträge," *Hamburger Monatshefte für Auswärtige Politik* (1936): 139.

114. Walz, *Völkerrechtsordnung*, 77.

115. H. Richter, "Völkerrecht," *Deutsches Recht* 4 (1934): 206.

116. Walz, "Nationalsozialismus und Völkerrecht," 476.

117. Walz, "Treuegedanke," 524.

118. Messerschmidt, "Revision," 74.

119. Gürke, "Grundzüge," 10 f.

120. Kranz, "Nationalsozialistisches Völkerrechtsdenken," 9.

121. Gürke, *Volk und Völkerrecht,* 50.

122. Nicolai, *Rassengesetzliche Rechtslehre,* 48.

123. Kranz, "Nationalsozialistisches Völkerrechtsdenken," 10.

124. Schmitt, "Reichsbegriff," 308.

125. Walz, "Nationalsozialismus und Völkerrecht," 474.

126. E. Tatarin-Tarnheyden, "Völkerrecht und organische Staatsauffassung," *Archiv für Rechts- und Sozialphilosophie* 29 (1935–36): 316.

127. Walz, *Völkerrechtsordnung,* 147.

128. Gürke, "Grundzüge," 7.

129. Gürke, *Volk und Völkerrecht,* 35.

130. Ibid., 18.

131. Carl Schmitt, "Faschistische und nationalsozialistische Rechtswissenschaft," *DJZ 41* (1936): 620.

132. Kraus, "Weltbild," 2422.

133. Walz, *Völkerrechtsordnung,* 83.

134. Ibid., 89.

135. Ibid., 98.

136. Ibid., 85, 88.

137. Ibid.

138. Ibid., 78

139. Walz, *Völkerrechtsordnung,,* 78.

140. Carl Schmitt, "Reich—Staat—Bund" (1933), in *Positionen und Begriffe im Kampf mit Weimar—Genf—Versailles 1932–1939* (Hamburg, 1940), 192.

141. Gürke, *Volk und Völkerrecht,* 23.

142. Carl Schmitt, "Reich und Raum: Elemente eines neuen Völkerrechts," *Zeitschrift der Akademie für Deutsches Recht* 7 (1940): 202.

143. Jahrreiß, "Wandel der Weltordnung," 528.

144. Walz, *Völkerrechtsordnung,* 148.

145. Schmitt, "Reichsbegriff," 304.

146. Ibid., 305.

147. Ibid., 303.

148. Carl Schmitt, "Völkerrechtliche Formen des modernen Imperialismus," in *Positionen und Begriffe im Kampf mit Weimar—Genf—Versailles 1932–1939* (Hamburg, 1940), 179.

149. Walz, *Völkerrechtsordnung,* 79.

150. Schmitt, "Reichsbegriff," 307.

151. Ibid., 311.

152. Gruchmann, *Großraumordnung,* 126.

153. Schmitt, "Reichsbegriff," 307 ("den Begriff einer konkreten Großraumordnung zu finden, der beiden entgeht und sowohl den räumliche Maßen unseres heutigen Erdbildes als auch unseren neuen Begriffen von Staat und Volk gerecht wird").

154. Ibid., 312.
155. Carl Schmitt, *Die Wendung zum diskriminierenden Kriegsbegriff* (Munich, 1937), 52f.
156. Gruchmann, *Großraumordnung*, 141.
157. Ibid.
158. Walz, *Völkerrechtsordnung*, 97.
159. Ibid.
160. Schmitt, "Völkerrechtliche Formen des modernen Imperialismus," 162.
161. Ibid.
162. Schmitt, "Raum und Großraum," 164.
163. Schmitt, "Großraum gegen Universalismus," 299 ("Besitzargumentation des Status quo der heutigen Vertragslage").
164. Ibid., 296.
165. Ibid., 297.
166. Schmitt, "Raum und Großraum," 179.
167. Gruchmann, *Großraumordnung*, 22; more extensively: Werner Daitz, *Lebensraum und gerechte Weltordnung: Grundlagen einer Anti-Atlantikcharta* (Amsterdam, 1943).
168. Jahrreiß, "Wandel der Weltordnung," 525.
169. Reinhard Höhn, "Großraumordnung und völkisches Rechtsdenken," *Reich, Volk, Lebensraum* 1 (1941): 260.
170. Roger Diener, "Reichsverfassung und Großraumverwaltung im Altertum," in ibid.; 178; Höhn, "Großraumordnung," 259.
171. Walz, *Völkerrechtsordnung*, 146.
172. Ibid., 142.
173. Höhn, "Großraumordnung," 269 (referring to Schmitt).
174. Walz, *Völkerrechtsordnung*, 143.
175. Bilfinger, "Staatengleichheit im Völkerrecht," 434.
176. H. H. Dietze, "Vom deutschen Verfassungsrecht zum europäischen Verfassungsrecht," *Deutsches Recht* 11 (1941): 809; Bilfinger, "Staatengleichheit," 494.
177. Schmitt, *Völkerrechtliche Großraumordnung*, 4.
178. Höhn, "Großraumordnung," 259.
179. Jahrreiß, "Wandel der Weltordnung," 521.
180. Diener, "Reichsverfassung," 229 ("[die] Form großräumiger politischer Gestaltung").
181. Ibid.
182. Huber, "Positionen und Begriffe," 39.
183. Schmitt, "Reichsbegriff," 303.
184. Schmitt, *Völkerrechtliche Großraumordnung*, 6; Schmitt, "Reich und Raum," 202.
185. Höhn, "Großraumordnung," 262 ("daß ganz bestimmte geschichtsmäßige Völker für ganz bestimmte Räume Verantwortung tragen").
186. Hofmann, *Legitimität gegen Legalität*, 221.
187. Huber, "Positionen und Begriffe," 39.
188. Hofmann, *Legitimität gegen Legalität*, 216.
189. Schmitt, *Völkerrechtliche Großraumordnung*, 48 (in relation to Werner Best).
190. Gruchmann, *Großraumordnung*, 130.

191. Küchenhoff, "Großraumgedanke," 68.

192. Ibid. On the concept of "leadership" (*Führung*), see Heinrich Triepel, *Die Hegemonie: Ein Buch von führenden Staaten* (Stuttgart, 1943).

193. Gruchmann, *Großraumordnung*, 131.

194. Ibid., 133.

195. Bilfinger, "Staatengleichheit im Völkerrecht," 494.

196. Bristler, *Völkerrechtslehre*, 10.

197. Ibid., 67.

198. Ernst Wolgast, "Nationalsozialismus und internationales Recht," *Deutsches Recht* 4 (1934): 198.

199. Gruchmann, *Großraumordnung*, 144.

200. Küchenhoff, "Großraumgedanke," 48.

201. Ibid.

202. Ibid.

203. Gerhard Jentsch, "Lebensraum," cited in Gruchmann, *Großraumordnung*, 21.

204. Ibid.

205. Küchenhoff, "Großraumgedanke," 57 ("biologisch gebundener Lebensräume").

206. Ibid., 62.

207. Ibid., 44.

208. Höhn, "Großraumordnung," 286.

209. Küchenhoff, "Großraumgedanke," 61.

210. Walz, *Völkerrechtsordnung*, 143.

211. Ibid., 141.

212. Schweizer, *Grundlage der Staatengleichheit*, 50.

213. Werner Daitz, *Das Selbstbestimmungsrecht der Lebensräume* (Berlin, 1941).

4. THE CATASTROPHE BEFORE THE CATASTROPHE

1. Cited by Benno Cohn, one of the two chairmen of the German Zionist Organization, in his report "Summons of the representatives of German Judaism before the Gestapo (Eichmann) in spring 1939" (German); reported in a meeting of the "Circle of Zionists from Germany" on April 1, 1958, in Tel Aviv; transcribed by Dr. Kurt Jakob Ball-Kadurie, Yad Vashem Archives, 01/125; published in Document 1 of Kurt Jakob Ball-Kadurie, "Die illegale Einwanderung der deutschen Juden," *Jahrbuch des Instituts für Deutsche Geschichte* 4 (1975): 415–17.

2. Cited in David Ben-Gurion, *Miscellaneous Writings*, ed. Gershon Rivlin (Tel Aviv, 1982), 5:397–98 (Hebrew); original in the Labor Party archive, 23/28, 41; see also Yoav Gelber, "Zionist Policy and European Jewry," *Yad Vashem Studies* (hereafter *YVS*) 13 (1979): 199.

3. Ben-Gurion, *Miscellaneous Writings*, 398.

4. See, for instance, Lenni Brenner's tendentious interpretation in his *Zionism and the Age of the Dictators* (London, 1938), 149 f.

5. See Dan Diner, "The Yishuv in Light of the Holocaust," *Ha'Zionut* 13 (1988): 301–8 (Hebrew).

6. See Herbert A. Strauss, "Jewish Emigration from Germany: Nazi Policy and Jewish Response (I)," *Yearbook of the Leo Baeck Institute* (hereafter *YLB*) 25 (1980): 328.

7. See Yehoshua Porath, *The Palestinian Arab National Movement: From Riots to Rebellion, 1929–1939* (London, 1977), 274–94.

8. See Michael J. Cohen, "British Strategy and the Palestine Question, 1936–1939," *Journal of Contemporary History* 7 (1972): 157–83; Michael J. Cohen, "Appeasement in the Middle East: The British White Paper on Palestine, May 1939," *The Historical Journal* 16 (1973): 571–96; Gabriel Sheffer, "The Involvement of Arab States in the Palestine Conflict and Arab-British Relationship before World War II," *Asian and African Studies* 10 (1974–75): 59–78.

9. Such a decision was made, for instance, in the British Cabinet meeting of November 14, 1938; see the Cabinet Paper 27/651, cited in Martin Gilbert, "British Government Policy towards Jewish Refugees, November 1938–September 1939," *YVS* 13 (1979): 129.

10. Gelber, "Zionist Policy," 199.

11. See Charles Wighton, *Heydrich: Hitler's Most Evil Henchman* (London, 1962) 167; Bernhard Lösener, "Als Rassereferent im Reichsministerium des Inneren," *VfZ* 9 (1961): 264–313. Uwe Dietrich Adam, *Judenpolitik im Dritten Reich* (Düsseldorf, 1972), 209 ff.

12. See Salomon Adler-Rudel, *Jüdische Selbsthilfe unter dem Nazi-Regime* (Tübingen, 1974), 115f.

13. See Artur Prinz, report of September 1945, "Die Gestapo als Feind und als Förderer der jüdischen Auswanderung" (copy of the text in the Wiener Library, Tel Aviv University, P.II f., no. 792), published as "The Role of the Gestapo in Obstructing and Promoting Jewish Emigration," *YVS* 2 (1958): 205–18.

14. Ibid., 205.

15. Ibid., 206.

16. See the excellent study by Jacob Toury, "From the Forced Emigration to Expulsion: The Jewish Exodus over the Non-Slavic Borders of the Reich as a Prelude to the 'Final Solution,'" *YVS* 17 (1986): 60 f.

17. Ibid.

18. See Strauss, "Jewish Emigration," 351–52.

19. See Herbert Rosenkranz, *Verfolgung und Selbstbehauptung: Die Juden in Österreich 1938–1945* (Vienna, 1978).

20. See Bruce F. Pauley, *Hitler and the Forgotten Nazis: A History of Austrian National Socialism* (Chapel Hill, N.C., 1981).

21. See Yisrael Benari, *The Evacuation Policies of Jabotinsky and His Prediction of the Fate of Poland's Jews* (Tel Aviv, 1968) (Hebrew).

22. See the vivid account of Juliane Wetzel, "Auswanderung aus Deutschland," in *Die Juden in Deutschland 1933–1945: Leben unter nationalsozialistischer Herrschaft*, ed. Wolfgang Benz (Munich, 1988), 433–38.

23. See two articles in *YLB* 27 (1982): Jacob Boas, "Germany or Diaspora? German Jewry's Shifting Perceptions in the Nazi Era, 1933–1939," 117; and Peter Baldwin, "Zionist and Non-Zionist Jews in the Last Years before the Nazi Regime," 87–108, as well as one in *YLB* 30 (1985): Jehuda Reinharz, "The Zionist Response to the Antisemitism in Germany," 105–40.

24. In "German-Jewish Internal Politics under Hitler, 1933–1938" (YLB 29 [1984]: 3–25), Jacob Boas has clearly delineated the shift: "Thus in 1903 Heinrich Stahl had returned from a trip to Palestine convinced that the place could not be made fit for human habitation; in 1936 they believed that only Palestine could save the Jews" (Jüdische Rundschau, April 12–May 8, 1938, 36); "Eva Reichmann-Jungmann likewise returned full of praise for the Jewish settlements after visiting Palestine around the beginning of 1938" (newspaper of the Centralverein, February 24, 1938, 17); "and by the end of 1935 even the RjF [Reichsvereinigung jüdischer Frontsoldaten] called for furthering the work there" (Jüdische Rundschau, October 10, 1935, 40).

25. See Abraham Margaliot, "The Problem of the Rescue of German Jewry during the Years 1938–1939: The Reasons for Delay in Their Emigration from the Third Reich," in Rescue Attempts during the Holocaust, ed. Yisrael Gutman and Efraim Zieroff (Jerusalem, 1977), 252.

26. See Dirk Blasius, "Zwischen Rechtsvertrauen und Rechtszerstörung: Deutsche Juden 1933–1935," in Zerbrochene Geschichte: Leben und Selbstverständnis der Juden in Deutschland, ed. Dirk Blasius and Dan Diner (Frankfurt am Main, 1991), 121–37. The point was made most clearly by the revisionist ("state") Zionist Georg Kareski: "German Jews have lost their legal equality, but they at least have legal grounding under their feet" (cited in Abraham Margaliot, "The Reaction of the Jewish Public in Germany to the Nuremberg Laws," YVS 12 [1977]: 91); on Kareski, see Francis R. Nicosia, "Revisionist Zionism in Germany," YLB 32 (1987): 231–67.

27. Margaliot, "Reaction of the Jewish Public," 86, 90.

28. Ibid., 94.

29. See Kurt T. Grossmann, "Zionist and Non-Zionist under Nazi Rule in the 1930s," Herzl Yearbook: Essays in Zionist History and Thought 4 (1961–62): 329–44; Hans Mommsen, "Der nationalsozialistische Polizeistaat und die Judenverfolgung vor 1938," VfZ 10 (1962): 68–87, above all document 2, 78; Boas, "Germany or Diaspora," 20 ff.

30. See Chaim Schatzker, "The Jewish Youth Movement in Germany in the Holocaust Period (part 1)," YLB 32 (1987): 166.

31. Still instructive in this regard is Hannah Arendt, The Origins of Totalitarianism (New York, 1951), 261; see also Michael R. Marrus, The Unwanted: European Refugees in the Twentieth Century (New York, 1985).

32. See Celia Heller, On the Edge of Destruction: Jews of Poland Between the Two World Wars (New York, 1977); Pawel Korzec, Les juifs en Pologne: La question juive pendent l'entre-deux-guerres (Paris, 1980).

33. See Erwin Viefhaus, Die Minderheitenfrage und die Entstehung der Minderheitenschutzverträge auf der Pariser Friedenskonferenz 1919: Eine Studie zur Geschichte des Nationalitätenproblems im 19. und 20. Jahrhundert (Würzburg, 1960); Pawel Korzec, "Polen und der Minderheitenschutzvertrag (1919–1934)," Jahrbücher für die Geschichte Osteuropas 22 (1974): 515–55.

34. See Emmanuel Melzer, "Relations between Poland and Germany and Their Impact on the Jewish Problem in Poland (1935–1938)," YVS 12 (1977): 193–94.

35. Ibid., 206.

36. See Leni Yahil, "Madagascar—Phantom of a Solution for the Jewish Ques-

tion," in *Jews and Non-Jews in Eastern Europe,* ed. Bela Vago and George L. Mosse (New York, 1974), 316 f.

37. See David Engel, "The Frustrated Alliance: The Revisionist Movement and the Polish Government-in-Exile, 1939-1945," *Studies in Zionism* 7 (1986): 11-37.

38. See Ezra Mendelson, "The Dilemma of Jewish Politics in Poland: Four Responses," in *Jews and Non-Jews in Eastern Europe 1918-1945,* ed. Bela Vago and George L. Mosse (New York, 1974), 203-19.

39. See Margaliot, "Rescue of German Jewry," 250 ff.

40. Ibid., 258.

41. Ibid., 247-66. Margaliot refers to an article from the *Gazeta Warszawska* that was reprinted in London in *World Jewry,* April 19, 1935.

42. See Nana Sagi and Malcolm Lowe, "Research Report: Pre-War Reactions to Nazi Anti-Jewish Policies in the Jewish Press," *YVS* 13 (1970): 402.

43. Ibid., 403. See Edwin Black, *The Transfer Agreement: The Untold Story of the Secret Pact between the Third Reich and Jewish Palestine* (New York, 1984); Werner Feilchenfeld et al., *Ha'avara Transfer nach Palästina und Einwanderung deutscher Juden 1933-1939* (Tübingen, 1972; Schriftenreihe wissenschaftlicher Abhandlungen des Leo Baeck Instituts 26); Francis R. Nicosia, *The Third Reich and the Palestine Question* (Austin, 1985), 29-49.

44. Melzer, "Relations between Poland and Germany," 208.

45. Ibid., 216-17.

46. A peripheral cause of the decree was the fear that through the appropriation of shares in Poland's Galician oil industry owned by Jewish stock investors living in Austria, the German Reich could gain influence over this energy sources.

47. See Salomon Adler-Rudel, "The Evian Conference on the Refugee Question," *YLB* 13 (1968): 235-73; Michael Mashberg, "American Diplomacy and the Jewish Refugees, 1938-1939," *Yivo Annual of Jewish Social Science* 15 (1974): 339-65; Henry Feingold, *The Politics of Rescue: The Roosevelt Administration and the Holocaust, 1938-1945* (New Brunswick, 1979); David S. Wyman, *Paper Walls: America and the Refugee Crisis, 1938-1941* (Amherst, 1968); Saul S. Friedman, *No Haven for the Oppressed: United States Policy towards Jewish Refugees, 1938-1945* (Detroit, 1973), 229-30.

48. Wyman, *Paper Walls,* 43-51.

49. Mashberg, "American Diplomacy," 346.

50. Ibid., 340n. 3 (citing the *New York Herald Tribune,* July 16, 1938).

51. Ibid., 341.

52. See (with extensive citations) Herbert A. Strauss, "Jewish Emigration from Germany: Nazi Policy and Jewish Response (part 2)," *YLB* 26 (1981): 358.

53. Ibid., 302.

54. Mashberg, "American Diplomacy," 346.

55. See Joshua B. Stein, "Great Britain and the Evian Conference of 1938," *Wiener Library Bulletin* 29 (1976): 40-52.

56. Mashberg, "American Diplomacy," 348.

57. Ibid., 356.

58. Strauss, "Jewish Emigration (part 2)," 344.

59. Nicosia, *Third Reich,* 158.

60. Shlomo Z. Katz, "Public Opinion in Western Europe and the Evian Conference of July 1938," *YVS* 9 (1973): 133.

61. Wyman, *Paper Walls*, 14–22, 210–11.

62. See Haim Genizi, "American Non-Sectarian Refugee Relief Organizations, 1933–1945," *YVS* 11 (1976): 216.

63. Taylor commented, "We accomplished the purpose for which the Intergovernmental Meeting in Evian was called" (cited by Mashberg, "American Diplomacy," 358).

64. See Shabtai Beit-Zvi, *Post-Uganda Zionism in the Crisis of the Holocaust* (Tel Aviv, 1977), 180 f. (Hebrew).

65. Ibid., 181–82.

66. "The Jewish People and Palestine: Statement by Dr. Weizmann made before the Palestine Royal Commission in Jerusalem on November 25, 1936," in *Chaim Weizmann: Statesman, Scientist, Builder of the Jewish Commonwealth*, ed. Meyer W. Weisgal (New York, 1944), 304–28.

67. Toury, "From the Forced Emigration to Expulsion," 67.

68. See Trude Maurer, "Abschiebung und Attentat: Die Ausweisung der polnischen Juden und der Vorwand für die Kristallnacht," in *Der Judenpogrome 1938: Von der "Reichskristallnacht" zum Völkermord*, ed. Walter H. Pehle (Frankfurt am Main, 1988), 52–73.

69. See Nicosia, *Third Reich*, 159 f.; Jürgen Rohwer, "Jüdische Flüchtlingsschiffe im Schwarzen Meer, 1934 bis 1944," in *Das Unrechtsregime*, ed. Ursula Büttner (Hamburg, 1986), 2:201 f.; Jon and David Kimche, *The Secret Roads: The "Illegal" Migration of a People* (Westport, Conn., 1976).

5. THE LIMITS OF REASON

In order to portray Max Horkheimer's changing position on anti-Semitism, I have focused my account on a few texts drawn from the years 1939–1944/45, thus necessarily forgoing treatment of his position on Judaism in general as well as related themes, such as the analysis of authority or of the significance of religion.

I wrote this essay in 1984 when I was teaching at Odense University in Denmark. Its text remains basically unchanged and does not reflect some shifts in perspective since then or take into account more recent literature on the topic such as Detlev Claussen, *Grenzen der Aufklärung* (Frankfurt am Main, 1987) or Rolf Wiggershaus, *The Frankfurt School: Its History, Theories and Political Significance* (Cambridge, 1994). In the discussion and notes I cite Horkheimer's texts by their abbreviated titles, adding the page numbers of their English versions—where available—in square brackets (in some cases I have modified the translations):

DA   *Dialektik der Aufklärung* (completed in 1944), in *Gesammelte Schriften: Dialektik der Aufklärung und Schriften 1940–1950* (Frankfurt am Main, 1987), 16–290; translated as *Dialect of Enlightenment* (New York, 1972)

"VS"   "Vernunft und Selbsterhaltung" (written in winter 1941–42), in ibid., 320–50; translated as "The End of Reason," in *The Essential Frankfurt School Reader*, ed. Andrew Arato and Eike Gebhardt (New York, 1982), 26–48

"JE"   "Die Juden und Europa" (written in early September 1939), in *Gesammelte Schriften: Schriften 1936–1941* (Frankfurt am Main, 1988), 308–31; translated as "The Jews and Europe," in *Critical Theory and Society: A Reader,* ed. Stephen Bronner and Douglas Kellner (New York, 1989), 77–94

"BV"   "Zum Begriff der Vernunft" (written in 1951), in *Gesammelte Schriften: Vorträge und Aufzeichungen 1949–1973* (Frankfurt am Main, 1985), 22–35

CIR   *Critique of Instrumental Reason* (New York, 1974); originally *Zur Kritik der instrumentallen Vernunft* (written in 1944, published as *Eclipse of Reason* [Oxford, 1947])

N   *Notizen 1950–1969 und Dämmerung* (Frankfurt am Main, 1974); translated as *Dawn and Decline: Notes 1926–1931 and 1950–1969* (New York, 1974)

1. Martin Jay, "The Jews and the Frankfurt School: Critical Theory's Analysis of Anti-Semitism," in *Permanent Exiles: Essays on the Intellectual Migration from Germany to America* (New York, 1985), 90, stresses the young Horkheimer's *"facile* dismissal of specifically Jewish problems" (italics added).

2. Ibid., 91. Elsewhere, Jay falls prey to a misunderstanding with substantive foundations by interpreting Horkheimer's resignation after the annihilation of the Jews as a turn toward a profession of Zionism: "Not until after the war did Horkheimer come to the melancholy conclusion that Zionism had been the only way out for the Jews of Europe" (Martin Jay, *The Dialectical Imagination: A History of the Frankfurt School and the Institute of Social Research, 1923–1950* [Boston, 1973], 308n. 92). The approach taken by Erich Cramer, *Hitlers Antisemitismus und die "Frankfurter Schule": Kritische Faschismustheorie und geschichtliche Realität* (Düsseldorf, 1979), is problematic. An ex post facto perspective does not allow us to trace the dramatic entwinement of theory and existential experience involved here.

3. Jay, *Dialectical Imagination,* 32, points out that at the time the Jewish members of the institute denied that their Jewish origins had any significance whatsoever.

4. Thus, before the war, Horkheimer attributed no significance to anti-Semitism in its own right (Jay, *Dialectical Imagination,* 133). The institute drew up a project for a study of anti-Semitism only in 1939: "Research Project on Anti-Semitism," *Studies in Philosophy and Social Science* 9 (1941): 124–43.

5. Cilly Kugelmann pointed out the following paradox to me: precisely those Jews with primarily political reasons for fleeing the Nazis—i.e., Jews such as Horkheimer—were the ones who left Germany early enough to escape the collective death sentence the Nazis passed on the Jews. In the first phase of Nazi rule, those Jews who perceived themselves above all as Jews usually did not see sufficient grounds to leave. Within the context of National Socialism, their self-image as Jews in itself comprised a biographical trap. This inversion of Jewish sensibility, on the one hand, and behavior that turned out correct in the light of Nazism, on the other, should help qualify judgments cast on members of the Frankfurt School in relation to anti-Semitism.

6. In a late remark (*N,* 161, in the aphorism "Deception," 1961–62), Horkheimer (hereafter M.H.) implicitly made clear the difference in the approach to the phenomenon of Nazism in its various phases: "The fact that National Socialism came to power in Germany is explicable, although what it did is inconceivable."

7. See *N,* 202 ("One Who Escaped," 1966–69): "People like me, not just gener-

ally like me, but specifically, that is, Jews, who looked and thought like Jews, like my father and my mother and like me, for the very reason that they were like that, at the end of years of awful fear, after unspeakable humiliation, inconceivable forced labor, beatings, and torment, were slowly tortured to death by the thousands in the concentration camps, because they looked and thought like Jews. . . . I should find satisfaction and peace in myself because my life testifies to senseless, unearned chance, the injustice, the blindness of all of life, because I should be ashamed still to be here."

8. In *Karl Marx and the Radical Critique of Judaism* (London, 1978), 148 ff., Julius Carlebach argues that "On the Jewish Question," helped bring about an intellectual breakthrough for the anti-Semitic stereotype of the trader as Jew. Carlebach provides an annotated bibliography on the essay (438-39) and explores the intellectual and social background of the actively assimilatory attitude toward the Jews predominant on the traditional left; in an extended discussion, he takes a positive position on M.H. (234 ff.).

9. Helmut Dubiel and Alfons Söllner characterize the text as "a political essay rather than a theoretical text"; moreover, Horkheimer treats German fascism in "an astonishingly economistic manner." See M.H., "Die Nationalsozialismusforschung des Instituts für Sozialforschung" in *Wirtschaft, Recht und Staat im Nationalsozialismus* (Frankfurt am Main, 1981), 7-31. Dubiel had earlier assessed the text differently, stating (in *Wissenschaftsorganisation und politische Erfahrung: Studien zur frühen kritischen Theorie* [Frankfurt am Main, 1978], 62; in English, *Theory and Politics: Studies in the Development of Critical Theory* [Cambridge, Mass., 1985]) that Horkheimer adopted the "continuity thesis" formulated by Pollock and Marcuse in 1933-34—fascism as the political form adequate to fully developed monopoly capitalism—and "specified it with the greatest possible precision and compactness in 'The Jews and Europe.'" Further, "the phenomenon of anti-Semitism as well, particularly the National Socialist form, is explained politically and economically."

10. Among these, above all Werner Sombart, *Die Juden und das Wirtschaftsleben* (Munich, 1928); Otto Heller, *Der Untergang des Judentums* (Vienna, 1931); Abraham Léon, *Kapitalismus und Judenfrage* (Munich, 1971). For a critical examination of Sombart and Max Weber, see Toni Oelsner, "The Place of the Jews in Economic History as Viewed by German scholars," *YLB* 7 (1962): 183-212.

11. Jay, "The Jews and the Frankfurt School," 91.

12. In *The Dual State: A Contribution to the Theory of Dictatorship* (New York, 1969), Ernst Fraenkel has shown how, in the Nazi state, the sphere of circulation and the corresponding forms of commerce and law could continue to function unimpaired despite political dictatorship and the exclusion of the Jews. In their critique of the equation of capitalism with the market, "Zum sozialwissenschaftlichen Potential der Kritischen Theorie," in *Kritischer Pessimismus und die Grenzen des traditionellen Marxismus,* ed. Wolfgang Bonß and Axel Honneth (Frankfurt am Main, 1982), 179 ff., Barbara Brick and Moishe Postone have demonstrated how critical theory's reliance on a form of "traditional Marxism" is a theoretical weak point.

13. The significance of the "socialization conflict" for M.H. and other representatives of the Frankfurt School in the development of their socially critical attitude has been pointed out by Hans Dieter Hellige, "Gesellschaftskonflikt, Selbsthass und die Entstehung antikapitalistischer Positionen im Judentum: Der Einfluss des Anti-

semitismus auf das sozialverhalten jüdischer Kaufmanns- und Unternehmerssöhne im Deutschen Kaiserreich und in der K. u. K.-Monarchie," *GuG* 5 (1979): 517. Helmut Gumnior and Rudolf Ringguth, *Max Horkheimer* (Reinbek, 1973), 7–9, cite an early biographical document in which his strong, emotional rejection of his own social origins finds expression: "Who is complaining about suffering? You and I? We are cannibals complaining that the flesh of the slaughtered gives us stomachaches. . . . You sleep in beds, wear clothes produced by people who are starving, people we drive with the tyrannical whip of our money, and you don't know how many women have fallen at the machine which produces the material for your 'cutaway.' Others are burned alive by poisonous gasses, so that your father continues to get the money you use to pay for your therapy—and you find it awful that you can't read more than two pages of Dostoyevsky. We are monsters, in fact we're not tormented enough. It's downright ridiculous, as if a butcher at the slaughterhouse were to brood about his white apron getting bloody" (letter to his cousin Hans, unpublished, Horkheimer Archive, Stadt- and Universitätsbibliothek Frankfurt).

14. In *Dämmerung* (1934), whose aphorisms date to the period from 1926–31, M.H.'s formulations on the Jews were far more pointed and intransigent. Under the title "Belief and Profit," he wrote: "The Jewish capitalists get all worked up about anti-Semitism. They say that what they hold most sacred is under attack. But I think that they get so unspeakably annoyed only because something about them is being threatened that yields no profit, yet cannot possibly be changed. If contemporary anti-Semitism were aimed at religion rather than 'blood,' many of those who are most outraged at it would renounce this unprofitable thing they hold most sacred 'with a heavy heart'" (*N*, 260 [43]).

15. Ibid.

16. On the presumedly instrumental significance of anti-Semitism, he writes: "The hatred of the Jews belongs to the ascendant phase of fascism. . . . It is used as a means of intimidating the populace by showing that the system will stop at nothing. Politically, the pogroms are aimed more at the spectators than at the Jews" ("JE," 4:328 [92]).

17. See Carl-Friedrich Geier, *Kritische Theorie: Max Horkheimer und Theodor W. Adorno* (Freiburg and Munich, 1982), 13: "If it did not itself sound cynical with respect to what happened at Auschwitz, then one might speak of Auschwitz as the *thema probandum* of critical theory; Auschwitz is the immediate evidence for the validity of the basic thesis of the historical construction in *Dialectic of Enlightenment,* according to which civilization itself calls forth the anticivilizational, the destructive, and intensifies it in the further course of history."

18. See Moishe Postone, " Nationalsozialismus und Antisemitismus: Ein theoretischer Versuch," in *Zivilisationsbruch: Denken nach Auschwitz*, ed. Dan Diner (Frankfurt am Main, 1988) 242: "No analysis of National Socialism can do it justice if it cannot explain the extermination of the European Jews."

19. See "The German Jews," *CIR*, 117: "The attempt to convert an anti-Semite is to some extent a contradiction in terms."

20. In a discussion following M.H.'s lecture "Über das Vorurteil" (On prejudice) (Cologne, 1963), Alphons Silbermann formulated the thesis that "prejudice is part of the structure of society" (35–36). It cannot be made to disappear, but it must be kept from reaching an "explosive state." M.H. responded by asking Silbermann a

question directed at the distinction between psychic latency and the social circumstances that actualize that latency: "Do you believe that prejudice itself exploded, that prejudice itself is the grounds for explosion?" Silbermann responded affirmatively and elaborated: "I believe that the program of education—'enlightenment' is not a particularly good term—that the educational program, call it a 'fight' against something or whatever you will, can only aim at keeping social prejudice from becoming explosive. It will never disappear, because it's a social given, inherent in human beings on both psychological and sociological grounds. . . . It's not a matter of anti-Semitism, it's a question of social prejudice."

21. Hatred of the Jews "is the secret resentment of one's own religion" (ibid., 34).

22. M.H. later corrected his original thesis that religious anti-Semitism was connected with Christianity. "With Christianity? Kierkegaard would say: with the Christians. For the hate practiced by Christians in the world is not immanent to Christianity" (ibid., 33).

23. Leo Löwenthal also collaborated on the first three of the seven sections of "Elements of Anti-Semitism." See Jay, "The Jews and the Frankfurt School," 281n. 34.

24. Ibid., 96.

25. M.H., *Die Sehnsucht nach dem ganz Anderen: Ein Interview mit Kommentar von Helmut Gumnior* (Hamburg, 1970), 11.

26. M.H., *Die Sehnsucht nach dem ganz Anderen*, 11.

27. *N*, 101 [165].

28. Ibid.

29. The aphorism "Hated Mirror Image" (*N*, 101 [165]).

30. The aphorism "On Anti-Semitism" (*N*, 28 [131]).

31. The aphorism "On the Metaphysics of Hatred of the Jews" (*N*, 164).

32. M.H., "The German Jews" (*CIR*, 116).

33. Ibid. See also the aphorism "A Particular Kind of Anti-Semitism," which alludes to an identification with his parents.

34. M.H., "Über das Vorurteil," 10.

35. "I believe that when a young person has been instilled with an abhorrence of these horrors, it is not necessary to speak above all of the atrocities committed upon the Jews" (ibid., 33).

36. The aphorism "After Auschwitz" (*N*, 213).

37. M.H., *Die Sehnsucht nach dem ganz Anderen*, 62.

6. BEYOND THE CONCEIVABLE

1. See Isaiah Trunk's remarks during the discussion in *The Holocaust as Historical Experience: Essays and a Discussion*, ed. Jehuda Bauer and Nathan Rotenstreich (London, 1981), 268.

2. Rezsö Kasztner (Rudolf Kastner), 1906–57, journalist, lawyer, leading figure in the Rumanian and Hungarian Zionist movements, was head of Budapest's Jewish Rescue Committee and negotiated with Eichmann in 1944 for the sake of gaining time. In the process, the SS allowed first 318, then 1,368 Jews to leave Bergen-Belsen for Switzerland. In Israel in 1953, he was slanderously accused of collaboration. In June 1955 a court recognized a portion of the accusations, referring to "a pact with the devil." In the course of the 1958 appeal, he was fully exonerated—although he

did not live long enough to learn of this, having been assassinated on a Tel Aviv street. The Israeli controversy over Kastner became part of the election contest between the Labor Party (Mapai) and the Zionist Revisionist Herut Party. See Ernest Landau, ed., *Der Kastner-Bericht über Eichmanns Menschenhandel in Ungarn* (Munich, 1961).

3. Hannah Arendt, *Eichmann in Jerusalem: A Report on the Banality of the Evil* (London, 1963). The response to Arendt's book culminated in Isaiah Trunk's groundbreaking study of the councils, *Judenrat: The Jewish Councils under Nazi Occupation* (New York, 1972).

4. *Eichmann*, 104. Arendt bases her argument on Raul Hilberg, *The Destruction of the European Jews* (Chicago, 1961) who discovers within the dynamic of the Final Solution a historical continuum of Jewish behavior in the face of their persecutors (257–66). For his part, Hilberg has distanced his thesis as much as possible from Arendt's; see Raul Hilberg, "The Judenrat: Conscious or Unconscious 'Tool,'" in *Patterns of Jewish Leadership in Nazi Europe 1933–1945* (proceedings of the Third Yad Vashem International Historical Conference, April 1977), ed. Yisrael Gutman and Cynthia J. Haft (Jerusalem, 1979), 61–63.

5. *Eichmann*, 109.

6. Yisrael Gutman, "The Concept of Labor in Judenrat Policy," in *Patterns of Jewish Leadership in Nazi Europe 1933–1945*, ed. Yisrael Gutman and Cynthia J. Haft (Jerusalem, 1979), 158–59.

7. On the wider context in which Arendt's perspective is situated—a context marked by an extreme tension between universalist and particularist values vis-à-vis Jewish identity and the Holocaust—see Dan Diner, "Hannah Arendt Reconsidered: On the Banal and the Evil in her Holocaust Narrative," *New German Critique* 71 (1997): 177–90.

8. Originally formed in the face of the German army's advance in North Africa, the Palmach was the elite corps of the *yishuv*'s military forces, the Hagana. It became renowned for its daring and dedication in the 1948 Arab-Israeli war and is associated in Israel with an elite ethos.

9. Nathan Alterman, *Between Two Roads: Excerpts from a Diary*, ed. Dan Laor (Tel Aviv, 1989) (Hebrew), 19 f.

10. See the extended treatments in Jacob Robinson, *And the Crooked Shall Be Made Straight: The Eichmann Trial, the Jewish Catastrophe, and Hannah Arendt's Narrative* (New York, 1965), 152 ff.; Trunk, *Judenrat*, 3 ff.; H. G. Adler, *Theresienstadt 1941–1945: Das Antlitz einer Zwangsgemeinschaft: Geschichte, Soziologie, Psychologie* (Tübingen, 1960).

11. See Herbert Rosenkranz, "Austrian Jewry: Between Forced Emigration and Deportation," in *Patterns of Jewish Leadership in Nazi Europe 1933–1945*, ed. Yisrael Gutman and Cynthia J. Haft (Jerusalem, 1979), 71; Herbert Rosenkranz, *Verfolgung und Selbstbehauptung: Die Juden in Österreich 1938–45* (Vienna, 1978), 115 f.; Robinson, *And the Crooked*, 153.

12. Jacob Robinson, Introduction to Isaiah Trunk, *Judenrat: The Jewish Councils under Nazi Occupation* (New York, 1972), xxix.

13. Yosef Kermisz, "The Judenrat in Poland," in *Patterns of Jewish Leadership in Nazi Europe 1933–1945*, ed. Yisrael Gutman and Cynthia J. Haft (Jerusalem, 1979), 77; Gutman, "Concept of Labor," 156.

14. Ibid., 167.

15. Aharon Weiss, "The Policies of the *Judenräte* in southeastern Poland," *Yalkut Moreshet* 15 (1972): 59–122 (Hebrew); Aharon Weiss "The Jewish Police in the Generalgouvernement and in Upper Silesia during the Holocaust" (Ph.D. diss., Hebrew University, Jerusalem, 1974) (Hebrew).

16. See the note that Czerniaków left the communal authorities: "Worthoff and his colleagues (from the resettlement staff) came by and requested that I prepare a transport of children for tomorrow. My bitter cup is now filled to the brink, as I cannot deliver defenseless children to their deaths. I have decided to make my exit. Do not consider this an act of cowardice or flight. I am powerless—my heart is breaking from sadness and pity, I cannot bear it any longer. What I do will bring the truth home to everyone and perhaps steer them toward the right course. I am aware that I am leaving you a difficult legacy" (*Im Warschauer Ghetto: Das Tagebuch des Adam Czerniaków 1939–1942* [Munich, 1986], 28). For the English edition see Raul Hilberg et al., eds., *The Warsaw Diary of Adam Czerniakow: Prelude to Doom* (New York, 1982). For a comparative study concerning the different reactions of the Jewish leadership see Aharon Weiss, "Jewish Leadership in Occupied Poland—Postures and Attitudes," *YVS* 12 (1977): 335–65.

17. Cited in Weiss, "The Policies of the *Judenräte*," 98.

18. See Jehuda Bauer, "Jewish Leadership Reactions to Nazi Policies," in *The Holocaust as Historical Experience*, ed. Jehuda Bauer and Nathan Rotenstreich (London, 1981), 186.

19. See Shmuel Krakowski, "The Opposition to the Judenräte by the Jewish Armed Resistance," in *Patterns of Jewish Leadership in Nazi Europe 1933–1945*, ed. Yisrael Gutman and Cynthia J. Haft (Jerusalem, 1979), 191.

20. Bauer, "Jewish Leadership," 186–87; Nachman Blumenthal, *Conduct and Actions of a Judenrat: Documents of the Bialystock Ghetto* (Jerusalem, 1962).

21. Dov Levin, "The Fighting Leadership of the Judenräte in Small Communities," in *Patterns of Jewish Leadership in Nazi Europe 1933–1945*, ed. Yisrael Gutman and Cynthia J. Haft (Jerusalem, 1979), 146.

22. Yitzhak Arad, "The Judenräte in the Lithuanian Ghettos of Kovno and Vilna," in *Patterns of Jewish Leadership in Nazi Europe 1933–1945*, ed. Yisrael Gutman and Cynthia J. Haft (Jerusalem, 1979), 109.

23. Gutman, "Concept of Labor," 179.

24. Bauer, "Jewish Leadership," 187.

25. Gutman, "Concept of Labor," 164–65.

26. Trunk, *Judenrat*, 410.

27. Ibid., 403.

28. Hilberg, "The Judenrat," 38. See also Saul Friedländer's remarks in *The Holocaust as Historical Experience: Essays and a Discussion*, ed. Jehuda Bauer and Nathan Rotenstreich (London, 1981), 256 f.

29. Lucy Dawidowicz, ed., *A Holocaust Reader* (New York, 1976), 273–87.

30. Trunk, *Judenrat*, 385–87.

31. Taking up Arendt's theme of collaboration, Leslie Epstein's novel *King of the Jews* (New York, 1980) focuses on the fate of both the ghetto and Rumkowski.

32. Ibid., 413.

33. See Krakowski, "Opposition to the Judenräte," 198; Gutman, "Concept of Labor," 171.

34. Krakowski, "Opposition to the Judenräte," 200.

35. Cited in Robinson, *And the Crooked,* 179.

36. Cited in ibid., 180.

37. Ibid., 187.

38. Friedrich Hielscher, *Fünfzig Jahre unter Deutschen* (Hamburg, 1954), 362, 365. On Hielscher's testimony, see Shaul Esh, "A German in the Lodz Ghetto," *Amat* 11 (1964): 34–46 (Hebrew).

39. Robinson, *And the Crooked,* 184.

40. Ibid., 186.

41. Ibid., 223, citing Shaul Esh, "The Dignity of the Destroyed: Towards a Definition of the Period of the Holocaust" (1962).

42. Joseph Walk, "The Religious Leadership during the Holocaust," in *Patterns of Jewish Leadership in Nazi Europe 1933–1945,* ed. Yisrael Gutman and Cynthia J. Haft (Jerusalem, 1979), 384.

43. So Yitzhak Arad, "Discussion," in *Patterns of Jewish Leadership in Nazi Europe 1933–45,* ed. Yisrael Gutman and Cynthia J. Haft (Jerusalem, 1979), 189.

44. Uriel Tal's remarks in *The Holocaust as Historical Experience: Essays and a Discussion,* ed. Jehuda Bauer and Nathan Rotenstreich (London, 1981), 237.

45. See Gutman, "Concept of Labor," 168.

46. See Hilberg, "The Judenrat," 38.

7. HISTORICAL UNDERSTANDING AND COUNTERRATIONALITY

1. See Martin Broszat and Saul Friedländer, "A Controversy about the Historicization of National Socialism," *YVS* 19 (1988): 1–47.

2. Johann Gustav Droysen, *Grundriß der Historik* (1868; Munich, 1960), 9.

3. See Wilhelm Dilthey, "Der Aufbau der geschichtlichen Welt in den Geisteswissenschaften" (1910–27), in *Gesammelte Schriften* (Stuttgart, 1958), 7:148; Gérard Gäfgen, *Theorie der wirtschaftlichen Entscheidung: Untersuchung zur Logik und ökonomischen Bedeutung des rationalen Handelns* (Tübingen, 1974), 54.

4. Gäfgen, *Theorie der wirtschaftlichen Entscheidung,* 278; see also Karl-Otto Apel, *Die Erklären-Verstehen Kontroverse in tranzendentalpragmatischer Sicht* (Frankfurt am Main, 1979), 15.

5. Ibid., 26.

6. William H. Dray, "Überlegungen zur historischen Erklärung von Handlungen," in *Methodologische Probleme der Sozialwissenschaften,* ed. Karl Acham (Darmstadt, 1978), 158.

7. Apel, *Die Erklären-Verstehen Kontroverse,* 26.

8. Gäfgen, *Theorie der wirtschaftlichen Entscheidung,* 24.

9. Norbert Elias, "Der Zusammenbruch der Zivilisation," in *Studien über die Deutschen* (Frankfurt am Main, 1989), 397.

10. Hannah Arendt, "Die vollendete Sinnlosigkeit," in *Hannah Arendt: Nach Auschwitz. Essays und Kommentare,* ed. Eike Geisel and Klaus Bitterman (Berlin, 1989), 29.

11. George I. S. Shackle, "Time and Thought," *British Journal for the Philosophy of Science* 9 (1958–59): 290.

12. See Yisrael Gutman, "The Concept of Labor in Judenrat Policy," in *Patterns of

Jewish Leadership in Nazi Europe 1933–45, ed. Yisrael Gutman and Cynthia J. Haft (Jerusalem, 1979), 151–80.

13. See Arnold Gehlen, "Probleme einer soziologischen Handlungslehre," in *Soziologie und Leben: Die soziologische Dimension der Fachwissenschaften,* ed. Frank Altheim et al. (Tübingen, 1952), 33.

14. See F. H. Knight, *The Ethics of Competition and Other Essays,* 2d ed. (Salem, N.H., 1955), 74: "Efficiency is a value category."

15. See Otto von Zwiedineck-Südenhorst, "Der Begriff homo oeconomicus und sein Lehrwert," *Jahrbücher für Nationalökonomie und Statistik* 140 (1934): 521.

16. See Karl Acham, "Über einige Rationalitätskonzeptionen in den Sozialwissenschaften," in *Rationalität: Philosophische Beiträge,* ed. Herbert Schnädelbach (Frankfurt am Main, 1984), 34. See also G. Hartfiel, *Wirtschaftliche und soziale Rationalität: Untersuchungen zum Menschenbild in Ökonomie und Soziologie* (Stuttgart, 1968).

17. See Paul Diesing, "The Nature and Limitations of Economic Rationality," *Ethics* 61 (1950–51): 13: "Economic rationality is at the same time a concrete and universal descriptive principle and a normative principle." In his *Theory of Justice* (Cambridge, Mass., 1971), John Rawls probably goes furthest in this direction; for him, utility calculations serve as a basis for morality (25). Gäfgen, *Theorie der wirtschaftlichen Entscheidung,* notes that modern decision theory has led to a resurrection of utilitarianism: "Economics then becomes a formal ethics, as in Bentham" (7).

18. Gäfgen, *Theorie der wirtschaftlichen Entscheidung,* 89.

19. See Gunnar Myrdal, "Das Zweck-Mittel-Denken in der Nationalökonomie," *Zeitschrift für Nationalökonomie* 4 (1933): 310.

8. ON RATIONALITY AND RATIONALIZATION

1. This essay's text and notes refer to the following publications by Götz Aly and Susanne Heim:

VdV   *Vordenker der Vernichtung: Auschwitz und die deutschen Pläne für eine europäische Ordnung* (Hamburg, 1991)

SuJ   *Sozialpolitik und Judenvernichtung: Gibt es eine Ökonomie der Endlösung? Beiträge zur nationalsozialistischen Gesundheits- und Sozialpolitik* (Berlin, 1987)

BuM   *Bevölkerungsstruktur und Massenmord: Beiträge zur nationalsozialistischen Gesundheits- und Sozialpolitik* (Berlin, 1991)

2. On the epistemological constitution and practical realization of economic rationality, see Gérard Gäfgen, *Theorie der wirtschaftlichen Entscheidung: Untersuchung zur Logik und ökonomischen Bedeutung des rationalen Handelns* (Tübingen, 1974), 18 ff., 53 ff.

3. On the discussion of this thesis, see Wolfgang Schneider, ed., *"Vernichtungspolitik": Eine Debatte über den Zusammenhang von Sozialpolitik und Genozid im nationalsozialistischen Deutschland* (Hamburg, 1991); and Hermann Graml, "Irregeleitet und in die Irre führend: Widerspruch gegen eine 'rationale Erklärung von Auschwitz,'" *Jahrbuch für Antisemitismusforschung* 1 (1992): 286–95.

4. On the universal anti-Semitic demand for "productivization" of the Jews,

see the still instructive study by Tamar Bermann, *Produktivierungsmythen und Anti-semitismus: Eine soziologische Studie* (Vienna, 1973).

5. For a comparative assessment of the economic and ideological rationale in the mass annihilation, see Ulrich Herbert, "Arbeit und Vernichtung: Ökonomisches Interesse und Primat der 'Weltanschauung' im Nationalsozialismus," in *Ist der Nationalsozialismus Geschichte? Zu Historisierung und Historikerstreit*, ed. Dan Diner (Frankfurt am Main, 1987), 198-236.

6. On the negative connotations of "utilitarianism" in the German philosophical tradition and in everyday usage, see Wolfgang Köhler, "Zur Geschichte und Struktur der utilitaristischen Ethik" (Ph.D. diss., Frankfurt am Main, 1983), 16; on the role of ethics in economics, see, e.g., Amartya Sen, *On Ethics and Economics* (Oxford, 1978). Sen makes a historical distinction between an ethically self-ensuring political economy and a technological "engineering approach" and places the orientation common to both tendencies, namely, "self-interest maximization," in a total societal context. At its center, one's own self-preservation and that of the total system are an internal limit.

7. See Rolf Sieferle, *Bevölkerungswachstum und Naturhaushalt: Studien zur Naturtheorie der klassischen Ökonomie* (Frankfurt am Main, 1990), 7-11.

8. Achim Bay, "Der nationalsozialistische Gedanke der Großraumwirtschaft und seine ideologischen Grundlagen" (Ph.D. diss., Erlangen-Nuremberg, 1962), points to the ideology of *Lebensraum* as the *Weltanschauung*-linked aspect of the sphere dominated by *Großraum*. In this context, it was crucial to replace all liberal economic principles, including the category of a world market, by political intervention (45). Since autarchy is made subservient to political aims, the factor of cost, otherwise effective, has little impact.

9. Georges Bataille, *The Accursed Share: An Essay on General Economy* (New York, 1991), investigates the extended preeconomic concept of economy in primitive societies, one that is not based on economic utility and accumulation. The nonprofit orientation of this thinking, which views conspicuous expenditure and consumption in particular as an enhancement of status, could still be a useful source for some as yet untried approaches in interpreting the Final Solution; see 48, 84.

10. Paul Diesing, "The Nature and Limits of Economic Rationality," *Ethics* 61 (1950-51): 13, makes it clear that "economic rationality is at the same time a concrete and universal descriptive principle and a normative principle."

11. Ultimately, what was at stake in the conference was finding a rationale for Heydrich's "authority of empowerment" concerning the "Final Solution of the Jewish Problem." On this, see the instructive article by Eberhard Jäckel, "Die Konferenz am Wannsee: Wo Heydrich seine Ermächtigung bekanntgab—Der Holocaust war längst im Gange," *Die Zeit*, January 17, 1992, 33-34.

12. The 1944 *Gesetz zur Behandlung Gemeinschaftsfremder* (law on the treatment of persons alien to the community), which did not come into force owing to the war situation, likewise does not exceed the boundaries of "social-hygienic" guidelines in any way.

13. George Shackle, "Time and Thought," *British Journal for the Philosophy of Science* 9 (1959): 290, coined the following memorable formula: "Rationality means something only for the outside observer."

14. See Hans Mommsen, "Realisierung des Utopischen: 'Die Endlösung der Ju-

denfrage' im Dritten Reich,'" *GuG* 9 (1983): 381–420. Heim and Aly refer to this article only in order to suggest Mommsen's ignorance of the participation by members of his academic discipline in the Nazi enterprise (*SuJ*, 8).

15. See Albrecht Ritschl, "Die NS-Wirtschaftsideologie—Modernisierungsprogramm oder reaktionäre Utopie?," in *Nationalsozialismus und Modernisierung*, ed. Michael Prinz and Rainer Zitelmann (Darmstadt, 1991), 48–70.

16. For a similarly monocausal approach, though utilizing another rationale, see Arno J. Mayer, *Why Did the Heavens Not Darken? The "Final Solution" in History* (New York, 1989). Mayer regards the ideological anti-Bolshevist motive as absolute, deriving from it all other aspects of the mass annihilation.

17. Hitler argued in terms of sociopolitical considerations, and the authors regard those considerations as especially significant: "Hungary, just as well as Slovakia, could put the Jews in concentration camps. If it did, it would open up many possibilities for its own native population by the vacating of positions occupied by Jews, thus providing the tolerant countrymen with career opportunities previously closed to them because of the Jews" (*VdV,* 358). However, other themes suggesting other obvious motives are known to have been broached in the meeting with Horthy: Hitler compared the Jews to insect pests and also blamed Bolshevism on them. Moreover, earlier German expressions of a desire to deport the Hungarian Jews have been documented.

18. A comprehensive documentation is provided by Randolph L. Braham in two works, *The Destruction of Hungarian Jewry* (New York, 1963) and *The Politics of Genocide*, 2 vols. (New York, 1981). An instructive survey can be found in Laszlo Varga, "Ungarn," in *Dimensionen des Völkermords: Die Zahl der jüdischen Opfer des Nationalsozialismus*, ed. Wolfgang Benz (Munich, 1991), 331–52.

19. At times Heim and Aly seem to desire to hedge the implications of their own argument against specificity. We are told, for example, that just as in the case of the "mass murder of German mentally ill patients and of the Polish, Yugoslav, and Soviet population . . . utilitarian aims *were also discernible* in the murder of the European Jews" (*VdV,* 11; italics mine).

20. I discuss this difference at greater length in chapters 10 and 12 of this book.

21. See Detlev J. K. Peukert, "Die Genesis der 'Endlösung' aus dem Geiste der Wissenschaft," in *Zerstörung des moralischen Selbstbewußtseins: Chance oder Gefährdung? Praktische Philosophie in Deutschland nach dem Nationalsozialismus*, ed. Forum für Philosophie, Bad Homburg (Frankfurt am Main, 1988), 24–48. In contrast with Aly and Heim, Peukert proceeds quite clearly from the premise of a very broad, multicausal genetic matrix for the Final Solution but tends to accord developments in the human sciences a certain causal significance qua historical subject, over and beyond political circumstances and events.

22. For a critical approach to such a focus, see Dirk Blasius, "Die 'Maskerade des Bösen': Psychiatrische Forschung in der NS-Zeit," in *Medizin und Gesundheitspolitik in der NS-Zeit*, ed. Norbert Frei (Munich, 1991), 268.

23. In a similar manner, the authors conflate the Nazi measures of annihilation and Stalinist mass murder and have no qualms about using Nazi sources to back up the conflation. On the problems of assuming such an identity between Nazi and Stalinist totalitarianism, see chapter 11 below.

9. HISTORICAL EXPERIENCE AND COGNITION

1. "Martin Broszat and Saul Friedländer: A Controversy about the Historiciza-tion of National Socialism," *YVS* 19 (1988): 1–47; triggered by Saul Friedländer's ar-ticle, "Some Reflections on the Historisation of National Socialism," *Tel Aviver Jahr-buch für deutsche Geschichte* 16 (1987): 310–24. That article was itself a response to Broszat's "Plädoyer für die Historisierung des Nationalsozialismus," *Merkur* 40 (May 1985): 373–85.

2. See the pioneering first chapter in George M. Kren and Leon Rappoport, *The Holocaust and the Crisis of Human Behavior* (New York, 1980), 13 ff. The ideas of these two authors converge with my own.

3. For some related thoughts on the epistemological and social "situatedness" of knowledge in ethnography and its hermeneutics, see Clifford Geertz, "Being There, Writing Here," *Dialogue* 2 (1989): 58–63.

4. Leopold von Ranke, *Geschichte der romanischen und germanischen Völker 1495–1535* (Berlin 1874), vii; on the significance of the Rankean approach, see S. J. Re-nier, *History: Its Purpose and Method* (London, 1950), 130 f.

5. Leopold von Ranke, "Politisches Gespräch," in *Sämtliche Werke* (Leipzig, 1867–90), 49–50, 328 ff.; Leopold von Ranke, *Weltgeschichte* (Leipzig, 1888), part 9, sec. 2, xi. In addition, see George Iggers, *Deutsche Geschichtswissenschaft: Eine Kritik der tradi-tionellen Geschichtsauffassung von Herder bis zur Gegenwart* (Munich, 1971), 116 f.

6. See Heinrich August Winkler, "Deutschland vor Hitler," in *Der historische Ort des Nationalsozialismus*, ed. Walter H. Pehle (Frankfurt am Main, 1990), 11–30.

7. See Kren and Rappoport, *The Holocaust and the Crisis*, 14.

8. See Raul Hilberg, *Sonderzüge nach Auschwitz* (Frankfurt am Main, 1987).

9. See Franz Neumann, *Behemoth: The Structure and Practice of National Social-ism* (London, 1942). On the importance of Neumann for the historiography of the Nazi system, see Raul Hilberg and Alfons Söllner, "Das Schweigen zum Sprechen bringen: Ein Gespräch über Franz Neumann und die Entwicklung der Holocaust-Forschung," in *Zivilisationsbruch: Denken nach Auschwitz*, ed. Dan Diner (Frankfurt am Main, 1988), 175–200.

10. See for instance Hans Mommsen, "Hannah Arendt und der Prozess gegen Eichmann," foreword to new edition of Hannah Arendt, *Eichmann in Jerusalem* (Mu-nich, 1986), i–xxxvii.

11. See Hannah Arendt's letter to Karl Jaspers, August 17, 1946, in *Hannah Arendt-Karl Jaspers Correspondence, 1926–1969*, ed. Lotte Köhler and Hans Saner (San Diego, 1993), 51–56.

12. Raul Hilberg, *Die Vernichtung der europäischen Juden* (Berlin, 1982), 738.

13. See among others Hans Mommsen, "Die Realisierung des Utopischen: 'Die Endlösung der Judenfrage' im Dritten Reich," *GuG* 9 (1983): 381–420; Martin Broszat, *Der Staat Hitlers* (Munich, 1969); Gerhard Hirschfelder and Lothar Ketten-acker, eds., *"Der Führerstaat": Mythos und Realität* (Stuttgart, 1981). For a compre-hensive summary see Ian Kershaw, *The Nazi Dictatorship: Problems and Perspectives of In-terpretation* (London, 1985), chap. 4, "Hitler: 'Master in the Third Reich' or 'Weak Dictator'?," 61–81.

14. See Raul Hilberg, "Tendenzen in der Holocaust-Forschung," in *Der historische Ort des Nationalsozialismus*, ed. Walter H. Pehle (Frankfurt am Main, 1990), 71–80.

15. Both Arendt's phrase and the perspective to which it is linked interact with the powerfully *universalistic* impulses articulated in her Eichmann book. As I have argued in "Hannah Arendt Reconsidered: On the Banal and the Evil in Her Holocaust Narrative" (*New German Critique* 71 [1997]: 177–90), such impulses represent one pole of the peculiar tension between an extreme humanist universalism and an equally extreme Jewish particularism revealed in her approach to the phenomenon of Eichmann. In the same article, I identify such a tension with that between a Western and an Eastern European historical and existential vantage: a theme considered within an Israeli context in chapter 11 here. I also argue in chapter 12 that by its very nature "humanizing" universalism is generally linked to German as opposed to Jewish historical memory—i.e., to that mnemonic collective bound up with the perpetrators rather than the victims.

16. See Fernand Braudel, "Histoire et sciences sociales: La longue durée," *Annales* 13 (1958): 725–53; and his *Ecrits sur l'histoire* (Paris, 1969), 41–83.

17. See Ulrich Herbert, "'Die guten und die schlechten Zeiten': Überlegungen zur diachronen Analyse lebensgeschichtlicher Interviews," in *"Die Jahre weiß man nicht, wo man die heute hinsetzen soll": Faschismuserfahrung im Ruhrgebiet—Lebensgeschichte und Sozialkultur im Ruhrgebiet 1930 bis 1960*, ed. Lutz Niethammer, 2d ed. (Bonn, 1983).

18. Martin Broszat et al., *Von Stalingrad zur Währungsreform: Zur Sozialgeschichte des Umbruchs in Deutschland* (Munich, 1988). In their introduction, xvi–xlix, the authors use the concept of "schlechte Zeit" (bad times)—yet without any mention of the contrapuntal notion of "good times." The authors explain that one reason they chose "the slogan-like title" *From Stalingrad to Currency Reform* was to "emphasize the period-overarching perspective of social history" (xx).

19. On the constitutive conditions of Jewish memory, see Yosef Hayim Yerushalmi, *Zachor: Jewish Memory and Jewish History* (Washington, D.C., 1982). For a critique of this essay, see Amos Funkenstein, "Collective Memory and Historical Consciousness," *History & Memory* 1 (1989): 5–26; see also Saul Friedländer, "Die Shoah als Element in der Konstruktion israelischer Erinnerung," *Babylon: Beiträge zur jüdischen Gegenwart* 2 (1987): 10–22.

20. For a comprehensive treatment, see Hans Walter Schmuhl, *Rassenhygiene, Nationalsozialismus, Euthanasie: Von der Verhütung zur Vernichtung "Lebenunwerten Lebens," 1890–1945* (Göttingen, 1987).

21. See Karl A. Schleunes, "Nationalsozialistische Entschlussbildung und die Aktion T4," as well as Raul Hilberg, "Die Aktion Reinhard," both in *Der Mord an den Juden im Zweiten Weltkrieg: Entschlussbildung und Verwirklichung*, ed. Eberhard Jäckel and Jürgen Rohwer (Stuttgart, 1985), 70–83, 125–36, resp.

22. See the approach based on history of science utilized by Detlev J. K. Peukert in "Die Genesis der 'Endlösung' aus dem Geiste der Wissenschaft," in *Zerstörung des moralischen Selbstbewußtseins: Chance oder Gefährdung? Praktische Philosophie in Deutschland nach dem Nationalsozialismus*, ed. Forum für Philosophie, Bad Homburg (Frankfurt am Main, 1988), 24–48.

23. Kershaw, *Der NS-Staat,* 166, is inclined to trace the historian's choice of historical perspective vis-à-vis the Holocaust (universal or particularistic) to emotions bound up with origin, but not to derive it from the historical phenomenon itself. His apodictic statement that "non-Jewish historians . . . necessarily [have] a different perspective than Jewish historians" cannot be accepted, when considered against the backdrop of what he calls "religious cultural eschatology." In his debate with Saul Friedländer (note 1 above), Martin Broszat takes a similar approach. Friedländer, on the other hand, argues for a "fusion of horizons" (46).

10. VARIETIES OF NARRATION

1. Gordon A. Craig, *Europe Since 1815* (New York, 1974).

2. See Lucy Dawidowicz, *The Holocaust and the Historians* (Cambridge, 1991) and, more recently, Tony Kushner, *The Holocaust and Liberal Imagination: A Social and Cultural History* (Oxford, 1994). On the "Anglo-Saxon" mode of perception, see esp. 205 ff.

3. On the systematic difference between German and English historiography, see James Joll, "National History and National Historians: Some German and English Views of the Past," 1984 Annual Lecture, German Historical Institute of London (London, 1985), 3–25. Joll puts forward the thesis that English historiography is focused primarily on continuity, German historiography on rupture.

4. See Lothar Kettenacker, "Preußen in der alliierten Kriegsplanung, 1939–1947," in *Studien zur Geschichte Englands und der deutsch-britischen Beziehungen: Festschrift für Paul Kluke,* ed. Lothar Kettenacker et al. (Munich, 1981), 312–40, esp. 319–20.

5. See Klemens von Klemperer, *Die verlassenen Verschwörer: Der deutsche Widerstand auf der Suche nach Verbündeten 1938–1945* (Berlin, 1994), 103 ff.

6. See Martin Gilbert, *Auschwitz and the Allies* (London, 1981).

7. On the significance of language symbolism in construction of meaning, see two works by Paul Ricoeur, *Time and Narrative,* vol.1 (Chicago, 1984–88) and *The Rule of Metaphor: Multi-Disciplinary Studies of the Creation of Meaning in Language* (London, 1978), as well as the work of Hayden White, *Tropics of Discourse: Essays in Cultural Criticism* (Baltimore, 1985).

8. Peter Burke, "Geschichte als soziales Gedächtnis," in *Mnemosyne: Formen und Funktionen kultureller Erinnerung,* ed. Aleida Assmann and Dietrich Harth (Frankfurt am Main, 1991), 289–304, esp. 296–97.

9. On the criminology relating to collective criminal acts, see Herbert Jaeger, *Verbrechen unter totalitärer Herrschaft* (Frankfurt am Main, 1982), esp. 380 ff; Adalbert Rückerl, *NS-Verbrechen vor Gericht: Versuch einer Vergangenheitsbewältigung* (Heidelberg, 1982); Jürgen Weber and Peter Steinbach, eds., *Vergangenheitsbewältigung durch Strafverfahren? NS-Prozesse in der Bundesrepublik Deutschland* (Munich, 1984).

10. On this phenomenon within Jewish memory see Dan Diner, "Gestaute Zeit: Massenvernichtung und jüdische Erzählstruktur," in *Kreisläufe: Nationalsozialismus und Gedächtnis* (Berlin, 1995), 123–39.

11. See, e.g., the narrative developed by Cynthia Heller in *At the Edge of Destruction,* 2d ed. (Detroit, 1994).

12. See chapter 8 above.

13. New York, 1996.

14. Götz Aly, *"Endlösung": Völkerverschiebung und der Mord an den europäischen Juden* (Frankfurt am Main, 1995), 29 ff. A notewothy aspect of Aly's new approach to the Holocaust as an "ethnic cleansing" that ran out of control is that it appears to follow closely the central argument of Andreas Hillgruber in his widely discussed *Zweierlei Untergang: Die Zerschlagung des Deutschen Reiches und das Ende des europäischen Judentums* (Berlin, 1986), which is well known as one of the texts that sparked the *Historikerstreit*. We read there, "The mass expulsion of the Germans [after 1945] from a quarter of the territory of the Reich within the borders of 1937 marked a provisional endpoint to the process inaugurated by the idea of a *völkisch* cleansing of German land. The process led to the struggles of nationalities on the periphery of Europe in the First World War, and, in its wake, in Turkey, for the first time to a genocide of the Armenians and the mass expulsions of the Greeks from Asia Minor. The extermination and resettlement policies of Hitler and Stalin, in their respective spheres of interest during the 1939–40 period of their alliance, continued such 'population exchanges'; starting in June 1941, the mass murder then reached an extremity in Hitler's 'Eastern War.' The Jews were meant to be exterminated, first in Poland and throughout the east, then in all German-ruled continental Europe" (66–67).

15. See, e.g., the announcement of upcoming books by a distinguished German publishing house that also stresses its interest in bringing notable works on the Holocaust to the attention of the public. In commenting there on Gudrun Schwartz, *Die nationalsozialistischen Lager* (Frankfurt am Main, 1996), the publisher notes:

> The Europe of the Nazis was a Europe of camps. Not only were certain population groups particularly singled out for murder, forced labor, exploitation, or terrorization [and] confined in death camps, work camps, concentration camps, camps for POWs, or penal camps. Everyday Germans were also confined: those ethnic Germans brought "home into the Reich," and many others who found themselves almost constantly in some sort of transit, vacation or training camp, or other sort of *Lager*. (Fischer Taschenbücher, "Programmschau Mai bis Oktober 1996," 61)

16. This document (Bundesarchiv Koblenz, R22, no. 4209) notes that "Reichsleiter Bouhler and Dr. Brand have been given the responsibility to expand the authority of doctors, later to be specifically named, so that, based on human judgement, incurable patients can, after a critical assessment of the condition of their health, be granted euthanasia."

17. Hans Mommsen makes this point convincingly. See "Die Realisierung des Utopischen: 'Die Endlösung der Judenfrage' im Dritten Reich,'" *GuG* 9 (1983): 381–420.

18. For an extreme example of this trend see Zygmunt Bauman, *Modernity and the Holocaust* (Oxford, 1989). The recent important study of Ulrich Herbert, *Best: Biographische Studien über Radikalismus, Weltanschauung und Vernunft 1903–1989* (Bonn, 1996), on one of the masterminds of the Gestapo and main security office of the Reich, appears to herald an opposing tendency in research that will once more focus intensely on the ideological dimension.

19. On the preservation of the distant past in a religious form, see Maurice Halbwachs, *Les cadres sociaux de la mémoire* (Paris, 1925).

20. The Gutman and Krakowski book was published in New York, 1986; the Lucas book in Lexington, Mass., 1986.

21. In this regard, the diaries of Victor Klemperer, *Ich will Zeugnis ablegen bis zum Letzten: Tagebücher 1931–1945,* ed. Walter Nowojski, 2 vols. (Berlin, 1996) take on an exceptional importance. Klemperer evokes the everyday reality of a German Jew in the Third Reich who was not engulfed by the Holocaust. His notes and comments thus reflect an experience that a "German" memory is prepared to accept (hence the popularity of the diaries), especially since Klemperer himself experiences a transformation of his identity (and thus of his memory) under Nazism into a Jewish one. The diaries constitute an unusual personal testimony in which the two perspectives nearly coalesce—though admittedly under the special circumstances so favorable for Klemperer, which "precluded" an awful fate.

11. NAZISM AND STALINISM

1. Robert Conquest, *The Harvest of Sorrow: Soviet Collectivization and the Terror-Famine* (New York, 1986), 3.
2. Both Hannah Arendt (*The Origins of Totalitarianism* [New York, 1951], 2:390) and Ernst Nolte (*Der Europäische Bürgerkrieg 1917–1945* [Berlin, 1987]) base their arguments on the latter event.
3. Maurice Halbwachs, *La mémoire collective* (Paris, 1950).
4. Ernst Nolte, "A Past That Will Not Pass Away (A Speech It Was Possible to Write, But Not to Present)," *YVS* 19 (1988): 71–73.
5. Adam Smith, *An Inquiry into the Nature and Causes of the Wealth of Nations* (1776; New York, 1937), 99.
6. See David J. Dallin and Boris I. Nicolaevsky, *Forced Labor in Soviet Russia* (New Haven, 1947) 105.

12. CUMULATIVE CONTINGENCY

1. For the current interest in deconstructing Israeli national founding myths, see Yael Zerubavel, "The Death of Memory and the Memory of Death: Masada and the Holocaust as Historical Metaphors," *Representations* 45 (1994): 72–100.
2. An example of the intervention of a nonhistorian in the public sphere is the article by the writer Aharon Megged, "The Israeli Impulse for Suicide," *Ha'aretz,* June 10, 1994 (Hebrew), which sparked the current debate.
3. On the deep layer of intercultural relations between Western and Eastern European Jewry, see Steven E. Aschheim, *Brothers and Strangers: The East European Jews in German and German Jewish Consciousness, 1800–1923* (Madison, 1982); and Shulamit Volkov, "The Dynamics of Dissimilation: *Ostjuden* and German Jews," in *The Jewish Response to German Culture: From Enlightenment to the Second World War,* ed. Jehuda Reinharz and Walter Schatzberg (Hanover, 1985) 195–211.
4. "Is it admissible to build everything on this catastrophe? And isn't it pure chance that we have survived in Palestine? Wasn't Hitler at the gates of the country? . . . Hitler did not plan to annihilate only the diaspora, but *Jewry,* all Jews everywhere. We have saved ourselves by *pure chance*" (Yaakov Zerubavel at the Congress of the World Organization of Poalei Zion, January 1945, cited in *Davar,* February 5, 1945 [Hebrew] [italics in the original]).

5. Tom Segev, *The Seventh Million: The Israelis and the Holocaust* (New York, 1993), although not acknowledging sufficiently the specific historical context of his subject, is of great importance for a public questioning of the dominant chronography.

6. An early and amateurish, but nonetheless important, study is S. B. Beit-Zvi, *Post-Ugandian Zionism in the Crucible of the Holocaust* (Tel Aviv, 1977) (Hebrew). Most of the studies written about the *yishuv*'s relation to the diaspora during the years of catastrophe somehow relate to this book, either explicitly of implicitly. See Dina Porat, *The Blue and Yellow Stars of David: The Zionist Leadership in Palestine and the Holocaust, 1939–1945* (Cambridge, Mass., 1990); Shabtai Teveth, *Ben Gurion, The Burning Ground: 1886–1948* (Boston, 1987); and Yehiam Weitz, *Awareness and Helplessness: Mapai Confronting the Shoah: 1943–1945* (Jerusalem, 1994) (Hebrew).

7. For the new trend of defending diaspora culture in Israeli discourse, see Amnon Raz-Krakotzkin, "Exile within Sovereignty: Toward a Critique of the 'Negation of Exile' in Israeli Culture," *Teoriyah u-Vikoret* 4 (1993): 23–55 (Hebrew).

8. See Dan Diner, "The Yishuv in Light of the Holocaust," *Ha'Zionut* 13 (1988): 301–8 (Hebrew).

9. For the trend of focusing on the experience of non-Zionist Jews in the displaced persons' camps, see Josef Grudczinsky, "Something Is Missing in This Story," *Ha'aretz*, May 3, 1995 (Hebrew).

10. For an early approach in counterhistory, see Yigal Eilam's still important study, *Introduction to a Different History of Zionism* (Ramat Gan, 1972) (Hebrew).

11. On the metaphor of compressed time see Dan Diner, "Gestaute Zeit: Massenvernichtung und jüdische Erzählstruktur," in *Kreisläufe: Nationalsozialismus und Gedächtnis* (Berlin, 1995), 123–39.

12. For an instructive study on nineteenth- and twentieth-century Polish and Polish Jewish literature as an indication of Polish-Jewish relations, see Israel Bartal and Magdalena Opalski, *Poles and Jews: A Failed Brotherhood* (Hanover, N.H., 1992).

13. For an outspoken "Western" reaction, see the letter by Hans Kohn, former head of the Jewish National Fund and later renowned historian of nationalism, to Dr. Feiwel, November 21, 1929: "Having come to this country [as immigrants], we were duty bound to come up with constitutional proposals which, without doing serious harm to Arab rights and liberty, would have also allowed for our free cultural and social development. But for twelve years we pretended that the Arabs did not exist and were glad when we were not reminded of their existence." Cited by Paul R. Mendes-Flohr, ed., *A Land of Two Peoples: Martin Buber on Jews and Arabs* (Oxford, 1983), 98–99.

14. For the phenomenon of transforming (Arab) land (*terra*) into (Jewish) territory by social and economic means, see Dan Diner, *Israel in Palästina: Über Tausch und Gewalt im Vorderen Orient* (Königstein im Taunus, 1980), 38–64. See also Baruch Kimmerling's pioneering study, *Zionism and Territory: The Socio-Territorial Dimensions of Zionist Politics* (Berkeley, 1983), 106–46.

15. On Jewish labor in Palestine, see Anita Shapira, *Futile Struggle: The Jewish Labor Controversy, 1929–1939* (Tel Aviv, 1977) (Hebrew). For a pioneering critical approach in Israeli social sciences to the function of Jewish labor, see Gershon Shafir, *Land, Labor and the Origins of the Israeli-Palestinian Conflict, 1882–1914* (Cambridge, 1989), 45–90.

16. These planners frequently referred to the struggle between nationalities in

East-Central Europe as a model and example of the conflict between Jews and Arabs. See Franz Oppenheimer, *Collective Ownership and Private Ownership of Land* (The Hague, 1917); Abraham Granowsky (Granott), *Probleme der Bodenpolitik in Palästina* (Berlin, 1925), 31; and Shalom Reichmann and Shlomo Hasson, "A Cross-Cultural Diffusion of Colonization: From Posen to Palestine," *Annals of the Association of American Geographers* 74 (1984): 64.

17. The historically dramatic conflicts that have now reerupted in the volatile quake zone between the Baltic and the Adriatic (and beyond) are also characterized by drastic measures aimed at bringing about ethnic homogeneity. The transfer of one population group for the benefit of another was made legal in the Lausanne accords of 1923, when Greeks from Asia Minor and the Pontus, who had lived for millennia in the Orient, were forced to leave their ancient areas of settlement in favor of the Turkish population and to relocate to a new home in the Greek nation-state. See in this regard Arnold J. Toynbee, ed., *Survey of International Affairs, 1920–1923* (Oxford, 1925).The westward shifting of Poland and the associated transfer of the German population after 1945 must also be viewed in the context of the formation of homogeneous nation-states.

18. For the dramatic and problematic position of the liberal colonizer desiring to overcome ethnic inequality and racist perceptions of the other on the basis of universal values, see Albert Memmi, *The Colonizer and the Colonized* (Boston, 1967).

19. See, e.g., Menahem Begin to the Knesset (Israeli parliament), June 20, 1977, cited in Segev, *The Seventh Million,* 393.

20. This argument was put forward at the beginning of the ideological struggle for the transformation of Israeli identity after the 1967 war. See, for example, statements by Begin during a discussion with members of Kibbutz Ein Ha-Horesh, *Yediot Aharonot,* October 17, 1969.

21. See Eli Lobel, "L'escalade à l'intérieur de la société israélienne," *Partisans* 52 (March–April 1970): 131.

13. ON GUILT DISCOURSE AND OTHER NARRATIONS

1. See Karl Jaspers, *Die Schuldfrage: Von der politischen Haftung Deutschlands* (1946; Munich, 1996); in English, *The Question of German Guilt* (New York, 1947).

2. In *Vergangenheitspolitik: Die Anfänge der Bundesrepublik und die NS-Vergangenheit,* 2d ed. (Munich, 1997), Norbert Frei provides a comprehensive study of the discourse's early public, juridical, and political form.

3. See Anson Rabinbach's perceptive chapter on "The German as Pariah: Karl Jaspers' *The Question of German Guilt,*" in *In the Shade of Catastrophe: German Intellectuals between Apocalypse and Enlightenment* (Berkeley, 1997).

4. The spiteful scorn of Carl Schmitt's comments concerning Jaspers's thinking is exemplary. See, e.g., *Glossarium: Aufzeichnungen der Jahre 1947 bis 1951,* ed. Eberhart Freiherr von Medem (Berlin, 1991), 167, 256, 278, and 285.

5. Jaspers, *Question of German Guilt,* 51 ff.

6. Ibid., 79, 80.

7. Richard Matthias Müller has written an intelligent, if apologetically defensive,

essay on the *Schuldfrage* in *Normal-Null und die Zukunft der deutschen Vergangenheitsbewältigung* (Schernfeld, 1994).

8. See Hannah Arendt's remark in a letter to Jaspers dated August 17, 1946: "It seems to me these crimes can no longer be juridically grasped, and here precisely lies their monstrosity" (*Hannah Arendt-Karl Jaspers Briefwechsel 1926–1969,* ed. Lotte Köhler and Hans Saner [Munich, 1985], 90).

9. See my essay, written before the reunification, "Von der Bundesrepublik zu Deutschland," in *Gnade der geschenkten Nation: Zur politischen Moral der Bonner Republik,* ed. Hajo Funke (Berlin, 1988), 195.

10. See Jürgen Habermas's praise for Goldhagen, "Warum ein 'Demokratiepreis' für Daniel J. Goldhagen? Eine Laudatio," *Die Zeit,* March 12, 1997. Habermas here overlooks the new frontlines displaced to the *Historikerstreit.* From such a perspective, he goes so far as to gloss over the central historiographical controversy hovering behind Goldhagen's book—its opposition to Christopher R. Browning's approach in *Ordinary Men, Reserve Police Battalion 101, and the Final Solution in Poland* (New York, 1992). We consequently read, "The concluding step of [Goldhagen's] argument is based on a circumstance already pointed to by the title of Christopher Browning's exemplary study: that the perpetrators were, precisely, 'ordinary men.' With his 'ordinary Germans,' Goldhagen sharpens this thesis to a critical edge [*sic*]."

11. For a highly interesting study of the rhetorical figures used in those turn-of-the-century texts presenting guiltlessly perpetrated crime as an expression of modern "risk-based" society, see Stefan Andriopoulos, *Unfall und Verbrechen: Konfiguration zwischen juristischem und literarischem Diskurs um 1900* (Pfaffenweiler, 1996).

12. Jaspers conveys this reaction in *Question of German Guilt,* 100:

In tracing our own guilt back to its source we come upon the human essence—which in its German form has fallen into a peculiar, terrible incurring of guilt but exists as a possibility in man as such.

Thus German guilt is sometimes called the guilt of all: the hidden evil everywhere is jointly guilty of the outbreak of evil in this German place.

It would indeed be an evasion and a false excuse if we Germans tried to exculpate ourselves by pointing to the guilt of being human. It is not relief but greater depth to which the idea can help us. The question of original sin must not become a way to dodge German guilt.

13. In *Nazi Germany and the Jews: The Years of Persecution, 1933–1939* (New York, 1997), esp. 41–76, Saul Friedländer describes a wide range of borderline anti-Semitic phenomena, which together cohere into clear-cut anti-Semitism. In this way Friedländer's approach combines a micrological focus with considerations of system that preserve a sense of the wider picture.

14. Exemplary in this respect is Yves Ternon, *L'état criminel: Les génocides au XXe siècle* (Paris, 1995). Ternon does not distinguish between ethnically and socially based mass murders. The author's notion of "genocide against the Jews" is therefore problematic, as he does not treat its "particularity" either on the plane of empirical comparison or on that of ideational polemic.

15. For a comparative effort at universalizing genocide and memory, see Herbert Hirsch, *Genocide and the Politics of Memory: Studying Death to Preserve Life* (Chapel Hill, N.C., 1995).

16. This particularly applies to West European countries like France and Norway. The latter country was home to only several hundred Jews. This example quantitatively illuminates the fact that at least in the context of the Nazi anti-Jewish measures, we cannot speak of "ethnic cleansing."

17. In this respect, see the tendency manifest in the work of the best-selling author Alfred-Maurice de Zayas, including his new book, *A Terrible Revenge: The Ethnic Cleansing of the East European Germans, 1944–1950* (New York, 1994).

18. See the remarkable ersatz narrative of the directors Helke Sander and Barbara Johr in their film *BeFreier und BeFreite*. Its report of the rape of German women takes an anthropological angle—but unmistakably repeats a national discourse on the theme. See also the collection bearing the film's title (Munich, 1992) v; on the intrapsychic phenomena of transference and guilt see Dan Bar-On, *Legacy of Silence: Encounters with Children of the Third Reich* (Cambridge, 1989).

19. See Müller, *Normal-Null*, 101.

20. The groundwork for such a history began in the 1950s. See the multivolume work, Theodor Schieder, ed., *Dokumentation der Vertreibung der Deutschen aus Ost-Mitteleuropa* (1954–1960), each volume with a different year and place of publication. Some of Schieder's assistants on the project would later emerge as among Germany's most important historians. On the history and fate of the German prisoners of war, see Erich Maschke, ed., *Die deutschen Kriegsgefangenen des Zweiten Weltkrieges: Eine Zusammenfassung* (Munich, 1974).

INDEX

Adorno, Theodor W., 12–13; on Christianity, 111–13; *Dialectic of Enlightenment*, 6, 98, 104, 108–14, 115, 256n17
Aktion Reinhard, 168
Aktion T4, 151, 168
Alterman, Nathan, 119
Aly, Götz, 138–44, 182–83, 263n19; anticapitalism of, 155; critique of modernity, 149; methodology of, 150, 154, 157; rationalization thesis of, 139, 142–45, 158; sources of, 139–40, 144–45, 149–50; use of subjunctivity, 152
Anglo-Saxon culture: hostility of geopolitics to, 28, 34–36, 39; idea of state in, 53, 54; in international law, 54; political, 40
Anschluss, Austrian, 81, 83–84, 88, 89
Anschütz, Gerhard, 21
Anti-Semitism: American, 91; bourgeois, 114; as cause of Holocaust, 181, 224–28; Christian sources of, 111–13, 180, 257n22; conceptual approach to, 224–25; difference in, 111, 115; economic explanation for, 108, 113; equality and, 109; under fascism, 256n16; following Kristallnacht, 78; Friedländer on, 271n13; in geopolitics, 31; guilt for, 116; Haushofer's, 31–34; historical, 203; Horkheimer on, 97–116, 253, 254n4, 256nn14,16; ideology of, 3, 225; Jewish narratives of, 179–80; motives for, 107; under National Socialism, 100–104; in Nazi legal theory, 51–52, 57–58; as negative teleology, 181; opportunistic, 182; as paranoia, 108–10, 113, 114; of perpetrators, 182, 227; Polish, 86–87, 179; political, 109–10, 111, 255n9; as popular movement, 109; racial, 33, 111; rationality and, 106–7, 114; religious, 111–13, 115, 257n22; "scientific," 34; as suprahistorical phenomenon, 181; theoretical treatments of, 99; traditional, 210; transhistorical character of, 111; utility of, 104, 107; victims' perception of, 132
Antiuniversalism, 5; under *Großraum*, 73–74; in international law, 56
Arab-Israeli conflict, 203, 204, 210–11; concept of justice in, 213; European models for, 212, 270n16; of 1948, 258n8; of 1967, 216, 270n20; political perception of, 212
Arabs, Palestinian, 80, 212–14
Arendt, Hannah, 5, 268n2; correspondence with Jaspers, 271n8; *Eichmann in Jerusalem*, 118, 164, 182, 258nn3,4,7, 265n15; Jewish critics of, 166, 181
Armenians, genocide of, 267n14
Aryanization, of businesses, 143, 151
Auschwitz: in Allied bombing campaign, 176; "borders of," 215; death marches from, 188; Greek deportees in, 148; and historical construction, 256n17; Hungarian Jews in, 150, 152; metaphor of, 188, 189, 209, 215, 220; as mnemonic device,

Hilberg, Raul, 124, 165, 258n4

Hildebrand, Klaus, 47

Hilfsverein (relief organization), 81, 82

Hillgruber, Andreas, 267n14

Himmler, Heinrich, 142

Hindenburg, Paul von, 19, 23; appointment of Hitler, 5

Historikerstreit (1986), 219, 222, 271n10

Historiography: British, 174–76, 266n3; collective memory in, 173–86; Continental tradition of, 174–75, 266n3; modes of understanding in, 1; of National Socialism, 165–66, 264n9

Historiography, Holocaust, 4, 6, 131, 160–61; causality in, 183–84; continuity in, 183–84; Jewish versus German, 178, 180, 186; victim and perpetrator in, 163–64

Historiography, Israeli, 6, 201–5; Arabs in, 214; effect of Holocaust on, 203, 204–7; ethnocentricity in, 209; individual in, 204; territorialist approach to, 214–17; Zionism in, 213

History: Jewish, 203–4; and memory, 6, 167, 173; universal, 176

History, German: causality in, 3, 177; continuity in, 3; Holocaust debate in, 4, 219, 221–24, 271n10; interpretive models of, 1–2; nineteenth-century, 2

Hitler, Adolf: alliance with Italy, 48; appointment as Reichskanzler, 5, 24; deportation policy of, 152, 263n17; Euthanasia Decree of, 184; food policy of, 151–52, 156; on Haushofer, 47; invasion of Poland, 87; *Lebensraum* under, 48–49; *Mein Kampf*, 39, 47; military opposition to, 176; "Oath of Legality" of, 21–22; on *Raum*, 47; resettlement policy of, 267n14; rise to power, 17–18

Hitler's Willing Executioners (Goldhagen), 181, 219, 223

Hochhuth, Rolf, 219

Hofmann, Hasso, 246n105

Holland, de-Judaization of, 144

Holocaust: accomplices in, 165; "Anglo-American" perspective on, 174; anthropological interpretations of, 2–3, 226, 228–29; Arendt on, 258n4; banality of, 161, 166, 181, 182; causality of, 150, 177, 181–82, 183–84, 185; Christian consciousness of, 188, 189, 214, 227–

28; as civilizational break, 98, 104; as "cleansing," 267n14; criminal awareness of, 164, 165; culpability for, 178, 183–84; deconstruction of, 159; denial of, 170; division of labor in, 163–64, 166, 180; economic rationalization of, 138–44, 148, 154–55, 182, 262n4; effect on Federal Republic, 218–19; effect on Israeli historiography, 203, 204–7; effect on political culture, 177; epistemological understanding of, 2–3, 4, 6; ethnic identity in, 4; events preceding, 183–84; existential premises for, 4; food-supply thesis of, 150–52; foreseeability of, 99; as foundational event, 218; functionalist approach to, 224; as German crime, 191, 220; guilt for, 164, 165, 180, 181, 183, 219–23, 271n12; as historical crisis, 161; historical evaluation of, 1, 138; historiography of, 4, 6, 131, 160–61, 163–64, 178, 179–80, 183, 186; Horkheimer's critique of, 256n17; Hungarian Jews in, 150, 152; iconic meaning of, 188, 218; inconceivability of, 99, 167, 254nn6–7; as industrial event, 178, 180, 181–82; intentionality of, 138–39, 178, 186, 224; irrationality of, 106–7, 131–32, 136; juridical questions of, 164; memory of, 3–4, 178, 183, 185, 192–93, 205, 229; metaphor of, 188, 189, 209, 215, 220; as mnemonic device, 193; as modernization program, 139–42, 150; monocausal theories of, 6, 152, 263n16; monstrosity of, 166, 167, 180, 181, 271n8; multicausal approach to, 263n21; narratives of, 4, 6, 173–86, 179, 209; negative teleology of, 168, 179, 210, 217; omission from histories, 173; personal accountability for, 169; phenomenology of, 170, 266n23; in Polish consciousness, 194–95; posthumous awareness of, 190; prehistory of, 6, 210; procedures of, 189; rationality of, 131–32, 137, 139–45; relation to Kristallnacht, 78, 81; resistance to, 117, 119, 121–22; role of corporations in, 149; as social engineering, 139–42; socioeconomic explanations of, 142–45; standardizing of death, 179; suprahistorical importance of, 186; theological discourse on, 4, 228–29; theological

Jews *(continued)*
  compliance with Germans, 117; eastern
    versus western, 32, 34, 204, 211–214,
    268n3, 269n13; emancipation of, 101–
    2, 104, 109, 112, 205; expiation tax on,
    143; in geopolitical theory, 31; ghetto-
    ization of, 84; impact on German mem-
    ory, 193; knowledge of deportations,
    121; legal status of, 84–91, 168; linguis-
    tic conception of, 98; loss of assets, 87,
    143; as mnemonic entity, 229; negative
    election of, 189; non-Zionist, 269n9;
    perception of Nazi threat, 254n5; perse-
    cution of, 110; as political subject, 209;
    productivity of, 141, 145, 261n4; of
    Rhodes, 148, 149; social expulsion of,
    100; social metaphors concerning, 98;
    in sphere of circulation, 103, 109, 113,
    255n12; suppression of elites among,
    83, 88; as traders, 255n8
Jews, Austrian: effect of Anschluss on, 88;
    forced emigration of, 78, 82–83, 120–
    21; investments of, 252n46
Jews, Central European, 79; after Kristall-
    nacht, 81; settlement of Palestine, 210
Jews, Eastern European: emancipation of,
    204; immigration to America, 86; narra-
    tives of, 205; Nazi theory on, 141; self-
    identity of, 205; survivors among, 207
Jews, German: civil rights of, 34, 97; forced
    emigration of, 78, 93; legal status of,
    84–85, 251n26; narratives of, 205; un-
    der Nazi law, 85, 168; passports of, 83,
    93, 252n46; stigmatization of, 84
Jews, Hungarian: in Auschwitz, 150, 152;
    deportation of, 263n17
Jews, Israeli: collective identity of, 204–7,
    270n20; collective memory of, 203,
    206–7, 216; consciousness of, 205
Jews, Polish, 269n12; in Austria, 88; com-
    munity organizations of, 121; in death
    camps, 154, 183; emigration of, 157–
    58; evacuation of, 84; in Evian confer-
    ence, 90; expulsion of, 82; legal status
    of, 86–89; narratives of, 179, 210
Jews, Soviet, 183; under Stalin, 195
Judaism: in Christian memory, 189; cultural
    memory of, 193
Judenräte (Jewish councils), 117–29, 169;
    Arendt on, 118–19; elders of, 121, 126–
    28, 169; ethical dilemma of, 126–29,

  136; historical treatments of, 118; of
    Poland, 120–29; rabbis' advice to, 127–
    28; rationality of, 133–37; and resis-
    tance, 121–22, 208. *See also* Ghettos
Jurisprudence, in geopolitics, 28–29
Jus ad bellum, 75, 76
Jus gentium, 49, 53
Justice: in Arab-Israeli conflict, 213; as fair
    exchange, 115; Nazi concept of, 60, 65;
    under Nazi international legal theory,
    60–63

Kareski, Georg, 251n26
Kastner, Rudolf, 126, 257n2
"Kastner affair," 118
Katyn, murders at, 194–95
Kaufmann, Erich, 56, 64, 66
Kelsen, Hans, 18, 25; pure theory of law,
    51–52, 56
Kemp, Robert, 232n8
Kennedy, Ellen, 233n16
Kershaw, Ian, 266n23
Kiddush hachaim (rabbinical maxim), 128
Kiddush hashem (rabbinical maxim), 127
Kierkegaard, Søren, 257n22
King of the Jews (Epstein), 259n31
Kirchheimer, Otto, 12, 232n12, 233n15
Kirov affair, 192
Kjellén, Rudolf, 44
Klemperer, Victor, 268n21
Knowledge, "situatedness" of, 264n3
Kohn, Hans, 33, 238n32, 269n13
Kovner, Abba, 119
Krakowski, Shmuel, 186
Kristallnacht: consequences of, 93; continu-
    ity in, 5; effect on expulsions, 81–82,
    86; events preceding, 83, 84–93; Göring
    on, 143; modes of perception of, 78; re-
    lation to Holocaust, 78, 81; victims of,
    79
Kugelmann, Cilly, 254n5
Kulturrecht (culturally based law), 51

Laak-Michel, Ursula, 34, 37, 38
Labor: in death camps, 199; exploitation
    of, 145; forced, 197–200; in ghettos,
    120, 128, 199–200; in Palestine, 211,
    269n15; productivity of, 199; rational
    meaning of, 134–35; "rescue through,"
    122–23, 124–25, 134; value of, 113–
    14

Rosenblatt, Leon, 126–27
Rumania, Jewish policy of, 92
Rumkowski, Chaim, 123, 125, 259n31
Ruppin, Arthur, 92
Russia, cooperation with Germany, 37

SA, leadership of, 192
Sander, Helke, 272n17
Schädlinge (human pests), 168
Schapiro, Abraham Duber Cahan, 127
Schieder, Theodor, 272n20
Schlecher, Ludwig, 56, 76
Schleicher, Kurt von, 11, 19; dismissal of,
    24; in emergency of 1932, 23; *Querfront*
    plan of, 24; Schmitt's allegiance to, 20,
    232n4
Schmitt, Carl, 4, 5, 50; allegiance to Schlei-
    cher, 20, 232n4; ambiguity of, 11–12,
    232nn5,7; antiparliamentarianism of,
    235n39; on capitalism, 72; concept of
    Feind, 231n1; constitutional doctrines
    of, 18–21; on contractual obligation, 73;
    on deception, 34; decisionism of, 12;
    expedience theory of, 20; extraterrito-
    rial principles of, 74–75; on *Großraum*,
    71–77; *Gutachen* of, 19; at Handelshoch-
    schule, 233n16; influence on the left,
    12, 233n16; on Jaspers, 270n4; in Nazi
    Party, 25–26; political Catholicism of,
    23–24; political theory of, 11–12; post-
    humous reputation of, 12–13; postwar
    interrogation of, 232n8; in *Reichsexeku-
    tion*, 20; and rise of Nazism, 17; role in
    emergency decrees, 22–23; at Union of
    German Constitutional Theorists, 15–
    16; use of theology, 232n7, 233n17; on
    war, 70–72; before Weimar Supreme
    Court, 234n36. Works: "Diktatur und
    Belagerunszustand," 18; "Einwirkungen
    des Kriegszustandes," 18; "Gesunde
    Wirtschaft im starken Staat," 24, 232n4;
    "Der Hüter der Verfassung," 16; *Legalität
    und Legitimität*, 21–22; *Politische Theolo-
    gie*, 12, 18–19
Schücking, Walther, 19
Schuldfrage (question of guilt), 219–24
Schumpeter, Joseph, 72
Schwab, George, 20, 232n12
SD (Sicherheitdienst): collaboration with
    Yishuv, 92; emigration program of, 82

Second Reich (Wilhelminian), 175
Segev, Tom, 269n5
Self-interest: maximization of, 262n6; of
    National Socialism, 131
Sen, Amartya, 262n6
Seneca, 55, 62
Seraphim, Peter-Heinz, 141, 142
Siauliai ghetto, 125
Silbermann, Alphons, 256n20
Simon, Ernst, 33
Smith, Adam, 146, 198
Social Darwinism, 33, 40
Social Democratic Party, 15–16; neutraliza-
    tion of, 24
Social formation, capitalist, 28, 29; Hausho-
    fer's rejection of, 31
Society: bourgeois, 100, 105–6, 114, 149;
    emergencies in, 14–15; primitive,
    262n9;
Söllner, Alfons, 255n9
Sonderweg (special path), German, 1, 2
Sovereignty: basis of, 62; Hegelian, 68; loss
    of, 75; state, 64, 67–70
Soviet Army, rescue of Jews, 123
Soviet Union: in establishment of Israel,
    215; in geopolitical theory, 36, 37; Ger-
    man attack on, 38; partisan activity in,
    122. *See also* Stalinism
Sphere of circulation, 103, 109; account-
    ability of, 114; under dictatorships,
    255n12
SS (Schutzstaffel), 83, 92; conflict with po-
    lice, 124; emigration policies of, 257n2
Staatsboden (state soil), 42
Staatsvolk (state people), 51, 68; origin of,
    68
Stahl, Heinrich, 251n24
Stalingrad, defeat at, 167
Stalinism: arbitrariness of, 195–96, 198;
    forced collectivization under, 193–94;
    forced labor under, 197–98; mass mur-
    der under, 187, 263n23; National So-
    cialism and, 187–200, 263n23; negative
    equality under, 196; Poland under, 194;
    post-Communist discourse on, 197; re-
    settlement under, 267n14; victims of,
    191
State: Anglo-Saxon idea of, 53, 54; equa-
    tion with law, 57; in geopolitical theory,
    28, 43–44; liberal, 72, 73, 101, 262n8;

medieval, 52, 59; Nazi concept of, 51–52, 67–70; power-based, 56; racial basis for, 67; versus Reich, 50–51, 68–70; Schmitt on, 232n6; sovereignty of, 64, 67–70; territorial, 43, 73; universalization of, 53; *völkisch* notion of, 52, 57; world, 55
State law: biological basis for, 56; monistic theory of, 56, 76
State plurality, 69
States: conflicts between, 70–71; equality between, 59–60, 62
State socialism, 43
Strasser, Gregor, 24
Stresemann, Gustav, 44
Sudetenland crisis, 71, 88, 93

Tal, Uriel, 135
Täuschen (deception), 34
Taylor, Myron G., 90, 92
Tel Aviv, counterculture of, 202
Teleology. *See* Negative teleology
Tenenbaum-Tamaroff, Mordechai, 124
Ternon, Yves, 271n14
Territory: abstract idea of, 54; in international law, 69; predestination concept of, 63
Third Reich: Agency for the Four-Year Plan, 151; archives of, 184; British image of, 175; continuity with Federal Republic, 156; Haushofer on, 42; Interior Ministry, 82, 93, 143; main security office, 154; Ministry for Propaganda, 48; Prussian influence on, 176; *Rechnungshof*, 145; Reichsbahn, 148, 164, 165; *Reichskuratorium für Wirtschaftlichkeit*, 145; *Reichsvertretung*, 82, 85; Schmitt under, 25; Wehrmacht, 123
Thoma, Richard, 13
Time, compressed, 179, 201, 266n10, 269n11
Toury, Jacob, 250n16
Trade: freedom of, 54, 73; in geopolitical theory, 27, 35, 39, 40; in liberal state, 72, 73; role in Holocaust, 149. *See also* Market
Translatio imperii, American, 73
Treaty of Westphalia (1648), 53–54, 69
Treblinka, transports to, 144
Trunk, Isaiah, 118, 124, 257n1

Tyroleans, resettlement of, 48

Ukraine, atrocities in, 187, 193–94
Umschichtung (restratification), 141
Unequal Victims (Gutman and Krakowski), 186
Union of German Constitutional Theorists, 15–16
United States: belief in geopolitics, 38, 239n68; eugenics in, 169; in geopolitical theory, 34–36, 40; immigration laws of, 86, 91; isolationism of, 89–90
Universal empire, Spanish, 55
Universalism: and *Großraum*, 73; Horkheimer's, 103–4; humanist, 265n14; of international law, 53–58; Nazi critics of, 55; in post-Auschwitz culture, 170; of world order, 55
Universalization: of Holocaust, 4, 185, 228–29, 230; of state, 53
Untermenschen, 168
Upper Silesia, Judenräte of, 121, 123
Urbanization: and anti-Semitism, 32; in geopolitical theory, 30, 40, 41
Der Ursprung des Deutschen Trauerspiels (Benjamin), 12–13
Urvolk (primal people), 51, 63, 68
Utility: of anti-Semitism, 104, 107; as basis for morality, 261n17; in ethics, 134–35; in German philosophical tradition, 262n6; in Holocaust theory, 146–47, 263n19

Value, production of, 199
Verfassungswirklichkeit (constitutional reality), 12
Versailles treaty (1919): geopolitics following, 28, 38, 41, 48; modern state under, 54
Verstehen (understanding), 130–32, 137, 160
Victims: autonomy of, 133; behavior of, 3; choice of, 2–3; collective identity of, 154; collective memory of, 3–4, 178, 183; cooperation by, 117; of death camps, 133; eugenic definition of, 147; of euthanasia, 193; Germans as, 230, 272n20; guilt of, 116, 187; in Holocaust historiography, 163; knowledge of extermination, 6; of Kristallnacht, 79;

Library of Congress Cataloging-in-Publication Data

Diner, Dan, 1946–
    Beyond the conceivable : studies on Germany, Nazism, and the
Holocaust / Dan Diner.
        p.   cm. — (Weimar and now ; 20)
    Includes bibliographical references and index.
    ISBN 0-520-21345-9
    1. Holocaust, Jewish (1939–1945)—Historiography.   2. Ger-
many—Politics and government—1918–1933.   3. Holocaust,
Jewish (1939–1945)—Causes.   4. Holocaust, Jewish (1939–1945)—
Personal narratives—History and criticism.   I. Title.   II. Series.
D804.348.B49   2000
940.53′18′0072—dc21   99-047175

                            Text: 10/13 Baskerville
                         Display: Baskerville
                    Composition: G&S Typesetters
            Printing and binding: Haddon Craftsmen
                           Index: Carol Roberts